Culture
and C   ct

Culture, Trauma, and Conflict

Cultural Studies Perspectives on War

Edited by

Nico Carpentier

**Cambridge
Scholars**
Publishing

Culture, Trauma, and Conflict: Cultural Studies Perspectives on War

Edited by Nico Carpentier

This book first published 2007
This edition published 2015

Cambridge Scholars Publishing

Lady Stephenson Library, Newcastle upon Tyne, NE6 2PA, UK

British Library Cataloguing in Publication Data
A catalogue record for this book is available from the British Library

ISBN (10): 1-4438-7056-0
ISBN (13): 978-1-4438-7056-6

Dedicated to the memory of Usha Zacharias
(1961-2013)

TABLE OF CONTENTS

INTRODUCTION:
STRENGTHENING CULTURAL WAR STUDIES

NICO CARPENTIER

The ideological model of war

War, i.e. armed conflict between organized political groups, is still an omnipresent phenomenon. In the meantime, though, despite the fact it has been "the universal norm in human history" (Michael Howard 2001, 1), its highly disruptive and destructive nature has strongly decreased its social respectability and acceptability. Howard (2001,2) stresses the relative novelty of this development: "the peace invented by the thinkers of the Enlightenment, an international order in which war plays no part, had been a common enough aspiration for visionaries throughout history, but it has been regarded by political leaders as a practical or indeed desirable goal only during the past two hundred years."

Despite a theoretical and ethical consensus surrounding the desirability of structural peace, its implementation has proven difficult – witness the high number and horrible intensity of armed conflicts and genocides in the 20th and 21st centuries. The principled repulsion of war seems to become easily translated into a discourse about the acceptability of war in the last instance. It is precisely this paradox between the consensus surrounding the desirability of structural peace and the apparent unavoidability of armed conflict that legitimizes its continued analysis. The deep societal impact of war further strengthens this legitimization. This impact is partially related to the actions of the soldiers (or fighters) involved, engaging in what Joanna Bourke (1999, 1) calls "sanctioned blood-letting," supported by processes of hero making. Her *Intimate history of killing* – despite the growing distance between killer and killed – points to the problematic "association of pleasure with killing and cruelty" (Bourke 1999, 369).

The societal impact is not restricted to (semi-)military personnel; entire nations become symbolically engaged in this process of de-civilization. The loss of humanity is not confined to the actual battlefield sites; war tends to cannibalize on the social and absorb it. War touches the core of our politics, economics and cultures. The threat to the survival of the state and its citizens (and soldiers) creates the political legitimacy, and the political will to revert to extreme and counter-democratic means in order to reach the ultimate goal of winning the war. Truth is not necessarily the only "first casualty of war". As Aeschylus put it, the suspension of democracy and human rights often follows quite rapidly. In the *War and the media* collection, Aijaz Ahmad (2005, 22) for instance points to what he calls the domestic dimension of the "war on terrorism", which takes surveillance "to new extremes in an otherwise democratic country." In addition, the economic and financial structure of a nation is affected. During wartime, and especially during prolonged periods of conflict, the importance of the already important industrial-military complex increases – weighing heavily on the public purse. And finally, war affects the cultures of the warring parties. The edges of imagined communities at war, which are blurred in more normal circumstances, become impenetrable frontiers between "us" and "them", between the Self and the Enemy. All eyes become strongly focused on the (political) center, and citizen-soldiers voluntarily subject themselves to the leadership of a small political-military elite. There is little room for internal differences, as illustrated in the famous words of the German Emperor Wilhelm, in claiming during the First World War that he no longer wanted to hear of different political parties, only of Germans. U.S. President, George Bush, used an updated version of this dictum in his address to the Joint Session of Congress and the American People on September 20, 2001, when he said: "Either you are with us, or you are with the terrorists." And an inversed version was used by Russian president Vladimir Putin, who stated in his Crimea address on 18 March 2014:

> They act as they please: here and there, they use force against sovereign states, building coalitions based on the principle 'If you are not with us, you are against us.' To make this aggression look legitimate, they force the necessary resolutions from international organizations, and if for some reason this does not work, they simply ignore the UN Security Council and the UN overall.

These three examples show the crucial role that ideology – defined as sets of ideas that dominate a social formation – plays in generating internal cohesion and in turning an adversary into the Enemy. This transformation is supported by a set of discourses, articulating the identities of all parties involved. Together they form an ideological model that has structured most of the interstate wars[1] in the 20th and 21st centuries. Although each

war has its own history and context which makes it unique, wars are
nevertheless built on remarkably similar ideological mappings. So, on the
one hand, the complex series of events that compose a war appear to be
highly elusive and impossible to represent in their entirety; but on the
other hand, the core ideological models that have structured wars in past
decades tend to be fairly stable and compatible.

This ideological model of war is crucial to understanding modern
warfare, as its core structure allows us to better understand (and
counteract) the discourses, rhetorics and narrations of war. As Keen (1986,
10) put it: "in the beginning we create the enemy. Before the weapon
comes the image. We think others to death and then invent the battle-axe
or the ballistic missiles with which to actually kill them." This of course
does not imply that the processes of mediation and representation
completely overtake the practices and materiality of war (and of killing).
But in the (20th and) 21st century, interstate war in particular has become a
political transgression which requires a discursive build-up to legitimize
the use of extreme military violence, all of which makes it necessary to
(re)construct this ideological model of war.

For this (re)construction, we first turn to Galtung (see, for instance,
Galtung and Vincent 1992) who, from a Peace Studies perspective, has
pointed to the dichotomized nature of these discourses, grounded by
the key binary opposition of good and evil. The variations of the
good/evil dichotomy that structure the identities of both Self and
Enemy are manifold: just/unjust, innocent/guilty, rational/irrational,
civilized/barbaric, organized/chaotic, superior to technology/part of
technology, human/animal-machine[2], united/fragmented, heroic/cowardly
and determined/insecure. A second layer of dichotomies structures the
meanings attributed to the violent practices of both warring parties. These
dichotomies include, among others: necessary/unnecessary, last
resort/provocative, limited effects/major effects, focused/indiscriminate,
purposeful/senseless, unavoidable/avoidable, legitimate/illegitimate,
legal/criminal, sophisticated/brutal and professional/undisciplined.

The dichotomies in question can be defined as floating signifiers
(Laclau and Mouffe 1985, 112-113; Žižek 1989, 97), implying that these
signifiers have no fixed meaning but are (re)articulated before, during and
after the conflict and inserted into different chains of equivalence. At the
same time, the dichotomies play a key role as nodal points in hegemonic
projects, where they have become fixed (being attributed with specific
meanings) and are used to fix a wide variety of other discursive elements.
In short, both sides claim to be rational and civilized and to be fighting a
good and just war, laying responsibility for the conflict on the Enemy.

Both sides present their violent practices as focused, well-considered, purposeful, unavoidable, and necessary. Both sides construct their own (inversed[3]) ideological model of war.

The construction of the Enemy is accompanied by the construction of the identity of the Self as clearly antagonistic to the Enemy's identity. In this process, not only is the radical otherness of the Enemy emphasized, but also the Enemy is presented as a threat to "our own" identity. Ironically, the identity of the Enemy as a constitutive outside is indispensable to the construction of the identity of the Self, as the evilness of the Enemy is a necessary condition for the articulation of the goodness of the Self.

Apart from the identities of the Self and the Enemy, there is a third discursive position -- that of the Victim -- which is crucial to the ideological model of war. Here it is important to keep LaCapra's (723) words in mind: "'Victim' is not a psychological category. It is, in variable ways, a social, political, and ethical category." The identity of the Victim may range from abstract notions, such as world peace or world security, to more concrete notions, such as a people, a minority, or another nation. In some cases the Self becomes conflated with the Victim, for instance when the Self is being attacked by the Enemy. For instance, in the case of the Cyprus conflict, where Turkey invaded the island in 1974 and occupied more than one third of the island's territory, the Greek Cypriot Self is often articulated as Victim of this invasion. In contrast, the Turkish Cypriot Self is frequently defined as Victim of the intra-communal violence of the 1960s (and before). Papadakis' (2006, 78) analysis of the material produced by the Greek Cypriot and Turkish Cypriot Public Information Offices shows that these documents produced by both sides "literally screamed with pain. Their aim was to show who truly suffered, who suffered most, and who was to blame for this suffering." In other instances the Victim is detached from the Enemy, when a regime is seen to (preferably brutally) oppress its "own" people, or when in intra-state or civil wars the nation or people become divided into warring factions. An example here is the 2003 Iraqi War[4], where the dictatorship of Saddam Hussein and the ruling Ba'ath party was defined as victimizing the Iraqi people (and especially the Shiites and Kurds), and was simultaneously seen as a threat to world security because of its alleged possession of weapons of mass destruction (WMD) (see Carpentier 2007).

The Victim is intrinsically linked to the identity of the Self and the Enemy, as its being victimized contributes to the construction of the evilness of the Enemy. The Self's goodness emanates not only from the willingness to fight this evilness, but also from the attempts to rescue the

Victim. These three discursive positions – Self, Enemy and Victim – together form the core structure of the ideological model of war rendered in Figure 1-1. In this model, the Self and the Enemy are juxtaposed, and encircled by the dichotomies that structure their identities in an intimate relationship with the Victim.

Somewhat in the background, this model also contains the discursive positions of Supporters and Passive Allies, which belong to a similar cultural sphere and tend to reproduce (at least partially) the constructions of the identity of the Self and Enemy. Finally, Bystanders have no direct affiliations to the conflict or the warring parties and relate to the conflict from their own particular contexts, which do not necessarily include the identity constructions of the Self and Enemy (as produced by the Self).

Figure 1-1: The ideological model of war

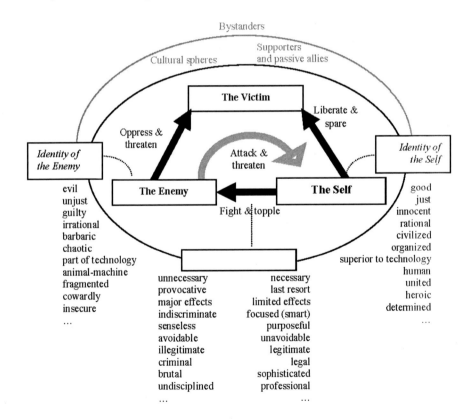

Of course, it should be kept in mind that these positions are discursive-ideological constructs, with an always-specific relationship to the complex mixture of events and practices, offering overarching frameworks of interpretation without which materiality remains unintelligible, but never able to capture the richness of these events and practices in their entirety. Following De Certeau's (1992) argument in the *Writing of history* and Laclau's (1996) argument in *Emancipations*, the unavoidable particularity of discursive translations needs to be emphasized. Moreover, the ideological model depicted in Figure 1-1 cannot be considered as being stable or fixed during (or before and after) war. From a Foucauldian perspective, it needs to be seen as the unstable overall discursive effect of a wide range of societal strategies aiming to define the Enemy and the Self. Although these ideological models of war are supported by hegemonic projects (of the state and/or the warring parties), different forms of resistance (outside as well as inside governments) permanently attempt to rearticulate them. Furthermore, the stream of events generated by the war could in many cases – often with the support of propaganda – become incorporated into the model, whereas other events require the model to be rearticulated. In extreme cases, events might even threaten the structural integrity of the ideological model. An example of such an extreme event is the Tet offensive during the Vietnam War, which severely crippled the Vietcong at the military level, and at the same time totally disrupted the U.S. ideological framework (see Hallin 1986). Within the discourse-theoretical frame, the term dislocation is used to refer to such moments of crisis. A dislocation can be defined as the destabilization of a discourse by events it is unable to integrate, domesticate or symbolize. Dislocations disrupt discourses and identities, but at the same time become the breeding ground for the creation of new identities (Laclau 1990, 39). Moreover, they bring to light the contingency of the social and, in doing so, become "the very form of temporality, possibility and freedom" (Laclau 1990, 41-43, summarized by Torfing 1999, 149).

Although the ideological model of war that constructs the identities of the Self and the Enemy is widespread, specific groups of actors tend to play a vital role in the hegemonization of this model. These groups may benefit from unequal power relations that increase the weight of their statements. A first group of actors is usually referred to as the state, and includes governments, parliaments, political parties, advisory bodies and, last but not least, the military. The state often holds decision-making powers, has to assume responsibility for waging the war, and is held accountable for the course of the war. However, its political function of representing and governing "the people" means that its statements (and actions) are also essential for establishing or supporting a hegemonic process. As war is considered to be a very specific condition, threatening the existence of numerous human beings and possibly even the survival of the state itself, it is not sufficient to legitimate the war as such. Next to military victory, mobilization of support from the "home front" (national unity) is a primary political objective legitimating hegemonic policies.

In addition to censorship, which aims to restrict the circulation of discourses, an instrument that is widely used for the purpose of hegemonization is, of course, propaganda. Characteristically, it is planned by organized groups, which can range from a small number of special advisors to large bureaucratic organizations responsible for propaganda and counter-propaganda efforts (Taylor 1995, 6; Jowett 1997, 75) This distinguishes it from hegemony, which is the relatively rigid but ultimately unstable result of a negotiative societal process determining the horizon of our thought within a specific social and temporal setting. Although propaganda can be instrumental in establishing hegemony, the societal construction of the collective will to fight a war transcends all propaganda efforts.

When attempting to further define propaganda, the parallel with ideology – again a much broader notion – is helpful. The traditional (rather negative) Marxist definition of ideology as false consciousness runs in parallel with the common sense view of propaganda as untruthful. Taithe and Thornton (1999, 1) describe this view as follows: "most readers will assume that [propaganda] is largely composed of lies and deceits and that propagandists are ultimately manipulators and corrupt." More neutral definitions of ideology as a set of ideas that dominate a social formation, allow for an approach that defines propaganda as a persuasive act with a more complex relationship towards truthfulness (Ellul 1973). Along similar lines, Taylor (1995) defines propaganda as the use of communication "to convey a message, an idea, an ideology ... that is designed primarily to serve the self-interests of the person or people doing the communicating."

Mediated representations of war

One of the major targets of the state's propaganda efforts is the mainstream media, which – as Kellner (1992, 57) remarks – should not be defined as hypodermic needles, but as "a crucial site of hegemony." A wide range of information management techniques has been developed in order to influence the (news) media's output. However, this is not to imply that the mainstream media are defenseless victims. Here, the media's specificity should be taken into account, both at the organizational level and at the level of media professionals' identities. The majority of the (Western) media can be seen as relatively independent organizations, with specific objectives and specific values. Even the most liberal normative media theories focus on the obligation of mainstream (news) media to independently inform their audiences and to use that independence to subject state practices to public scrutiny. Moreover, media professionals claim to have access to the description of factuality and to represent truth or authenticity, which potentially runs counter to (some of) the propaganda efforts of the states at war.

Unfortunately, this does imply that media organizations and media professionals can easily escape from the workings of the ideological model of war. Although both like to believe that they are outside the operations of ideology - what Schlesinger (1987) has called the macro-myth of independence – ideology as such, and the workings of the ideological model of war, are difficult to escape. A first point to be made here is that journalism is itself a professional ideology, as argued, for instance, by Deuze (2005) and Carpentier (2005). Secondly, ideology penetrates the representations that media professionals generate. If the discourses on the Enemy and the Self have been hegemonized and turned into common sense, they may become the all-pervasive interpretative frameworks of media professionals. At the same time, care should be taken not homogenize the diversity of media organizations and practices. In a number of cases the mainstream media have managed to produce counter-hegemonic discourses. They have provided spaces for critical debate, in-depth analysis and humor. They have also attempted to counter some of the basic premises of the ideological model, and tried to show the horror of war.

The mainstream media are not the only discursive machinery to attribute meaning to war. Other spheres, such as literature, the arts, the streets (as public spaces), film, cartoons, and popular culture, contain discourses that reproduce or disrupt the hegemonic discourses of war. An almost visionary example of the critical capacity of popular (music) culture can be found in George Michael's pop song and video clip *Shoot the Dog*, which was released before the onset of the 2003 Iraqi War. It contained a (rather amusing) critique of the dependant relationship of Britain with the U.S.A., depicting Tony Blair as Bush's puppy, thus attempting to disarticulate the homogeneous Western Self. In a statement about this song, George Michael made an explicit reference to the impending war in Iraq, when he posed the following question:

I have a question for you, Mr. Blair. On an issue as enormous as the possible bombing of Iraq, how can you represent us when you haven't asked us what we think. And let's be honest, we haven't even begun to discuss it as a society. So please Tony, much as we've all loved watching the best team we've had in 40 years at the World Cup, and much as we loved the Jubilee, now that we have some downtime, could we have a little chat about Saddam? (Michael 2002)

Recognizing pain, memory and trauma

The focus on ideology and representation has no ambition to ignore the materiality of war. War impacts on human bodies with almost unimaginable force. It destroys or mutilates them. It causes pain to them, and traumatizes them. The (individual) trauma is not only physical, but also psychological, well exemplified in the phenomenon of shell shock. Erikson (1976, 153) defines this individual trauma as "a blow to the psyche that breaks through one's defenses so suddenly and with such brutal forces that one cannot react to it efficiently."

But the impact of war does not end here. War does not start with the onset of actual hostilities. First the Enemy-Other needs to be created, which in principle requires painful detachment of that Enemy from the global Self (in other words from humanity), and in which ideology provides the anesthesia that blocks the pain of detachment. But this preparation also has a material component. Preparing for war requires a specific mindset, which is generated through a series of rituals. For soldiers this is achieved through military training, but civilians also engage in the performance of "homeland security" rituals. Such (self-)disciplining practices are strongly reminiscent of Foucault's (1978) descriptions in *Discipline and punish*, as the rituals involved act directly on the bodies of the soldiers and the civilians. The soldiers in particular are molded to become the docile killing bodies that will carry out the actual elimination of the Enemy.

War does not end when hostilities cease. The damaged and mutilated bodies remain. Memories of the disappeared bodies also remain, in some cases fed by institutionalized hope, as with the Cypriot Missing Persons (Sant Cassia 2005). And the traumatic memories of war remain. War is a dislocation that disrupts social and cultural structures, and that continues to do so after the violence ends. It is "a blow to the basic tissues of social life that damages the bonds attaching people together and impairs the prevailing sense of communality" (Erikson 1976, 153). War trauma is more than the aggregation of individual traumata. It is collective, a "'knot' tying together representation, the past, the self, the political and suffering" (Buelens, Durrant and Eaglestone 2014, 4), that continues to structure a culture, for generations and decades, in many predictable and unpredictable ways.

At the same time the harrowing memory of war forces us back to questions of ideology and representation. However hard our cultures try to materialize memory by enshrining it in memorials, museums, and other sites of memory, our representations are unavoidably all that we are left with. To use Eyerman's (2001, 12) words: "how an event is remembered is intimately entwined with how it is represented." As direct access to (past or present) events is a realist illusion, the discursive mediation of those events becomes a condition of possibility for their continued existence within a society or a culture. De Certeau's (1992) argument highlights the discursive-ideological struggle (or, to use Hall's phrase: "the struggle to signify") that lies behind these representational processes, in which the ideological model of war often prevails. The meaning attributed to events is not stable, but the result of a process of cultural negotiation. Although its hegemonic truths are protected, contestation and attempted renegotiations always remain possible.

This process of memorialization also implies forgetting. Historical knowledge creates a narrative of a series of events and attempts to mold the infinite details of people's lives (and deaths) into a systematic discourse, often reducing those lives to "causes, politics, leaders and results" (Lewis 2002, 270). Moreover, the processes of glorification of the Self and demonization of the Enemy are by default used to make sense of the loss, which also impacts on what is remembered and what is forgotten. Forty and Küchler (1999, 9) for instance refer to the commemorative activities that took place after the First World War. Their specific aesthetics and conventions were "in some people's view, a most misleading view of the war that had just been fought." Forty and Küchler add: "But it is surely an inevitable feature of memorials … that they permit only certain things to be remembered, and by exclusion cause others to be forgotten." Again, ideology plays a crucial role in this process of memorializing and forgetting.

Strengthening Cultural War Studies

The above discussion contains an (implicit) plea for recognition of the importance of ideology, representation, identity, pain, trauma, and power as analytic categories for War Studies. The importance of these concepts has increased markedly in the last decade – enough for Griffith (2001) to proclaim the cultural turn in (Cold) War Studies. But there continues to be a series of problems. Early versions of Cultural War Studies have not managed to permeate traditional War Studies, leading to a continued underestimation of the importance of these analytic categories in "mainstream" War Studies, and in a number of its subfields. Moreover, Cultural War Studies still has difficulties in defragmenting itself into a critical and fairly coherent – but open and interdisciplinary – subfield of War Studies, or of Cultural Studies. Establishing Cultural War Studies as a separate discipline would of course be self-defeating – a discipline would be too disciplining for any strand of Cultural Studies – but the nomadic nature of Cultural War Studies has prevented it from exerting much influence on either War Studies or Cultural Studies.

War Studies has become a vast field of study, and a diversity of academic subfields has produced an extensive collection of articles, readers and monographs on the issues of war and conflict. Not only have scholars working in the fields of History, Political Studies and International Relations contributed to this body of literature, but Media, Journalism and Communication Studies scholars also have contributed to long lists of publications, while Propaganda Studies has produced an equally extensive set of publications.

Although Propaganda, Media, Journalism and Communication Studies may seem promising for an approach to ideological processes, most of this literature is fairly traditional – albeit sometimes very critical – for instance, in analyses of the problems that journalists have to face when dealing with the military, the difficult relationships between media organizations and the military, and the way that propaganda affects media coverage. Of course, and fortunately, there are exceptions in this subfield that do place a stronger emphasis on ideology, representation and (popular) culture and, more generally, on the relationship between ideology, culture and conflict. But this list is much smaller. Examples that come to mind are *War, culture and the media. Representations of the military in 20th century Britain* (Stewart and Carruthers 1996); *Fighting fictions. War, narrative and national identity* (Foster 1999), *Watching Babylon. The war in Iraq and global visual culture* (Mirzoeff 2005) and *Monsters in the Mirror: Representations of Nazism in Post-war Popular Culture* (Buttsworth and Abbenhuis 2010). Other examples, from the subfield of Holocaust Studies, are *Narrating the Holocaust* (Reiter 2000); *Visual culture and the Holocaust* (Zelizer 2001), *Holocaust and the moving image* (Haggith and Newman 2005) and *The Generation of Postmemory: Writing and Visual Culture After the Holocaust* (Hirsch 2012). As Jeffords (2007, 238) remarks, also militarism is an area of Cultural Studies production, because it refers to "the complex set of social, political, economic, and cultural activities and institutions that support a society that engages in warfare."

And of course, there are authors that defy any classification, such as Paul Virilio (1989; 2002), Jean Baudrillard (1995), Slavoj Žižek (2002; 2004), Susan Sontag (2003) and Judith Butler (2009), who have published work on the role of specific cultural systems in war, such as cinema, the media, and photography. Nevertheless, the attention to ideology and representation in Propaganda, Media, Journalism and Communication Studies is still fairly new and limited, and the culturalist analyses are far from being all-pervasive.

Thus, although it might be too early to claim that the existence of a cultural turn can be expanded to War Studies in general, and it is definitely still too early to refer to an ideological turn in War Studies, Cultural Studies certainly has the potential to fill this gap. It has always exhibited a strong interest in the role that power, ideology and hegemony play in our contemporary conjuncture. Even in the early days of Cultural Studies, exemplified by *Policing the crisis* (Hall et al. 1978), it aimed to critically address the power imbalances in society, and the ways that ideology contributed to the maintenance of these imbalances and to the (self)disciplining of the members of these societies. Arguably, the critical project of Cultural Studies was even strengthened by its generating an opening for polysemy and agency to enter the stage, allowing a move beyond the subject theory of the powerless. Also, Cultural Studies has had a continuing intimate relationship with the concepts of identity, representation, othering and power (see Hall 1997) which makes it extremely suited to providing an ideological angle to War Studies, focusing on the representations that support the ideologies of war and the identities of the Self and the Enemy. Again, Cultural Studies has contributed strongly to the articulation of the concept of representation as part of the critical toolkit, and to revealing the sometimes problematic nature of our ways of seeing and thinking of ourselves and others, for instance in relation to gender, class, and ethnicity.

As already mentioned, a number of authors have published on war from a Cultural Studies perspective, and many more will undoubtedly do so. Also, a number of structuring initiatives have been taken, for instance through the establishment of the working group on *Culture and War* of the *Cultural Studies Association (U.S.)* and the *Journal of War and Culture Studies*. But given the societal and cultural impact of war, such initiatives are relatively few, and they have not managed to push ideology and representation to a higher position on the general War Studies research agenda. This generates an interesting paradox: traditional War Studies scholarship has neglected ideology and representation, and also in the fields that might overcome this shortcoming, none has managed to do so (yet).

One can speculate about the nature of this deficiency. One can look at the disinterest of the more traditional strands of academia in the Cultural Studies apparatus, and their preference for historical realities and factuality. One can look at Cultural Studies itself and carefully suggest the following explanations: the loss of popularity of the concept of ideology in Cultural Studies; its difficulties in looking beyond specific and localized imagined communities, and the conflation of Cultural Studies and the Study of Culture. Without showing much intellectual creativity, one can even blame the more celebratory strands in Cultural Studies that seek out audience agencies. A more positive approach to addressing this deficiency would be to call for a strengthening of Cultural War Studies[5] (a call supported by the present book).

War was pervasive in the 20th century, and so far the 21st century seems to hold little promise of improvement. War is still one of the world's most destructive forces, which on a daily basis touches the lives of millions of people: those who have lived through war (and continue to mourn the losses it has brought), those currently living the war, and those that will live a war still to come. The societal presence of what Knightly (1982) calls "the institution of war" is thus structural, in that it requires all possible perspectives to be put to work to increase our understanding of this pervasiveness and destructiveness, of this eternal repetition of the same. Cultural War Studies has an important role to play in adding to this knowledge, by putting the critical vocabulary (including ideology, representation, and power) of Cultural Studies to good use to analyze the constructions that push us towards a glorified killing of our fellow (wo)men and then try to make us forget the intensity and durability of the trauma.

At the same time a strengthened Cultural War Studies would contribute to Cultural Studies by putting ideology more firmly on its research agenda, and by sharpening its critical objectives. Cultural Studies should be more than a project that combines eloquent textual readings, in-depth analyses of (preferably resistant) consumption practices and a celebration of human agency, seasoned with some high cultural theory. Cultural Studies needs to engage with the horrific, the destructive, the violent-pornographic, the perverse, the vile and the prosaic in our present-day conjuncture, reassuming its key role of relentlessly uncovering the always hidden societal structures that generate oppression, suffering and death. From this perspective, war becomes a borderline case, in which the celebration of human agency might not be the first and best choice. However important and truthful our celebration of agency, resistance and pleasure – and not to ignore the potential of these concepts to theorize and understand the social – it is time to open Pandora's box and attempt to (re)orient the Cultural (War) Studies toolbox towards an analysis of what limits our agency, what destroys our resistance, what perverts our pleasure, and what structures our bare existence. Cultural Studies needs to go to war again.

The book

The main objective of the second edition of this book remains to make a modest contribution to the strengthening of Cultural War Studies. The book implicitly proposes a research agenda that would critically focus on the issues of ideology, representation, identities of Self and Enemy, power, pain and trauma, in relation to the oppressive forces of war. This is not to say that Cultural War Studies should cut its connections with the theoretical and empirical practices of Cultural Studies; these will allow Cultural War Studies to build on an intellectual apparatus whose strengths (and weaknesses) have been proven.

The starting point for this book project was a panel session – entitled *Representing the New Cold War* – at the *Fourth Annual Meeting of the Cultural Studies Association*. The conference in which this session took place was held at the George Mason University in Arlington VA, U.S.A., on April 19-22, 2006. A series of panels at this and other conferences can be seen as the seeds of Cultural War Studies, which for too long has been restricted to the underground of Cultural Studies. The second edition was prepared a few years later, in the summer of 2014, not accidentally 100 years after the beginning of the First World War.

The structure of this edited volume mirrors the research agenda discussed in the present introduction. The first part of the book focuses on the diversity of media that generate meanings and definitions of past and contemporary wars. These chapters are not restricted to the more traditional analyses of media content, but utilize these media products to reflect on the contemporary cultural condition(s) in the U.S.A. and Europe. Rebecca A. Adelman's chapter looks at the representations of war generated by the memorialization of killed soldiers in *Last Letters Home*. Christina Lane's analysis of the post 9-11 film *Flightplan* shows how this film facilitates the belief that the original (historical) trauma can be healed. Metasebia Woldemariam and Kylo-Patrick R. Hart's chapter takes us back to the Rwandan genocide, and its sometimes-problematic filmic representation in *Hotel Rwanda*. Karen J. Hall's chapter acts as a bridge between the first and second parts of the book in analyzing the hard-core representations of war that circulate on the Internet, and the ways these images of torn bodies reproduce the dominant ideological model of war.

The second part of the book moves (at least partially) away from media representations and focuses on torture and incarceration. The practices in the name of "war against terror" in the 21st century have caused a number of shifts in the articulation of human rights, and their relationship with the notions of a just war and justifiable (state) violence. The "use" of Guantánamo (and the disarticulation of its prisoners from the common forms of legal protection) has been defined – well within the framework of the ideological model of war – as regrettable but necessary and unavoidable in the war against terror. The "Ticking Time Bomb" argument has been articulated (as an alibi) to justify the increase in torture practices. Stephanie Athey's chapter offers an important counter-narration to this and similar arguments that legitimize (state) torture, showing its complexity, and especially its omnipresence before and after 2001. Usha Zacharias' chapter looks at what occurred at Abu Ghraib, and the notions of imperial citizenship that made it possible. Although the second part of the book is quite short, it acts as an important interruption, halting the narrative flow of the book to foreground the extreme violence of torture.

The third and final part of the book consists of five chapters on issues related to memory and trauma. A series of (late 19th and) 20th century conflicts and wars are revisited to demonstrate the cultural durability of war and the interconnection of these wars with present-day discourses and practices through the dialectics of remembering, commemorating and forgetting. Gordon Coonfield considers the flying of the flag after 9/11 as a ritual enactment by a traumatized nation. Vincent Stephens's chapter analyzes *A home at the end of the world* and *American pastoral* to illustrate the workings of traumatized citizenship and national identity. Marc Lafleur's chapter revisits the A-bomb artifact, and the way that its history is re-narrated, transforming it from a destructive tool into a celebration of technology and nationhood. Tina Wasserman looks at the work of the Israeli journalist Amira Hass, in order to thematize the difficult relationship between the two traumata that haunt the Middle East: the Holocaust, and the Palestinian Occupation. Finally, through the analysis of a 1937 film on the Dreyfus Affair, Nico Carpentier analyzes how a 19th century conflict becomes a grim portent of the horrors of the Second World War. In going back in time for more than a century, this chapter shows that analyses of cultural trauma should not remain confined to the present era, but require a historical dimension. This part of the book strongly reconnects with the first part in allowing for a reflection on the role of representational practices in the construction of memory and coping with trauma. This reconnection signifies the dynamic process between the representations of traumatic events through a diversity of media, on the one hand, and on the other hand the representations of these events embedded in our memories, that render the (near) past present.

The best way to end a book on an important but not so pleasant topic is to revert to warm words. So I here wish to convey my gratitude to the external and internal reviewers for their (really) appreciated comments, to the staff of CSP for their assistance and good care, and to the authors of this book for combining a professional attitude with great insights, which made my work a fascinating learning experience. Thanks.

But this is also the place to express sadness, as one of our authors, Usha Zacharias, passed away on September 30, 2013. To commemorate her work, this second edition is dedicated to her. It is always difficult to summarize a life in a few words, but I believe we should remember especially her academic work on the cultural politics of gender, media and citizenship, but also her work as an activist in labor and feminist circles and her work as a film-maker. A more detailed In Memoriam was published by Carter and Hegde (2014) in *Feminist Media Studies*.

Notes

[1] Although the focus of this introduction (and the entire book) is on interstate war, a similar argument could be made for intrastate wars.
[2] Haraway's (1991) discussion of these dichotomies has a specific focus on the human/machine dichotomy.
[3] It can be argued that the different ideological models constructed by the different warring parties are inversed, but still similar in their core structure. Galtung (2009, 105), for instance, emphasizes the structural similarities of perceptions: "There are important symmetries in the perception, they are to some extent mirror images of each other, through imitation and projection." Given my cultural embeddedness in Belgium and Western Europe, the development of this model was unavoidably influenced by this specific cultural affinity, despite all attempts at cultural-intellectual empathy, curiosity, and understanding.
[4] The various names ascribed to this conflict are in themselves problematic. Calling it the Second Persian Gulf War (and the 1991 Gulf War the First Persian Gulf War) tends to exclude the 'first' Persian Gulf War, namely the Iran-Iraq war (1980-1988). The absence of clear Western involvement seems to warrant its exclusion from the count. For this reason the more neutral '2003 Iraqi War' is preferred. Media are of course confronted with similar problems, and some made different choices, as Bodi (2004, 244-245) remarks: "Al Jazeera's tag for the conflict was 'War on Iraq', in contrast to the BBC's neutral 'War in Iraq' and Fox News' jingoistic 'Operation Iraqi Freedom' which merely parroted the Pentagon's

name for the conflict." Moreover, the Iraqi War that started in 2003 is lasting
longer than expected; for this reason also, the name '2003 Iraqi War' is preferred
to refer to the first period in this war, which started on March 19 2003 with the
bombing of Baghdad, and ended when the US president George Bush declared the
end of all major combat operations on May 1 2003, in his speech on the USS
Abraham Lincoln. This signaled a new phase in the Iraqi war, which Seib (2004, 1)
ironically calls the "postwar war."
[5] Although contributing to the establishment of peace should be the ultimate and
utopist horizon of Cultural War Studies, calling it Cultural Peace Studies would
only assist in hiding the omnipresence of war and (neo)imperialism.

Works Cited

Ahmad, Aijaz. 2005. Contextualizing conflict. The U.S. "war on
terrorism". In War and the media. Reporting conflict 24/7. Edited by
Daya Kishan Thussu and Des Freedman. London, Thousand Oaks CA,
New Delhi: Sage: 15-27.
Baudrillard, Jean. 1995. The gulf war did not take place. Bloomington IN:
Indiana University Press.
Bodi, Faisal. 2004. Al Jazeera's war. In Tell me lies. Propaganda and
distortion in the attack on Iraq. Edited by David Miller. London: Pluto
Press, 243-250.
Bourke, Joanna. 1999. An intimate history of killing. Face-to-face killing
in twentieth century warfare. London: Granta Books.
Buelens, Gert, Durrant Sam, and Eaglestone, Robert. 2014. Introduction.
In The future of trauma theory. Contemporary literary and cultural
criticism. Edited by Gert Buelens, Sam Durrant, and Robert
Eaglestone. London: Routledge, 1-8.
Butler, Judith. 2009. Frames of war. When is life grievable? London:
Verso.
Buttsworth, Sara, and Abbenhuis, Maartje M. (ed.) 2010. Monsters in the
Mirror: Representations of Nazism in Post-war Popular Culture. Santa
Barbara: ABC-CLIO.
Carpentier, Nico. 2005. Identity, contingency and rigidity. The (counter-)
hegemonic constructions of the identity of the media professional,
Journalism 6(2): 199-219.
—. 2007. Fighting discourses. Discourse theory, war and representations
of the 2003 Iraqi War. In Communicating war: Memory, media and
military. Edited by Sarah Maltby. Cambridge: Cambridge Scholars
Press.
Carter, Cynthia, and Hegde, Radha Sarma. 2014. In Memoriam—Usha
Zacharias. Feminist Media Studies 14(1): 3-4.

de Certeau, Michel. 1992. The writing of history. New York: Columbia University Press.

Deuze, Mark. 2005. What is journalism? Professional identity and ideology of journalists reconsidered, Journalism, Theory Practice & Criticism 6(4): 443-465.

Ellul, Jacques. 1973. Propaganda: The formation of men's attitudes. New York: Vintage Books.

Erikson, Kai. 1976. Everything in its path. New York: Simon and Schuster.

Eyerman, Ron. 2001. Cultural trauma: Slavery and the formation of African American identity. Cambridge: Cambridge University Press.

Forty, Adrian, and Küchler, Susanne (Eds). 1999. The art of forgetting. Oxford: Berg.

Foster, Kevin. 1999. Fighting fictions. War, narrative and national identity. London: Pluto Press.

Foucault, Michel. 1978. History of sexuality. Part 1. An introduction. New York: Pantheon.

—. 1979. Discipline and punish: The birth of the prison. New York: Vintage Books.

Galtung, Johan. 2009. Theories of conflict. Definitions, dimensions, negations, formations. Oslo: Transcend.

Galtung, Johann, and Vincent, Richard C. 1992. Global glasnost: Toward a new world information and communication order? Cresskill NJ: Hampton Press.

Griffith, Robert. 2001. The cultural turn in Cold War Studies. Reviews in American History 29(1): 150-157.

Haggith, Toby, and Newman, Joanna (Eds). 2005. Holocaust and the moving image. Representations in film and television since 1933. London: Wallflower.

Hall, Stuart (Ed.). 1997. Representation: cultural representations and signifying practices. London, Thousand Oaks CA and New Delhi: Sage Publications.

Hall, Stuart, Critcher, Chas, Jefferson, Tony, Clarke, John, and Roberts, Brian. 1978. Policing the crisis: Mugging, the state, and law and order. London: MacMillan.

Hallin, Daniel C. 1986. The "uncensored war". The media and Vietnam. Berkely, Los Angeles, London: University of California Press.

Haraway, Donna. 1991. A cyborg manifesto: Science, technology, and socialist-feminism in the late twentieth century. In Simians, cyborgs and women. The reinvention of nature. Edited by Donna Haraway. New York: Routledge, 149-181.

Hirsch, Marianne. 2012. The generation of postmemory: Writing and visual culture after the holocaust. New York: Columbia University Press.

Howard, Michael. 2001. The invention of peace. Reflections on war and international order. London: Profile Books.

Jeffords, Susan. 2007. War. In Keywords for American Cultural Studies. Edited by Bruce Burgett and Glenn Hendler. New York: NYU Press.

Jowett, Garth. 1997. Toward a propaganda analysis of the Gulf War. In Desert Storm and the Mass Media. Edited by Bradley Greenberg and Walter Gantz. Cresskill NJ: Hampton Press, 74-85.

Keen, Sam. 1986. Faces of the enemy. New York: Harper and Row.

Kellner, Douglas. 1992. The Persian Gulf TV War. Boulder CO, San Francisco CA, Oxford: Westview Press.

Knightley, Philip. 1982. The first casualty of war. London: Quartet.

LaCapra, Dominick. 1999. Trauma. Absense, loss. Critical Enquiry 25(4): 696-727.

Laclau, Ernesto, and Mouffe, Chantal. 1985. Hegemony and socialist strategy. Towards a radical democratic politics. London: Verso.

Laclau, Ernesto. 1990. New reflections on the revolution of our time. London: Verso.

—. 1996. Emancipations. London, Verso.

Lewis, Jeff. 2002. Cultural studies. The basics. London: Routledge.

McNair, Brian. 1998. The sociology of journalism. London, New York, Sydney, Auckland: Arnold.

Michael, George. 2002. Statement on *Shoot the dog*. Downloaded on March 15, 2004 from http://george.michael.szm.sk/Lyrics/lyrstdog.html.

Mirzoeff, Nicholas. 2005. Watching Babylon. The War in Iraq and global visual culture. New York: Routledge.

Papadakis, Yiannis. 2006. Toward an Anthropology of Ethnic Autism. In Divided Cyprus: Modernity, History, and an Island in Conflict. Edited by in Yiannis Papadakis, Nicos Peristianis and Gisela Welz. Bloomington: Indiana University Press, 66-83.

Reiter, Andrea. 2000. Narrating the holocaust. London: Continuum.

Sant Cassia, Paul. 2005. Bodies of Evidence: Burial, Memory and the Recovery of Missing Persons in Cyprus. New York: Berghahn Books.

Schlesinger, Philip. 1987. Putting "reality" together. London and New York: Methuen.

Seib, Phillip (ed.). 2004. Lessons from Iraq: The news media and the next war. The Lucius W. Nieman Symposium 2003. Milwaukee WI: Marquette University.

Sontag, Susan. 2003. Regarding the pain of others. New York: Farrar, Straus and Giroux.

Stewart, Ian, Carruthers, Susan L. 1996. War, culture and the media. Representations of the military in 20th century Britain. Trowbridge, Wilts: Flicks Books.

Taithe, Bertrand, and Thornton, Tim. 1999. Propaganda: A misnomer of rhetoric and persuasion? In Propaganda. Political rhetoric and identity 1300-2000. Edited by Bertrand Taithe and Tim Thornton. Phoenix Mill: Sutton Publishing, 1-24.

Taylor, Philip M. 1995. Munitions of the mind: A history of propaganda from the ancient world to the present era. Manchester: Manchester University Press.

Torfing, Jakob. 1999. New theories of discourse. Laclau, Mouffe and Žižek. Oxford: Blackwell.

Tuchman, Gaye. 1972. Objectivity as a strategic ritual: An examination of newsmen's notions of objectivity. American Journal of Sociology 77: 660-679.

Virilio, Paul. 1989. War and cinema: The logistics of perception. London: Verso.

—. 2002. Desert screen. War at the speed of light. London: Continuum.

Zelizer, Barbie (ed.). 2001. Visual culture and the Holocaust. New Brunswick NJ: Rutgers University Press.

Žižek, Slavoj. 1989. The sublime object of ideology. London: Verso.

—. 2002. Welcome to the desert of the real. London and New York: Verso.

—. 2004. Iraq: The borrowed kettle. London and New York: Verso.

PART I:

MEDIA REPRESENTATIONS OF WAR

"FORT LIVING ROOM": GENDER, RACE, CLASS, SEXUALITY, AND SENTIMENT IN THE HBO DOCUMENTARY *LAST LETTERS HOME*[1]

REBECCA A. ADELMAN

Introduction

Over the course of Operation Iraqi Freedom, the U.S. military sustained 4412 fatalities, and 66 more during the subsequent Operation New Dawn (Department of Defense 2014). Simultaneously, since the U.S. invasion the Iraq Body Count estimates that 126,155-140,903 Iraqi civilians have been killed (Iraq Body Count 2014). Before these numbers, one perhaps wonders what else there is to be said, what sense there is to be made.

And so, in many ways, this chapter is an inquiry into the unwieldy. This fundamental awkwardness is reflected in its lengthy title, and made more acute by the ungainly numbers with which it begins. Thus, insofar as it is conceptualized out of incomprehensibility, it proceeds from a position at an ironic distance from its central object, a documentary text which distills these counts into 60 minutes of cleanly edited film, telling a story that is otherwise unintelligible. The dexterity with which the film manages all the discourses (reduced to single words and crammed into the title of this article) is the location of its power and its danger, while its stark presentation provides an unintentional counterpoint to the difficulty of accessing information about the dead and the true nature of the conflict.

Once the dead are buried, the jobs of grieving and narration remain; tasks which are only made more urgent by each new casualty; the grief is endless, while the discourses must be elastic enough to accommodate every new loss. The HBO Films documentary *Last Letters Home: Voices of American Troops from the Battlefields of Iraq* (2004) reflects both of these demands for a war that has never lent itself to easy explanations. Like Vietnam, this war had been politically and culturally "discredited" (Walter 1999, 45; see also Harvey 2002, 197), and so its dead were uniquely difficult to commemorate, though mourning was, and is, imperative. Of necessity, the film borrows from codes of race, gender, sexuality, and class that teach us to value certain lives (and deaths) above others. Thus the film makes its message maximally comprehensible while mitigating the post-9/11 pain of the "affliction of the previously invulnerable" (Retort 2005, 5). These ideologies provide logic to the conundrum of so many dead and offer a way into the film, ultimately ensuring the success of its effort to evoke particular emotional responses.

The idea that the media is an economy is axiomatic. What is perhaps less obvious is that it is an economy with two currencies: actual money and emotional capital. Media outlets compete for shares of the market but also for monopolies on audience attention (Debatin 2002, 163), which is literally priceless, though it can certainly be bought. Affect is thus a commodity and a fundamental component of late capitalist markets (Massumi 2002, 45), which traffic in experiences, sensations, and events. As such a system, the media generates specific types of memories and "produces a particular kind of 'forgetting'" (Ashplant, Dawson, and Roper 2000, 70) through its narrations.

Stories that do not follow established patterns are scarcely intelligible (Galtung 2004, 187), and thus certain narratives endlessly regenerate themselves in a process that is predictable and pleasurable. Part of the routinization of narrative in the media relates to the idea of sentiment, insofar as popular media texts offer the opportunity to process emotions in a way that is standardized and satisfying. Viewers tuning in to *Last Letters Home*, then, expect to feel sadness, but can anticipate a sense of closure, delivered by the contained nature of the narrative, its suggestion of completeness, and its promise of catharsis. Mediated death, grief, and suffering are things that we know how to handle, their mastery guaranteed in the documentary by an elaborate and effective emotional apparatus.

Given that the first Gulf War lasted only a month and cost the United States less than 400 lives, at the outset of this one, Americans[2] did not anticipate the need to grieve for so many. As the War grew increasingly unpopular,[3] however, there was confusion and disagreement about what to do, and this perplexity shaped the cultural milieu into which the film arrived. How was it possible that the American nation could be saddened by the loss of its heroes, those who are arguably its best citizens insofar as service members embody ideal Americanness more precisely than any other group, without agitating widely for the most logical (if unfeasible) solution: a complete withdrawal of troops?

Luc Boltanski's (1999) analysis of the ethical implications of witnessing suffering provides one explanation. Many opponents of the war seemed to assume that sadness for the deaths of soldiers or empathy was a radical response, an obstacle to its engines. But for those who only experienced these losses secondhand, quite the opposite may very well be the case. Boltanski writes that "[T]o arouse pity, suffering and wretched bodies must be conveyed in such a way as to affect the sensibility of those more fortunate" (1999, 11); their appearances are always orchestrated, reframed in accordance with the spectators' desires. "[S]entimental pity," then, has a "hidden alliance with the social order" (1999, 139), as pitying creates a distance which keeps us from acting on behalf of those who suffer, while the barrage of deaths and images pushes us through a tiny, accelerated process of mourning again and again. Simultaneously, sentiment works alongside structures of racialization and gendering, reinforcing them by determining what sorts of bodies are worthy of admiration and pity (Wanzo 2009). Images of the war dead can work like nothing else to "create the illusion of consensus" in the national community (Sontag 2003, 6), and these losses are rendered intelligible through the rhetoric of sacrifice as they pass from private tragedy to public spectacle. Thus the media, while bound to report casualties, at least occasionally, generally does so in ways engineered to provoke an impotent kind of grief, rather than resistance to the incursion that demands it. To this norm, *Last Letters Home* is no exception.

Last Letters Home: Considering a requiem

After "9/11"[4], U.S. citizenship reemerged as a concept that was meaningful, fashionable (Barber 2003, 88), and eminently marketable. The invasion of Iraq proved more difficult to sell, but films about soldiers are always popular, particularly in the aftermath of September 11th, which created a "renewed appetite for war stories" (Dixon 2004, 1). Thus, shortly after the 2004 Presidential Election, on 11 November 2004 (Veteran's Day), HBO (a popular U.S. cable channel known for its edgy and political original programming) premiered a documentary featuring surviving family members of U.S. military personnel who died in Iraq. *Last Letters Home* was a timely contribution to the genre of the commemorative war text and another in the "long tradition of dual-use products resulting from the cooperation between the military and the film industry" (Thomas and Virchow 2005, 27).

The film, produced at a time when the occupation seemed less ill-fated (Kaplan 2005, 331) than it would subsequently prove to be, offers its audience the opportunity to mournfully participate in the national community while shouldering part of the military's funereal responsibility.[5] It capitalizes on what Wendy Kozol has astutely described as an "affective tug" surrounding depictions of American military personnel (2009, n.p.). In a strange departure from cable media business practice, which also might be explicable – at least partially – in terms of the potential for good public relations to follow from such a move, HBO decided to "open its signal, making the program available to almost all cable households" ("About the Film") on the night it premiered, expanding its reach. The documentary was regularly rebroadcast on all HBO channels, and HBO's website included a comprehensive section about it; interested viewers could learn more about the film and the families it features.

Last Letters Home is the work of Bill Couturié, who has developed a number of documentaries similar to this one. The project's website features an interview with him, in which he outlines his goal of making a film that is "Very honest, very direct." For Couturié, capturing and disseminating these stories is a "sacred duty." He asserts that his "point was not to make a movie about the political justification of the war [, but to] talk about the human cost of the war. And allow the audience … to make up their own minds."

Capitalizing on the "significant vogue" of documentary filmmaking (Tobias 1998, 1), particularly in the early days of the Global War on Terror when American audiences seemed especially hungry for information (Mellencamp 2006, 129), *Last Letters Home* was a commercial venture. The film was released at a moment when American public and popular cultures were troping the narrative of just war (Dixon 2004, 1) while managing the residual traumas of September 11th, that "ultimate form of reality television" (Debatin 2002, 167). Compared to coverage of the terrorist attacks and of the subsequent wars, *Last Letters Home* is stylized, even though it retains traces of the roughness integral to documentary film, and controlled. It references terror and war, but does so with an imperturbable calm, all the while provoking the audience to a particular kind of feeling.

This film has all the hallmarks of HBO original programming, as it is technically masterful, socially relevant, and emotionally compelling. It is a montage of 11 families reading their final correspondence from loved ones[6], interspersed with personal snapshots – now such a popular form of wartime photography (Davis 2006, 32)[7] – of the deceased. Each segment opens with a military portrait of the dead soldier, framed in black. The person's rank and full name appear in white lettering and below it a brief caption with the cause and place of death (i.e. "Killed by an explosion in Baghdad"). This information fades out and is replaced with a past-tense statement about the person's age (i.e. "He was 51"). The whole screen then dissolves into an image of their hometown. During the interviews, surviving family members share letters and e-mails which are alternately finished or incomplete, received before or after the soldier's death, and oddly prescient or painfully optimistic about the author's future. All segments end with another photo of the deceased, again captioned by their name and rank and their dates of birth and death. The segments run uninterrupted, and their identical format lends the text coherence and also invests it with a sense of military uniformity; upon closer inspection, though, the flimsiness of this illusion of sameness becomes clear.

The imperative of homogeneity echoes the goal of ultimate similarity in commemorations of those who have made the ultimate sacrifice, navigating a dialectic of the fundamental individuality of the war memorial and the collectivity there expressed (Ashplant, Dawson, and Roper 2000, 18). Benedict Anderson writes that in monuments to war dead[8], "names are stripped of all substantive sociological significance ... No class, no religion, no age, and no politics" (1998, 363); *Last Letters Home* stands askance to that, offering the simultaneous promise of non-discrimination while seeking quietly and insistently to highlight everything that disappears before Anderson's eyes. The constitutive lack of personalizing organization in the "scar" (Lin quoted in Rowlands 1999, 139) that is the Vietnam Wall, the anonymity that shrouds the Tomb of the Unknown Soldier, and the habits of repetition and sameness in memorializing war dead all inform the structure of the film. However, the contentions that there is equality in death or in American cultural responses to it seem fictions.

The documentary features letters read by the survivors of these people:

Table 2-1: Summary of *Last Letters Home*

Casualty	Race/Gender/Age (*)	Survivor(s)	Segment Time	Snapshots (Total)
Spc. Michelle M. Witmer	White woman, 20	Mother, father, sister	6:53	12 (14)
Pfc. Raheen Tyson Heighter	African-American man, 22	Mother [grandmother](**)	4:45	5 (7)
Sgt. Frank T. Carvill	White man, 51(***)	Sister [2 nephews]	3:30	6 (8)
Spc. Robert Allen Wise	White man, 21(****)	Mother, girlfriend	4:53	7 (9)
Capt. Joshua T. Byers	White man, 29	Mother, father [2 brothers]	4:46	5 (7)
2nd Lt. Leonard M. Cowherd	White man, 22	Wife, mother, father	5:05	9 (11)

Pfc. Francisco Martinez-Flores	Latino man, 21	Mother, sister	4:08	6 (8)
Capt. Pierre E. Piché	White man, 29	Mother, father [wife]	5:39	8 (10)
Spc. Holly J. McGeough	White woman, 19(****)	Mother, father	6:14	6 (8)
Pfc. Jesse A. Givens	White man, 34	Wife [2 sons (1 unborn)]	7:15	5 (7)

(*) Race/gender identity is inferred from phenotype and appearance in photos. Although we cannot know how any of the dead identified themselves in terms of race or gender, the creators of the film seem to have chosen subjects who were not ambiguously raced or gendered according to prevailing schemas.

(**) I have listed the survivors that appear on camera, [bracketing] those who are mentioned but not interviewed.

(***) This person is not visually or narratively coded as heterosexual.

(****) This family is visually or narratively marked as working-class.

Despite the differences in the details of each soldier's story, there is one important thing that all vignettes have in common: they commemorate each soldier through his or her *family*. Indeed, the only people who appear on camera are immediate family: parents and spouses. In this way, the film privatizes grief (by confining it to the sphere of the family) even as it makes it public (by broadcasting it). *Last Letters Home* reinscribes discourses about the centrality and integrity of the American family, privileging close relatives – rather than friends or families of choice – as the appropriate and rightful bearers of sadness and agents of mourning, while also using the figure of the family to domesticate what Judith Butler has described as the potentially destabilizing force of mourning (Butler 2000). *Last Letters Home* relies on the sentimental power of the symbol of the family to facilitate its affective project.

Commemorative labor:
The (a)political in *Last Letters Home*

We make sense of ourselves in the world by connecting "personal biography with historical events" (Eber and Neal 2002b, 178), but when we have no claim to the occurrences in question, we often seek to fuse ourselves emotionally to those who do. The media is a conduit in this process, insofar as "individuals do not actually experience events" (Debord 1995, 141) in societies where everything is mediated. Accordingly, most wars are remembered primarily through their representations (Calder 2004, 23), rather than through any other mode. *Last Letters Home* enables unification of the grieving self to the grieving nation, but this grafting is complicated by the dynamics of media consumption, which muddy the already problematic processes of identifying with the suffering other. What distinguishes collective traumas from individual disasters is that shared crises unite groups of people, while individual problems tend to isolate the sufferer from non-afflicted peers (McLean 2004, 65). Because the collective trauma of the terrorist attacks on the United States ostensibly unified the populace, a documentary such as this becomes particularly compelling, as it resonates with a new understanding of shared American identity, both amongst citizens and between citizens and the state (Anker 2012). Further, the ideological response to the attacks circumscribed the representational field so that "an overvisibility of controlled imagery causes an information overload that chokes ... other possible images" (Richard 2003, 133) and constructs our engagements with them.

But this history alone did not guarantee that *Last Letters Home* would be favorably received. It is also important to note that the United States privileges "martial citizenship" (D'Amico 2000, 105), epitomized by the "classic, immemorial labor of infantry" (Kaplan 2005, 361); as a culture and society, Americans prize military service above a range of other criteria for determining belonging and membership. Additionally, though Americans are fascinated with their military personnel, only a particular version of their suffering makes engaging entertainment. After all, the affliction of heroes is compelling not because they are weak but because they are strong (Boltanski 1999, 131). The grief of people featured in *Last Letters Home* is modulated, while the ubiquitous letters keep the film soundly in the ideological terrain of the heroic, even as the actual rhetoric of heroism is strangely absent from the text of the film.

Considering the tendency to invoke the language of heroism when speaking of war dead, the film's relative silence here is odd, but not entirely shocking. Perhaps the most plausible explanation for it lies in the documentary's methodical avoidance of controversial claims, for the seemingly innocuous designation of a fallen soldier as a "hero" might in fact index far more than a simple honorific. Given the context of an unpopular war and a divided national audience, explicitly deeming one of its victims a 'hero' might elicit deeply polarized responses: whether, as was the case in Vietnam, anti-war skepticism about whether or not a U.S. soldier on this mission could actually qualify as heroic, or anti-war anger at the circumstances that produced the occasion for this kind of sacrifice. Furthermore, the category of "hero" is jealously guarded, the boundaries carefully policed – would not there be some in the audience who would balk at expanding it to include a female soldier, a nonheterosexual soldier, a soldier who is not white?

Last Letters Home successfully dodges the more complicated questions of American patriotism and also of foreign policy. Non-Western countries have long been "missing" from U.S. media (Galtung 2004, 227), and Iraq itself is not meaningfully present here, an absence which forecloses questions about the rightness of the war. Though a number of the soldiers commented disparagingly about Iraq, the film couches such articulations in safer terms while de-emphasizing that commentary. For example, in the section featuring the mother and girlfriend of Spc. Wise, the camera catches a quick post-script that reads: "IRAQ STINKS!" But his mother quickly interrupts as she reads the second post-script, in which he writes, "'There's no place like home (click)'" three times and then laments, "Damn! It didn't work again."[9] The notion of a soldier who misses the comforts of home, and situates that longing charmingly within a reference to popular culture, is far more manageable than the soldier who expresses misgivings about the U.S. military presence in Iraq.

One of the things that make the film appear innocuous is its seeming lack of a political agenda, which is especially striking if we consider the ease with which soldiers' words can be assimilated to an anti-war position.[10] *Last Letters Home* holds patriotic sadness and dissenting anger apart from one another by parsing them carefully at the level of narrative and distracting the viewer at the level of affect. Further, there are no angry survivors in the film, nor are there angry letters; there is nothing in the story which suggests that disagreement with the war is a logical response. Only sadness seems to make sense, and the film works so heavily on the viewers' emotions that it is difficult, after watching it, to take any kind of intellectual position at all. *Last Letters Home* relies on the "primacy of the affective in image reception" (Massumi 2002, 24), the capacity of affective response to overwhelm all others.

Just being sad, or even remorseful, however, is not enough, and so viewers are put to work despite their sorrow, invited to enact the ritual that might be understood as commemorative labor. The film's primary project is this revalued task of remembrance, as the thing without which "living activities ... would lose their reality at the end of each process and disappear as though they had never been" (Arendt [1958] 1998, 95). The job of commemorative labor is active, if not productive of tangible goods, but is also demanding, requiring careful attention to the stories and astute, if unspoken, comprehension of what they mean, and also serves the state that cannot afford to have its citizens immobilized by grief.[11] The wage is competitive in its way, and more than enough to ensure access to the affective post-9/11 American community. And at the risk of belaboring the metaphor, one might say that commemoration is a growth industry, whose opportunities for advancement will surely proliferate as various fights and wars against terrorism persist.[12]

Remembrance, however, is typically understood to be apolitical, simply the right and reasonable thing to do, and the notion of commemorative *labor* grates against our cultural intuitions about death, grief, and memory. But there is no categorically "proper way to remember" (Eber and Neal 2002a, 10), so commemorative labors must be structured in accordance with other ideological practices. This is particularly true in the case of otherwise incomprehensible deaths. "By rupturing human bonds, death threatens social solidarity; by affirming social bonds, the rituals of mourning reconstitute society" (Walter 1999, 21), and so the film seeks to control the messier aspects of the war with a reliance on the familiar rhetoric of race, class, gender, and (hetero)sexuality.

Grief sutured into narrative:
The stories in *Last Letters Home*

Turning now to the film itself, it is important to treat the vignettes in order, to preserve the thread of continuity that binds the film into a coherent whole and to acknowledge the deliberate nature of its construction. The film relies on certain ideological and thus affective juxtapositions in order to remain intelligible and provocative of its intended responses. In turn, the normative families win our sympathy easily, while those families which deviate highlight the normalness (and thus the grievability) of the others; after all, commemorative labor occasionally requires grieving for those who might otherwise seem ungrievable (this is part of the work of it), but always knowing the difference.

The first story features the family of Spc. Michelle M. Witmer. Hers is the only story that includes images of Iraq: two snapshot panoramas of Baghdad illustrate her mother's reading of an e-mail to her father. The message consisted largely of her writing about life-changing experiences in Iraq, thus stripping those pictures of the political charge they might have carried, locating them instead within a white woman's coming of age. Interestingly, Spc. Witmer's accounts of Iraq are among the most revealing; she asks her parents to "please pray for [her]" because being in Iraq is "no cakewalk." She wrote on the eve of an armored vehicle patrol, and notes that they had been trained to expect civilians to run in front of their tanks in an effort to stop them; she tells her family that she has been prepared to run people over if necessary, "even kids." The horror of this, "the classic tradition of unconventional war" (Kaplan 2005, 365), is undone, however, by the inclusion of 3 snapshots that show Spc. Witmer in uniform and the smiling company of Iraqi children. This opening story sets the tone for the rest of the film, striking a balance between the barbarity of war and the humanizing power of individual soldiers' narratives.

Having left the Witmers, the audience meets Cathy Heighter, the mother of Pfc. Raheen Tyson Heighter, an African-American man, her brief interview and lack of photos standing in glaring contrast to the preceding story. Generally, this representation of an African-American male soldier coheres with a pattern of imaging this group as excessively violent and physically powerful. Of the 5 pictures of Pfc. Heighter, two feature him holding an AK-47, while a third shows him flexing his muscles. The shortness of the segment relative to the one that precedes it and the lack of sentimentalizing photographs remind us again of the urgency of asking what deaths we "dismis[s]" (Brottman 2004, 177). The ending photo is also noteworthy; of all 11, it is the only one that is a posed portrait, a graduation picture of Pfc. Heighter in mortarboard and gown. This highly identifiable form of portraiture arguably functions to ease the American public into doing something unaccustomed: grieving for an African-American man. This photograph affirms that Pfc. Heighter is a good citizen, unthreatening to all but the enemy, and radically expands the significatory possibilities for the vignette about his life. While the snapshots of him and his weapon invite fantasy about black hyper-masculinity, the portrait of him mediates the terrifying other side of that representation, assuaging white anxiety about uncontrollably violent blackness. Thus, his death becomes a tragedy rather than a relief.

Perhaps the most inscrutable segment is the next one, that of Sgt. Frank T. Carvill. It is the shortest of all 11 stories, and because of this and its not unrelated lack of interviews with immediate family, one might ask why the documentary invites us to overlook the death of this man, survived by his sister and her sons. His last letter home was addressed to the boys, while this tribute contains the most patriotic signifiers: a snapshot of Carvill on a boat with his nephews in FDNY and NYPD baseball caps, another of Sgt. Carvill posed with a group of men before a U.S. flag. The unusual preponderance of symbols of Americanness here, in a piece that exhibits so many other striking differences from its neighbors, works as a compensation for the lack of normative family structures ordering the narrative of Sgt. Carvill's life; he is not survived by a wife or children of his own, but is instead established as a worthy subject of grief by his patriotism and nobility.

A different kind of revision is required in the representation of the mother and girlfriend of Spc. Robert Allen Wise. These women live in a trailer, and the audience learns this before we see their faces, in the opening shot of their home, which Spc. Wise calls "Fort Living Room," an expression that poignantly captures the pervasiveness of American militarization. In his last letters, he wrote to his mother about life in the desert and going 20 days without a shower, and sent his girlfriend drawings of the house imagined for them. Indeed, the dominant theme of this section is "home"; after all, "IRAQ STINKS." The language of domesticity and the longing for things quintessentially American (expressed in anticipation of a trip to "Olive Garden and DQ" as soon as he returns) contrasts with his family's non-traditional housing and living arrangements. Because the American Dream is not understood to include a mobile home, Spc. Wise's fluency with the appropriate desires for suburban consumption militates against otherwise disruptive perceptions of low class status. Moreover, the film makes clear that Spc. Wise aspires to something apparently better in its careful recounting (via his girlfriend) of his plans, an emphasis on goals which seems to echo the decision to end the story of Pfc. Heighter with the official portrait, both signifying upward mobility and thus, worthiness of grief.

Having managed to commemorate Spc. Wise, *Last Letters Home* returns to more normative and navigable terrain with the parents of Capt. Joshua T. Byers. The deceased is a white man, marked as middle-class by his parents' disclosure that they were returning from vacation when they got the news of their son's death, identified as heterosexual through the inclusion of a wedding picture at the end of his story, and defined as upwardly mobile by his report that he was expecting a promotion to a command position. The film does not accentuate anything that might make Capt. Byers legible as different: the segment is neither noticeably long nor noticeably brief, and the focal point is truly the grief of his parents, especially his otherwise stoic father, whose crying forces a cut while he collects himself. There is no need to establish Capt. Byers as a worthy cause for grieving; such a response is obvious, and his segment punctuates the more complicated stories that precede and follow it.

2nd Lt. Leonard M. Cowherd was newly married when he was killed in Karbala. He is survived by his wife and his parents, and their stories are told separately within a single section of the film; his wife – who reads an incomplete letter that the military forwarded after his death – begins. Cynthia Enloe notes that "military wives have long been the subject of shifting policy calculations" (2000, 155), and this dynamic discursive legacy is evidenced and imaged here. They become visible only during

times of national crisis, and are mobilized in strategic ways,[13] always as
nobly suffering; Sarah Cowherd is thus located within an iconographic
precedent. Her portion of the story is brief; either because her letter was
short or because she does not quite fulfill our vision of the good military
wife. She confesses to crying uncontrollably when she learned that her
husband would be deployed, and though this is a touching expression of
love, it is also a deviation from the ideal patriotic woman, willing to
sacrifice her husband for her nation. Moreover, we gather from context
that 2nd Lt. Cowherd is not long dead at the time of filming, but a quick
shot of Mrs. Cowherd holding a photograph clearly shows her newly-
manicured fuchsia nails. Because "[G]rief is surrounded by expectations"
(Walter 1999, 121) with which we are all familiar, something about Mrs.
Cowherd's mourning seems amiss. So that this man might be properly
remembered, then, the film splits his time between his widow and his
parents; this is the only segment that crosses between two locations. His
parents relay a far more detailed piece of correspondence, and their grief is
above reproach. In the last letter they received from their son, he quotes
the Bible and asserts that he has "stayed the course," a clear echo (whether
intentional or not) of President Bush's rhetoric of persistence against all
odds.[14]

Whereas 2nd Lt. Cowherd's parents fill the representationally problematic
gaps left by his wife's interview, the mother and sister of Pfc. Francisco
Martinez-Flores cannot, by virtue of their ethnic difference, adequately
make the case for the importance of their loss. Indeed, because he wrote to
his family in Spanish, and his mother's English is limited (the only time
she spoke English was when she apologized, saying "Sorry" for crying),
his sister had to translate. The film thus relies on the sentimental
momentum allowed by the previous segments and the power of the story
of Pfc. Martinez-Flores' physical death, which is exceptionally graphic: he
drowned in his tank. It is the impact of this type of death that makes this
segment powerful; we are not a nation inclined to grieve over someone so
thoroughly marked as non-white (Cacho 2012).[15] The sheer horror of
dying like this is magnified by the fact that his sister leafs through a photo
album of water-damaged pictures, developed posthumously, and
(presumably, or at least potentially) trumps the ambivalence that viewers
might feel when confronted with the death of a man of color. We might
also consider that some viewers could relish the thought of a man of color
dying thusly, a more troubling explanation for the attention paid to the
precise manner of his death.

The following segment, featuring the parents of Capt. Pierre E. Piché
on the banks of a river in Starksboro, VT, requires no such embellishment,

but does contain an interesting rupture in the apolitical veneer of the documentary. Capt. Piché, we learn, had been preparing to go to graduate school for teaching when he was sent to Iraq. He told his parents he was trying to "roll with the punches" of military life, but admitted that he could not wait to get out, being certain that he had adequately done his duty after a year at war. He was proud, he wrote, to defend his country, but he did not want to do it long-term; though he is "not an idealist," he feels like he needs to do something he can believe in. What logically follows from this is a declaration that this war does not qualify, but instead, his mother immediately began talking about how he wanted to be a teacher, reading only intermittently from the letter. This might suggest creative editing or careful prompting from the interviewer, or it may have been spontaneous; the facts of the situation are less relevant than the film's avoidance of any prolonged discussion of a soldier's doubt in his mission. At the same time, however, Capt. Piché's misgivings also receive the most narrative latitude. It is difficult to imagine that the film would have permitted these articulations to go undisciplined if a less ideal(ized) soldier had issued them. If these critiques had come from a soldier who was of color or working class, they would have raised the specter of conscription by circumstance of the poor and the non-white in the U.S. military, which may well have been too much for a text already so freighted. And so viewers are quickly returned to ground that is less ideologically shaky.

The articulate reserve of Capt. Piché's parents stands in stark contrast to the less refined speech of the survivors of Spc. Holly J. McGeough.[16] The Zasadnys, her parents, begin by relaying an anecdote from their daughter about doing "poop duty," a chore related to the lack of toilet facilities in Iraq. Though the family's home looks sufficiently suburban, they are marked as lower-class by their incorrect syntax and the content of the letters that they read. As Barbara Ehrenreich points out, one of the most common rhetoric of working class representation is "mental inferiority" (1995, 42), and the Zasadnys' seeming amusement over matters related to defecation and their slight but noticeable errors in grammar (i.e. "I seen the man ...") identify them as deviating from standard, accepted, ostensibly educated forms of speech. In Holly's letter to her mother, she comments that Christmas is approaching and asks that if she "decides to get drunk, [she] ha[s] a Captain Morgan and Dr. Pepper for me," a clear departure from middle-class norms about proper holiday observances. She also tells her mother that when she gets back, they will go shopping and she (Mrs. Zasadny) "won't need those pills anymore." The gaze of the camera is detached here, and places spectators in the position of benevolent condescension, allowing them to revel in the feeling of their own compassion, sympathizing from a distance with the masses. At the same time, the interviewer seems uneasy with the unmediated display of lower-class whiteness. In one of his few recorded intrusions into the narrative, he prompts Mrs. Zasadny, "And when did you get the card?" – as if to end this as quickly as possible.

Last Letters Home concludes with the story which is the easiest for it to tell but is, perhaps for that very reason, also the hardest to watch. It features the widow of Pfc. Jesse A. Givens,[17] who was pregnant with their second son when she received the news of his death. He mailed his last letter home with instructions to read it only if he did not return; she received it upon her release from the hospital after childbirth. Mrs. Givens' patriotism is literally present on her body, as she is wearing a sweater with an U.S. flag in the shape of a heart.[18] Just out of focus in the background is a brightly-colored pile of children's toys. The camera displays no uneasiness with Mrs. Givens. This segment is by far the longest, and in a deviation from the talking-head style typical of documentary framing, Mrs. Givens is occasionally shot (usually when she cries) from a low angle, more reflective of narrative film cinematography. She is, in many ways, the documentary's perfect subject: grieving appropriately, her blond femininity accented by her pregnancy and production of two sons, happily and loyally married; she has "lost the love of [her] life." Thus, Mrs. Givens sits and cries quietly at the confluence of the "three interlinked locations of guaranteed national Goodness: The Unborn, The (heroic) Dead, and The Living" (Anderson 1998, 360ff.) who persevere in the hope for "[a]nother chance, another chance" (Anderson 1998, 364) for their country to get it right.

Quantifying the incalculable in *Last Letters Home*

From there, the film dissolves, as Mrs. Givens' story provides the air of closure so common in televised war stories (Willis 2005, 116) but also futurity, made real in their sons, while the credits highlight the essentially cinematic character of the text. This conclusion is artificial, as the list of war dead continued (and continues still, in various ways) to grow exponentially beyond the documentary's diegetic domestic space, and so provides a specious ending, as all memorials do (Rowlands 1999, 131). There is no room here for the truth that "[I]mperialism ... is about never-ending involvement" (Kaplan 2005, 349). At the same time, filmic convention arguably allows viewers to take distance from what they have seen, enacting a separation from the grief they have witnessed. In this way, the documentary is sadly ironic, commemorating a war that is not over and confining its image of bereavement to the tiniest fraction of survivors.

Simply considering the film in qualitative terms, however, and thus allowing our analysis to remain at the level of the narrative, leaves other representational injustices undocumented, and makes it difficult to claim decisively that something is awry. The continual march of the film, from soldier to soldier, family to family, all over the country, is as lulling as it is disorienting. Keeping track of the details of so many stories that all have roughly the same ending is difficult, and so it is useful to look at what is clear and quantifiable.

This alternative is a significant divergence from the logic of the film, and so holds the potential to navigate a way around the smokescreen so lovingly and deliberately erected by the emphasis on the inexpressible and the collective, which implies that demystification and specificity are both unnecessary and crass. Certainly, quantitative analysis runs the risk of distracting us from the film's potential to provide a meaningful story about the consequences of the war. But this very interruption of its narrative is an important intervention, which might ultimately offer the survivors a kind of commemorative justice, a different way of fulfilling the film's implicit promise of recognition.

Last Letters Home seems to guarantee a democratic forum for the cultivation and experience of patriotic grief, as it assembles a community of mourners and sympathizers. Yet the collapse of all these stories into a single narrative obfuscates their uniqueness and their relationships to one another. In *Disagreement: Politics and Philosophy*, Jacques Rancière (1999, 103) repeatedly critiques the representational logic of post-democracy:

> As a regime of opinion, the principle of post-democracy is to make the troubled and troubling appearance of the people and its always false count disappear behind procedures exhaustively presenting the people and its parts and bringing the count of those parts into line with the image of the whole.

According to Rancière, "the people" are misrepresented by the very instruments – the public opinion poll, the census, and other tabulations – that are ostensibly designed to give them a voice. These instruments permit the "the people" to appear only through their collectivity, expressed in tallies and percentages. In these cases, data about quantitative totals masquerades as a truthful and accurate reflection of popular beliefs.

We might imagine the narrative of *Last Letters Home* as the allegedly democratic "image of the whole," in which the parts have been added and made to amount to a story, which eclipses the difficult truths of individual dramas it contains. In distinction to this aggregate, the numbers I derive from the story and provide here offer a representation of the individual families that comprise it. I am seeking, then, to use a quantitative method to reveal the intricacies of the dynamics of collective mourning in the film.

The radical shift in perspective afforded by quantitative analysis reveals some telling and troubling disparities within the film. First, among the four shortest segments, one commemorates the death of a nonheterosexual man, and two are in honor of the only soldiers of color represented here. Next, two of the three longest segments focus on the two white female soldiers, while the longest focuses on the grief of a young white wife and mother. Finally, the longest segment was more than twice as long as the shortest, while the segments that featured the most personal, humanizing snapshots had approximately twice as many as those that included the fewest.

Table 2-2: Segment Times of *Last Letters Home*

Shortest								Longest	
Carvill	Martinez-Flores	Heighter / Byers	Wise	Cowherd	Piché	McGeough	Witmer	Givens	
3:30	4:08	4:45/ 4:46	4:53	5:05	5:39	6:14	6:53	7:15	

- Difference of 3:45 from shortest to longest
- Average time was 5:19

Table 2-3: Snapshots of *Last Letters Home*

Fewest					Most	
Heighter / Byers / Givens	Carvill / Martinez-Flores / McGeough	Wise	Piché	Cowherd	Witmer	
5	6	7	8	9	12	

- Total pictures (including snapshots) in a segment ranged from 7-14
- Average number was 6.9 (8.9 total pictures)

With the film analyzed in this way, its ideal subject becomes clear, evidenced in the unequal allotment of commemorative space to those who deviate from the collective fantasy of the perfect (white, male, heterosexual) soldier and its simultaneous relocation of women as privileged objects of the gaze. This is not an argument for a redistribution of grief and memory according to a vacuous liberal vision of equality, which affords recognition to marginalized bodies primarily on the condition that their suffering be made public and available for consumption (Abbas 2010).

Rather, it is an effort to query the felicity of the persistent cultural promise of commemorative justice enacted by *Last Letters Home* and so many other texts.

The avarice with which time is allocated to the deaths of soldiers of color might only be reflecting military reality, in which the myth of meritocracy contrasts with racialized assignment of rank and status (D'Amico 2000, 107). And though the film purports to treat all of its subjects identically, I would argue that it is organized according to a racist logic that is "inferential" rather than "overt," a hallmark of most liberal treatments of racial issues (Hall 1981, 20), and that it alternately silences and spectacularizes the deaths of soldiers of color, always accenting their difference.

In addition to this ordering, implicit racism, there is also a class hierarchy here. The working class is not underrepresented in this film, as it typically is in mass media (Ehrenreich 1995, 40), and though not present in proportion to its 60-70% of the population (Ehrenreich 1995, 40), there are two families marked as non-middle class. But there is also a class-based division of labor, since those two families are left with the task of recounting the nastier, embodied aspects of war. The working class is required to do hard work in the film, just as they are generally charged with performing the most difficult and dangerous (and necessary) labor in actuality. So when the Wise women chuckle about what the soldiers call the "stink of the desert rose" and the Zasadnys relate the details of "poop duty," we are provided with key information, essential to our understanding of the experience of warfare, but which other survivors could not be expected to relay. The film leaves matters of class in ambivalent tension; it must make the deaths of the (white) lower class seem noteworthy, while preserving the artifice of middle-class superiority.

By featuring the families of soldiers who are working class or of color, the documentary proceeds with the appearance of a liberal equality, a suggestion of sameness under the categories of "American" and "soldier" in the "worldwide fraternity" (Kaplan 2005, 13) that is the United States military. Simultaneously, the relative underrepresentation of the poor and people of color occludes the extent to which the poor and people of color are, by most estimates, overrepresented in the U.S. military, especially in its most dangerous positions. Again, the documentary is doubly insulated: enacting the promise of inclusivity while sidestepping questions about military justice.

Heterosexism, like so many other ideological imprimaturs, may not appear to be operative in the documentary and never finds an overt articulation; nevertheless, it functions powerfully to make *Last Letters*

Home work as a sentimental text. The film's emphasis on family hints at an organizing logic prizing heteronormative formations; accordingly, the majority of the deceased are marked as heterosexual through marriage or by default. Yet, there is one who is not: Sgt. Carvill. (Not) coincidentally, his segment is the shortest of the film. There is no suggestion that Sgt. Carvill is married; he is merely avuncular. Interestingly, one of the few snapshots reproduced in his story shows him, his two nephews, and another man holding hands and jumping into a pool. That man may, of course, be his brother-in-law or another relative, but vagueness remains in the representation of his sexual orientation. This is not, of course, to suggest anything about Sgt. Carvill; instead, it is a comment on a pattern in the film, manifest in the correspondence between the comparatively impersonal nature of this segment and the lack of heteronormative narrative.

This ambiguity bears an affinity to the status of sexual orientation in the U.S. military in general. Sgt. Carvill's unmarked difference is precisely that which was mandated at the time by "Don't Ask Don't Tell".[19] This, however, raises the question of why the filmmakers opted to include him at all; we might cite the film's putative effort at the establishment of equality between the soldiers it features, or suggest that his story functions as an argument for a liberal America, blind to divisions of any sort. However, no matter the intention, the outcome seems to be the same: providing tacit approval for silence about nonheterosexuality in the military while also preserving the film's claim to diversity. It is noteworthy, thus, that Sgt. Carvill's story features heavily in Couturié's interview with HBO, in which he claims Carvill as communal property and identifies his death as a communal loss, opining that "We're going to miss Frank," the collective pronoun referring to the American people. While the emphasis on his heroism (Sgt. Carvill rescued people from the World Trade Center on 9/11) is well-deserved, it also functions to justify his inclusion in the film and thus in our grief, all the while refusing to ask and failing to tell anything too personal.

The version of heteronormativity by which *Last Letters Home* is organized also informs the gender dynamics of the film, which operate according to a particular logic of white womanhood that accentuates the roles of women as wives, mothers, and nurturers, even when they are also soldiers. Thus, it is revelatory that the two longest segments (by far) are those that feature white women: the loss of Spc. Witmer (6:53) and the widow of Pfc. Givens (7:15); the relatively small number of snapshots included in the latter segment suggests, for example, that Mrs. Givens is the true focus of this story. Motherhood figures heavily in both, obviously in the case of Mrs. Givens as the newly widowed mother of two young sons, and implicitly, hauntingly in the strategic choice to include snapshots of Spc. Witmer with Iraqi children.

There is a way in which the dead female soldier is incomprehensible, given the always vexed question of women in the U.S. military and the association of military violence with manhood. Yet the need for fighting bodies and the absence of a draft has necessitated the presence of women in the military, and their legal exclusion from the front line has proven difficult to enforce in a war where there is functionally no such thing. Despite all this, however, *Last Letters Home* smoothly answers these questions by recourse to the nexus of white womanhood and sentimentality, visualized in the grieving widow, the daughterless mother, and the female soldier whose death foreclosed her presumable future. The documentary does not feature stories of any female casualties who were also mothers, a loss that would be almost impossible to negotiate while preserving neutrality. Indeed, insofar as the promise of the new beginnings of birth and childhood are essential to political life (Arendt [1958] 1998, 108), the thought that this war is killing American mothers and thus circumscribing the potential of politicized natality would be too much for the documentary to bear.[20]

All of these omissions belie the film's claim of pure verisimilitude but are important not only for the exclusions they reflect. They are worth considering because the exclusions themselves and their opaque disguises make the film work. As it occludes difference and its politics, *Last Letters Home* smoothes the mechanisms by which militarized commemorative labor can be undertaken, so that the viewers have only to think about death in a way that is safe and controlled, blinded to the injustices that preceded or surrounded it.

At the same time, the film is a consumer good, designed for proper functioning and easy consumption. And so, despite the production team's expressed commitment to faithfully document the "human cost" of the war, it is perhaps the opposite which is the final outcome. At least, that is, to the extent that successfully watching the whole story of the grief of these families, in this commodified but ostensibly unmediated form, makes it feel manageable and finite, when it is not, in reality, likely to be either. Pain is the only thing that defies expression (Arendt [1958] 1998, 50), a sensation that can only be put into words after it has ceased. The relative ease, then, with which these survivors recount the most intimate details of the deaths of their loved ones de-realizes the pain of (their) loss, while also suggesting that it is bounded and surmountable.

Last Letters Home is framed, on the one hand, as a humanist tribute, in which all markers of difference disappear. At the same time, it rewrites those specificities in ghostly and indelible script across the bodies of the dead and those who survived them. In this paradox, the film relies on uncontroversial signifiers: home, the nation, love, and loss, as it enacts a peculiar movement. Though all of these have histories that are intimately connected to definitions of race, gender, class, and sexuality, the awful genius of this film is that it temporarily suspends the urgency of those questions in favor of a larger, more emotional project, which leaves the politics of remembrance unspoken and uninterrogated. Thus affective response continues to look apolitical, while the film indirectly necessitates that we rethink how affect matters in politics (Protevi 2009). The ruse of a pure grief rests on the simple invitation extended by *Last Letters Home*, the way it beckons its viewers into "Fort Living Room" and asks only that the audience sympathize with those who reside there. In exchange, spectators are moved, entertained, and required to do nothing more than consume the images with a quiet, almost military, resolve.

Notes

[1] I owe tremendous thanks to the many people who have helped me bring this project to fruition, particularly Dr. Philip Armstrong for his careful readings, re-readings, and expansive commentary. A correspondence with a friend (who requested anonymity) of one of the soldiers featured in the documentary challenged my thinking on many issues in unique and important ways, and I am deeply grateful for the insights he provided.

[2] Americans refers here to the United States of America; and not to the American continent.

[3] For one set of polling data that provides a snapshot of popular opinion about the war around the time that *Last Letters Home* was released, see the report of the Pew Research Center (2008).

[4] I have put "9/11" in diacritical marks to indicate the distance between the event and the signifier it has become. So as not to exaggerate the extent to which this reality and its representation are separable, however, I have not included them around every reference. Still, one might imagine them there, faintly, at all times.

[5] This service is particularly valuable because the US military has struggled to perform it satisfactorily, prohibiting media at funerals, attempting to suppress casualty figures, and implementing automated processes for death notices from the Department of Defense. For more on the state's bureaucratic and methodical approaches to the management of war dead, see Capdevila and Voldman (2006).

[6] The small number of soldiers featured is striking, though the number 11 has symbolic importance in American military history (for example, Veteran's Day, formerly Armistice Day, is observed on November 11th [11/11] of every year, to commemorate the eleventh-hour signing of the Armistice which signaled the end of World War I. Of course, it would have been all but impossible to responsibly

represent the deaths of all the military personnel who had perished in the War before the film was made; these 11 people are metonyms for all the dead, a replacement that is replicated in many other memorializing texts and artifacts. With the exception of constructions like the Vietnam Wall, we are rarely confronted with an individualized tally of casualties. In this way, monuments to few individuals are recognizable as substitutes for itemization of sacrifice.

[7] Davis specifically cites the Abu Ghraib photos, but his observation holds generally as well.

[8] Of course, war memorials often do mention rank as a distinguishing feature, and the individual graves on war cemeteries often include references to religion. Moreover, memorials have been built to celebrate the sacrifices made by specific nations. World War One examples are the Canadian National Vimy Memorial (in Vimy, France), and in its proximity a site commemorating the "Dead of the Moroccan Division" and the "Indian Memorial to the Missing". For a more detailed history of American memorials, see Doss (2010).

[9] Here, Spc. Wise is alluding to the iconic film *The Wizard of Oz,* in which Dorothy, the protagonist, magically transports herself home by clicking her heels together three times and repeating this incantation.

[10] The editor of this volume suggested that the uncanny ability of the film to simultaneously reveal the suffering caused by the death of a soldier and avoid sustained anti-war critique is distinct for nations at war. I thank him for pointing out the strangeness of this combination and the particular "field of tension" where this film is thus located.

[11] On the politics and potential of protracted sadness, 'bad feelings,' and depression, see Cvetkovich (2012).

[12] In this formulation, I diverge from analyses like that of Timothy Cole, who argues that this war is a "textbook case of rhetorical mobilization for war, without any concomitant requirement that the public must contribute to and sacrifice for the cause beyond supporting the troops and trusting the administration to aggressively protect its citizenry" (2005, 140). Of course, the effort required of Americans during the GWOT is minimal compared to that demanded by conflagrations like World War II. But the fact that we Americans can have all the sugar and butter (and gasoline) that we want doesn't mean that everything is effortless.

[13] We might, for example, consider the figure of Cindy Sheehan in these terms.

[14] Lauren Berlant's (2011, 1)description of 'cruel optimism' may be relevant here. In her terms, "a relation of cruel optimism exists when something you desire is actually an obstacle to your flourishing."

[15] Cacho also reminds us of the violence that often attends efforts to endow these deaths with the 'value' that they might otherwise be denied (2012, 147-168).

[16] There is an inconsistency within the film with respect of the spelling of her last name. The first time it appears, it is spelled "McGeogh" but at the end of the segment, it is spelled "McGeough," which matches the return address on her envelope.

[17] Pfc. Givens died the same way that Pfc. Martinez-Flores did, by drowning in a tank, but there is no similar attention to those details in this segment.

[18] Many of the female survivors featured in the film wore tops emblazoned in similar ways, and not a few had pictures of their deceased loved ones on them. On the gender politics and political idealization of the 'security mom,' see Grewal (2012).
[19] DADT was the controversial legislation passed in 1993 under U.S. President Bill Clinton which forbade non-heterosexual service people from disclosing anything about their sexual orientation or practice (on penalty of dishonorable discharge), and conversely mandates that their superiors cannot require them to reveal any such information. The policy was repealed in 2011 .
[20] Not unpredictably, American viewers seem to be less squeamish about the thought of dead Iraqi mothers, and occasional stories about Iraqi orphans and the institutions created to house them do make their way to the news.

Works Cited

Abbas, Asma. 2010. Voice Lessons: Suffering and the Liberal Sensorium. Theory and Event 13(2): n.p.

Anderson, Benedict. 1998. The Spectre of Comparisons: Nationalism, Southeast Asia, and The World. New York: Verso.

Anker, Elisabeth. 2012. Heroic Identification, Or "You Can Love Me Too – I Am So Like the State." Theory and Event 15 (1): n.p.

Arendt, Hannah. [1958] 1998. The Human Condition. 2nd ed. Chicago: The University of Chicago Press.

Ashplant, Timothy G., Dawson, Graham, and Roper, Michael. 2000. The Politics of War Memory and Commemoration. In The Politics of War Memory and Commemoration. Edited by T.G. Ashplant, Graham Dawson, and Michael Roper. London: Routledge.

Barber, Benjamin R. 2003. The War of All Against All: Terror and the Politics of Fear. In War After September 11th. Edited by Verna R. Gehring. Lanham, MD: Rowman and Littlefield.

Baukus, Robert A., and Strohm, Susan M. 2002. Gender Differences in Perception of the Media Reports of the Gulf and Afghan Conflicts. In Communication and Terrorism: Public and Media Responses to 9/11. Edited by Bradley S. Greenberg. Cresskill, NJ: Hampton Press.

Berger, Arthur Asa. 2004. Ads, Fads, and Consumer Culture. Advertising's Impact on American Character and Society. 2nd ed. Lanham, MD: Rowman and Littlefield.

Berlant, Lauren. 2011. Cruel Optimism. Durham: Duke University Press.

Boltanski, Luc. 1999. Distant Suffering. Morality, Media, and Politics. Translated by Graham Burchell. Cambridge: Cambridge University Press.

Bratich, Jack Z. 2003. Cultural Studies, Immanent War, Everyday Life. 9/11 in American Culture. Edited by Norman K. Denzin and Yvonna S. Lincoln. Walnut Creek, CA: AltaMira Press, 2003.

Brottman, Mikita. 2004. The Fascination of the Abomination. The Censored Images of 9/11. In Film and Television After 9/11. Edited by Wheeler Winston Dixon. Carbondale, IL: Southern Illinois University Press.

Brown, William J., Bocarnea, Mihai, and Basil, Michael. 2002. Fear, Grief, and Sympathy Responses to the Attacks. In Communication and Terrorism: Public and Media Responses to 9/11. Edited by Bradley S. Greenberg. Cresskill, NJ: Hampton Press.

Butler, Judith. 2000. Antigone's Claim: Kinship Between Life and Death. New York: Columbia University Press.

Cacho, Lisa Marie. 2012. Social Death: Racialized Rightlessness and the Criminalization of the Unprotected. New York: New York University Press.

Calabrese, Andrew. 2004. Toward a Political Economy of Culture. In Toward A Political Economy of Culture: Capitalism and Communication in the Twenty- First Century. Edited by Andrew Calabrese and Colin Sparks. Lanham, MD: Rowman and Littlefield.

Calder, Angus. 2004. Disasters and Heroes. On War, Memory, and Representation. Cardiff: University of Wales Press.

Capdevila, Luc, and Voldman, Danièle. War Dead: Western Societies and Casualties of War. Translated by Richard Veasey. Edinburgh: Edinburgh University Press.

Cole, Timothy. 2005. The Political Rhetoric of Sacrifice and Heroism in US Military Intervention. In Bring 'Em On: Media and Politics in the Iraq War. Edited by Lee Artz and Yahya R. Kamalipour. Lanham, MD: Rowman and Littlefield Publishers, Inc.

Cvetkovich, Ann. 2012. Depression: A Public Feeling. Durham: Duke University Press.

D'Amico, Francine. 2000. Citizen-Soldier? Class, Race, Gender, and Sexuality, and the U.S. Military. In States of Conflict: Gender, Violence, and Resistance. Edited by Susie Jacobs, Ruth Jacobson, and Jennifer Marchbank. London: Zed Books.

Davis, Walter A. 2006. Death's Dream Kingdom: The American Psyche Since 9/11. London: Pluto Press.

Debatin, Bernhard. 2002. "Plane Wreck with Spectators": Terrorism and Media Attention. In Communication and Terrorism: Public and Media Responses to 9/11. Edited by Bradley S. Greenberg. Cresskill, NJ: Hampton Press.

Debord, Guy. 1995. The Society of the Spectacle. Trans. Donald
Nicholson- Smith. New York: Zone Books.

Dixon, Wheeler Winston. 2004. Introduction: Something Lost – Film
After 9/11. In Film and Television After 9/11. Edited by Wheeler
Winston Dixon. Carbondale, IL: Southern Illinois University Press.

Doss, Erika. 2010. Memorial Mania: Public Feeling in America. Chicago:
University of Chicago Press.

Eber, Dena Elisabeth, and Neal, Arthur G. 2002a. Introduction: Memory,
Constructed Reality, and Artistic Truth. In Memory and
Representation. Constructed Truths and Competing Realities. Edited
by Dena Elisabeth Eber and Arthur G. Neal. Bowling Green, OH:
Bowling Green State University Popular Press.

—. 2002b. Epilogue: The Individual and Collective Search for Identity. In
In Memory and Representation. Constructed Truths and Competing
Realities. Edited by Dena Elisabeth Eber and Arthur G. Neal. Bowling
Green, OH: Bowling Green State University Popular Press.

Ehrenreich, Barbara. 1995. The Silenced Majority. Why the Average
Working Person has Disappeared from American Media and Culture.
In Gender, Race, and Class in Media: A Text-Reader. Edited by Gail
Dines and Jean M. Humez. Thousand Oaks, CA: Sage.

Enloe, Cynthia. 2000. Maneuvers: The International Politics of
Militarizing Women's Lives. Berkeley, CA: University of California
Press.

Folkerts, Jean, and Lacy, Stephen (eds.). 2004. The Media In Your Life:
An Introduction to Mass Communication. 3rd ed. Boston: Allyn and
Beacon.

Forces: U.S. & Coalition / Casualties. Updated regularly.
http://www.cnn.com/ SPECIALS/2003/iraq/forces/casualties (accessed
10 September 2006).

Forty, Adrian. 1999. Introduction. In The Art of Forgetting. Edited by
Adrian Forty and Suzanne Küchler. Oxford: Berg.

Frankenberg, Ruth. 2002. Whiteness as an "Unmarked" Cultural Category.
Sociology: Exploring the Architecture of Everyday Life. 4th ed. Edited
by David M. Newman and Jodi O'Brien. Thousand Oaks, CA: Pine
Forge Press.

Galston, William A. Introduction. 2003. In War After September 11.
Edited by Verna R. Gehring. Lanham, MD: Rowman and Littlefield.

Galtung, John, and Vincent, Richard C. 2004. U.S. Glasnost. Missing
Political Themes in U.S. Media Discourse. Cresskill, NJ: Hampton
Press.

Gergen, Kenneth J. 1998. History and Psychology. Three Weddings and a Future. In An Emotional History of the United States. Edited by Peter N. Stearns and Jan Lewis. New York: New York University Press.

Gray, Bettina. 1998. The Intimate Moment. The Art of Interviewing. In The Search for Reality. The Art of Documentary Filmmaking. Edited by Michael Tobias. Studio City, CA: Michael Wiese Productions.

Grewal, Inderpal. 2012. "Security Moms" in Twenty-First-Century U.S.A. In The Global and the Intimate: Feminism in Our Time. Edited by Geraldine Pratt and Victoria Rosner. New York: Columbia University Press.

Grimes, William J. 2004. Cable Television. In Media Selling. Broadcast, Cable, Print, and Interactive. Edited by Charles Warner and Joseph Buchman. 3rd Ed. Ames, IA: Iowa State Press.

Hall, Stuart. 1981. The Whites of Their Eyes: Racist Ideologies and the Media. In Silver Linings. Some Strategies for the Eighties. Edited by George Bridges and Rosalyn Brunt. London: Lawrence and Wishart.

Harvey, John H. 2002. Perspectives on Loss and Trauma. Assaults on the Self. Thousand Oaks, CA: Sage.

Hoffner, Cynthia, Fujoka, Yuki, Ibrahim, Amal, and Yi, Jiali. 2002. Emotion and Coping With Terror. In Communication and Terrorism. Public and Media Responses to 9/11. Edited by Bradley S. Greenberg. Cresskill, NJ: Hampton Press.

Iraq Coalition Casualty Count. Updated regularly. http://icasualties.org/oif/ (accessed 10 September 2006).

Internet Movie Database (IMDB). 2006. "Bill Couturié Filmography." http://www.imdb.com/name/nm0184322 (accessed 2 June 2006).

Johnson-Cartee, Karen S. 2005. News Narratives and News Framing. Constructing Political Reality. Lanham, MD: Rowman and Littlefield.

Kaplan, Robert D. 2005. Imperial Grunts: The American Military on the Ground. New York: Random House.

Kelly, Liz. 2000. Wars Against Women. Sexual Violence, Sexual Politics, and the Militarised State. In States of Conflict. Gender, Violence, and Resistance. Edited by Susie Jacobs, Ruth Jacobson, and Jennifer Marchbank. London: Zed Books.

Kozol, Wendy. Battlefield Souvenirs and Ethical Spectatorship. Text of paper presented at Feeling Photography Conference. University of Toronto. Toronto, ON. October 17, 2009.

Last Letters Home: About the Film. 2004. http://www.hbo.com/docs/programs/lastlettershome/about (accessed 18 February 2005).

Last Letters Home: Crew Bio. 2004. http://www.hbo.com/docs/programs/
lastlettershome/crew/index.html (accessed 21 August 2006).

Last Letters Home: Voices of American Troops from the Battlefields of
Iraq. 2004. 60 minutes. New York: HBO Films.

Massumi, Brian. 2002. Parables for the Virtual. Movement, Affect,
Sensation. Durham: Duke University Press.

McChesney, Robert W. 2004. The Problem of the Media. U.S.
Communication Politics in the Twenty-First Century. New York:
Monthly Review Press.

McLean, Scott. 2004. The War on Terrorism and the New Patriotism. In
The Politics of Terror. The U.S Response to 9/11. Edited by William
Crotty. Boston: Northeast University Press.

Mellencamp, Patricia. 2006. Fearful Thoughts: U.S. Television since 9/11
and the Wars in Iraq. In Rethinking Global Security: Media, Popular
Culture, and the "War on Terror". Edited by Andrew Martin and
Patrice Petro. New Brunswick: Rutgers University Press.

Mosco, Vincent. 2004. Capitalism's Chernobyl? From Ground Zero to
Cyberspace and Back Again. In Toward A Political Economy of
Culture. Capitalism and Communication in the Twenty-First Century.
Edited by Andrew Calabrese and Colin Sparks. Lanham, MD:
Rowman and Littlefield.

Mumford, Laura Stempel. 1998. Feminist Theory and Television Studies.
In The Television Studies Book. Edited by Christine Geraghty and
David Lusted. Arnold, NY: St. Martin's Press.

O'Sullivan, Tim. 1998. Nostalgia, Revelation, and Intimacy. Tendencies in
the Flow of Modern Popular Television. In The Television Studies
Book. Edited by Christine Geraghty and David Lusted. Arnold, NY:
St. Martin's Press.

Patraka, Vivian. 2002. Spectacular Suffering. Performing Presence,
Absence, and Witness at U.S. Holocaust Museums. In In Memory and
Representation: Constructed Truths and Competing Realities. Edited
by Dena Elisabeth Eber and Arthur G. Neal. Bowling Green, OH:
Bowling Green State University Popular Press.

Pew Research Center. 2008. Public Attitudes Toward the War in Iraq:
2003-3008. March 19, 2008.
http://www.pewresearch.org/2008/03/19/public-attitudes-toward-the-
war in-iraq-20032008 (accessed July 16, 2014).

Protevi, John. 2009. Political Affect: Connecting the Social and the
Somatic. Minneapolis: University of Minnesota Press.

Rancière, Jacques. 1999. Disagreement: Politics and Philosophy. Trans.
Julie Rose. Minneapolis: University of Minnesota Press.

Retort (Iain Boal, T.J. Clark, Joseph Matthews, Michael Watts). 2005. Afflicted Powers. Capital and Spectacle in a New Age of War. New ed. London: Verso.

Reynaud, Patricia. 2002. Simple Minds, Complex Distinctions. Reading Forrest Gump and Pleasantville Through the Lens of Bourdieu's Sociological Theory. In Memory and Representation. Constructed Truths and Competing Realities. Edited by Dena Elisabeth Eber and Arthur G. Neal. Bowling Green, OH: Bowling Green State University Popular Press.

Richard, Birgit. 2003. The World Trade Center Image Complex. A Critical View on a Culture of the Shifting Image. In 9/11 in American Culture. Edited by Norman K. Denzin and Yvonna S. Lincoln. Walnut Creek, CA: AltaMira Press.

Rowlands, Michael. 1999. Remembering to Forget: Sublimation and Sacrifice in War Memorials. In The Art of Forgetting. Edited by Adrian Forty and Susanne Küchler. Oxford: Berg.

Ruggiero, Tom, and Glasscock, Jack. 2002. Tracking Media Use and Gratifications. In Communication and Terrorism. Public and Media Responses to 9/11. Edited by Bradley S. Greenberg. Cresskill, NJ: Hampton Press.

Ryan, John, and Wentworth, William M. 1999. Classical Sociological Theory and Mass Media. In Media and Society. The Production of Culture in the Mass Media. Boston: Allyn and Bacon.

Sloyan, Patrick J. 2003. What Bodies? In The Iraq War Reader. History, Documents, Opinions. Edited by Micah L. Sifry and Christopher Cerf. New York: Touchstone Books.

Sontag, Susan. 2003. Regarding the Pain of Others. New York: Farrar, Straus and Giroux.

Spigel, Lynn. 1998. The Making of a TV Literate Elite. In The Television Studies Book. Edited by Christine Geraghty and David Lusted. Arnold, NY: St. Martin's Press.

Stearns, Peter N., and Lewis, Jan. 1998. Introduction. In An Emotional History of the United States. Edited by Peter N. Stearns and Jan Lewis. New York: New York University Press.

Stempel, Guido H. III, and Hargrove, Thomas. 2002. Media Sources of Information and Attitudes about Terrorism. In Communication and Terrorism. Public and Media Responses to 9/11. Edited by Bradley S. Greenberg. Cresskill, NJ: Hampton Press.

Step, Mary M., Finucane, Mary O., and Harvath, Cary W. 2002. Emotional Involvement in the Attacks. In Communication and

Terrorism. Public and Media Responses to 9/11. Edited by Bradley S. Greenberg. Cresskill, NJ: Hampton Press.

Sterritt, David. 2004. Representing Atrocity: From the Holocaust to September 11. In Film and Television After 9/11. Edited by Wheeler Winston Dixon. Carbondale, IL: Southern Illinois University Press.

The Iraq Body Count. Updated regularly. http://www.iraqbodycount.net/ database (accessed 16 July 2014).

Thomas, Tanja, and Virchow, Fabian. 2005. Banal Militarism and the Culture of War. In Bring 'Em On. Media and Politics in the Iraq War. Edited by Lee Artz and Yahya Kamalipour. Lanham, MD: Rowman and Littlefield.

Tobias, Michael. 1998. Introduction: The Search for Reality. In The Search for Reality. The Art of Documentary Filmmaking. Edited by Michael Tobias. Studio City, CA: Michael Wiese Productions.

United States Department of Defense. Updated regularly. Casualty Status Update. http://www.defense.gov/news/casualty.pdf (accessed July 16, 2014).

Wagner, Robert W. 1998. The Family Filmed. In The Search for Reality. The Art of Documentary Filmmaking. Edited by Michael Tobias. Studio City, CA: Michael Wiese Productions.

Wakshlag, Jack. 2002. Introduction: Reflections on Media in Times of Crisis. In Communication and Terrorism. Public and Media Responses to 9/11. Edited by Bradley S. Greenberg. Cresskill, NJ: Hampton Press.

Walsh, Katherine Cramer. 2004. Talking About Politics. Informal Groups and Social Identity in American Life. Chicago: University of Chicago Press.

Walter, Tony. 1999. On Bereavement. The Culture of Grief. Buckingham: Open University Press.

Wanzo, Rebecca. 2009. The Suffering Will Not Be Televised: African American Women and Political Storytelling. Albany: State University of New York Press.

White, Jonathan. 2001. Terrorism and the Media. In Terrorism: An Introduction. 3rd Ed. Belmont, CA: Wadsworth Thomson Learning.

Willis, Susan. 2005. Portents of the Real. A Primer for Post-9/11 America. London: Verso.

Wilson, Clint C. II, and Gutierrez, Felix. 1995. Communication, Media, and Society. In Race, Multiculturalism, and the Media. From Mass to Class Communication. 2nd Ed. Thousand Oaks, CA: Sage Publications.

Zingrone, Frank. 2004. The Media Symplex. At the Edge of Meaning in the Age of Chaos. Cresskill, NJ: Hampton Press.

GOOD GRIEF:
THE CULTURAL WORK OF *FLIGHTPLAN*
AND THE VANISHING LADY TALE

CHRISTINA LANE

Introduction

The memorial and tribute television programs released within the immediate aftermath of 9/11 notwithstanding, (North) American media industries refrained from depicting direct representations or realistic portrayals of the events of 9/11, especially in mainstream movies, between the fall of 2001 and, roughly, the fall of 2005. Indeed, Paramount deleted graphic scenes from Ben Affleck's 2002 airplane thriller, *The Sum of All Fears*, and studios digitally erased the twin towers out of films such as *Serendipity* (2001) and *Spiderman* (2002). Luke Howie, in *Terror on the Screen: Witnesses and the Reanimation of 9/11 as Image-event, Popular Culture, and Pornography*, reflects on such visual subtraction. After describing his personal experiences of watching the 9/11 attacks and aftermath on live television ("the whole event was drowned in images"), he remarks, "I [eventually] witnessed popular television shows, some set in New York City, return to the air.... When *Friends* returned for the eighth season, in late September 2001, something was missing. It took me a few moments to process the reality that the Twin Towers, which had once littered the background images of the opening credits and the scene transitions, were gone. Simply and quietly they had been airbrushed out of the shot, as though their disappearance had not been dramatic and globally witnessed" (Howie 2011, 5).

In 2006, as if a "fifth anniversary" pact had been made between television networks, major studios (whose development departments had had projects waiting in the wings since the month of the attacks) and (American) audiences, the industry issued a succession of explicit portrayals. *Flight 93* (A & E, January 2006), *United 93* (Universal Studios, April 2006), *World Trade Center* (Paramount, September 2006), *On Native Soil: The Documentary of the 9/11* Commission Report (Court TV September 2006), and the ABC mini-series docu-drama *The Path to 9/11*

(September 2006) all re-visit and re-play traumatic accounts of the terrorist attacks of 9/11.

Several films were also released with 9/11-related settings, plots, images, and political themes that would have been deemed too sensitive even one year or two years earlier. *Syriana* (Warner Bros., December 2006), for example, sees U.S. foreign policy through a multiplicity of – and often highly politicized – vantage points. Steven Spielberg's *Munich* (Dreamworks, December 2006) probes the "Black September" terrorist plot of the 1972 Olympics in Germany, in order to re-contextualize contemporary U.S. politics of terrorism.

Flightplan, released prior to the aforementioned titles (November 2005), conjures up a number of 9/11 elements – a terrorist threat on a plane, white Americans' suspicious fear of Arab men, a pervasive presence of surveillance and technology – in notable ways.[1] *Flightplan*, like the films that followed, rehearses a certain series of relatable events, and implies a specific set of questions: How will Americans, as a collective, ascribe meaning to what happened on 9/11? Who were they before the attacks and who are they after it? What does it mean to survive such an event as a nation?

Flightplan is unlike those other films, however, in that it draws on a separate set of source texts – myths, models, and cinematic and literary narratives – that engage feminist responses to these questions. In the film, a recently widowed Kyle Pratt (Jodie Foster), who is accompanying her husband's bodily remains on a transatlantic flight from Berlin to New York, loses her six-year old daughter, and begins to suspect that the plane is being hijacked. Because she is an aeronautical engineer who, as it happens, has helped design this state-of-the-art, double-decker plane, she attempts to take the flight into her own hands. As she becomes increasingly out of control, Kyle begins to embody a terrorist threat to the pilots, crew, and passengers. By the third act of the film, the major plot twist has been revealed: the Air Marshal (Peter Sarsgaard), and the only person on board that she thought was her ally, kidnapped her daughter, placed a time bomb in her husband's coffin, and plans to use her perceived insanity in a ploy to put millions of dollars in his own bank account. Kyle's only option for rescuing her daughter (held captive in the cargo hold) and minimizing possible danger to innocent bystanders is to take her vigilante role to an extreme, playing the raving lunatic terrorist everyone thinks she is, until she has the chance to beat the fraudulent Air Marshal through hand-to-hand combat and bring her daughter to safety.

In understanding the feminist possibilities of *Flightplan*, what I propose to be the "feminist subconscious" of the film, a major factor is of course Jodie Foster's star persona, which shall be considered below and has been examined at length in previous scholarship (see Rich 1991, Mizejewski 1992, Lane 1993, Staiger 1993, Hollinger 2012). Even more central, however, are two earlier films in which the trope of the Vanishing Lady – *The Lady Vanishes* (Alfred Hitchcock 1938) and *Bunny Lake is Missing* (Otto Preminger 1965) – is activated in ways that negotiate certain social and cultural anxieties related to the film's historical context. These films mobilize themes of grief and loss, but specifically, women's intense feelings – as they correlate to the psychoanalytic pre-Oedipal stage. In other words, as a character longs for a time "that can no longer be" or a place "that perhaps never was," she also opens up within the film a rehearsal space for traumatic feelings in war, catastrophe, or major social upheaval.

The Lady Vanishes is an obvious root text for *Flightplan*. Its protagonist, Iris Henderson (Margaret Lockwood) suffers a bump on the head upon boarding a train to London and soon thereafter receives comfort from an elderly governess Miss Froy (Dame May Whitty). On appearance, Miss Froy boasts a frumpish tea-and-tweed personality, but she is really a British Intelligence Officer traveling to London with crucial information which the Nazis are trying to intercept. (The bump on the head was caused by a flowerpot, which was actually intended to kill Froy.) Iris falls asleep and, upon waking, Miss Froy has disappeared and all of the other passengers deny ever seeing her. She enlists the assistance of Gilbert (Michael Redgrave), a jovial folk musician who takes a romantic interest in her and they eventually uncover the espionage plot. But for much of the film, Iris finds herself in the position of having to defend not only her memory but her ability to see, know, and take action, especially in the face of male authority figures who attempt to undermine her agency. Distorted camerawork, multiple exposures, and superimpositions suggest that Iris, whose very name calls attention to the crucial act of looking, questions whether or not she can trust the memory of what she has seen. And because the purpose of her train trip is to submit herself to a wedding about which she is very ambivalent, her journey represents a patriarchal rite-of-passage that is symbolically about loss and confinement.

Furthermore, Iris's plea for the other passengers to "wake up" is as much about national politics as it is about gender politics. Many of the characters who have been trying to convince her that she suffers from an unstable mind have been part of the Nazi spy ring. Importantly, several characters (such as two men trying desperately to make it to a cricket match) have had no knowledge of the Nazi presence on the train; they simply ignore Iris for selfish reasons. This opens up in *The Lady Vanishes* a space for critique of those British who were being complacent about the rise of fascism in the thirties, which, the film suggests, came very close to complicity.

Even closer in plot to *Flightplan* than *The Lady Vanishes*, however, is *Bunny Lake is Missing*, a film that has received little scholarly attention to date. Based on a 1957 American pulp novel by Evelyn Piper, this film is transplanted by Preminger to 1960s swinging London. Ann Lake (Carol Lynley) has just arrived from the States with her brother Stephen (Keir Dullea) and young daughter Bunny (Suky Appleby). The mother leaves Bunny off at her new school, spends a day preparing her new apartment, and upon returning, is told that Bunny has never *been* at the school. As police involvement ensues, she is assisted by Lieutenant Newhouse (Laurence Olivier) who slowly uncovers a pathological childhood relationship she shared with her brother, which included his implied emotional abuse of her. It is ultimately revealed that Stephen has kidnapped Bunny, out of jealousy over his rival niece, but not before the film has taken Ann back into a role-play game, where she becomes both a younger version of herself and a semblance of her own daughter at the same time.

Bunny Lake is Missing works through a number of themes, including the obvious psycho-social conflicts of insinuated incest. This theme is not exploited, however, except for the purpose of illustrating the degree to which Ann can give herself over to seeing the world through Stephen's eyes. That is, she suffers from the same instability of vision and crisis of authority as Iris in the Hitchcock film. The most central conflict for Ann, though, involves the decision that she has made to raise Bunny out of wedlock, which connects her crisis of authority to the film's broader social context (in the U.S. and in Britain).

As she fights to prove that Bunny indeed exists, characters continue to question her daughter's legitimacy, which raises the "origin story" of Bunny's illegitimacy in relation to Ann's unmarried status: Ann's own (proto)feminist issues of reproductive freedom in an era that was on the cusp of the women's movement.[2] *Bunny Lake is Missing*, then, is not about national trauma per se: rather, it uses the theme of psychoanalytic trauma as a stand-in for cultural conflict. Dahlia Schweitzer (2010, 1) observes, *Bunny Lake is Missing* is a story about a woman who stands up to the men around her; but even more so, it is about a woman "struggling to be heard, to be seen, to *exist*". The film signals a political boiling point for "women who are consistently pushed aside, ignored, lost in the cracks, and who fight to be acknowledged, to prove that they are right, that they are, whatever the question may be" (Schweitzer 2010, 1).

Looking at *Flightplan* through the window:
With an eye toward *The Lady Vanishes*

In a *Village Voice* article published upon *Flightplan*'s release, Devin
McKinney explores in detail various renditions of the Vanishing Lady tale,
proceeding back to the Great Exposition in Paris in 1889. In "Frightplan:
Toward a Cultural History of the Vanishing Lady—with a Nod to Jodie
Foster," McKinney tentatively hypothesizes that *Flightplan* taps into one
of the driving emotions that "the legend's tellers usually *don't* catch,"
which is grief (2005, 16). I will analyze the film more closely in an effort
to prove his hypothesis correct; however, I will further show that some of
those films he dismisses (he calls *Bunny Lake* an "unfocused thriller" by a
"jaundiced auteur"; he says *The Lady Vanishes* has "soundstage clutter"
and its terror "feels thin") convey the very same psychic trauma. In order
to best be attuned to the grief described by McKinney – and to appreciate
these films' status as trauma films – it is necessary to place their themes of
loss in the psychoanalytic framework of the mother-daughter, Pre-Oedipal
bond and to value this bond's symbolic function for feminism.

But first let us turn to the origins of the Vanishing Lady story and
McKinney's suggestion that it repeatedly emerges according to the
psychic needs of a particular era. The legend, which has never been
verified as fact or fiction, was first recounted in detail by Algonquin
Roundtable writer Alexander Woollcott in the 1934 "While Rome Burns."
As the story goes, a woman and her elderly mother traveling from India
arrive at the Paris Exposition and check into their hotel when the mother
falls ill. After a long series of events and obstacles, beginning with the
hotel concierge calling a doctor and then telling the woman that her
mother needs a special medicine, the daughter returns to the hotel to find
that the mother has disappeared. The staff denies ever having met either of
them. It is ultimately revealed that a cover-up has taken place because the
initial doctor's visit yielded a diagnosis of bubonic plague, which had the
potential to scare the crowds away from the Exposition.

According to McKinney, Woollcott is deeply troubled by the Vanished
Lady: "he regrets that the story has lost its original 'content of grief' and
become a cocktail anecdote. 'The story of this girl's ordeal,' [Woollcott]
writes, 'long seemed to me one of the great nightmares of real life'" (qtd.
in McKinney 2005, 16). So haunted by it, Woollcott went on try to verify
its authenticity, achieving no success. McKinney, now himself interested
in the ghosts of the "Lady," has tracked all possible versions and dates of
the story, and honed in on one in particular that helps him connect the tale
to *Flightplan*.

It is a passage in Ernest Hemingway's *The Torrents of Spring* (1926). An elderly waitress relays a missing mother story to the book's narrator, ending with, "I never saw Mummy again. Never again. Not even once." The narrator eventually says, "There's more than that...I'd stake my life there's more than that." And the waitress replies, "Sometimes, you know, I feel there is...I feel there must be more than that. Somewhere, somehow, there must be an explanation. I don't know what brought the subject into my mind this morning" (Hemingway 1926, 36). McKinney declares, "Now there, if you let yourself hear it, is grief – for the damnable enigma of loss. And years later, a numb wonderment at the suddenness of its recurrence. Woollcott might have approved" (2005, 16). McKinney (2005, 16) goes on to say:

> *Flightplan*'s renewal of the legend may resonate with humanity's recent losses to terror attack and natural disaster—just as the story's popularity throughout the 1920s may have been a specter of the Great War and the influenza epidemic of 1918. These too have been years of wholesale loss and sudden, inexplicable grief for millions.

This connection might explain why long sequences in *Flightplan* convey the ambience of an extended funeral, as tight close ups on the protagonist's face carry the weight of her intense maternal longing. In other thriller films, Jodie Foster plays stoic, as in *Silence of the Lambs* (1991), or angry, as in *Panic Room* (2002), an apt comparison since in the latter she stars as a mother who will stop at nothing to protect her daughter. Here, however, she is stricken with grief. Her relentless presence (assured by the fact that she appears in nearly every scene) – and the camera's preoccupation with the emotional expressions on her face – saturate the film with an overwhelming and oppressive sense of sorrow. This has to do with her character's losses, yes, but *Flightplan* is governed by a less tangible haunting, the ghost of 9/11 which exists at the outer edges of the film's frame.

Some recent theories on trauma have suggested that films which target audiences on a deeply emotional level may negotiate cultural experiences in more provocative or productive ways than those that use codes of realism, logic, or intellectual analysis. Most specifically, E. Ann Kaplan's *Trauma Culture: The Politics of Terror and Loss in Media and Literature* brings together psychoanalytic and neuro-scientific theories regarding how individuals cope with trauma in an effort to better understand national media responses to 9/11. She finds psychiatric studies on the brain most helpful in theorizing how affect and empathy should not be underestimated as we consider cinematic representations of trauma. Taking as her point of departure that these studies apply to those who have lived through direct or indirect (secondary, or even collective) events such as wars, disasters, or catastrophes, Kaplan (2005, 34) explains:

> In arguing that trauma is a special form of memory, [these theorists] stated that in trauma, the event has affect only, not meaning. It produces emotions – terror, shock, fear – but perhaps above all the disruption of the normal feeling of comfort. Only the sensation sector of the brain – the amygdale – is active during trauma. The meaning-making one (in the sense of rational thought, cognitive processing), namely the cerebral cortex remains shut down because the affect is too much to be registered in the brain.

So while the "higher" regions of the brain – those where critical analysis or abstract thought takes place – may be able to function after such an event, a return to the original site of trauma means a return to a territory of emotions, pre-cognition, and sub-conscious thought.

To make a claim for the usefulness of such theories is not to suggest that a "direct" lived experience of physical or emotional trauma is *equal* to a heavily mediated and indirect trauma. How does one make sense of the differences between an experience of an escape down the stairwell of a burning tower, crawling through the trenches of a warzone, surviving a brutal rape, or watching an image of a plane crash on a television screen? What *does* seem to be at issue is that the heavy degree of mediation of 9/11 magnifies rather than dilutes its affective impact. By way of proliferated technology and an endless repetition of images, American citizens (as viewers) witnessed, negotiated, and frequently "owned" the trauma of 9/11, but they often did so subconsciously and subliminally. What they continually said on live newsfeeds and in Internet chat rooms was that watching the planes hit the Twin Towers was "like watching a movie."

Therefore, the cinematic experience of an affective journey such as Jodie Foster's character's – and the identification with her maternal grief and her ultimate victory – may invite audiences away from reason and logic and toward a sub-conscious healing process. This is less about re-enacting the events of 9/11 in procedural form (as *United 93* and *World Trade Center*, at times, attempt to do) or making analytical meaning out of them (as some other films tries to do). Rather, the more contemplative sequences in *Flightplan* simply allow an audience to "be" in that center of the brain, or more aptly put for film scholars, to revel in the excesses of maternal melodrama. Then, as the film progresses, she becomes more active, even aggressive, in ways that promise the possibility of regaining control over the events.

Because *Flightplan* produces associations with the subconscious and the maternal, it engages with what is defined in psychoanalytic terms as the pre-Oedipal phase. This represents a stage in a girl's development before she passes through the Lacanian mirror stage and, obviously, the oedipal phase. As a symbolic space, it can be understood as an early time of female bonding, where the daughter experiences diffuse boundaries and mother-love. In this phase, the girl's state might be defined as "pre-cognitive" or "pre-language" (although she is occasionally surfacing to a language she is beginning to comprehend) as she experiences moments of plenitude and wholeness near the mother's body.

Because this stage may also be associated with activities such as breastfeeding or gazing at the mother's eyes, it is defined by a lack of boundaries. That is, both mother and child may not know where "one stops and where the other begins." This phase has been appropriated by psychoanalytic feminists as an imaginary, all-female space, potentially outside of patriarchal language – or pre-patriarchy. It conjures up longing, nostalgia, and loss, for a time and space that is impossible to return to, that indeed may never have existed at all. So, even for women who go through so-called normal heterosexual, feminine socialization, occasional moments of longing for a lost "maternal" time will erupt in everyday life, often having to do with what is not possible within the confines of patriarchy. Feminist film theory has made use of such psychoanalytic constructs as the pre-Oedipal phase, the mirror stage, and, now, the psychic space of trauma as one lens through which to examine cinematic representations of female relationships.

There is one specific *Flightplan* passage in which all of these connections – affect, grief-related trauma, the pre-Oedipal bond, and the Vanishing lady tale – come together. And it happens to be, as we will see, the moment that most directly references *The Lady Vanishes*. In this sequence, Kyle has woken up from a knock on the head and is beginning to believe what those on the plane are telling her. She has been informed gradually by the pilot and crew that her daughter never boarded the plane, her husband's apparent fall was actually a suicide, her daughter died during her husband's act of suicide, and she herself cannot be trusted because she has been heavily medicated (not true) as a result of all of these events. As she opens her eyes, she finds that she is under the close scrutiny of the Air Marshal and a therapist (a passenger who has volunteered to help).

A distorted shot offers Kyle's point of view. In soft, breathy whispers, the unnamed therapist (Greta Scacchi) asks, "How are you feeling? Are you in pain?" to which Kyle does not respond. The therapist continues, "So many of my patients come to me after a loss, to grieve. Sometimes, it's just stopping, allowing the pain to come." Kyle lets out an obedient sigh, indicating that she is acquiescing to a new possible reality: perhaps she really *is* in denial that Julia has died. This scene is framed in soft focus and it mobilizes the aesthetic codes that the film has so far associated with sadness and a lost time: Jodie Foster is illuminated with a halo light and draped with aquamarine colors. The mise en scene appears washed with Kyle's inner struggle – in a way that evokes oceanic or amniotic undertones. In fact, her close ups appear to be swimming in amniotic fluid to the point where she might be perceived as being in an "in utero" state.

And the overemphasis of the therapist on words specifically referencing "feeling" or "pain," even the way that she speaks these words, reinforces the sense that the scene itself is swimming in a sea of affect. The therapist goes on, "When something is too overwhelming, we deny it. We choose to believe something else ... it feels better than the truth." Kyle whispers in agreement, "So much better."

Then the tone of the scene begins to shift. Scacchi's character is not part of the criminal plot that will eventually play out; she means well for Kyle, in that she believes the mother has indeed lost her child. She continues talking and Kyle sinks further into despair, coming to grips with her new reality as a grieving mother. As the counseling session ensues ("But it's impossible to move on if we haven't accepted, if we haven't grieved. Sometimes it helps to think of an image ..."), Kyle turns to look out the window, as if in search of that very image—an imaginary site or visual space she can create that will enable her to maintain an attachment with Julia apart from her current experience.

As much as this space is about preserving their mother-daughter bond in death, it calls upon the original connection of the pre-Oedipal phase. The hope for healing can be found, the film suggests, through a return to the subconscious, which in this case is determined solely by female bonds. Furthermore, one of the most interesting aspects of the pre-Oedipal phase is that it is not a one-sided rite-of-passage experienced solely by the daughter. Given its associated lack of boundaries and its ritualistic nature, a daughter's pre-Oedipal phase may be just as powerful for a mother, as the mother is returned to a stage of pre-cognition and daughterhood.

This is why the film's focus on Kyle's efforts to find, or re-find, a psychic space in order to more easily grieve her loss is so significant. In fact, as she looks out the window in search of "an image," there is a literal pause – an extended suspension of time – as she gazes out into the night sky and a series of reflections of her face form on the window. As the camera lingers here, the double image of the mother's face and the "unrepresentable,"--- that which is searched for, longed for, and grieved for – forms a screen that is open to projection, similar to other screens that will appear in *The Lady Vanishes* and *Bunny Lake is Missing*.

Kyle's reverie abruptly ends, however, as the reality of Julia's physical presence on the plane reveals itself. The picture that the daughter has traced earlier with her finger on the glass re-appears in the reflection of the mother's face in the window. So the daughter's inscription and the mother's image meet almost as an eruption, a symbolic flash which testifies to the power of their bond. And what does the flash look like? The picture that Julia has left behind is a heart, the most affective symbol of all. This leaves little doubt that affect is at the heart of the film.

Fig. 3-1: Flightplan screenshot 1: reflection of the mother's face

Genealogically speaking, this sequence draws on what Patrice Petro (1986, 124) calls the "emotive power of maternal psychic energy" in *The Lady Vanishes*. In order to fully appreciate the emotional undercurrents of the mother-daughter bond in *Flightplan*, it is essential to re-visit the conversation between Iris and Miss Froy to which the above sequence alludes and to digress slightly for the purpose of discussing the ultimate meaning of this conversation for the film. This occurs in a dining car just after Iris has woken up from a nap (her first of two) and is complaining about the bump on her head. Miss Froy comforts her by offering to treat her to tea. Once at their table, the conversation is designated as a separate, female space carved out only for the two of them – they remain the exclusive focus of the camera throughout and Miss Froy sets the tone by initially requesting "a pot of tea for two please."

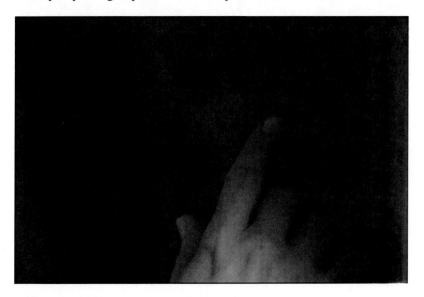

Fig. 3-2: Flightplan screenshot 2: the picture of a heart

In her analysis of this scene, Petro foregrounds its many subconscious qualities. For example, it opens with "a superimposed image of smoke, faces, and train wheels, coded to be read as dreamlike" and closes with another "shot of train wheels," so that the rhythm of the train (at other times too) "provides for Iris's entry into an earlier psychic realm" (1986, 127). (Significantly, whereas this scene is bracketed off as different from the rest of the film, *Flightplan* starts off as surreal and tries to sustain a dream-like effect for as long as possible.)[3] In addition, when Miss Froy first pronounces her name, Iris mishears it as "Freud," creating yet another textual slippage into the psychoanalytic realm.

Fig. 3-3: The Lady Vanishes screenshot 1: Miss Froy writing

Furthermore, because this meeting is being coded cinematically as a possible hallucination, the entire exchange is "rendered in ambiguous terms" as though it may be taking place outside of "proper consciousness" (1986, 127). All of this is reinforced, I would add, by the broader psychic tableau provided by the panoramic window against which they converse. At the moment when Iris mispronounces the governess's name as Freud and the train whistle blows loudly, causing the latter to scribble "Miss Froy" on the glass for clarity, the inscription of her name blends into their shared dream-landscape. So the picture window itself offers up a projection screen for Iris where the real and surreal aspects of Miss Froy blur together in the moment and in her memory.

All of these elements come together, then, to stage this sequence as a mise en scene for that "maternal psychic energy." Iris's bond with Miss Froy is powerful for many reasons. After all, she will eventually make the decision to escape a conformist marriage and, more importantly, she will rally the rest of the passengers into action against the fascists. Petro attributes Iris's newfound power to the female desire she finds "on the margins of the Oedipal/paternal relations." She specifically suggests that the film provides "a textual movement through which affectual desire is activated for the spectator by focusing upon the heroine's search for the

Fig. 3-4: The Lady Vanishes screenshot 2: Froy written on the window

mother and for what rapidly becomes the lost object of her original desire" (Petro 1986, 124).

This means that each assertion on Iris's part that Miss Froy has existed ("She was on this train. I know she was. And *nothing* will convince me otherwise.") is also an insistence that her brief connection with the older woman be recognized by the public, not buried into the margins of her mind. It will be the re-appearance of that name – when Iris re-sees the handwriting on the window later in the film – which will bring the marginal back to the center. Not only will the community affirm her bonds with Miss Froy, but her perceptiveness will have proven effective in stopping the Nazis.

Perhaps the most utopian move of the film is the final "crescendo" moment when Gilbert, Iris, and Miss Froy are reunited at the London Foreign Affairs Office, in a way that not only re-forges the symbolic mother-daughter bond, but also foresees a triangular family which would allow that bond to survive and flourish. As Gilbert and Iris are called into the office for him to deliver the secret musical code, he pauses, realizing he has suddenly forgotten the tune. Off-screen, a piano begins to play the music that has escaped his mind, and so he and Iris proceed toward the piano and, hence, into the office. The camera, sandwiched between the couple, tracks with them as it gradually reveals Miss Froy as the person playing the piano. She is alive and well, apparently just as surprised to see them as they are to see her. She clasps each of their hands and the film fades on the happy embrace of the three characters.

To the extent that Iris and Gilbert have been brought into the pre-Oedipal fold, then, they have also achieved a state of wholeness and plenitude with an image of the British matriarchy. Miss Froy's cover as governess is not coincidental, for the maternal subtext of the film images a Mother England that had an imperial history and would not let its citizens down. As the Nazi plot unfolds on the train, the film celebrates those characters that show courage and band together. In general, although this film could be easily passed off as light entertainment and it has been interpreted by some (especially Raymond Durgnat) as reflecting a relaxed moral attitude on Hitchcock's part toward the war, *The Lady Vanishes* represents a subtle rallying war-cry against isolationism (Durgnat 1974, 155-157). In this way, Miss Froy – and the Vanishing Lady trope, more broadly – was perhaps functioning in its historical moment at the level of national iconography, a symbol to haunt the nation as it was haunting Iris.

Looking at *Flightplan* through the mirror: With an eye toward *Bunny Lake*

It is not a window but a mirror that assumes this role as a maternal psychic screen in *Bunny Lake is Missing*. In one of the film's most powerful moments, Ann returns home to find all of Bunny's clothes and toys missing. A visually stunning shot tracks back on Ann's hand as she gropes along a shelf where her daughter's things once were. A large mirror hanging over the shelf offers up a second image of the empty space as Ann looks into a void, expecting one vision only to finding another. She turns her head in unison with the camera, so that her face is framed in extreme close up and her hand covers her gasping mouth. She wears the expression of someone whose entire reality has just shifted abruptly into nightmare.

As an allusion to Jacques Lacan's theory of the mirror stage, this scene places Ann regressively back in the child's position of fragmentation. That is, one understanding of the mirror stage is that as a child moves into the world of (patriarchal) language, her experience of her image in the mirror offers up the illusion of wholeness and coherence. A maternal figure may also function as a mirror, providing this image of wholeness, in addition to the plenitude associated with the pre-Oedipal phase. So moving through the mirror stage is about negotiating one's sense of identity fragmentation with that of coherence and patriarchal (or other kinds of power), which will be a continual back-and-forth process throughout adult life.

Ann's moment in the mirror makes for a remarkable crisis then. As a mother faced with a non-image of her daughter, the void produces an obliteration of her own sense of coherence. This throws her across to the other side of the mirror, converting her back into the child-role. Such a role has been chasing her since childhood, anyway, the film has suggested, such as when she looks at a photograph of a girl and cannot discern whether she is seeing her daughter or herself. There are two traumatic dimensions to existing on the daughter-side of the mirror. The first is that she is thrust symbolically back in her brother's hands where, as a girl, she was forced to play childhood games ruled by a logic that only made sense within his psychotic mind. The second is that, as a daughter with no mother, she now confronts the *other* void, living in a world of fragmentation with no reassurance of plenitude.

So where does she go? Well at this particular moment, fascinatingly, she turns directly to an African mask that hangs on her bedroom wall. This charged object has taken on thematic significance in one of the film's opening scenes, when her new landlord, played creepily by Noël Coward, offers it to her. "It's a mask," he says, "You can wear it if you like. I believe it's marvelous for fertiliating." Annoyed, Ann answers back, "That's not my problem," in a tone that suggests she is issuing a rebuff to

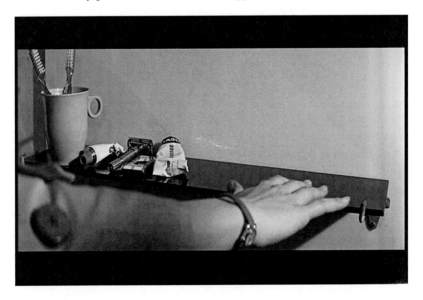

Fig. 3-5: Bunny Lake is Missing screenshot 1: Ann's moment in the mirror

Fig. 3-6: Bunny Lake is Missing screenshot 2: panic 1

Fig. 3-7: Bunny Lake is Missing screenshot 3: panic 2

what she perceives as a sexual advance on his part. But his "slip of the tongue" is telling, considering that "fertiliating" – fertility, reproduction, sexual freedom – is precisely "her problem," not in the way she means it, but because Bunny's existence puts her at a societal and psychological disadvantage.

By turning from the mirror to the mask, she goes back to the original crisis of "fertiliating." Her psychic solution will be to unmask the mask, to own her right to have made her choices to have given birth to Bunny, and, by the end of the film, she will leave behind all of the dolls, toys, and playhouses that have haunted her world, so that she may claim her own legitimacy and her daughter's as well. By re-birthing herself, Ann's character is thus part of a proto-feminist movement that will gain its own authority in the decade(s) to come.[4] In other words, the look of horror on Ann's face in this mirror scene reflects a fear of the voiding of the self. Ann "exists far outside the limits of the societal norm" (Schweitzer 2010, 3). Her story calls for social change.

So all three films are driven by a subconscious motor that uses mother-daughter bonds to tap into cultural longings for what never was, what might not ever be, or what once was but will never be again. *Flightplan* and *Bunny Lake* differ from *The Lady Vanishes* and the original "Paris Exposition" tale, of course, in that they revolve around the mother-figure's loss (and not the daughter-figure's loss). In other words, they convert the "disappearing subject" from mother to daughter so that the search is not so much for the past but for the future. Given *Bunny Lake*'s historically rooted engagement with feminist politics (especially when one considers the narrator's voice in the novel) and a long history of feminist iconography surrounding Jodie Foster, this is not surprising. It appears that the tale undergoes "proto-feminist" and then "post-feminist" revision, transforming the daughter to the mother so as to allow the adult woman to re-birth herself.

Reality check

Having gained greater insight into what it means for a mother-figure and a daughter-figure to meet "in the looking glass," it is worth examining other contemporary aspects of *Flightplan*, including the impact that Jodie Foster's presence has on the film's maternal register. As performer and star, Jodie Foster participated in a very long and public mother-daughter narrative of her own, which began off-screen in the early 1970s. The child actress was managed by her publicity-agent mother Brandy Foster, who enjoyed equal parts publicity for herself and, as the daughter has since noted in numerous interviews, took great pleasure in blurring the boundaries of their relationship for a variety of obvious reasons. A 1994 *Vanity Fair* article gives the actress an opportunity to voice this symbiosis for herself:

> Jodie speaks of her [mother] now with a detachment that seems new. "I didn't choose my own movies until I was 16," she observes, "[so] I couldn't help but be in a position where I was putting forth her personal agenda about what was important for her in *her* life, and playing people that she felt a personal connection to .... *She* wanted those victims to survive. *She* wanted me to be someone who was substantial on her own, and I became that person" (Schnayerson 1994, 170).

Their relationship had been further governed by a role reversal, according to Jodie Foster, in which she played the maternal figure, in part because the child actress was the sole breadwinner for the single mother of four children.

In an insightful *Sight and Sound* essay entitled "Mother Courage," Linda Ruth Williams analyzes various meanings of "Foster as mother" and "Foster as daughter," which took on even more significance once the star had two sons of her own but refused to reveal any details regarding the origin of their father. Commenting on the frequency with which she plays fatherless or husband-less characters, Williams claims, "Foster the celebrity single mother, herself the daughter of a single mother, has given us three remarkable lone-parent portraits in the last ten years" (referring to *Panic Room, Anna and the King, Little Man Tate*), noting also her roles as a bereaved daughter (in *Contact, Nell,* and *Silence of the Lambs*) (Williams 2002, 13). She highlights *Nell* as specifically embodying "a weird way with language; single mothers and orphans alike, Jodie Foster's characters are incompletely repressed, struggling for a linguistic precision with which to paper over the cracks" (Williams 2002, 13). It is precisely this struggle which makes Jodie Foster the ideal candidate to play the mother in *Flightplan*. And it is a scene such as the one explored above – when the very moment that she is "in between the cracks" of grief collides with a "precise" sign written by her daughter's hand – that explains why the vanishing lady trope lives in a nation's collective memory.

Without Jodie Foster, this film may not have worked as a trauma film at all then. This is particularly significant given that it was originally written as a father-son story, set to star Sean Penn. According to the production history, while the project was in development, producer Brian Grazer reached an epiphany and declared, "Our protagonist needs to be a woman and she needs to be Jodie Foster."[5] If *Flightplan* had gone forward as a male-centered film, it may have had even more problems with plot, story, and theme than it does as released, given that Jodie Foster and the emotional scene work are the major elements holding it together. As a melodrama, I believe the film works; as a thriller, it is best understood as a stage set, with actors, blocking, and props in place, inhibited by too much cultural inertia to put its play into motion.[6] In processing the events of 9/11 logically and rationally, *Flightplan* fails because it carries so many charged images and narratives that it apparently does not know what to do with them.

In fact, the loose constellations of 9/11-related moments in the film are worth noting. In an obvious way, Kyle represents the war widow, doing the woman's work of bringing her husband home. She can therefore be extracted out of the plane and envisioned as a participant in the media landscape of the "9/11-widow" that has become part of the American national consciousness. In fact, when read this way, she is not just any bereaved wife, but the widow of the "falling man." Is it any coincidence that her husband's death occurred as the result of a fall from a building? And that "what really happened at the point of the fall" becomes a point of preoccupation for the film? (The film reveals that the husband was pushed to his death, as part of the hijacking plot, which means that his death shifts from accident to suicide to murder as the narrative unfolds, with accompanying flashbacks.)

Esquire's Tom Junod wrote a seminal piece on the "falling man", contemplating the image of the people who jumped from the World Trade Center as the buildings were burning. He specifically refers to one photograph, of an unknown man in freefall whose body vertically aligns with the towers and, with one knee bent looks, if only temporarily, resigned and free. Junod comments, "One of the most famous photographs in human history became an unmarked grave, and the man buried inside its frame – the Falling Man – the Unknown Soldier in a war whose end we have not yet seen" (Junod 2002, 7).

In addition to these figures, once Kyle realizes her daughter is in danger, she becomes an embodiment of the "Let's roll" mentality ascribed to the male passengers who fought back on United 93, the mentality later appropriated by President George W. Bush in his efforts to assert his militaristic masculinity. (It might be argued that her embodiment is cathartic, because the audience can feel a powerful "let's roll" wave without drowning in the violent reality of the actual attack.) In addition to the war widow, falling man, and passenger heroes, *Flightplan* also features the potentially dangerous Arab men, the air marshal (who comes to symbolize the dangers of unchecked surveillance measures), and the complacent "Don't Bother Me" American bystanders. *Flightplan* takes in an array of figures, images, and ideological threads, but appears to short-circuit in any efforts to process them in a culturally productive and articulate way, unless it is understood as an affective experience.

The "feminist subconscious" of *Flightplan* is most evident when the movie is compared to other 9/11 trauma films. Take *United 93* or *World Trade Center*, for example. A pseudo-documentary, procedural film, *United 93* prides itself on realism to the point of hiring actual flight attendants and pilots to play the parts of airline characters in order to increase verisimilitude. The director Paul Greengrass attempts to recreate what transpired on the United Flight Number 93, including the hijacking of the plane, the passengers' efforts to stop the terrorists, and the subsequent crash in Shanksville, Pennsylvania. As the story was taken up immediately after the attacks and transformed into an official narrative of heroism by the media and the Bush administration, it is important to remember that many versions of masculinity were represented on that flight beyond the one-dimensional "Let's Roll" variety. For example, Mark Bingham was openly gay and his mother made a point of this whenever she went on national media outlets to discuss his heroic actions; however, all of the male characters looked and acted the same in the film.

United 93 suffers from stereotypical gender roles with one-dimensional male characters and passive, hysterical women. The film's treatment of the female flight attendants is particularly negative, culminating in a scene where a male passenger grabs a weak, simpering flight attendant by the hair and growls, "Stewardess, are you listening to me?" In other words, he reverses roles of power, takes away her "voice," and rolls back the professional gains women have made in the aviation industry (in abolishing the word "stewardess" from its vocabulary) all in one fell swoop.

In the meantime, the other two narrative spaces of *United 93* – the air traffic control unit and Defense Command Site – are undeniably male, governed by a cacophony of impersonal, men's voices and dominated by their point of view as they view the attacks on the World Trade Center through a series of flat-screen monitors. In fact, the screens which mediate 9/11 for these characters provide an effective counterpoint to those represented in the above three films. In this setting, the televisions and computers make for a highly technologized and militarized lens through which to re-visit a historically traumatic moment.

World Trade Center, on the other hand, deliberately tries to balance the stories of its male and female characters. Oliver Stone tells the true story of two New York Port Authority police officers who became trapped underneath the rubble of the Trade Center concourse just after the attacks, paying nearly equal attention to the suffering borne by the men's wives and families during the hours that they do not know whether their husbands are alive or dead. *World Trade Center* is not understated in its theme; in fact, it is very heavy-handed (and clichéd) in its message that these husbands have taken their wives and loved ones for granted and they can find meaning in 9/11 by re-evaluating the "little moments" that ordinarily pass them by.

While there are moments of action in *World Trade Center*, it is best categorized as a male melodrama. The relationship between the male characters *is* open to a progressive psychoanalytic or anti-oedipal narrative reading. Sergeant John McLoughlin (Nicholas Cage) starts off as a higher-ranking father figure for Patrol Officer Will Jimeno (Michael Peña). The opening act of the film establishes the Port Authority officers' confidence in him as he leads them to the crash site; however, once the two men are pinned underneath the debris, John is clearly impotent as Will calls out for reassurance. When the film draws to a close, few efforts are made to re-secure John's masculinity or paternal authority. Both men lie in hospital beds together, as brothers in survival. Cut to two years later and they enjoy a celebratory picnic, but they are both limping as the result of permanent injuries to their legs. Rather than grasp toward phallic power as a solution for resolving the anxiety of the towers going down, *World Trade Center* seeks healing in the symbolic emotional site that these two men have created underground in those hours of desperation -- a site which resembles a womb more than a phallic image. And, because the film's attention is focused elsewhere, it also looks for healing in the women's experiences.

World Trade Center underscores that although the wives have an "indirect" relationship to the trauma of their husbands, it is a trauma nonetheless. This film attends to the domestic context of the suffering of John's wife, Donna (Maria Bello), and Will's wife, Allison (Maggie Gyllenhaal). Significantly, a central theme concerns the fact that Allison is pregnant with a baby girl in so much as the naming of the baby comes to have symbolic meaning, both for the survival of the couple's love for each other and the spirit of future "post-9/11" generations. As the film draws to a close, the final scene reveals that Will's preferred name (Olive) has won out. Though no mention is made of the fact, Allison's original favorite "Alisa" is of course derived from her own name, which means that, with her active and willing participation, the tighter connection between Allison and "Alisa" has been cut off. The power of naming forfeited by the mother – in such a way that deprives *World Trade Center* of its feminist possibilities. In its effort to provide Will, somewhat crippled in his

masculinity, with the opportunity for regeneration through his connection
to his new daughter, the film disempowers the very mother figure whose
interests it was apparently very concerned with at the story's start.

So Allison and Alisa do not take their place among other sets of
characters such as Kyle and Julia, Ann and Bunny, or Iris and Miss Froy.
Placing *Flightplan* alongside *United 93* and *World Trade Center* is
illuminating in part because it may help us to see Hollywood's mediation
of a very specific set of cultural anxieties at the same time with roughly
the same demographic in mind. But what precisely is *Flightplan*'s appeal,
given that it was not marketed as a "woman's picture" and yet there were
very few complaints echoed in reviews about the number of melodramatic
moments contained in this supposed thriller? Its box office and DVD
rental receipts indicate that the Vanishing Lady tale is a great draw for
male and female audiences alike, and that the possible appeal of an
affective, subconscious experience of a post-9/11 film is not divided along
gender lines.

In hypothesizing what the mother-daughter theme means for male
viewers, *Flightplan* might be seen in relation to the cycle of "masculinity
in crisis" films which began in the late 1980s, backlash movies such as
Falling Down (1993) in which the anxiety-ridden male character fears his
changing world. Have post 9/11 films brought the "falling down man" into
a fetal position – no longer suffering from anxiety but now stricken with
grief – in such a way that *Flightplan* provides relief and solace? *World
Trade Center* certainly hints at this, as it invites audience members to
experience the excruciating suffering of its two male protagonists in the
womb-like cavern of the World Trade Center rubble.

Regardless of how one might answer these open questions, the
connections between *Flightplan*, *The Lady Vanishes*, and *Bunny Lake is
Missing* suggest that the Vanishing Lady tale will live on. But so will the
incredible feeling of loss that it bears. And the never-ending quality of
loss, the on and on-nesss of it, is the very part of the original story that all
three films elide. For in each movie, the mother and daughter figures are
reunited, sealing up the hole that is in the whole, so to speak. The
reconnection – the re-finding of that psychic space – is not a real
possibility, according to Freudian theory, however. Instead, it is an illusion
perpetuated by the films whose endings provide a promise of possible
closure.[7] All three translations of the tale, then, facilitate a belief that the
original (historical) trauma can be healed, whereas the tale of the mother
and daughter at the Paris Exposition does not. As McKinney puts it, "Tell
a story once, and the ending is written. Tell it again and again, recasting

the details but preserving the dread, and it goes on forever – like loss itself" (McKinney 2005, 16).

Notes

[1] *Flightplan*'s script had been in development before 9/11 and it went through dramatic revision as soon as the attacks occurred.

[2] In this way, Preminger's choice of Olivier in the part of Ann's ally is a strategic breakthrough, given that, decades earlier in *Rebecca* (1940), he had played a character who had become obsessed with the sexual transgressions of a promiscuous woman. Here, the Inspector spends all of his time trying to understand Ann's struggles to be sexually and independent (*as* a woman), in a way that allows Preminger to morally redeem both Olivier and Hitchcock by the end of the film.

[3] The opening sequence provides an entryway into the narrative through the subjective, destabilized perceptions of Kyle as she returns home from viewing her husband's body at the morgue. Intermittent flashes of her view of the coffin, a tube train racing past her as she sits on a platform, and a nighttime walk with her husband are interspersed with other random images so that the film's language is first born through Kyle's subconscious.

[4] For insightful analysis of the relationship between Piper's novel and Preminger's film, see Esther Sonnet (2009). She suggests that the film adaptation de-emphasizes the political implications of the novel, choosing instead to prioritize the psychoanalytic dimensions.

[5] Brian Grazer explains this in the featurette on the *Flightplan* DVD.

[6] Kyle's confrontation scene with the Arab men is a good example of this. Becoming frantic, she makes up her mind that a group of Arab men, and one man in particular, must be responsible for kidnapping her daughter. She runs down the aisle of the plane, creating a disturbance among the passengers and crew. The Arab man sees her coming towards him and stands up defensively. The beginning of the scene is filmed so as to make him look guilty and menacing. But as the clash between Kyle and him continues, he is framed as increasingly sympathetic. Her point of view becomes less reliable. Meanwhile, in the background, an irritating, stereotypically "American" passenger voices a chorus of anti-Arab sentiment.

The scene can only go so far, however, and then it gets "stuck." The stand-off truly becomes a "stage," and the characters appear to be actors who do not have pages for the next lines. Kyle lunges at the man only to be subdued by the Marshal. The attack provides the Arab character with one last opportunity to make a plaintiff cry (to the characters and the audience) about how painful it is to live under constant scrutiny. But even and especially after the build up of the camera's frenetic pace and the eruption of physical violence, the film does not seem to know what to do with the conflict it has initiated. Kyle, still convinced that the Arab men are a threat, takes off down the aisle again.

[7] *Flightplan* offers the most conservative ending of all, wherein, the daughter wakes up, oblivious to all of the narrative action that has occurred and asks her

mother the all-American, children's question, "Mommy, are we there, yet?" Kyle
assures her, "Not yet. Almost").

Works Cited

Durgnat, Raymond. 1974. The Strange Case of Alfred Hitchcock.
    Cambridge: MIT Press.
Hemingway, Ernest. 1926. The Torrents of Spring. London: Jonathan
    Cape.
Hollinger, Karen. 2012. Jodie Foster: Feminist Hero? Pretty People:
    Movie Stars of the 1990s. Edited by Anna Everett. New Brunswick,
    NJ: Rutgers University Press.
Howie, Luke. 2011. Terror on the Screen: Witnesses and the Reanimation
    of 9/11 as Image-event, Popular Culture, and Pornography.
    Washington, D.C.: New Academia Publishing.
Junod, Tom. 2003. Falling Man. Esquire 140(3): 199.
Kaplan, Ann E. 2005. Trauma Culture: The Politics of Terror and Loss in
    Media and Literature. New Brunswick, NJ: Rutgers University Press.
Lane, Christina. 1995. The Liminal Iconography of Jodie Foster. Journal
    of Popular Film and Television 22(4): 149-153.
McKinney, Devin. 2005. Fright Plan: Toward a Cultural History of the
    Vanishing Lady—with a Nod to Jodie Foster. Village Voice,
    November 8, Arts Section.
Mizejewski, Linda. 2004. Hard-boiled and High-heeled: The Woman
    Detective in Popular Culture. New York and London: Routledge.
Petro, Patrice. 1986. Re-Materializing the Vanishing "Lady". Feminism,
    Hitchcock, and Interpretation. In The Hitchcock Reader. Edited by
    Marshall Deutelbaum and Leland Poague. Ames: University of Iowa
    Press.
Rich, Ruby B. 1991. Never a Victim: Jodie Foster, a New Kind of Female
    Hero. In Women and Film. A Sight and Sound Reader. Edited by Pam
    Cook and Philip Dodd. Philadelphia: Temple University Press.
    Originally published in Sight and Sound, vol. 1, no. 8 (December
    1991).
Schnayerson, Michael. 1994. Jodie Rules. Vanity Fair May, 174.
Schweitzer, Dahlia. 2010. Who is Missing in Bunny Lake? Jump Cut: A
    Review of Contemporary Media. 52. Summer: 1-3.
Sonnet, Esther. 2009. Evelyn Piper's Bunny Lake is Missing (1957):
    Adaptation, Feminism, and the Politics of the 'Progressive Tekst'.
    Adaptation 2(1): 65-86.

Staiger, Janet. 1992. Taboos and Totems. Cultural Meanings of Silence of the Lambs. In Film Theory Goes to the Movies. Edited by Jim Collins, Hillary Radner, and Ava Preacher Collins. New York and London: Routledge.

Williams, Linda Ruth. 2002. Mother Courage. Sight and Sound May: 12-14.

MEDIA, GENOCIDE AND *HOTEL RWANDA*

METASEBIA WOLDEMARIAM
AND KYLO-PATRICK R. HART

Introduction

In 1999, the writer Keir Pearson heard a remarkable story. Five years earlier, his friend John was in Tanzania listening to a shocking radio broadcast: the on-air journalist was inside the Hôtel des Mille Collines in Kigali, Rwanda, describing survival in the hotel while, outside of it, genocide raged on. John explained how the Rwandan hotel manager, Paul Rusesabagina, would ultimately save the more than 1,200 people who took refuge at the hotel. Fascinated, Pearson called the Rwandan Embassy in Washington, D.C. As he asked about Rusesabagina, the woman on the phone said she was a Mille Collines survivor. Starting with her, Pearson began interviewing genocide survivors on three continents. The result was the first draft of the *Hotel Rwanda* screenplay.

When *Hotel Rwanda*, directed by Terry George, was released in 2004, it received critical praise for its depiction of the 1994 Rwandan genocide. Yet films that focus on genocide often spark controversy; aside from issues about the filmmakers' agendas and biases, in the public arena, critics and scholars alike debate the manner by which such films represent "historical reality." Rosenstone (2004, 2006) has argued that the historical film is not just a vehicle to transmit an objective past. Rather, such films often provide a way to think about the past through the visual metaphors they present. As he notes, one can "see the historical film as part of a separate realm of representation and discourse, one not meant to provide literal truths about the past (as if our written history can provide literal truths) but metaphoric truths which work, to a large degree, as a kind of commentary on and challenge to traditional historical discourse" (Rosenstone 2004, 163).

Representing genocide

Most discourse about genocide representations since WWII has focused on the Holocaust; as Gilman points out, "The murder of the Jews moved from being one aspect of the crimes of the Nazis to being their central, defining aspect over half a century. Over the past decade or so, it has evolved from a specific, historical moment to the metaphor for horror itself" (Gilman 2000, 281). As such, the late twentieth century saw an anxious revival of analysis in relation to memory, the Holocaust and how it is represented. Books such as Daniel Goldhagen's *Hitler's Willing Executioners* (which examines the role of "average" Germans) and Pierre Vidal-Naquet's *Assassins of Memory* (which focuses on those in France who denied the Holocaust) played a significant role in this revival (Said 2000, 175).

The concern with how traumatic historical events such as genocide are represented (and accordingly remembered) certainly applies to the Rwandan genocide of 1994, which has been the topic of several books, articles and documentaries. A quick Google search of "Rwandan Genocide" will bring up thousands of web pages. On some level, then, the genocide can be said to have infiltrated at least a segment of the U.S. cultural and intellectual memory, although this raises questions about how the Rwandan genocide is (and should be) framed and remembered. Arguably, the Rwandan Genocide is framed more in terms of the West's moral failure to intervene (which, although largely true and certainly significant, hardly reveals much about nature of genocide) rather than a complex tragedy that deserves critical, historical analysis. Moreover, these representations tend to relocate Africa as a continent of tribal warfare and ethnic strife. In the process, the historical, political and cultural forces that motivated the 1994 genocide become obscured. As Newbury and Newbury (1999, 293) explain, "the concept of 'genocide' is tied in the general literature so strongly to the concept of 'ethnic struggle' that the Rwandan genocide of 1994 is simply assumed to be ethnic in its origins, as well as in its effects."

Representational limits

In relation to the Holocaust, the most publicly discussed and represented genocide of the twentieth century, there have long existed conflicting viewpoints about how – and whether – it can be adequately represented. In "Does the Holocaust Lie Beyond the Reach of Art", Nobel Laureate Elie Wiesel has claimed that the Holocaust, in one sense, lies beyond representation as those who were not there cannot "know" it while those that lived through it are unable to fully depict it: "Since we [survivors] are incapable of revealing the Event, why not admit it. ... I tell of the impossibility one stumbles upon in trying to tell the tale" (*New York Times*, 17 April 1983).

Wiesel has argued that while anyone can write about it, there should be limits to representations of the Holocaust, a theme that is taken up in Saul Friedlander's edited collection *Probing the Limits of Representation* (1992), in which various authors debate the meaning of historical truth and representation. In his introduction, Friedlander makes clear that he believes that the Holocaust, like other historical events, is open to interpretation and representation. He cautions, however, that it tests our "traditional conceptual and representational categories, an 'event at the limits'" (in Jenkins 1997, 389). Largely concerned about whether certain claims to "truth" might take precedence over others, Friedlander also has said, quite famously, that "there are limits to representation which should not be but can easily be transgressed" (1992, 3).

For some, the concern is based on the reality that Holocaust representations have become a staple in U.S. popular culture; there is a danger of sliding into kitsch as the Holocaust is packaged and distributed as entertainment. This commodification of the Holocaust (the Shoah-business as it is sometimes disparagingly referred to) extends beyond film: Mengele twins have appeared on the television talk show *Geraldo,* a Holocaust cookbook has been published, and Holocaust museums are listed as tourist sites. One such museum even offers visitors the chance to buy, for only $39.95, a replica of a boxcar used to transport victims to concentration camps. For a donation to the museum of at least $5,000, visitors are presented with an original spike from the Treblinka concentration camp (Rapaport 2002, 56-57).

Others have pointed to the fact that the mainstreaming of this tragedy means that it has become quite common to speak of the "Holocaust film" as though it composes a distinct genre. Such uncritical usage implies that, like a western, a musical or film noir, there exist ideological conventions to which the "Holocaust film" adheres. This is ethically problematic as the conventional organizing practices of genre may "order the world" in a reassuring manner for audiences, persuading some that this ordering is not the result of the generic form or from the audiences' own abilities to impose structure, "but is, rather, immanent in the world itself prior to its generic reconception" (Langford 1999, 24).

This genre/generic approach to Holocaust representations in Hollywood productions – such as the film *Schindler's List* (1993, directed by Steven

Spielberg) or the televised series *Holocaust* (1978) – has been roundly condemned by many survivors and scholars alike[1]. For example, in "Trivializing the Holocaust: Semi-Fact and Semi-Fiction," Wiesel has stated about the television series *Holocaust*: "All I know is that the witness does not recognize himself in this film. The Holocaust *must* be remembered. But not as a show." (*New York Times*, 16 April 1978).

A second set of representational problems is related to the African continent. African and Africanist scholars have long decried the manner by which generic structures have been applied to visual representations of the continent, precisely because they may leave audiences with a certain view of reality regarding what is inherently "African." Colonial photography set the stage for how an entire continent of various peoples were transformed, through repetitious images, into a generic indigenous mass requiring "civilizing missions" and the presence of the European to somehow rehabilitate them. Early cinematic representations closely followed this model; films such as *Sanders of the River* (1933, directed by Alexander Korda) emphasized the role of the white officer in maintaining peace among natives (Harding 2003, 70). Alternately, Africa has been used as an exotic, dangerous backdrop within which things "happen" to the Euro-American stars, and Africans themselves (regardless of locality) play secondary characters at best.

When *Hotel Rwanda* premiered in 2004, it did not invite such criticism, perhaps because, unlike the Holocaust, it was not perceived as a singular event whose representation required much critical analysis. Part of the reason must be due to the fact that most U.S. mainstream media outlets that covered the tragedy in 1994 did so as though it were yet another dark crisis emanating from the equally dark continent. To American audiences, the genocide was frequently represented as based on tribalism that, somewhat consistent with early cinematic renderings of Africa, only Western/U.N. intervention could solve.

News media and Rwanda

But as ample research has made clear, the fault did not necessarily lie with lazy journalists relying on stereotypical African images. The concept of genocide is so strongly linked to the notion of ethnic or tribal enmity that it became the easiest explanation as to what happened in Rwanda in 1994. It is no surprise, therefore, that U.S. media coverage zeroed in on this explanation; the genocide was largely framed as tribal warfare with Hutu massacring Tutsi.

Furthermore, financial and other considerations led many U.S. news outlets to severely downsize the number of reporters on the continent. The relatively small numbers of U.S. journalists based in Africa were responsible for representing the entire continent to American audiences. Some have argued that covering the vast and complex issues in several countries meant these journalists were generally ill equipped to cover the Rwandan genocide during the initial crisis stages (Livingston and Eachus 2000, 213-214). Analysis of U.S. television coverage of the genocide additionally demonstrates that journalists with little knowledge about the country were flown in to file stories alongside the few journalists in Africa-based bureaus. The result was that "journalists relied on stereotypes – thoroughly tested by news organizations in stories set in other African countries...that characterized the genocide in Rwanda as the result of some inexplicable, uncontrollable primordial tribalism that drove Hutus and Tutsis to murder" (Fair and Parks 2001, 36). Journalists were often unable to clearly distinguish between who the "good" guys and the "bad" guys were, as television convention requires. Consequently, the genocide itself received far less coverage than the refugee crisis that ensued.

For the most part, print media faced the same constraints; journalists relied on simplistic and formulaic analyses to explain the genocide to their audiences. Numerous examples can be found in one of the most important U.S. newspapers, *The New York Times*. For instance, a headline from 9 April 1994 reads "Terror Convulses Rwandan Capital as Tribes Battle." Two days later, an article explains that the plane crash that killed Rwanda's President Habyarimana "ignited one more round of the tribal bloodletting that has plagued this part of Africa for centuries" (*New York Times*, 11 April 1994, A12).

Another possible reason that there remains a paucity of research and critique in relation to any limits of representation posed by the 1994 Rwandan genocide generally, and *Hotel Rwanda* in particular, is that the genocide has not greatly penetrated American public memory or consciousness and, where it has, it has not done so as a singular event: the genocide continues to be regarded as tribalism compounded by the moral failure of nonintervention on the part of the U.S., the U.N. and European states. The articles and books, both academic and popular, devoted to this tragedy tend to try to explain what happened and why[2], rather than analyze representational strategies[3]. Finally, of course, one has to consider the fact that the Rwandan genocide (perhaps because it occurred only twelve years ago and in Africa) has not often been a cinematic "object".

Of the handful of feature films dealing with the subject (see Dauge-Roth 2010, 191), *Hotel Rwanda* has been the most commercially and critically successful. Made on a budget of about USD 17.5 million, the movie brought in at least USD 23 million at the U.S. box office, and over USD 10 million internationally. This is a respectable figure for a film that director Terry George initially had difficulty raising money to make. Although Hollywood studio executives liked the screenplay, they could not imagine *Hotel Rwanda* being commercially successful: it was about genocide, it was located in Africa, and the key roles were written primarily for African and African-American actors. George and producer A. Kitman Ho secured funding and tax relief from various countries, and they eventually signed a distribution deal with MGM/UA. This, George has said, freed him from the constraints that studio financing would have placed on him, such as forcing him to use favored actors (Morales 2004).

Cinematic representations

How does one justify making a film such as *Hotel Rwanda* that tries to tell a given truth about atrocities without turning it either into a voyeuristic narration that arouses audiences, or into kitsch? How does one represent the unrepresentable? This becomes relevant when we consider that visual media tend to influence and shape our memories of traumatic events more than books and other print media (Rapaport 2002, 64). Furthermore, in the twentieth century, public memory of war "has been created less from a remembered past than a manufactured past, one substantially shaped by images in documentaries, feature films, and television programs" (in Hoskins 2001, 336). Our historical imagination is accordingly greatly influenced by cinematic texts as well as other modes of artistic expression. It is for this reason that the immediacy of images offered by film "seems to have an advantage over literature in the quest for "realistic" representation…. Cinema transmits versions of history to these younger generations, and, more importantly, becomes instrumental in forming contemporary discourses of the past, present, and future" (Stimmel 2005, 102). *Hotel Rwanda* has no pretenses of being a film that explores all aspects of the genocide. Its highly positive critical reception and its commercial success in the West as a film about Africa and genocide makes it a relevant film to analyze. Moreover, the later denouncements of the central figure in the film (Paul Rusesabagina) by the Rwandese government and by survivors' organizations, questioning his heroism[4] (Waldorf 2009) add to the relevance of the analysis.

Hotel Rwanda

Hotel Rwanda is based on the real-life experiences of Paul Rusesabagina (played by Don Cheadle), hotel manager of the luxurious Hôtel des Mille Collines in Rwanda's capital, Kigali, during the 1994 genocide. The film details how Rusesabagina, a man initially concerned only about those close to him, moves his family and a few others into the relative safety of the hotel. Before long, and as Western powers and the U.N. abandon Rwanda to its fate, Rusesabagina converts the hotel into a refugee camp for more than 1,200 Tutsi and Hutu who would otherwise have been massacred. The film's focus is on how Rusesabagina manipulates his contacts within the genocidal regime to keep the refugees alive, as well as the manner in which Rwanda was abandoned by the fleeing Western powers and by the U.N.

Because director Terry George hoped to attract the widest possible audience, the PG-13-rated *Hotel Rwanda* is not a gory film. George has said that he hoped the film could be used as an educational tool in schools; a film depicting too much genocidal violence might not have been suitable for such purposes (Netribution 2006). While at least part of the decision to not graphically display genocide is based on financial considerations, scholars have also noted that viewers are repelled by visceral art. Such images not only invite issues of censorship, but some authors have also claimed that these images may not convey what genocide is about as their explanative powers are reduced to images (Feinstein 2005, 32), although this position has been questioned (Sontag 2003).

Films about such traumatic events face representational dilemmas: how does one convey the horror of genocide without being exploitative? For example, while she finds there are several levels of reception in relation to *Schindler's List*, Hansen is primarily interested in the rejection the film faced from critical intellectuals. She finds that this critique centers on several factors: the film is a Hollywood product and accordingly part of the Shoah-business; the narrative fiction technique employed is not adequate (especially as it employs a classical – or generic, as Langford might say – narrative style replete with both melodramatic moments and at the same time, a "realist" approach by recycling images of the Holocaust from other films, documentaries and stills); the film's subjective point of view belongs to perpetrators; and, finally, the film violates taboos by representing the unrepresentable. Hansen notes that critics seem to agree that one of the most egregious of such transgressions in *Schindler's List* occurs when a group of Jewish women is accidentally deported to Auschwitz and forced into a shower room where they believe they will be gassed. As they huddle fearfully, they are delighted to discover that the shower is actually one of water rather than gas (Hansen 1996, 296-301).

While the intention here is not to draw comparisons between *Schindler's List* and *Hotel Rwanda*, it is instructive to analyze the latter in relation to the critique of representational strategies that the former utilizes. *Hotel Rwanda*'s narrative technique relies on melodramatic moments, especially hair-raising last-minute rescues. At the same time, its use of real-life images (such as President Clinton on the cover of an issue of *Time* magazine, Rwanda's President Habyarimana and the then-rebel leader Kagame on TV screens, real-life and recreated radio announcements, etc.) serves to highlight the fact that the film is depicting actual events. Adding legitimacy to the aura of reality, the film concludes with text that explains what has happened to various characters (for instance, Rusesabagina and his wife adopted their nieces and moved to Belgium).

One cannot overlook some of the melodramatic moments in *Hotel Rwanda* as simple narrative devices to maintain the audience's attention. Melodrama, especially in the form of last-minute rescues, often serves viewer's voyeuristic impulses. In this film, last-minute rescues lead to empathy with the survivors. For instance, the closing scenes portray Rusesabagina and his wife dramatically reunited with their presumably orphaned nieces. Ending with this happy image, the film turns genocide into a story of survival; the dead remain largely forgotten.

But perhaps some aspects of the realistic approach in *Hotel Rwanda* remain more problematic. On the one hand, the film's use of radio announcements – both recreated and actual – have strong explanatory powers about local hate propaganda as well as the West's moral failures. On the other hand, by equating genocide with tribalism, the film fails to move beyond stereotypical characterizations of Africa generally and of Rwanda in particular. By recycling simplistic generalizations that many mainstream U.S. journalists relied on in 1994, the film's potential explanative powers are severely compromised, especially if we recall that people remember and learn about such traumatic events through visual media. Furthermore, the realistic tendency serves to legitimize the seeming historical accuracy of the film.

A spontaneous genocide?

Hotel Rwanda begins with a bustling scene at what appears to be a normal African market. There are soldiers pushing people around, but the upbeat music doesn't make for a tense atmosphere. Rusesabagina is driven past a roadblock where he gives money to a soldier who recognizes him. They share a pleasant greeting before Rusesabagina continues on to the airport, where some Europeans give him rare Cuban cigars and he also collects an icebox full of lobsters for the hotel. Shortly thereafter, we see a businessman[5] puffing on a cigar that Rusesabagina has clearly provided to him. On the table is a doctored photograph of the businessman alongside the real President Habyarimana. After throwing Rusesabagina a Hutu Power shirt, the businessman advises Rusesabagina that it is time to "join his people." Rusesabagina, now identified as a Hutu, sidesteps the issue by saying "time is money."

As the two men walk through the warehouse, a crate of machetes spills to the floor. The businessman leans down to pick up one of the machetes, saying: "A bargain buy from China. Ten cents each." The camera cuts to Dube, a hotel employee driving Rusesabagina, who looks on anxiously. In the foreground, we see part of the machete as the businessman explains that he will make a profit from the machetes. Dube's troubled-looking face is perhaps the first visual inkling the audience receives that the machetes signify something ominous. This moment of recognition is not expanded upon, and the film misses the opportunity to better explicate the years of planning behind the 1994 genocide.

On the drive back, Dube says to Rusesabagina that the businessman is "a bad man. I've heard him on the radio telling the Hutu to kill all the Tutsi," to which Rusesabagina replies, "Rutaganda and his people, they are fools, Dube. Their time is soon over. Anyways, this is business." There are several scenes hinting at impending doom: Rusesabagina's neighbor is beaten by soldiers who have labeled him a rebel spy; Thomas, Rusesabagina's Tutsi brother-in-law, begs to take his sister into exile before the killings begin. Rusesabagina ignores all of these warnings, as he is convinced that nothing major will happen. Rusesabagina is accordingly stunned when the killings erupt; for him, none of these brief incidents signifies that the long-planned genocide is actually underway. Thus, like mainstream coverage in 1994, the genocide is framed as spontaneous and ethnic in *Hotel Rwanda*.

Representing radio

When the plane carrying Rwanda's President Habyarimana was shot down as it was preparing to land on the night of 6 April 1994, it was quite clear (as described later) that the massacres that began hours afterwards were not a spontaneous eruption of ethnic warfare. On the contrary, the killings had been carefully planned for years by the extremists. Although

Hotel Rwanda misinforms audiences about this aspect of the genocide, it very efficiently uses radio as a cinematic device.

As the most widely available medium in Rwanda, radio was the most effective tool to propagate hate (Chalk 2000, 96-98). *Hotel Rwanda* reminds us of radio's significance during the genocide. The hate station *Radio-Télévision Libre des Mille Collines* (RTLM) is mentioned (and heard) several times throughout the film. This successfully conveys the horrifying nature of the broadcasts. For example, we hear an announcer exhorting Hutu men to "taste those Tutsi whores before they die." In the background, we see a woman being manhandled by two members of the militia; it is clear that she is about to be raped, if not killed.

The use of radio broadcasts propels the narrative of genocide in crucial ways. In the film, Habyarimana's death is confirmed as Rusesabagina listens to RTLM. We hear the order to kill Tutsi as it is announced on the radio. Significantly, George also uses radio broadcasts to frame Western responses to the genocide as well as to inform us of the incredibly fast rate of killing. From the very beginning of the film, radio informs us of why extremists are fomenting hatred. As the opening credits roll, we hear a radio being tuned to a station identified as RTLM. The screen turns black as we hear an announcer say:

> Read our history. The Tutsi were collaborators for the Belgian colonialists. They stole our Hutu land. They whipped us. Now they have come back, these Tutsi rebels. They are cockroaches. They are murderers. Rwanda is our Hutu land. We are the majority. They are a minority of traitors and invaders. We will squash the infestation. We will wipe out the RPF rebels. This is RTLM, Hutu Power radio. Stay alert. Watch your neighbors.

The second key instance in the film that loosely defines the genocide as based on ancient enmity between Hutu and Tutsi occurs not on the radio but during an exchange at a bar in the hotel. A Western journalist asks about the actual difference between Hutu and Tutsi. The reply he receives is: "The Belgians used the Tutsis to run the country. Then, when they left, they left the power to the Hutus, and of course the Hutus took revenge on the elite Tutsis for years of repression." As discussed below, the Belgian policy of politicizing racial identity certainly did lay the groundwork for genocide and the ensuing Western discourse of ancient ethnic grievances as the catchall explanation of what caused it. But here we face a conundrum. On the one hand, and following Rosenstone's (2004, 163) thesis, historical film texts can be seen as a "separate realm of representation and discourse" that provides metaphorical truths, rather than literal truths, about a subjective past. On the other hand, *Hotel*

Rwanda focuses on recent history that has generally not been well understood. Rwanda's more distant colonial history remains even more opaque for most Western audiences; if historical film texts are a way of explicating the past, then *Hotel Rwanda*'s history lesson falls short. Furthermore, while Rusesabagina is portrayed as ultimately heroic (and rightly so), one is left with the impression that he is the sole Rwandan concerned with saving others[6]; other Rwandans are portrayed as survivors, as killers, or, much less frequently, as victims.

Rwandan identities

If memory is influenced by visual media, one needs to be concerned about the manner by which *Hotel Rwanda* leaves the impression that the genocide is spontaneous. Furthermore, because ethnic hatred is represented as the root cause of the genocide, it is imperative to briefly review scholarly analysis of Hutu and Tutsi in Rwanda. There is overwhelming consensus that the position that the genocide occurred as a result of ancient "tribal bloodletting" is not only overly simplistic, but it is also misguided. Such a position further obscures the complex, competing narratives that continue to exist in Rwanda about identity and about genocide.

Mamdani (2002) has argued that Hutu and Tutsi are neither cultural nor ethnic identities; there existed social systems through which some prosperous Hutu, over time, became Tutsi and other systems through which poorer Tutsi were absorbed as Hutu. Although these "movements" were not statistically large in number, they were considered socially significant enough to be named. Mamdani further argues against the belief that the distinction lies in "market-based" identities according to which Hutu were cultivators while Tutsi owned cattle; instead, he says that these are political identities tied to notions of power.

> The clearest proof that Hutu is not an ethnic but political identity is provided by the Hutu of northern Rwanda: before being incorporated into the state of Rwanda, they were known as Bakiga, just like their cousins in western Uganda. With incorporation into the state of Rwanda, they became Hutu. Rather than a transhistorical identity, Hutu was really a transethnic identity of subjects, all of those who came to be subjugated to Tutsi power in Rwanda.
> ...
> To understand the historical formation of Hutu and Tutsi, one needs to look at the historical formation of the Rwandan state, not the developments of markets or communities speaking a single language. The simple fact is that Hutu and Tutsi were not ethnic identities. Just as Hutu

was a subject identity, an identity of all those subjugated to power in Rwanda before Belgian colonization, Tutsi was an identity of power. It is not that all Tutsi were in power, but simply that all were associated with power. For example, in the colonial period, all whites–including poor whites–were associated with power. The association may not have made them all rich, but this gave even the poorest of whites an exemption from the most degrading treatment reserved for those not white (Mamdani 2002, 499).

Colonialism would add another (still existent) notion: according to Belgian policy, Hutu and Tutsi became racial identities. Classifying the numerical majority Hutu as Bantu and the minority Tutsi as Hamitic (thus a "foreign, civilizing influence"), the colonial system cemented the racial ideology by forcing Rwandans to carry identity cards that branded the bearer as either Hutu or Tutsi. The result was that one's status became fixed; it was virtually impossible to undergo the social system of transformation as described above[7] (Mamdani 2002, 499). Tutsi were afforded academic and bureaucratic opportunities that were generally not available to Hutu. The very small educated Hutu elite, led by the country's future first post-independence President, were determined to end Tutsi domination as Rwanda neared political independence; by 1959, a socio-political revolution had begun (with Belgian assistance), which resulted in Tutsi chiefs and bureaucrats being replaced with Hutu counterparts. For these Hutu elite, then, racial classification was a necessary doctrine. The Belgian formulation of Hutu and Tutsi as two different races was not discarded after independence; instead, radical elements manipulated the notion of racial difference up to, and beyond, 1994 (Hintjens 1999, 254-256).

After 1959, the conflation of political goals with racial identities meant that Tutsi were often scapegoated; thousands fled Rwanda during successive waves of political violence that targeted them. These refugees (and their descendents) were refused repatriation under the policies of Rwanda's second president, Habyarimana, who led the country from 1973 until his death in 1994. Metaphorically at least, these Tutsi became the "Jews of Africa" (Mamdani 2002, 500). In 1990, the Rwandan Patriotic Front (RPF) composed almost exclusively of Tutsi soldiers that had grown up in exile, mounted an attack against President Habyarimana's government (Newbury and Newbury 1999, 294-295; Melvern 2004, 19-84).

The 1990 RPF incursion gave extremists in and closely allied to Habyarimana's government the excuse to argue for great expansion of security forces. The army's size grew from about 7,000 troops in 1989 to more than 30,000 troops by 1994. Furthermore, international emergency relief supplies provided to the government were purportedly used to buy arms. Rwanda also faced a severe economic crisis as the price of coffee, a primary national cash crop, had fallen drastically in the mid 1980s. Meanwhile, the World Bank demanded structural adjustment and there was international pressure for the country to democratize. In the face of such crises, Habyarimana's rhetoric blamed merchants, traders and intellectuals for Rwanda's woes. Tutsi largely filled these occupations as they were generally barred from political and administrative posts (Hintjens 1999, 256-257).

More ominously, all Tutsi in Rwanda were labeled as being RPF supporters. Hutu extremists framed the conflict with the RPF as one between Hutu and Tutsi; the conflict was defined as "us" versus "them" (Newbury and Newbury 1999, 304). This racist ideology served as "pseudo-justification for the more fundamental goal of regime survival under sharp conditions of socioeconomic crisis and growing political opposition" (Hintjens 1999, 242). It was under such economic and political pressure that, by 1991, Habyarimana's political party had formed the most infamous militia group: the Interahamwe. Initially, the Interahamwe was composed of mostly unemployed, uneducated youths for whom life seemed to hold little opportunity. Although the Interahamwe was a civilian militia, members received military training, and their campaign of organized killing had started as early as 1991. The Interahamwe militia was well organized; it had a strong internal structure and committees devoted to research and development, social/legal affairs and propaganda (Melvern 2004, 25).

This was part and parcel of the campaign of hate propaganda mounted by the extremist hardliners. They targeted the RPF and by extension, all Tutsi as supposed RPF supporters. Accordingly, the journal *Kangura* was established to promote Hutu power and demonize Tutsi. By 1993, the now-infamous RTLM[8] radio station was established. Like *Kangura*, RTLM was devoted to rabid hate-propaganda based on conspiracy theories; these media outlets assured listeners that Tutsi were fomenting revolution against Hutu, that their ultimate goal was the extermination of Hutu, and that anyone who maintained relations with Tutsi was against the well-being of the Hutu majority. Hutu were exhorted to keep watch; those that maintained friendship, employed or married a Tutsi were branded as traitors (Melvern 2004, 49-56; Chalk 2000, 93-107).

As a tool of the extremists, RTLM did not neglect to vilify the U.N. mission in Rwanda; as an informant made clear to the head of the mission, the extremists planned to kill several peacekeepers to ensure Western withdrawal from the country (Gourevitch 1998, 102-106). In fact, ten

Belgian U.N. peacekeepers would be brutally killed in the first days of the genocide, effectively ensuring the withdrawal of most U.N. peacekeepers and Westerners from Rwanda (Melvern 2004, 151-162; 214-217).

White flight

Among the most powerful scenes in *Hotel Rwanda* are those depicting the West abandoning Rwanda. One scene portrays an exchange between Rusesabagina and a Western reporter who has videotaped a massacre in progress. Having seen the video, a shocked Rusesabagina nevertheless believes it will reap positive benefits, saying, "I am glad that you have shot this footage and that the world will see it. It is the only way we have a chance that people might intervene." The reporter[9], already coded as having covered other African tragedies, knowingly replies, "I think if people see this footage, they'll say, 'Oh my God, that's horrible,' and then go on eating their dinners."

The more visually and emotionally striking scenes occur when Westerners are evacuated from the hotel. As they make their way to the busses that will take them to safety, dutiful hotel employees hold umbrellas over their heads, evoking the days of colonialism and white power in Africa. Some of the departing Westerners are holding on tightly to Rwandan children with whom they obviously have very close connections. But the Western soldiers organizing the evacuation insist their mandate is to rescue foreign nationals only. Media cameras are on hand filming this "white flight." As the evacuation proceeds, a French priest and (presumably) the foreign and Rwandan nuns who serve with him make their way to the hotel. Children who seem to belong to a Catholic orphanage are part of the group of people headed by the priest. The priest thanks the Western soldiers who are organizing the evacuation, only to be told that "no Rwandans" can board the bus. As the priest argues, Rusesabagina steps forward, saying that the soldiers "are not here to help us.... Get your people on the bus. I will take care of the others." This specific exchange is painful to witness, as desperate human beings are being abandoned. Yet, from an African perspective, it can also be interpreted as an empowering moment: Rusesabagina personifies self-reliance, a common theme in the decades-old Pan African discourse.

As the Rwandans stand silently under the hotel eave, watching the busses roll away, the evacuees (including a dog) sit silently in the busses, watching the Rwandans in return. This last image conveys the sense of abandonment that many Rwandans felt as Western powers evacuated. The PBS documentary *Triumph of Evil* (1998) is damning of the white flight.

Most notably, the documentary alleges that the French embassy staff took the embassy dog while leaving their Tutsi local staff behind. According to the documentary, the staff was subsequently massacred.

What is interesting about Terry George's depiction of the white flight is that many of the evacuees are coded as sympathetic; they seem torn that their whiteness affords them sanctity while the blackness of the Rwandans condemns them to remain in a country torn by genocide. Furthermore, viewers are reminded that not all Westerners have abandoned Rwanda. A significant character in the film is Madame Archer, a member of the Red Cross who is constantly crossing through dangerous areas of Kigali to rescue orphans and deliver crucial medical supplies. Rather than blaming such individuals, *Hotel Rwanda* reserves special condemnation for the U.S. government (a spokeswoman is heard, in actual radio footage, waffling over why the government applies the term "acts of genocide" to Rwanda), France (denounced for supplying the Hutu army), the U.N. (characterized as an ineffectual organization), and, as discussed above, the Belgians, whose colonial policies are blamed for inciting ethnic hatred to begin with.

Conclusion

Rosenstone (2006), but also Gudehus et al.'s (2010) reception study on *Hotel Rwanda*, remind us that historical films need not be literal, that through visual metaphors they can effectively transmit a sense of what the past might have been like. And while we concur that metaphorical "truths" are part and parcel of historical film, we remain cautious about the manner in which *Hotel Rwanda* often presents events as literal truths.

Can one ever represent – or obtain – a "real" understanding of genocide, particularly through visual media? Part of the concern for scholars, as outlined in this chapter, has been the manner in which film narrative lends itself to melodramatic moments that objectify (and therefore trivialize) genocide. Yet is there any appropriate way to represent systematic elimination of a people? *Hotel Rwanda* has largely escaped some of the public criticism reserved for Holocaust representations, perhaps because the Rwandan genocide is not considered a "singular event" in public consciousness. But because *Hotel Rwanda* remains the most commercially successful feature film about the 1994 genocide, analyzing its representational strategies demands special attention. In 1994, far too many journalists pounced on the usual trope of African stereotypes that encouraged fatalistic attitudes about the continent. The usual African tribalism and ethnic enmity, compounded by colonial policies, were defined as the root causes of genocide. Such explanations gained (and have largely maintained) currency in public discourse about Rwanda's genocide, in spite of the fact that several noteworthy books, documentaries and journal articles tell us a different story that cannot be adequately summarized in brief headlines. *Hotel Rwanda* sometimes regurgitates simplistic and misguided formulations of Rwanda's history, especially as it relates the causes of genocide. And by interweaving actual historical images into a narrative essentially presented as real, the film's metaphorical truths take on an aura of literal truth. If, like several other cinematic representations of genocide, *Hotel Rwanda* ignites debate and research, perhaps Terry George will have produced his hoped-for educational tool in more ways than one.

Notes

[1] Some have come to the defense of *Schindler's List*. In her conclusion, Hansen (1996, 312) posits that to dismiss the film because of the 'a priori established unrepresentability' implies "missing a chance to understand the significance in the Shoah in the present, in the ongoing and undecided struggles over which past gets remembered and how."

[2] For instance, see Gourevitch (1998); Mamdani (2001); Melvern (2004).

[3] A notable exception is Dauge-Roth (2010).

[4] Ndahiro and Rutazibwa's (2008) book *Hotel Rwanda or the Tutsi genocide as seen by Hollywood* was particularly critical. Two years before, Rusesabagina (2006) had published his memoirs, with the title *An ordinary man: The true story behind Hotel Rwanda*.

[5] He is soon identified as the real-life George Rutaganda, one of the leaders of the infamous Interahamwe militia.

[6] For example, Janzen (2000), whose study focuses on a mayor and his staff who acted to save lives, notes that there were many such instances of people rescuing others during the genocide.

[7] While such social transformations occurred, Harrow says they were quite rare; making them significant served (and continues to serve) the interests of the current Tutsi-dominated government that downplays differences between Hutu and Tutsi. At the same time, Hutu extremists (and their virulent propaganda machine) perpetuated the idea that the "foreign" Hamitic Tutsi were bent on domination (Harrow 2005, 36-37). Whatever competing narratives exist, that they are utilized for current political purposes is not lost on Mamdani, who writes that: "When Rwandese intellectuals discuss the question of Hutu and Tutsi, you can trace sharp differences between two points of view. The Hutu point of view emphasizes that Hutu and Tutsi were always different, whereas the Tutsi point of view maintains they were the same people, divided–as in any 'normal' society–by circumstances of wealth or occupation. But there is one thing they seem to share in common: the

preoccupation with origins. And this preoccupation is the mark that colonialism has left on all of us" (Mamdani 2002, 499).
[8] RTLM's connection to the government was clear. It was founded with financial assistance from Habyarimana's son-in-law as well as other prominent members of Habyarimana's inner circle (Chalk 2000, 96).
[9] The first time this journalist is seen on-screen, he seems relieved to arrive for an assignment in Rwanda and to be staying at the comfortable Hôtel des Mille Collines. As he tells a colleague, it provides a change from other assignments where people have shot at them, effectively portraying Western journalists in Rwanda as uninformed and ignorant about the country about which they are reporting.

Works Cited

Braun, Robert. 1994. The Holocaust and problems of historical representation. History and Theory 33 (2): 172-197.
Chalk, Frank. 1999. Hate radio in Rwanda. In The Rwanda crisis from Uganda to Zaire. Edited by Howard Adelman and Astri Suhrke. New Brunswick NJ: Transaction Publishers, 93-107.
Dauge-Roth, Alexandre. 2010. Writing and filming the genocide of the Tutsis in Rwanda: Dismembering and remembering traumatic history. Plymouth: Lexington.
Fair, Jo Ellen, and Parks, Lisa. 2001. Africa on camera: Television news coverage and aerial imaging of Rwandan refugees. Africa Today 48(2): 34-58.
Feinstein, Stephen. 2005. Destruction has no covering: artists and the Rwandan Genocide. Journal of Genocide Research 7(1): 31-46.
Friedlander, Saul. 1997. Probing the limits of representation. The postmodern history reader. Edited by in Keith Jenkins. London: Routledge, pp. 387-391.
—. 1992. Introduction. Probing the limits of representation: Nazism and the final solution. Cambridge MA: Harvard University Press.
Gilman, Sander L. 2002. Is life beautiful? Can the Shoah be funny? Some thoughts on recent and older films. Critical Inquiry 26(2): 278-309.
Gourevitch, Philip. 1998. We wish to inform you that tomorrow we will be killed with our families: stories from Rwanda. New York: Picador.
Gudehus, Christian, Anderson, Stewart, Keller, David. 2010. Understanding Hotel Rwanda: A reception study. Memory Studies 3(4): 344-363.
Hansen, Miriam Bratu. 1996. "Schindler's List" is not "Shoah": The second commandment, popular modernism and public memory. Critical Inquiry 22(2): 292-312.

Harding, Frances. 2003. Africa and the moving image: Television, film and video. Journal of African Cultural Studies 16(2): 69-84.
Harrow, Kenneth W. 2005. "Ancient Tribal Warfare." Foundational fantasies of ethnicity and hatred. Research in African Literatures 36(2): 34-45.
Hintjens, Helen M. 1999. Explaining the 1994 genocide in Rwanda. The Journal of Modern African Studies 37(2): 241-286.
Hoskins, Andrew. 2001. New memory: mediating history. Historical Journal of Film, Radio and Television 21(4): 333-346.
Janzen, John M. 2000. Historical consciousness and a "Prise de Conscience" in genocidal Rwanda. Journal of African Cultural Studies 13(1): 153-168.
Jenkins, Keith (ed.). 1997. The postmodern history reader. London: Routledge.
Langford, Barry. 1999. "You cannot look at this." Thresholds of unrepresentability in holocaust film. Journal of Holocaust Education 8(3): 23-40.
Livingston, Steven, and Eachus, Todd. 1999. Rwanda: U.S, policy and television coverage. In The Rwanda crisis from Uganda to Zaire. Edited by Howard Adelman and Astri Suhrke. New Brunswick NJ: Transaction Publishers, pp. 209-228.
Mamdani, Mahmood. 2001. When victims become killers: colonialism, nativisim and genocide in Rwanda. Princeton NJ: Princeton University Press.
—. 2002. African states, citizenship and war: A case-study. International Affairs 78(3): 493-506.
Melvern, Linda. 2004. Conspiracy to murder: the Rwandan genocide. London: Verso.
Morales, Wilson. 2004. Hotel Rwanda: An Interview with Director Terry George and Paul Rusesabagina, Blackfilm, December, http://www.blackfilm.com/20041217/features/terryandpaul.shtml (accessed May 14, 2006).
Ndahiro, Alfred, Rutazibwa, Privat. 2008. Hotel Rwanda or the Tutsi genocide as seen by Hollywood. Paris: L'Harmattan.
Netribution. 2006. Interviews: Terry George. Framing Rwanda. http://www.netribution.co.uk/2/content/view/104/267 29 January (accessed May 14, 2006).
Newbury, Catherine, and Newbury, David. 1999. A catholic mass in Kigali: Contested views of the genocide and ethnicity in Rwanda. Canadian Journal of African Studies 33(2/3): 292-328.

Rapaport, Lynn. 2002. Hollywood's Holocaust: Schindler's List and the construction of memory. Film & History 32(1): 55-65.

Rosenstone, Robert A. 2004. Confessions of a postmodern historian. Rethinking History 8(1): 149–166.

—. 2006. History on film/film on history (History: concepts, theories and practice). New York: Pearson Longman.

Rusesabagina, Paul. 2006. An ordinary man: The true story behind Hotel Rwanda. London: Bloomsbury Publishing.

Said, Edward. 2000. Invention Memory and Place. Critical Inquiry 26(2): 175-193.

Sontag, Susan. 2003. Regarding the Pain of Others. New York: Farrar, Straus and Giroux.

Stimmel, Joanna K. 2005. Between globalization and particularization of memories: screen images of the Holocaust in Germany and Poland. German Politics and Society 23(7): 83-105.

Waldorf, Lars. 2009. Revisiting Hotel Rwanda: genocide ideology, reconciliation, and rescuers. Journal of Genocide Research 11(1): 101-125.

PHOTOS FOR ACCESS: WAR PORNOGRAPHY AND US-AMERICA'S PRACTICES OF POWER

KAREN J. HALL

Let the atrocious images haunt us. Even if they are only tokens, and cannot possibly encompass most of the reality to which they refer, they still perform a vital function. The images say: This is what human beings are capable of doing – may volunteer to do, enthusiastically, self-righteously. Don't forget.
—Susan Sontag, Regarding the Pain of Others (2002)

Introduction

From at least the time of the U.S. Civil Rights Movement and through the Vietnam anti-war movement, U.S. political activists could rely on a strategy of revelation. Jim Crow, lynching, My Lai and later Watergate served as emblems of what was most foul in the era's structures of social and political power. These crisis points, for many citizens, reinforced an ideological belief that if all the facts were known, those in power would create and follow just policy. The role of the righteous citizen, therefore, was to make all the facts known. Power attempted to subsume the public voice, however, in order to manufacture consent, and those who resisted had to struggle to be heard so that right, not might, would prevail.

In the current U.S. information economy, ideas and intellectual property circulate at an alarming volume and rate. Though still the largest military force in the world, the U.S. is no longer the powerful producer of goods it once was. Manufacturing has been left so far behind in the U.S. that even the manufacture of consent has been subsumed in the information age.

Revelation has lost its power in an age where cynicism trumps belief. When discussing current events, the phrases I most often hear from U.S. citizens include, "you just don't know who to believe," "I don't have enough information to know for sure," and "I don't believe anything anymore." The shape of the dominant U.S. popular imagination has changed its character. Once entrusted to leaders believed to be benevolent, the U.S. collective imagination was the compliant end product of dominant power's consent manufacturing process. Now in the information age, the U.S. collective imagination seems afloat without a compass, and an increasingly large sector of the dominant part of society has adopted a stance of cynicism, the contemporary version of dropping out of the sociopolitical arena. Whereas the first condition helped to uphold a national naïve ignorance that masqueraded as innocence, cynicism works to disable the national political will; decisions cannot be made until all the facts are in, and even U.S. children know the facts can no longer be trusted. Thus, this mythical force of the U.S. collective imagination has lost the power to recognize that decisions are made actively. Things just happen.

More than any other cultural site, the Internet has served to aid the increase of ideas and opinions to which U.S. citizens are exposed. Although the Internet has been lauded by many as a new public space full of potential, the Internet is also a sight where U.S. citizens produce for global consumption propagandistic material more jingoistic and vulgar than anything the U.S. state could ever have dared to make. The Internet provides at least some web publishers and surfers a place to express their enthusiasm for war, and their productions are often a sort of cottage industry of consent manufacturing. Their productions have the potential to further confuse and defuse the power of revelation on which the anti-war movement continues to rely. Like laid off government workers from the culture wars, these independent publishers reproduce and often ramp up the state propagandistic voice.

A short history of war on the Web

Arguably, the first use of the Internet in a military and political conflict was the 1989 Tiananmen Square uprising. The Internet at this time was quite new, however, and the activities that were about to come into being – cyber-war, netwar, and hactivism – had yet to be named (Conklin 2003). Once the Internet became user friendly, it was used strategically by the Chiapas in their struggle with the Mexican government as well as by the Tamil Tigers in Sri Lanka (Taylor 2002). By the time of the NATO air strikes on the former Yugoslavia in 1999, the Internet and the public's use of it had matured.

The Serbs and the Yugoslav military were outmatched by NATO military capabilities, but the various groups involved in the conflict had fairly equal access to the Internet. Despite this even technological starting ground, it was the Serb forces that were far more able to make use of the Internet to convey their perspectives in an attempt to win the hearts and minds of a worldwide audience of users. Propaganda was distributed on the Internet before the bombing even began and was cited by high-level decision makers. NATO spokesman Jamie Shea justified a military response in Kosovo due to the Serbian massacre of Kosovars, and cited numbers that were reported on an Internet site run by the Kosovo Liberation Army. This official use of information provided by an Internet source lent hitherto unprecedented authority, credibility and significance to wartime Internet projects. The Internet was also instrumental in keeping traditional media venues alive. When Milosevic shut down the independent radio station (B92), it sent its signal to Amsterdam via the Internet, and the BBC then sent it back to Yugoslavia by satellite. Although slow to respond, "Milosevic fought back on the Internet and the Serb diaspora assisted. They created pro-Serb Web sites, blitzed pro-Kosovo news groups with pro-Serb mailings and even mail-bombed the NATO Web site" (Boggs 2006). Individuals in combat areas sent e-mails to journalists in an attempt to influence the stories they wrote. Tom Regan of the *Christian Science Monitor* received a message from a Serb in a combat zone that had a virus attached. When activated, it then e-mailed an impostor message to all of Regan's contacts (Boggs 2006).

By the time of the 2003 Iraq War, millions of users around the world were participating in conversations and reading news on the web. The norm on websites which attract anonymous users to highly polarized debate and which allow users to post comments replicates the abrasively confrontational counterpoint of the infamous Fox news program, *The O'Reilly Factor*. Rather than the moderating style of Tim Russert or Bob Schieffer on *Meet the Press* (NBC) or *Face the Nation* (CBS), posters flame and reflame each other, rehearsing their own deeply held convictions rather than listening to and considering those of others posting to the board. These flame wars abound on bulletin boards which garner mass appeal and mistake uninformed, illogical, and unjustified opinion for argument. Flaming is one way that elements of the discourse of the dominant media are shaping discourse in many sectors of the web. Careful monitoring and upholding the critical argumentative engagement of the community of users takes a substantial commitment of time and resources by the web host. Websites that offer casually monitored, anonymous posting are greater in number than those that are thoughtfully monitored, and therefore assert a greater force on perceptions of the dominant norm in the Internet environment.[1] In addition, online environments are not only confrontational, but play a significant role in the legitimization of particular conflicts and in the recruitment of supporters and fighters for both sides, as, for instance, the conflict in Syria has shown.[2]

Hacking, or hacktivism, is related to flaming as a form of Internet argumentation. Instead of attempting to silence an individual with insults as is the purpose of flaming, hacktivism attempts to silence an entire webpage. Hackers either change webpage content or replace pages with those of their own creation. During the opening days of the Iraq War, hacking increased dramatically with targeted sites including the U.S. National Centre for Agricultural Utilization Research, the U.S. Navy, and al-Jazeera. A London security firm recorded 1,000 incidents during the first week of the war alone (*Wired* 2003 and *BBC News* 2003). The full strength of these types of cyber-attacks was demonstrated not that much later, in 2007 in Estonia, when a distributed denial-of-service attack from Russia took out many of the European country's servers (Landler and Markoff 2007).

Also the Internet's capacity to distribute audiovisual material plays a significant role, as Robert Fisk (2004) reported in *The Independent*:

> The "resistance" or the "terrorists" or the "armed Iraqi fighters"—as US forces now refer to their enemies—began with a set of poorly made videos showing attacks on American troops in Iraq. Roadside bombs would be filmed from a passing car as they exploded beside US convoys. Guerrillas could be seen firing mortars at American bases outside Fallujah. But once the kidnappings began, the videos moved into a macabre new world.

When they are posted and receive publicity in the media, videos made by insurgents in Iraq (and other areas of conflict) are viewed in record numbers. According to a CNN report by Jeff Greenfield: "internet tracking reported...that video of the Berg beheading had replaced porn and celebrity items as the most frequently searched item on the net." Unlike the war in Kosovo, the forces fighting in opposition to the U.S. and coalition forces did not focus their energy on creating or influencing established information sources. The most spectacular and widely covered aspects of the Iraq netwar have largely been comprised of graphically violent videos and photos. Many U.S. Internet users have focused a great deal of outrage at their enemies for resorting to what they see as inhumane, barbarous methods, but it is not only the forces fighting in opposition to the U.S.-led coalition who are using these tactics. This fact became forcefully apparent when the photos of prisoner humiliation at Abu Ghraib became an internationally covered news story.

Softcore netwar

A fairly common example of one genre of web production in the U.S.-led netwar against Iraq is a short film titled, *Iraq Fighting*, made available on Metacafe, a website where individuals can upload their short films and receive viewer feedback.[3] In this film, viewers see U.S. soldiers firing into the abandoned streets of Fallujah. The camera occasionally cuts to the faces of the soldiers, but spends most of its time looking in the direction that the soldiers are firing. Occasionally the tip of one of the soldier's automatic weapons appears in the frame, reminiscent of first person shooter video game screens. One element that distinguishes this video from the games is that after darkness falls, the soldiers go to investigate the area they have been firing upon and film the dead bodies of the Iraqis they killed in the firefight. Unlike a video game, the fallen enemy does not disappear but lies in a static, fuzzy camera shot as evidence of a day's work.

This genre of video, which I will call "raw combat," typically features U.S. soldiers or private military personnel, employed by companies such as Blackwater and engaged by the U.S. as mercenaries, firing on urban positions or driving through urban streets.[4] U.S. individuals are visible and audible while Iraqis rarely appear. Occasionally, as in the case of the Kevin Sites' footage, viewers can see U.S. soldiers kill Iraqis, but more often, weapons are fired into an anonymous landscape.[5] This is true at least in part because the soldiers and journalists filming the action do not have the technological capability to view the targets at which the soldiers are firing. Their lenses are only capable of capturing the action at close range. Because these camera operators have greater access to and a higher degree of safety with U.S. operatives, video viewers see the war over the shoulders of U.S. individuals "as if they were there" on the scene, looking through American eyes. However, because they often cannot see what the soldiers actually see, viewers see a far tamer, more sanitized war "reality." This is even true of the raw combat shot using the camera technology in the Apache attack helicopters. In these short films, the subjects appear as white images on a black field due to the fact that the film records heat signatures.[6] Audio tracks are comprised of soldiers communicating with base command centers, reporting what they see, receiving orders to engage, confirming orders, exploding targets and killing people, then reporting the results back to base. While these films expose viewers to actual war killings, viewers do not see faces, expressions, blood, or any detail of the victims' humanness or the environments' beingness.

At the time of my visit, *Iraq Fighting* had been viewed 72,233 times and visitors had left 84 comments. A brief sampling of comments helps to characterize what flaming on the internet can look like:

- God Bless the Troops...
  Every One!!
  by Trufflehunter 12th March
- Nice hsow [sic] yet!
  Em, nice show, yet, if the troops are so good how come they still cannot control Iraq and get rid of the terrorists? The number of terrorists and terrorist attacks are increasing not decreasing. I am puzzled!
  by die_hard_Jordanian , 27th July
- the US troops are good
  but terrorists aren't easy to fight. hiding amongst civilians, etc... they're sneaky sons of b***hes.
  by getoverit , 6th August
- more dead terrorists
  love to see it
  by rifleman 68 , 1st May
- All Americans and British can go suck binladens d**k
  Then he might forgive you. You can be his slaves and binladen can f**k with allah after that. hahahahahahhaha.
  by suck my , 20th July
- you can blow us up with a nuke
  before we ask him for forgiveness. and forgiveness for what, by the way?
  by getoverit , 6th August

The Internet has made possible an international dialogue, but in this case, the only participants are jingoistic nationalists. This conversation would be more appropriate if the participants had been watching a video game rather than raw footage captured during actual combat. When viewing war on the Internet, however, the experience of watching and commenting is similar enough to viewing combat-style video games that they have not been moved to an alternative discursive realm. From the comfort of their PCs, "rifleman 68" can celebrate death, "suck my" can threaten American and British users, and "getoverit" can go so far as to imagine a nuclear attack against the U.S. Raw combat productions introduce authentic war images in citizens' imagination while they sit at their computers. Those users removed from combat zones can practice hyper-masculine war cheers and pro-militarist opinions, at times cheering in unison with fellow posters sitting at computer screens inside combat zones, establishing a truly powerful militarist hyper link.

Another form of war media prevalent on the Internet is comprised of a montage of still photos and action footage overlaid with a music soundtrack, a genre I'll refer to as "war theatre." These productions showcase the might of the U.S. military. Missiles are launched, tanks thunder, jets roar, soldiers pose, and all manner of hardware and weaponry assert the dominance of the U.S. *Bomb Saddam* by Grouchymedia is an example of such a production. The video features the song, *Bombs Over Baghdad* by Outkast, played over a montage of military recruiting and training films, and promotional videos produced by weapons manufacturers. *Bomb Saddam* was made with the intent of supporting and thanking the troops. It is one of hundreds of war theater productions broadcast on the Internet. Inspired by military recruiting advertisements, Hollywood propagandistic war movies and countless other media productions, U.S. citizens are now taking upon themselves the task of creating propaganda that supports the troops and rallies the home front. Propaganda production can satisfy the pleasures of fulfilling a civic duty to support the state, give producers the pleasure of creating and distributing a work of their own making, and occasionally, as was the case for Grouchymedia producer, can bring notoriety and fifteen minutes of fame.[7]

War theater also includes productions made by military personnel to record memories from their deployment. *Battleforce 3/327 Iraq deployment video* is a typical sample from this category of shorts.[8] The video features a variety of still photos and live action footage displaying weaponry and all the soldiers who make up the unit. Rock songs and two military press announcements makeup the soundtrack. Death is referenced in two sections of the video: first the death photos of Uday and Qusay Hussein are shown while the soundtrack plays the military announcement that the men have been killed along with a warning that the soldiers should not brag about this event; in order to assert their prowess, "There's no need to talk. All you have to do is walk." Death is referenced near the end of the video when fellow soldiers are shown parading in front of the boots, gun and helmet of the soldiers who have died in the unit. There is no depiction of death beyond these two references, however, which distinguishes war theater productions from the videos I discuss below under the category of war porn.

Live from Iraq is a war theater production that has received more than the typical amount of media attention. This video accompanies the rap album produced by soldiers while deployed in Iraq who recorded the tracks under the group name, $4^{th}25$. Like other examples in this genre, the video features a montage of footage and stills set to accompany the soldiers' rap song.[9] The images featured in the video have been collected on a website associated with the album, 4[th]25.com, which was run by Big Neal, a member of the group. What distinguishes this production from others in the genre is its purposeful existence to market a commodity. The video is part of a campaign of press releases to promote the rap album of the same name. Thus, *Live from Iraq* brings the war theater production out of the amateur realm of entertainment and into the entertainment industry.

Hardcore netwar

Feminism's analysis of pornography has led to a non-sexist, though gendered, definition most typically characterized as a dominant and dominating voyeuristic gaze at a feminized, commodified subject. Pornography operates via a system of exposure that degrades, objectifies and dehumanizes its subject in such a way that the abuses depicted in the subject matter of the pornography are implicitly condoned and endorsed.[10] Produced for the sole benefit of the masculine subject, feminine sexuality is constructed by the masculine pornographic gaze and sold back to the culture in the multi-billion dollar pornography market. What is objectionable about pornography is its existence in a dehumanizing, abusive system that exploits the feminine for profit, not the exposure enacted in its content.

When applied to the voyeuristic gaze of war, pornography's definition needs to change very little. The gender dynamics of masculinity and femininity are echoed as are the power relationships between domination and subjugation. War pornography that celebrates the destruction of war, the torn and exposed bodies, the severed limbs, the hated Enemy made vulnerable and opened to the eyes of the Self, degrades and dehumanizes its subjects and turns them into objects. It encourages and authorizes the agents of its gaze. Based on this definition of war pornography, I have designated the production of the most graphic and disturbing genre of Internet war productions "war porn."

In video form, war porn productions look like *U.S. Marines OIF 11*.[11] The soundtrack for this video is A Perfect Circle's *Counting Bodies Like Sheep to the Rhythm of the War Drums*. Any irony intended by the songwriter, Tool's Maynard James Keenan, was lost on the makers of this war porn video. The piece begins with a montage of graphic images: photos of Iraqi prisoners of war are followed by gory photos of Iraqi war dead. The juxtaposition and progression of these images suggestively condone if not promote the illegal practice of murdering prisoners. These images are then followed by a series of black screens that pose the following questions: "Do you feel remorse for these men?"; "Do their deaths upset you?"; and "Have you forgotten?" The final question is followed by footage of the second passenger plane flying into the World Trade Center.[12] Then follows video footage released on the Internet by Iraqi insurgency groups depicting the destruction of U.S. vehicles by improvised explosive devices (so-called "ieds") and two shots that show dead U.S. soldiers. These clips are prefaced by a red on black screen that proclaims, "They Will Pay in Blood." The theme of this screen returns in a photo of a Caucasian hand holding a dead grasshopper against the background of an urban desert landscape. Black screens follow that read, "And he shall rain fire from the heavens," "Returning the plagues to the desert," "Smiting all but the chosen." These biblical-styled proclamations are then followed by film footage captured by the weapons systems in attack helicopters. Viewers see what the pilots saw: targets are sighted, locked onto, and then detonated by missiles. Supposed enemy locations are obliterated in a flash of heat represented as white light on the screen. The video ends with footage of an Iraqi detainee shooting himself in the head with a pistol while in custody and a final black screen proclaims, "There will be no virgins awaiting your arrival."

An amateur pornography website called nowthatsfuckedup.com (NTFU) became an archive for war porn like *U.S. Marines OIF 11*. The site required browsers to pay for a subscription in order to gain access to photos men took of their wives and girlfriends. The site's owner, Chris Wilson, learned that military service personnel stationed in Afghanistan and Iraq could not gain access to his site because online credit card verification companies marked their payments as questionable due to the country from which they originated. He decided to set up a system so that service men could submit a photograph to prove that they were deployed in either of these two countries and in exchange, he would give them free access to the website.

The site is no longer in existence; however, it was not closed down because of the war porn content. The sheriff of Polk County, Florida prosecuted Wilson for violations of sexual obscenity laws. The amateur photographs men took of their wives and girlfriends were deemed obscene and inappropriate for circulation in Polk County. The U.S. military took no legal action against the website or its owner and the Pentagon claimed it could find no connection between the pictures and any of its service personnel. By allowing its continued presence on the web, the military establishment gave passive endorsement to this media presence. In fact, Wilson created a new website, Barbecue Stopper, and uploaded all of the war photos which can still be viewed.[13] The sexual pornography was eradicated in the name of decency, but representations of the carnage of war remain.

At first Wilson received many photos I would categorize within the war theater genre. Photos showed soldiers posed with their weapons, their buddies, and their units. Street scenes, desert scenes and sunsets over the desert were just some of the subjects depicted in the 1,699 photos in the "Pictures - General-Iraq-War-Images" section of NTFU. Soon, soldiers began to submit war porn photos and videos in order to gain free access to NTFU's pornography library. Among the more than 200 photographs housed in the "Pictures-Gory-Iraq-War-Images" section of NTFU, browsers could find all manner of corpses, body parts, and ruptured internal organs.

A tighter, more apt yoking of the violence fueled by militarist masculinism may never have existed than that found on NTFU.[14] The violence extends beyond the frames of the photographs and into the comment and response sections beneath each image. Individual comments drip with jingoism and macabre humor. Beneath a photograph of a man whose chest cavity has been torn open and most of the skin covering his head and face has been burned away, one contributor left this comment: "Will that be crispy or original sir..." and another pondered, "wonder if it will be an open casket." When one poster argued that animals had clearly caused some of the tissue damage, the soldier who posted this photo replied:

> NO animals got to him before our guys. My buddy that took these was a few blocks away when they heard the snap/boom of the transformers. It was less than 10 minutes between the incident and when they showed up. If you will, please note the BURNS in the areas you mentioned (which accounts for there being no broken bones). And YES, electricity DOES do this to people. There are plenty of documented (in actual Pathophysiology texts) cases and photos of entrance and exit (electrical) wounds causing MASSIVE tissue damage; which is what happened here: this guy was burned/fried to a crisp.

Another poster left the following comment complete with icon: "Fuck me that's gonna sting in the morning! let's hope he remembers not to splash on the Aftershave... " A soldier gives this description for a less gory overhead photo of a bombed area of the desert in which two corpses lie in the frame:

> Pic from iraq, insurgent casualties from 500lb bombs dropped by F16s near Baqubah. Notice the body dead center, and the one next to the upper

car missing limps [sic]. There are many more where this came from if you
want to see.

The jocular responses include:

Boom Baby! thats awesome...post more please
wonder how many were standing where now the hole is? thanks to all our
brave soldiers for taking the fight to them, come home safe all.
nah, that's a little bomb. An F-16 can carry 2,000 lb bombs. Now that's a
bomb.
Was the bomb laser guided or just dropped for fun?

The dehumanization and devaluing of individual lives deemed to be
enemies by U.S. citizens is evident in these civilian posts, and it is
articulated in a forthright, moralistic manner by a military officer:

That's an American Lying center photo. Check the Uniform. I have no
problems laughing at the dead insurgents or looking at these photos. But as
SSgt in the USAF I'm inclined to ask that the dead Americans (our
Brothers in Arms) be given the proper respect they deserve.
Thank you,
V/R
SSgt "SOLO" Pittman

The comments left by visitors to NTFU are damaging to the image of
the U.S. and its military, but even more troubling is the U.S. government's
refusal to respond decisively to a situation in which U.S. personnel are
behaving in an inhumane and unprofessional manner.
   In a *New York Times* article from September 2005, Thom Shanker
reported that "an Army inquiry has found no evidence to prove that U.S.
military personnel sent graphic photographs of Iraqi war dead to an
Internet site in exchange for online pornography." The Pentagon did ban
military personnel from visiting the site, but this ban only meant that
soldiers could not access the site from government computers. A very
large number of soldiers have their own computers in Iraq and have
managed to gain access to the Internet.[15] From their own computers,
soldiers were free to visit NTFU as often as they wished.

Visual subjectivity

   Nicholas Mirzoeff (2005) argues in his book, *Watching Babylon: The
War in Iraq and Global Visual Culture*, that the constant stream of visual

imagery from the war in Iraq demands new theories for subjectivity and reception. Whereas Althusser's analysis of subjectivity was based upon interpellation, the subject responding to the hail, Mirzoeff relies on the work of Jacques Rancière who modified the command of power: no longer does power speak, "Hey, you" to the subject. In the twenty-first century, power commands the subject to "move along" and asserts "there's nothing here to see." Subjects of power can be equated with vehicles moving in traffic; their purpose is to keep moving, to circulate. Mirzoeff points out, however, that no one believes the statement that there is nothing to see. Everyone understands there is something to see, but those being commanded to move along do not have the authority to look (Mirzoeff 2005).

In addition to the problem of circulation, visual subjectivity must also negotiate the pervasiveness of imitation. In the logic of the visual culture from the Iraq War, images are treated as if they are the transparent products of technology, capturing a slice of unmediated reality that testifies to the status and condition of the material world. Within such a system, the visual is assumed to achieve "immediacy and relative efficacy by reducing reading to a matter of recognition, which is then thought to solicit mimesis" (Morris 2004). Thus, just as power attempts to determine who has the authority to look, the dominant visual logic attempts to predetermine how subjects will interpret what they are authorized to see – through a process of recognition based on imitation rather than a process of seeing based on critical reflection. This naturalized, patriotic interpretive mode responds to war imagery by internalizing the look of the source of power that seeks to determine who has the authority to see. This look has already situated its political standpoint. It glances at an image and recognizes without words where it fits in the flow of power. To internalize this look, then, curtails a heuristic of questions and discovery. To ponder the relationship between the local and the global, the subjectivity of the gazer and the gazed upon, is constructed as unnatural and unpatriotic. To enact patriotic looking is to imitate the power dynamics of the voyeur, the gaze that seeks pleasure in the power to access the forbidden exposed only for his or her view.

It must come as no surprise then that the individuals who posted responses to war photographs on NTFU reproduced the voyeuristic, nationalistic, militaristic discourse that produces them. By internalizing the gaze of power, the gaze that insists, "Move along! There's nothing here to see" when flag-draped coffins are at hand as well as when soldiers celebrate the deaths of Iraqis, these individuals submit to an inverted mimetic reproduction of reality. Their version of the world is the product of power's selective interpretation of the real as it appears in war theater and war porn. Although these very same individuals insist that only those who have been in combat can criticize the actions of war, many have not come to their own interpretation through experience, but through the internalization of dominant power. They see with the eyes of a soldier.

Visitors to NTFU recognize that they have a special entitlement: they are allowed to look at Iraqi dead as a form of entertainment and pleasure; they are encouraged to find the torture and desecration of the enemy desirable. While they are enjoying the power of looking, they are discouraged from thinking analytically about what any of this means for self, country, enemy or war. In order to access the power of the gaze, to gain knowledge of reality that only those authorized to see are permitted to obtain, demands the suspension of the verbal and the analytical. This curtailment of verbalized articulation is what Rosalind Morris (2004) had in mind when she claimed in her essay, *Images of Untranslatability in the War on Terror*, that "[T]he Empire of Images displays rather than explains itself. It demands imitation not understanding."[16] Within this logic, critical communication is abandoned and only naturalized common sense can be spoken: "He's burned and dead. Good work. Come home safely." Those empowered by American militarized masculinity like to look, and they are not compelled to explain what or how they see. To speak about desire and pleasure creates public relations problems and undermines the validity of proclamations concerning the war project's goal to establish freedom and democracy.[17]

U.S. military training demands a loss of self and a reconstruction in power's image. Thus, when service personnel imitated the process by which professional journalists assert their authenticity and credibility, i.e. submitting photographs that illustrate their experience, they were simply following the rules of a different yet similar professional code. Just as photographs assert that journalists have experienced what their stories claim, the military image posts were designed to prove the men were stationed overseas and thus were entitled to free access to NTFU's pornography boards. NTFU's owner, Chris Wilson reminded visitors of the relationship between photorealism and verisimilitude in his warning that "There have only been a few people cheat from this but I do now know what kind of pics to expect from the guys over there. So please do not waste my time if you are not a military person by just posting Iraq pics you found on CNN or something."[18] Some soldiers may have posted war porn as a conscious strategy, reasoning that graphic photographs from a combat scene are the most authentic images of war as well as the least reproduced by the U.S. media, and therefore the most likely to be accepted for free access. The context of the website was more powerful in determining how the images would be interpreted, however, than any individual's dubious rationale and intentions.

The context within which the photographs were placed limited the polysemic nature of the images: the photographs could only mean one of two things, either that the sender was deployed overseas in a combat area or that the sender was a poser trying to steal free access to pornography. If the images remained on the site, they had been accepted as authentic; thus their meaning in this context was transparent and stable: the individual who posted the image was a U.S. service person deployed in Iraq or Afghanistan and this was a piece of his reality. The meaning of the photograph had become external to the content of the photograph. The meaning was linked in a cause and effect relationship to the newly gained access of the sender. The horror visited upon the subject of the photograph became almost meaningless: "He's burned and dead. Good work. Come home safely."

The soldiers' photographs of Iraqi war dead can be seen as an imitation of the U.S. government's decision to publish death photos of Uday and Qusay Hussein, and then later Abu Musab al Zarqawi. Although the historical practice of memorializing war feats with trophy photos is a long one, the practice is usually a private one that reaches a selective audience. While soldiers' trophy photos were turned into postcards and mailed through the postal service, they still reached a more limited audience than cable and Internet broadcasts of trophy photographs now reach. Despite the prevalence of highly binarized logic popular in the U.S. today – you're either with us or against us, with us or with the terrorists – dominant power readily treats the law as ambiguous and open to interpretation when it suits the purposes of power. For example, Capt. Chris Karns, a Centcom spokesman, acknowledged that there are Department of Defense regulations and Geneva Conventions against mutilating and degrading dead bodies, but claimed that he was unsure about regulations concerning photos of dead bodies (Glaser 2005). When the U.S. government treats international codes of conduct as indeterminate and practices power via an immoral if not illegal display of its war kills, individual soldiers have a powerful example to imitate. The government's practice lends legitimacy to the individual's practice, and together, they have built a mighty and gruesome archive of war propaganda.

The impunity with which the U.S. government and American individuals reject the spirit of the Geneva Code regulations, both in their practices in the fields of combat and in their representations of those practices in speeches, policies and the media, degrades the power of law in dangerous ways. Just before the Abu Ghraib incidents, Attorney General Alberto Gonzales stated that the Geneva Conventions were "trite" law (Crane 2006). Law scholars David Crane and Fred Bryant argue that attitudes such as the one held by Gonzales signify that the U.S. has lost the moral high ground in the fight against terrorism: "The United States was the final bulwark against the onslaught of impunity, terror, and tyranny. That bulwark is crumbling; terror camps, GITMO, Abu Ghraib, and Haditha are examples of how much those walls have crumbled" (Crane 2006). Currently in the U.S., the conventions of taste are more prevalent in the establishment of boundaries of acceptable action than domestic or international law.

Law of taste

When the media speaks of issues of taste, they are using a thinly veiled code for standards which, when followed, can predict a stable audience and market rating. Jacqueline Sharkey refers in her analysis of television coverage of the Iraq War to a study by the Project for Excellence in Journalism which monitored 40.5 hours of coverage of the war by ABC, CBS, NBC, CNN, and Fox. The study discovered that early in the conflict about half the reports from embedded journalists showed combat action, but not a single story depicted people hit by weapons. Taste, and the ethics of not-showing, was the most common justification given by the media for this depiction of victimless war. CNN's policy for war coverage was characterized in the following way: "We take very seriously our responsibility to tell the story as accurately and comprehensively as we can. At the same time, we're mindful of the sensibilities of our audience." Lester Crystal, executive producer of *The NewsHour with Jim Lehrer*, was even less ambiguous: "For taste purposes, you don't show people in agony on the air. You don't show a lot of dead bodies" (Sharkey 2003). Taste thus becomes yet another mode by which economics determine war policy.

Current media practices create an environment within the U.S. where those with Internet access and a desire to see some of the material effects of war are able to do so, while those who rely on broadcast news programming see only a very selective, consumer-friendly, death-free version of reality. While I would not want to see war porn on cable or network broadcasting, a number of characteristics distinguish war images which invite the ethical process of witnessing the effects of war from images that appeal to nationalistic voyeurism. The subjects depicted in the three genres of Internet war media I discuss above are almost entirely male. Propagandistic war imagery generally includes spectacular displays of weaponry. When U.S. soldiers appear in the same frame with enemy dead, often they are depicted standing around the bodies as if oblivious to their suffering while taking a break from their duties; the dead are not mourned or grieved over by anyone in the photo's frame. In the most hard core war porn, U.S. military personnel are shown celebrating the deaths of Iraqis, high-fiving each other, giving the thumbs up and grinning, or flexing their biceps in a jubilant show of strength.

In contrast, when an alternative process of viewing is invoked, war imagery includes men, women and children, combatants and non-combatants. Neither weapons nor the machinery of war are glorified. The suffering of the living – human, animal and environment – is the central focus of such imagery. Photos within this category that depict graphic death and wounding frequently include aid workers or community and family members trying to rescue the victims, mourning them, and grieving their loss. Thus, the rhetoric of what I will call "war's witness" asserts the humanity of victims of war in the face of injustice. By avoiding these war images, U.S. broadcast media rejects the responsibility of educating consumers about the material effects of war. By operating according to the rules of taste, the sanitized version of war they offer makes war more palatable.

Beyond issues of representation, the standards for a tasteful war are as indeterminate as the standards of decency where pornography is considered: "terrorism, terrorists and terror itself have become the political pornography of modernity: one knows terrorism with certainty only when, literally, one sees it" (Der Derian 2005). Laws are made with the intention of establishing fair and just standards. Even still, the legal trial system operates within a system of logic that accepts that meaning is arbitrary. The Geneva Convention states clearly that "[T]he wounded and sick shall be collected and cared for," but standards of care vary across time and place. Law, therefore, attempts to account for contextual variations in a variety of ways. One way is to seek the interpretation of an impartial judge. In the case of the above statement from the Geneva Convention, the provision goes on to state "An impartial humanitarian body, such as the International Committee of the Red Cross, may offer its services to the Parties to the conflict." An impartial body can then determine the standards of acceptable care. Where law attempts to rely on structures to impart impartiality and equality, taste is a wholly individual matter. By definition, taste is a personal preference derived from one's own bodily experience. No one would dispute that national origin and cultural background shape an individual's sense of what is tasteful, proper, and inoffensive; individual free will and right are held to be the ultimate arbiters of taste. Matters of taste are arbitrary and need no evidence, proof or justification. Therefore one cannot defend oneself against allegations based on taste as one can in a system of law.

The legal case against NTFU asserted that by law, the amateur sexual pornography on the site was illegal to distribute in Polk County, FL. The state had the right and responsibility to eliminate the images because the photographs were indecent. The war porn remained on the site until the domain name was taken over by the Polk County Sheriff's Office. The photos were then transferred over to barbequestopper.com, where they remained until 2006.[19] Both the law and the community standards of taste in Polk County deemed the war porn allowable. Thus, the power and impact of the war porn on NTFU goes far beyond any specific quality or meaning of the images. Their very existence and the context of their display express their power. The photographs assert that not only do Americans have the moral right to kill Iraqis, but they have social legitimacy to look at the products of their awesome killing power in an entertainment, not a humanitarian or current events, context. No policeman dare stand by photos of enemy war dead and tell Americans to move along. Americans are authorized by birthright. While some individuals, like myself, may pretend they can cling to a moral high ground and pronounce their abhorrence of distasteful war practices, structurally, all American citizens bear the burdens and pleasures of the power of the war gaze.

The images produced by the U.S. war gaze are haunting tokens of the power to perpetrate violence, yet they reveal only one side of violence. The war gaze exposes the U.S. warrior nation's shadow – its proclivity to find pleasure in the destruction it has wrought. The force of this gaze is so powerful that even when citizens wish to show the nature of war, they are more likely to produce war porn than war's witness. Unschooled and unpracticed in the discourse of this alternative act, citizens revert to known discourses and trained behaviors. Chris Wilson claims he wished to show the true side of war on nowthatsfuckedup.com, the version that the rules of good taste censor, the version that shows us what human beings are capable of doing. His motives were to produce alternatives, but what he generated was closer to the U.S. cultural dominant than he intended.

Increasingly, the Internet is asserting itself as a force in the creation of public taste. As a larger audience comes to rely on the Internet for news and entertainment, it is possible that the polysemic images made available by global producers will challenge, perhaps even determine, the tastes of the U.S. public. For now, however, dominant interests and practices continue to shape productions on the web facilitating state agenda rather than challenging them. U.S. citizens enter the Internet environment and reproduce the ideological messages and ways of seeing that dominant U.S. power has trained them toward, even to the extent that they produce the propaganda that the government is not allowed to create.

Notes

[1] Although new standards influenced by technology are not inherently degrading or less than old standards, in the case of the style of argument I refer to here, communication and argument are the decided losers. As defined on the popular Internet resource Wikipedia, flaming is characterized as follows:

> "A flame is typically not intended to be constructive, to further clarify a discussion, or to persuade other people. The motive for flaming is often not dialectic, but rather social or psychological. Sometimes, flamers are attempting to assert their authority, or establish a position of superiority.... Most often however, flames are angry or insulting messages transmitted by people who have strong feelings about a subject. Finally, some consider flaming to be a great way to let off steam, though the receiving party may be less than pleased."

[2] See, for instance, http://edition.cnn.com/2014/06/03/world/meast/syria-defector-recruits-westerners/.

[3] *Iraq Fighting* can be viewed at http://www.metacafe.com/watch/82292/iraq_fighting/. Similar videos can be seen by entering "Iraq war" into this search engine or the many others like them.

[4] Blackwater, which later changed its name into Xe Services and Academi, in its own words, is "a professional military, law enforcement, security, peacekeeping, and stability operations firm who provides turnkey solutions" (http://www.blackwaterusa.com/about - no longer online). Academi argues to be "a completely separate company from the former Blackwater" that is an "elite security services provider" (http://academi.com/faqs/). Hired by the U.S. government to perform in Iraq, Blackwater personnel are featured in a war music video entitled, "Black Water mercs having fun in helicopter in Iraq," http://www.youtube.com/watch?v=_ukhFo80Z4w&NR (no longer online). The sound track and camera angles are reminiscent of 1980s television shows such as *Magnum P.I.* or *The A Team*; the military-violence-for-hire (by Western states) is distinctly twenty-first century.

[5] The video is available along with Alex Chadwick's news article about the event, No court-martial for marine taped killing unarmed Iraqi, 2005, *NPR* http://www.npr.org/templates/story/story.php?storyId=4646406.

[6] A example of this kind of footage is the video footage from a US Apache helicopter in 2007, released by Wikileaks, showing the deaths of Reuters journalist Namir Noor-Eldeen and several others (see

https://www.youtube.com/watch?v=5rXPrfnU3G0 and
http://collateralmurder.com/).
[7] Grouchymedia's first video production, *Taliban Bodies* was captured on national
television when a U.S. service person had it up on his computer screen during the
filming of an NBC program, *Ship at war: Inside the* Carrier Stennis. When Ryan
Hickman, producer of Grouchymedia, saw his video on the sailor's computer, he
asked his local NBC affiliate for a copy of the program and his West Palm Beach
news station did a feature story on the creation of the video (see
http://www.grouchymedia.com/videos/taliban_bodies/nbc.cfm).
[8] The video was online at http://www.youtube.com/watch?v=Umpz3y-09nE (no
longer online).
[9] The video is available at https://www.youtube.com/watch?v=jMbkIZKErAc. The
Facebook page of the group is https://www.facebook.com/pages/4th25-Fourth-
Quarter/228986923785016.
[10] Among the many feminist theorists who have contributed to the study of
pornography from whom I have learned, I drew most directly from Diana Russell's
work for this definition.
[11] The video was available at http://www.youtube.com/watch?v=dCp3vy_y99Y
(no longer online).
[12] Although it may be surprising to individuals consuming media from outside the
U.S., the linkage between the events of 9/11 and Saddam Hussein has been made
so many times by the Bush government and the U.S. media that a 2006 Zogby poll
showed that 46% of Americans believe the two were connected
(http://www.zogby.com/news/ReadNews.dbm?ID=1169).
[13] The photos were available at http://www.barbecuestopper.com/warpictures/.
[14] While it is true that al-Qaeda uploads and distributes its videos to Internet
servers that are able to stay in business due to the profit raised by their distribution
of pornography, this coincidence of war pornography with sexual pornography is
one of pragmatic necessity rather than conscious and chosen affiliation as with
NTFU. My thanks to Tom Keenan of Bard College's Human Rights Program for
sharing this insight.
[15] Cary Voss, writing for the online magazine, *Localist*, reports on the state of
Internet access, both military sanctioned and individually improvised, in her
article, *Hacking Iraq* (http://www.localistmagazine.com/iraq.htm).
[16] See p. 406.
[17] Nevertheless, such ideas do sometimes get stated aloud as was the case when
Lieutenant General James Mattis, a U.S. Marine stated: "Actually, it's quite fun to
fight them, you know. It's a hell of a hoot. It's fun to shoot some people, I'll be
right up front with you. I like brawling . . . You go into Afghanistan, you've got
guys who slap women around for five years because they didn't wear a veil . . .
You know, guys like that ain't got no manhood left anyway, so it's a hell of a lot of
fun to shoot them" (http://www.abc.net.au/news/2005-02-04/its-fun-to-shoot-
some-people-us-general/630776).
[18] The complete rules are as follows:

116 Photos for Access

"If you are a U.S. Soldier stationed in Iraq, Afghanistan, or any other combat area and would like free SUPPORTER access for the site, you can post real pictures you or your buddies have taken while you have been deployed.

This section is for the gory ones so that people who do not wish to see that kind of stuff can just not go in here. I also do not want already published pictures that were taken by news people. This is supposed to be an area where we can see pictures posted by soldiers themselves.

Just post your pics like you normally would and when I see them I will approve you for free access to the wife and g/f area. There have only been a few people cheat from this but I do now know what kind of pics to expect from the guys over there. So please do not waste my time if you are not a military person by just posting iraq pics you found on CNN or something.

Keep up the good work over there guys, we love seeing your pics."

[19] The last trace of http://www.barbecuestopper.com/warpictures/ on the Wayback Machine (archive.org) is dated 7 December 2006.

Works Cited

Anti-war hackers target websites. 2003. BBC News. http://news.bbc.co.uk/2/hi/technology/2871985.stm (accessed 12 September 2006).

Boggs, Carl. 2006. Pentagon strategy, Hollywood, and technowar. New Politics 11(1). http://www.wpunj.edu/newpol/issue41/Boggs41.htm. (accessed 12 September 2006).

Campbell, David. 2006. Horrific Blindness: Images of Death in Contemporary Media. Journal for Cultural Research 8(1): 55-74.

Conklin, David B. 2003. The internet in war: the case of Kosovo. Paper presented at Midwest Political Science Association. Chicago, Illinois, April 3-6, 2003.

Crane, David M., and Bryant, Fred E. 2006. Losing the moral high ground: The US and the rule of law. Jurist Legal News and Research. http://jurist.law.pitt.edu/forumy/2006/06/losing-moral-high-ground-us-and-rule.php

Der Derian, James. 2005. Imaging terror: Logos, pathos and ethos. Third World Quarterly 26(1):23 – 37.

Fisk, Robert. 2004. Terror by video: How Iraq's kidnappers drew their inspiration from horrors of Chechnya. http://www.robert-fisk.com/articles422.htm (accessed 14 September 2006).

Glaser, Mark. 2005. Porn site offers soldiers free access in exchange for photos of dead Iraqis. Online Journalism Review.

http://www.ojr.org/ojr/stories/050920glaser/ (accessed 14 September 2006)

Greenfield, Jeff. 2004. Transcripts CNN http://transcripts.cnn.com/TRANSCRIPTS/0405/21/lol.01.html (accessed 12 September 2006).

Griffin, Michael. 2004. Picturing America's "war on terrorism" in Afghanistan and Iraq: Photographic motifs as news frames. Journalism 5(4): 381–402.

Kahney, Leander. 2003. Internet stokes anti-war movement. Wired http://www.wired.com/news/culture/0,1284,57310,00.html (accessed 14 September 2006).

Kellner, Douglas. 2003. September 11, spectacles of terror, and media manipulation. A critique of Jihadist and Bush media polit." Logos 2(1): 86-102.

Landler, Mark, and Markoff, John. 2007. Digital Fears Emerge After Data Siege in Estonia. New York Times, 29 May 2007.

Mirzoeff, Nicholas. 2005. Watching Babylon: The War in Iraq and Global Visual Culture. New York: Routledge.

Morris, Rosalind C. 2004. Images of untranslatability in the war on terror. interventions 6: 401-/423.

Rainey, James. 2005. Portraits of War: Unseen Pictures, Untold Stories. http://www.latimes.com/news/nationworld/nation/la-na-iraqphoto21may21,0,2732182.story?page=5&coll=la-home-headlines (accessed 14 September 2006).

Risen, James, and Lichtblau, Eric. 2005. Bush lets U.S. spy on callers without courts. The New York Times http://select.nytimes.com/gst/abstract.html?res=F00F1FFF3D540C758 DDDAB0994DD404482 (accessed 12 September 2006).

Russell, Diana. 1994. Against Pornography. The Evidence of Harm. Berkeley, California: Russell Publications.

Shanker, Thom. 2005. Army inquiry finds no evidence G.I.'s gave war photos to web. New York Times http://select.nytimes.com/gst/abstract.html?res=F40D12F839540C7A8 EDDA00894DD404482&n=Top%2fReference%2fTimes%20Topics% 2fPeople%2fS%2fShanker%2c%20Thom (accessed 12 September 2006).

Sharkey, Jacqueline. 2003. The TV war. American Journalism Review May/June: 4.

Sontag, Susan. 2002. Regarding the Pain of Others. New York: Farrar, Straus Giroux.

Taylor, Philip M. 2002. The world wide web goes to war, Kosovo 1999. In
    Web.Studies, Rewiring Media for the Digital Age. Edited by David
    Gauntlett. New York: Oxford UP.
War hack attacks tit for tat. 2003. Wired.
    http://www.wired.com/news/conflict/0,2100,58275,00.html (accessed
    12 September 2006).
Zelizer, Barbie. 2005. Death in Wartime: Photographs and the "Other
    War" in Afghanistan. Press/Politics 10(3): 26-55.

PART II:

INCARCERATION AND TORTURE

ABU GHRAIB, WAR MEDIA AND THE GRAY ZONES OF IMPERIAL CITIZENSHIP[1]

USHA ZACHARIAS

Prologue

Excerpt from the press conference held by the former U.S. secretary of state, Donald Rumsfeld, at NATO headquarters, Brussels, Belgium:

QUESTION: Regarding terrorism and weapons of mass destruction, you said something to the effect that the real situation is worse than the facts show. I wonder if you could tell us what is worse than is generally understood.
RUMSFELD: Sure. All of us in this business read intelligence information. And we read it daily and we think about it and it becomes, in our minds, essentially what exists. And that's wrong. It is not what exists.

I say that because I have had experiences where I have gone back and done a great deal of work and analysis on intelligence information and looked at important countries, target countries, looked at important subject matters with respect to those target countries and asked, probed deeper and deeper and kept probing until I found out what it is we knew, and when we learned it, and when it actually had existed. And I found that, not to my surprise, but I think anytime you look at it that way what you find is that there are very important pieces of intelligence information that countries that spend a lot of money, and a lot of time with a lot of wonderful people trying to learn more about what's going in the world, did not know some significant event for two years after it happened, for four years after it happened, for six years after it happened, in some cases 11 and 12 and 13 years after it happened.

Now what is the message there? The message is that there are no "knowns." There are things we know that we know. There are known unknowns. That is to say there are things that we now know we don't know. But there are also unknown unknowns. There are things we don't know we don't know. So when we do the best we can and we pull all this information together, and we then say well that's basically what we see as the situation, that is really only the known knowns and the known unknowns. And each year, we discover a few more of those unknown unknowns.
—Secretary Rumsfeld press (2002)

The unknown known

The theme of this chapter is inspired by a comment made by philosopher Slavoj Žižek at the Rethinking Marxism 2003 conference plenary session (Žižek 2003; 2004). Adding to Rumsfeld's categories of "known knowns" – that which the U.S. administration knows and admits that they know; the "known unknown" – that which the U.S. administration knows that they do not know; and the "unknown unknown" – that which the U.S. administration does not know that they do not know; Žižek suggested a fourth category. This category, Žižek said, would reveal the ideology of the other three: the category of the "unknown known" – that which the U.S. administration knows but does not admit that they know. This chapter carries forward Žižek's insight to argue that this play between knowing and not knowing is central to imperial citizenship and sovereign power as it is deployed in administration rhetoric. I use the specific instance of media coverage of Abu Ghraib to illustrate how uncomfortable public knowledge is dealt with by evoking a "state of exception" as well as the civilizational superiority of U.S. democracy. Scholarly work on war media and rhetoric since 9/11, I argue, also inadvertently reproduces the nationalist citizen-subject who can potentially correct U.S. democracy from within, even as they are pliant to media messages and war rhetoric. The knowledge the administration produces and the critique of that knowledge still remain within strongly nationalistic boundaries which, consequently, promote the sovereign power of the security state by leaving little room for transnational dialogue or intervention – even in the case of torture as international political practice.

The realm of pure truth

I begin by revisiting Rumsfeld's remarks on Iraq's weapons of mass destruction, which won a 2003 Foot in the Mouth award from Britain's Plain English Campaign for the most baffling statement made by a public figure (Rummy rant wins 2003). Diverging from Žižek's focus on the known/unknown, the statement can be read for its covert logic of imperial supremacism and racial suspicion. The object of the known/unknown, as Rumsfeld makes clear, are "important countries, target countries". These "target countries" alone can occupy the space of the "unknown" in Rumsfeld's three-term game. In this sense, the known/unknown – what we know and what we do not know – are both about those target countries, while the "we" that knows or knows that it does not know, remains outside the target area. The known knowns, the known unknown, and the unknown

unknown are all known by a central sovereign Knower. The Knower who knows what it does not know occupies a position of omniscience, where the Other is always the target of its knowledge. Within this epistemological frame there is room to question the known and the unknown, but no room to question the Knower who mediates both. Rumsfeld's deployment of the idea of absolute knowledge – or of the all-Knowing Knower – lays the ground for the legitimization of sovereign power. In Foucault's words, "We are subjected to the production of truth through power and we cannot exercise power except through the production of truth" (1972, 93).

Once we reduce the Knower and its target, Known, to the United States and its "target country", Iraq, we can now re-read the statement for its racial logic, where the Other is always suspect, since it is never fully knowable, and it can never claim utter transparency, since it has no space within the Sovereign Knower that can actually know the known and the unknown. The dark, opaque unknown and its constant evasion of the knower's gaze are metaphors that melt into centuries-old epistemological tropes about the Orient as unfathomable mystery. The unknowability in turn creates the desire to master, to know, to render transparent – legitimating the will for power. As Said's (1979) work demonstrates, the Occident's production of knowledge about the Orient is part of the Occident's will to govern the Orient. Still, it is important to note that the latest discourse of sovereignty by virtue of civilizational superiority transcends the older binaries of colonial epistemology of white knower and dark unknown – and this epistemological trope's justification of the relationship between the knower and unknown as a relationship of power and governance. Instead of the colonial production of knowledge allied to the will to power, this new form of imperial sovereignty explicitly uses the absence of knowledge to stage a military occupation. The clue to this vital ideological shift in post 9/11 imperial power lies in the unknown unknown: the things we did not know in the past, may not know now, and may not know later (since we did not know in the past). The rhetorically posited knowledge of the unknown unknown legitimizes military action not on the ground of a present threat, an impending threat, or a past threat, but just from the atemporal, Omniscient position of being able to Know the Other as always-already threatening. As Rumsfeld went on to explain in the press conference, "the absence of evidence is not the evidence of absence." Here we double back to the all-knowing Self as ground for the evidence, this time made not on the logocentric assumption of self-presence alone, but the metaphysical claim of omniscience, since the Self not only knows itself but absorbs all other forms of knowledge through its logic of absence. The whole discourse of known/unknown is built on the stated premise that one is always already looking at "important countries, target countries"; in short, one is always already within the realm of already revealed Truth. The "unknown unknown" also rhetorically creates a "state of exception" that perennially justifies sovereign power. The play between "knowing" and "not knowing" as a means of justifying civilizational supremacy, and thus sovereign power, continues into the discourse around Abu Ghraib, as I will attempt to show.

The citizen's civilizational journey

In this context, critiques of wartime media since 9/11 face the fundamental challenge of rearticulating assumptions about the models of citizenship that undergrid them. Although the concept of citizenship remains marginal to media studies, recent work has done much to dislodge the idea of citizenship as an unchanging political essence, and instead foregrounded the semiotic, performative, rhetorical and discursive dimensions of citizenship (Asen 2004, Barnhurst 1998, Miller 1983, Murphy 2003, Zaeske 2002). These studies, however, still retain the nation-state as the imagined boundary of the citizen-subject. In contrast, other media scholars have displaced the set of naturalistic ties that firmly bind citizenship (real or rhetorical) to territoriality, nationality, and sovereignty (Shah 1999, Tapia 2005, Cammaerts and Van Audenhove 2005, Neilson 2002). Such a rethinking is persuaded by the work of scholars such as Balibar (2003), Ong (1999), and Sassen (2003) who have dealt with the question of citizenship in transnational contexts as well as the context of globalization, where nation-states no longer seem to enjoy the political and economic sovereignty that once made boundaries powerful. Yet in war media studies, the citizen-subject evoked is an invariably nationalist subject. Cutting across war media studies paradigms is the silent presence of the free-willed yet economically, culturally, or linguistically drugged first world citizen. The U.S. citizen, who is the subject of these writings, appears to be burdened by pre-existing stereotypes of Arabs/Muslims that are part of collective consciousness (Merskin 2003) or weighed down by the rhetoric of presidential binary discourse that produces moral certitude (Coe et al. 2004) or carried away by the mythical resonance of dominant media editorials (Lule 2002). The citizen-subject is also swayed by religious rhetoric, whether it is that of the community of the covenant (Bostdorff 2003) or of the exorcism (Gunn 2004), neither of which naturally enters into the state-citizen political or legal pact. The citizen is unable to assert agency in the theoretical paradigm of political economy, for here, the propaganda model affirms the supremacy of the manipulative media (Herman and Chomsky 1988). Nor can the citizen be trusted to act against a media climate of war hysteria or a society of the spectacle (Kellner 2002, McChesney 2002). Within the cultural studies paradigm, there is a startling contrast between the willingness of the citizen to produce resistant and negotiated readings of fictional media texts, such as romances and soap operas, and their "cultural dope" mode when they are confronted with war news. The studies cited above, then, retain a model of liberal citizenship, with a citizen who withdraws from the realm to which they rightly belong, that of constituting power in the citizen-state compact, but who may or may not awaken to action at a time of crisis.

Propaganda analysis of the media that rely on political economy epistemologically reproduces this essentially decent citizen whose almost perennial ignorance of U.S. foreign policy has to be corrected by the media, which invariably fails to communicate in the public interest, if one may so hyperbolically put it. Take, for example, the influential critique of Herman and Chomsky: "The U.S. media do not function in the manner of a propaganda system of a totalitarian state. Rather they permit – indeed, encourage spirited debate, criticism, and dissent, as long as these remain faithfully within the system of presuppositions and principles that constitute an elite consensus, a system so powerful as to be internalized largely without awareness" (1988). The five filters of the propaganda model: concentration of ownership, primacy of advertising income, strategic news sources, disciplining flak, and anti-communism enable elite consensus and prevent the citizen from effective intervention in the political process. Thus, for instance, in the case of Cambodia and East Timor, the media did not provide "facts" or "analyses that would have enabled the public to understand the issues or the bases of government policies…" and "they thereby assured that the public could not exert any meaningful influence on the decisions that were made." This, they state, is "quite typical of the actual 'societal purpose' of the media on matters that are of significance for established power; not enabling the public to assert meaningful control over the political process." Recently, Chomsky re-asserted the significance of the propaganda model for Iraq, stating that "government-media" propaganda was able to convince the people that Iraq is an imminent threat and that Iraq was responsible for September 11" (Chomsky 2003).

The propaganda model is based on the model of the sleeping decent citizen who could potentially awaken through "organization and self-education" from ignorance to take steps for "democratization of social life and for meaningful social change." The history of international intervention happens in the diurnal rhythm of the waking and the sleeping life of this political citizen. The interplay between politics and economy is played out through the figure of this citizen-subject: if the citizens do not know their nation's international politics, it is because of the monopolistic media economy and its lop-sided filers. The political lack is transferred to the sphere of the economy, where the helplessness of the political citizen is obvious and natural in face of the disempowerment in economic citizenship.

It is also perfectly explicable, it appears, that the citizen goes back to political sleep after the horrors of each post-atrocity revelation that tells the story of adventures abroad. This model appears to hold true even for critical media analysis of propaganda, which Kellner defines as "a particular mode of persuasive discourse that mobilizes ideas, images, arguments, rhetoric, and sometimes disinformation and lies to induce people to agree with specific policies and actions." Kellner states: "propaganda attempts to overcome divisions of opinion and to persuade people that policies they might have opposed, such as war, are right, good, and just" (1992, 235). The figure of the manipulated citizen, as we saw with Chomsky, returns: this time it is neither Indonesia nor East Timor but Iraq 1991. Thus Kellner (1992, 7) argues, from the paradigm of critical theory, that the "media helped to create an environment, that in conjunction with other social factors, helped mobilize consent to the Bush administration's war policies". The "tribal drum of television," he writes, "turned the population into often frenzied supporters of the U.S. military intervention in the Middle East" (1992, 7). This argument is repeated when, in post 9/11 U.S., it is seen that television "whipped up war hysteria" (Kellner 2002) or when the mainstream media's control of the public sphere ends up producing patterns of "thought and behavior congruent with corporate capitalism" (Kellner 2004). The unquestionably firm relationship between political citizenship and economic citizenship creates a democratic crisis that leaves the subject of the nation-state a voiceless actor.

The "primacy of the media economy" argument was reiterated in an editorial for the timely special issue of *Television & New Media*. The editorial writers identified six "casualties of war" in the media sphere from 9/11 to the fall of Kabul. "Independent inquiry was the first under threat, already rendered vulnerable by a century of interlocked interests of government, news, media corporations, and Hollywood," they write. This in turn damaged "public knowledge of war conditions in Afghanistan, the threat of anti-terrorist laws to harm civil liberties, the invitation to war profiteering in U.S. economic stimulus laws, the use of polls in the propaganda effort, and the mangling of history" (Lewis et al. 2002). Once again, we are presented with a historically contextualized, but largely similar set of reasons for the lack of information in the public interest. This ideologically arranged marriage of politics and economy generates a circular reasoning where the economy remains the unknown before which politics must surrender its possibility of knowledge. To be fully politically informed and to function as a political actor, it appears, one must first have full economic citizenship. The political citizenship of this social actor remains in abeyance since it is constantly colonized by the U.S. military/corporate sector. Economy shortcircuits the political; the explanation is ready before politics can be articulated, a phenomenon Žižek calls "postpolitical" (Žižek 1997, 999).

The kind of civilizational transformation imagined – from deficient economic citizenship to full political citizenship – also undercuts the political system that this hypothetical citizen, as subject of a capitalist democracy, is meant to support. Biesecker's (1998) point that democracy cannot be treated as an ahistorical given is particularly relevant here, as are studies of citizenship cited earlier that refuse to treat it as an unchanging political essence. However, what is more pertinent to this chapter are the implications of this particular model of political citizenship, or rather, the rhetorical reinvention of such a citizen-subject with regard to international issues. What ought the world that is constituted in and through imperial policy do while this fictional citizen-subject is shielded by its rhetorically produced "unknowing" condition? Does this decent imperial citizen that persistently recurs as a rhetorical figure in state, media, and academic discourses really belong to the sphere of political ontology, as it appears to do? Or is this unknowing citizen – who does not know what the government is up to because the media does not function in the public interest – a necessary fiction in our militaristic politics (and its counterpart, the knowledge produced about U.S. militaristic politics) since Vietnam? Is not the passive assumption of this idea of citizenship, or the rhetorical reinvention of such a citizen, itself arguably a fallacy?

Italian philosopher Agamben's (1995) work is significant in this context for its theorization of sovereign power and the state of exception. Prior to the state-citizen contract organized on the grounds of birth and nationality, he argues, is the phenomenon of sovereign power. He uncovers a novel dimension of state power that is primarily self-constituting; one that does not require a democratic mandate from the "constituting power" of the people that a concept like citizenship may imply. Sovereign power – the power to govern over bare life and the power to eliminate bare life – constitutes itself, not through a juridical domain, but through a logic that puts sovereignty in a position to decide what shall be deemed rule and exception. Sovereign power "creates and defines a space in which the juridical order has validity" just as it creates a state of exception, or a suspension of order in which the juridical relationship can be replaced by the direct power of violence. Sovereign power constitutes itself in and through the state of exception because it has the power to define rule and exception. Thus Agamben states there is a "hidden point of intersection" between the juridical institutional model of power, and the biopolitical model of power. In doing so, Agamben develops and moves beyond Foucault's concept of biopower, in which the state has the power to include in its technologies of governance the "biological life" – or death – of populations as a whole (Foucault 1978). Agamben shows how the biopolitical model of power – the power to govern the life and death of populations – can be enabled only through sovereign power, a form of power that is both inside and outside the juridical order, and which constitutes itself through a state of exception. The state of exception – which is not chaos, but the "suspension of order", the exception to the juridical realm – is integral to the constitution of sovereign power.

In a state of exception, the "citizen", who is the fictional subject of our understanding of the media, is a dangerous ontological assumption; not simply because this figure sanctions political passivity and thus endangers democracy in the U.S. alone, but because they epitomize a civilizing narrative that effectively conceals their silent rhetorical deployment in the legitimization of sovereign imperial power. It also obscures the ambiguities of citizenship at a time when nation/colony, home/empire distinctions are relegated to the gray zones necessitated by a global war on terror. As Žižek points out, since 9/11, the U.S. is operating under the logic of a state of emergency, since it is in a state of war. However, for the majority of people, daily life goes on since war is the "business of state agencies". In other words, he states, "we are entering a time in which a state of peace itself can be a state of emergency" (2004, 107). To paraphrase Arendt: Eichmann is normal according to the "normal" of Nazi-Germany (1963, 26). The fictional citizen-subject, in other words, appears to be all the more fictional when a democracy begins to operate from a state of exception.

What is problematic about deploying the politically sleep prone citizen as an epistemological tool in wartime, is its silent legitimization of sovereign power. This citizen-subject, mostly asleep, yet claiming a dormant political life that can be awakened through media revelations, operates within the curious ironies of the known unknown, once again, with a racial-military coding. Communication in the public interest balances against its opposite, communication that is not necessarily in the public interest, through a logic of foreclosure and disclosure. The foreclosure/disclosure hypothetically produces the essentially good, normal, humanist citizen-subject, who, armed with alarming, true knowledge, will awaken to public interest, and protest against the militaristic citizen-subject who has journeyed out to police the world. In either case, the saving of public interest remains with us, the "American" (read nationalist) citizen-subject, shortcutting the possibility that an anti-imperialist politics is not a nationalist project. Such is the frightening lesson of Abu Ghraib, to which I will turn to now.

There was no real dearth of coverage of Abu Ghraib on network news, although it was largely reported as a marginal and extreme fallout of the war on Iraq. As of May 15, 2005, news archive searches for Abu Ghraib yielded 385 results on CNN, 734 news items on ABC, 1038 stories on MSNBC, and 999 stories on CBS[2]. My focus in this chapter is primarily on the reports in May 2004, when the story first made its appearance. A timeline of the unfolding torture trail, as well as key documents, and the inquiry reports (Taguba, Schlesinger, Fay, Church) conducted so far are all available at www.aclu.org, including details of the case that has been filed against Rumsfeld by the American Civil Liberties Union. As I describe below, the figurative references to the "state of exception" and the normalizing of the state of exception can be seen throughout in the discourses of power deployed to handle the crisis of Abu Ghraib.

Imperial citizenship: us and them

The problems of assuming "civilized citizenship" as an epistemological premise can be traced in the way Abu Ghraib was both normalized and/or justified as a state of exception even in the initial context of its media revelation. The rhetoric surrounding torture, I argue here, shows how the citizen who travels from the unknown to knowledge – as an epistemological figure – is appropriated into the technologies of governance. The state, in this context, is able to play upon the ontological assumptions of the model of citizenship described above in order to contain the public images of torture that challenged its projected image as sole defender of freedom and democracy.

The torture of Iraqi prisoners at Abu Ghraib was a classic case of communication (inadvertently or otherwise) in the public interest that was made possible by CBS *60 Minutes* and the *New Yorker* magazine that acted as the airing spaces for the political rifts within U.S. army and intelligence. Presenting the University of Georgia's Peabody Award in broadcasting excellence to CBS for breaking the Abu Ghraib story, Horace Newcomb, director of the award, called it an "important moment" in television of 2004 (CBS wins Peabody 2003). Seymour Hersh, who traced the "chain of command" for torture in painstaking detail in his series of articles in the *New Yorker*, notably won the National Press Foundation Award, 2004, the Ron Ridenhour Courage award 2004 (named after the journalist who broke the story of the My Lai massacre in Vietnam), and the fifth George Polk award, 2004. By all criteria, Abu Ghraib was a successful media feat of exposure, an example of investigative journalism and reporting. The citizen-subject of wartime communication certainly began the civilizational journey from the unknown to the known at this moment: few could plead not guilty to witnessing the widely-circulated images of abuse that, as Sontag (2004) noted, was now far more infectious through the digital images linked up to the Internet. The images of Specialist Charles Graner, Pfc. Lynndie England, or Spc. Sabrina Harman posing playfully with naked Iraqi male bodies piled into pyramids, the hooded Iraqi man waiting for electrocution on a box, the Iraqi man crawling on the floor, held on a leash by Lynndie England, and finally, the attack dogs menacing a nude, bound Iraqi male prisoner with their homophobic, pornographic and sadistic resonance were certainly arresting enough to outstrip channel-switching instincts.

What of the citizen-spectator of these images, confronted with this new unknown unknown? To trace the citizen's civilizational journey, let us turn to the way in which these spectacular images of Iraqi prisoner torture by U.S. soldiers and military intelligence units at Abu Ghraib was normalized by the administration through a logic of exception. The leading defence of the administration in terms of media strategy was to treat torture as an unknown unknown and to term the interrogation methods as "abuse". This was done so consistently from a nationalist perspective – that is, without any sense of the responsibility that the U.S. had to its occupied territory and the citizens of that territory. Abu Ghraib called into question the problems of imperialism and citizenship: the blurred categories of nation/colony, state of law/ state of exception, free citizen/colonized subject. There could clearly be no discourse of international human rights, given the ambiguous status of the U.S. vis-à-vis the Geneva Convention, and no particular claim of Iraqi citizenship, given that Iraq was occupied territory.

Both Bush and Rumsfeld responded to the Abu Ghraib images with covert racial logics of American exceptionalism and of civilizational supremacism that categorized the images as representing deviant, perverse human behavior, and not the everyday realities of war by other means. These disclaimers of May 2004 must be seen in the context of Bush's nomination and the senate judiciary committee's confirmation of Alberto Gonzales as Attorney General of the United States in January 2005. Gonzales, by this time, was well known for his recommendation that prisoners in Afghanistan be denied the protection of the Geneva conventions, and also for his role in redefining torture to mean "procedures that would produce pain of an intensity akin to that which accompanies serious physical injury such as death or organ failure" (Danner 2004). Without explicitly denying knowledge of torture, Bush's televisual and rhetorical image appeared ignorant about both sanctioning torture as policy as well as regarding the specific interrogation methods at Abu Ghraib. Bush characterized Abu Ghraib as a "stain on the nation's honor", the consequence of "wrongdoing by a few" that should not reflect on the "thousands of U.S. military personnel serving and sacrificing in Iraq" (Bush: Abuse was 2004). Torture, and intelligence gathering, thus appeared to be a "state of exception" to the war in Iraq, rather than integral to it, as we see in later reports that note how more aggressive interrogation methods were deployed after the then-inexplicable rise of the Iraqi armed resistance (Danner 2004).

Testifying before the senate armed services committee on May 7, 2004, Rumsfeld said he had failed to recognize "how important it was to elevate a matter of such gravity to the highest levels" (Rumsfeld testifies before 2004). The "mistreatment", in his words that carefully avoided the use of the term torture, was "inconsistent with the values of our nation." He added that it was "inconsistent with the teachings of the military, to the men and women of the armed forces. And it was certainly fundamentally un-American". Rumsfeld, who made a flying trip to Abu Ghraib, also took a further plunge into the Unknown Unknown, when he said to a packed hall of U.S. soldiers, "I stopped reading the newspapers. I'm a survivor," a gesture greeted with thunderous applause in visual clips replayed on May 13, 2004 primetime ABC World News and BBC America World News transmitted by PBS. The apology he had offered to the Iraqi detainees before the senate armed services committee was not heard in Iraq. These public demonstrations of ignorance of the national debate occurred even as ABC World News reported on May 14, 2003, that the International Red Cross had checked fourteen detention facilities across Iraq, and had turned in a secret report to the Bush administration a year beforehand in May 2003, following which they met with Condoleeza Rice on January 15, 2004, and Paul Wolfowitz on January 16, 2004. (See www.aclu.org for a timeline of the torture policies, The Case against Rumsfeld).

Once torture became Known, it then became a Known Unknown: the administration now knew about Abu Ghraib, but not about torture being a widespread practice from Guantanomo Bay to Afghanistan to Iraq. More important, the prisoner torture was not "knowable" as an "American" act. In his May 10, 2004 weekly radio address, Bush said, "The brave and honorable soldiers, sailors, airmen, Coast Guardsmen and Marines who are serving and sacrificing in Iraq – not the few who have let us down – show the true character of America" (Bush: I have 2004). Torture thus appeared to be a dramatic and singular exception, and not the norm, and certainly not one that belonged to our national character. As the White House got increasingly defensive, Bush restated, "We do not condone torture. I have never ordered torture. I will never order torture. The values of this country are such that torture is not a part of our soul and our being" (Bush: I have 2004). The administration affirmed faith in the majority of the troops who they knew were good kids doing the job; as against the deviant Others, who had served up this "body blow" as Rumsfeld put it during his Baghdad trip (Rumsfeld visits Iraq's 2004).

Since torture was not integral to national character, the real question was how to do a makeover for the "Arab world"; yet another post 9/11 "rebrand America" project. Peter Jennings said on ABC World News May 11, 2004, that the administration was doing its best to overcome the serious setback, and to "tell the world that abusing prisoners was an aberration." Networks consistently portrayed Abu Ghraib as an exception, one that would be overcome by the stable norms of civilized citizenship that were the premises of western democracy. It was no wonder then, that all that was needed was a battle of images. ABC news reported Condoleeza Rice had appeared on three Arab networks, illustrating it with a clip in which she said "people will see" that the administration was determined to get to the bottom of the matter. CNN's Wolf Blitzer on May 10, 2004, commented that it was now up to Rumsfeld to "ride out the storm and to make it appear to America and the world that he is fixing it." Wesley Clark, then speaking for the Democrats, appeared on ABC news on May 11, 2004, to say that the question was "how seriously are we perceived to be taking the issue." *Time* magazine's Washington correspondent Timothy Burger appeared on CNN on May 10 (Mother's day) to say that the images would play right into the hands of extremists in the Arab world who "want to portray us as occupiers and anti-Arab, which is wrong, but that image will be portrayed especially in much of the Arab world, which has a government-controlled press which won't allow the other side of the story: that most Americans are good people, they're trying to do their best."

The rhetorical presentation of Abu Ghraib an "exceptional act" was based on the assumption of the national self as a known known: where there was a bright half of America that could interrogate itself, and a darker half that may be the semi-playful victims of a subterranean popular culture of hazing and sexual pranks. As Rumsfeld told the armed services committee, this incident too could be used to prove the civilizational code:

> However, terrible the setback, this is also an occasion to demonstrate to the world the difference between those who believe in democracy and in human rights, and those who believe in rule by terrorist code.
>
> We value human life. We believe in individual freedom and in the rule of law. For those beliefs, we send men and women of the armed forces abroad to protect that right for our own people and to give others who aren't Americans the hope of a future of freedom.
>
> Part of that mission, part of what we believe in, is making sure that when wrongdoings or scandal do occur, that they're not covered up, but they're exposed, they're investigated, and the guilty are brought to justice.
>
> Mr. Chairman, I know you join me today in saying to the world, judge us by our actions, watch how Americans, watch how a democracy deals with the wrongdoing and with scandal and the pain of acknowledging and correcting our own mistakes and our own weaknesses. (Rumsfeld testifies before 2004).

Once again, we see the epistemological trope of the known/unknown; this time too, it is drawn on the sovereign infallibility of "America" and its self-referential ability to uncover the Truth. The association of U.S. citizenship with human rights, justice, and freedom through the possibility of the corrective mechanisms of its democracy makes torture fundamentally a question of national character and national values; while refusing to acknowledge it as international practice, and a question of processes of transnational justice. The knowing/unknowing American national citizen was the subject of the torture debate even as the torture clearly concerned citizens and international organizations elsewhere in the world. Underpinning Rumsfeld's testimony is the notion of civilizational supremacy of a nation that is determined "to give others who aren't Americans the hope of a future of freedom." This discourse of the self-correcting, and therefore civilizationally superior form of American humanity was strengthened when U.S. citizen Nicholas Berg was beheaded by an alleged militant group just as Maj. Gen. Antonio M. Taguba, who conducted the investigation on Abu Ghraib, was testifying before the Congress in Washington D.C. The video of the beheading stated that this act was in revenge for the abuse of prisoners in Abu Ghraib, leading Senator John McCain to remark on May 11, 2004, on ABC World News: "It is terrible. It is tragic. It also shows the stark difference between Americans and these barbarians. We have found out about mistreatment of prisoners – we are addressing the issue completely. These people have no regard for humanity or common decency, which is why we have to win in Iraq." Wayne Allard, another senator, said in the same newscast that the incident illustrated the "difference between the way we do business, and so frequently our adversaries do business."

The ability to enact this difference between "us" and "them" became critical to the way in which the knowledge about Abu Ghraib was absorbed. Conservative talk radio picked up the theme, in Sean Hannity's words: "Do we now understand the difference between atrocity and mistreatment? Where is the outrage now?" (ABC World News, May 11, 2004). The knowing American who can perform the journey away from the unknown, who belongs to the America which can self-reflexively interrogate itself, know itself, and interrogate its own unknown, is held up as the civilizational difference from "their" world. The debate on torture constructed a citizen whose nationalist identity was constructed on the trope of the known/unknown: the citizen whose bright, visible, rational self can interrogate its darker self.

The Christian and the corrections officer

As seen in the reactions to Abu Ghraib, the founding narrative of democracy then rests on the knowing, civilizationally superior citizen who could be the corrective force that straightens out its errant, dark twin. Yet it is this very narrative of democracy that collapsed in the media revelation of Abu Ghraib. In other words, the civilizational narrative – that of the citizen who comes to their democratic senses when confronted with the failures of democracy – seems to have hit the rock of the transformed world of post 9/11 politics with Abu Ghraib. Thus Danner writes, "At least since Watergate, Americans have come to take for granted a certain story line of scandal, in which revelation is followed by investigation, adjudication, and expiation. Together, Congress and the courts investigate high-level wrongdoing and place it in a carefully constructed narrative, in which crimes are charted, malfeasance is explicated and punishment is apportioned as the final step in the journey back to justice, order, and propriety. When Alberto Gonzales takes his seat before the Senate Judiciary Committee today for hearings to confirm whether he will become attorney general of the United States, Americans will bid farewell to that comforting storyline" (Danner 2005).

The storyline of exposure, outrage, and correction – the bedrock narrative of a purely political democracy – disappeared, according to Danner, with the Bush nomination of Alberto Gonzales, who rewrote the definition of torture in a now publicized White House memo. Thus Danner added, "The senators are likely to give full legitimacy to a path that the Bush administration set the country on more than three years ago, a path that has transformed the United States from a country that condemned torture and forbade its use to one that practices torture routinely" (Danner 2005). Yet Danner's dramatization of the moment of the confirmation of Gonzalez bypasses the discursive thread that had all along been woven along with the normalizing of the exception, the visibility of Abu Ghraib, as a natural condition of rule. The breaking story of Abu Ghraib was simultaneously normalized as a state of exception to the existing state of war. The state of exception, or the state of war, naturalizes the borderline cases of the exception as an extension of the general state of war. This normalizing of the "exception to the exception" even as one accepts war as a normal, everyday, condition of the empire is evident if we travel the gray zone between torture as paralegal activity that potentially violates conceptions of human rights (the Geneva convention point of view), and torture as integral to war by other means in the larger gameplan of us vs them, civilization vs terrorism, freedom vs oppression, democracy vs dictatorship.

The belief in the comforting storyline of exposure, outrage, and correction ignores the way the terms of debate, and the very language in which it may be conducted, radically shifted after 9/11. As Žižek points out, Jonathan Alter wrote in *Newsweek* as early as 5 November 2001 as follows: "We can't legalize torture; it's contrary to American values. But even as we continue to speak out against human rights abuses around the world, we need to keep an open mind about certain measures to fight terrorism, like court-sanctioned psychological interrogation". And as if to suggest that the practice of "extraordinary rendition", or the transferring of detainees to nations outside the U.S. known for their brutal interrogation practices would be new, Alter added, "And we'll have to think about transferring some suspects to our less squeamish allies, even if that's hypocritical. Nobody said this was going to be pretty." Žižek writes that the liberal response, as articulated by Alan Dershowitz, was: "I'm not in favor of torture, but if you're going to have it, it should damn well have court approval." What is more dangerous than an explicit endorsement of torture, Žižek argues, is to "simply introduce it as a legitimate topic of debate" because such a move "changes the background of ideological presuppositions and options much more radically than outright advocacy" (Žižek 2003, 104).

It is in this context that Rush Limbaugh's much publicized comments make sense. Limbaugh characterized the incident as "no different than what happens at the Skull and Bones initiation, and we're going to ruin people's lives over it, and we're going to hamper our military effort, and then we are going to really hammer them because they had a good time. You know, these people are being fired at every day. I'm talking about people having a good time, these people, you ever heard of emotional release? You [ever] heard of need to blow some steam off? These were just boys and girls blowing off steam during a stressful situation. Let's not make an international incident out of it, for crying out loud" (Rush: MPs just 2004).

Appearing in two CBS interviews immediately after the Abu Ghraib photographs were released, Lynndie England was quoted in a CBS station interview in *60 Minutes* on May 12, 2004, echoing similar sentiments of "normal" war practices. "I guess it just goes with stuff that happens during war time," England told reporter Brian Maass in an interview with CBS station KCNC-TV. "Going in and interrogating, and doing what you're told. People probably think that, 'No, they thought of this on their own, and they were just doing this of their own free will, and this and that,'" said England. "It's not like we laid in bed one night and thought, 'Oh, I want to do this tomorrow, let's do this.' We didn't think of it" (The Pictures: Lynndie 2004). England's words capture the normalcy of the exception; or rather, the normalcy of torture during a state of exception.

The same argument was being used in the Abu Ghraib trials by Guy Womack, the defendant lawyer for Charles Graner, described as the "ringleader" of the Abu Ghraib torture incidents, who appears in the photographs along with Lynndie England. Arguing that his client was only following orders, and often earning praise from his superiors for his actions, Womack said, "Don't cheerleaders all over America form pyramids six to eight times a year? Is that torture?" (Booth 2005). This resonates with Limbaugh's way of normalizing Abu Ghraib through a cultural argument that juxtaposed the binaries, fun and work: why not have a little fun at the end of the working day? "Doing the job" may reflect the banality of evil in our times, but that is certainly a part of the civilized citizenship that makes it easier to both exceptionalize and normalize Abu Ghraib.

Curiously, it is the metaphor of "the job" that prevailed in the statements of various other actors in Abu Ghraib. Sabrina Harman, in an e-mail interview from Baghdad to the Washington Post, said it was that "her assignment" to break down the prisoners. "They would bring in one to several prisoners at a time already hooded and cuffed," Harman said. "The job of the MP was to keep them awake, make it hell so they would talk" (She's no stranger 2004). Similarly, in the CBS *60 Minutes II* interview, Lynndie England said she was instructed by persons in higher rank "to stand there, hold the leash" while she was being photographed; presumably, she too was following orders because she said she "didn't want to be in any picture" (The Pictures: Lynndie 2004). The civilian contract staff working for private security firms or for the intelligence and who were present in the prison also were apparently doing their job; as it turns out, so well that the two firms involved in the torture story, CACI International and Titan, won million dollar contracts from the Pentagon a day after Charles Graner was sentenced (Beaumont 2005). Defending Rumsfeld, Dick Cheney said: "Don Rumsfeld is the best secretary of defence the U.S. has had. People ought to get off his case and let him do his job." (NBC Nightly News, May 9, 2004). The anonymity of the job extended all the way up. After the senate had finished viewing the videotapes and photographs, Bush too rose to the occasion to give a speech to Republicans, and as Rick Santorium praised strong leaders "who are not afraid to step out and do what's right for America." On May 10, 2004, CBS nightly news reported that Bush also drove across town to the Pentagon to personally convey an endorsement for Rumsfeld: You are doing a superb job. Our nation owes you a debt of gratitude… Who can doubt that Iraq is better for being free?"

Perhaps the most powerful and truthful testimony to "doing the job" has come from Charles Graner, himself, whom Specialist Joseph Darby (the "whistle-blower" who turned in the CD of the photographs to his superior officer at Abu Ghraib) quoted as saying: "The Christian in me says it's wrong, but the corrections officer in me says I love to make a grown man piss himself" (Tanner 2005, Watson 2005). This insightful comment reflects on the two Americas, the moral America that is sentencing Graner, and the military America that trains the corrections officer in him. Graner's remark also draws attention to the "work" of the corrections officer; the job that's not Christian, but must be done. In an e-mail that the *New York Times* obtained, it turned out that Graner had been sending his "work diary" to friends and family in chatty messages that strikingly uses the semiotic code of work to naturalize his actions:

"The guys give me hell for not getting any pictures while I was fighting this guy," said one message, titled "just another dull night at work," with a photograph attached of a bound and naked detainee howling with pain, his legs bleeding. To an e-mail message about a Take Your Children to Work

Day event, he replied, "how about send a bastard to hell day?" attaching a photograph of a detainee's head bloodied beyond recognition (Zernike 2005).

Graner is significant because he is, in Foucauldian terms, the biopolitical body of the empire. That is, he is indistinguishable from the point where the totalizing state structures of imperial power and the processes of individualization or subjectivation merge into the political body, at once governed and governing. The words of followers are often more important than those of their leaders. Sending a photograph of him stitching a wound on a detainee's eye, Graner once again referred to the banal and absolute nature of his power, "Try doing this at home, and they'll lock you up if you don't have some type of license," adding, "Not only was I the healer, I was the hurter. O well life goes on" (Zernike 2005).

The citizen who can perform the civilizational journey, both "healer and hurter", and in the final analysis, or in the final solution, is simply playing their part in the floating signifier of the "job" in a state of exception; this is the new form of citizenship, especially the power of imperial citizenship, that we cannot afford to ignore. Indeed, it arguably illustrates Žižek's (2003) use of the phrase "liberal totalitarianism", the point where the everyday, innocuous metaphor of "doing the job" forms a continuum with the sovereign violence of the security state.

Abu Ghraib marked a significant difference in the way the revelatory moment of knowledge for the waking citizen is discursively handled, so that the entire effort is, almost as it were, to quickly naturalize any new atrocity. What has been striking about Iraq network coverage is that it marks a real difference from Gulf war 1991 in terms of its daily imagery from the terrain of war. The hyperreality of the media coverage and the packaging of the war as a "spectatorial video-game" that Shohat and Stam (1994) critiqued in Gulf war coverage have vanished in favor of the broad daylight and realtime bodies of the Iraqi armed resistance. However, the images of Abu Ghraib that Colin Powell compared to My Lai was devoured so quickly, so that by the time the third part of the Hersh story appeared, it had ceased to be the lead, and was replaced with the anxiously awaited handover of Iraq to the interim government.

Hersh himself commented in an interview to *Democracy Now*, "It's not as if there's any monopoly on critical reporting about the war. Even *The New York Times* had a marvelous story a month ago about a group of Marines that came back disillusioned with the lack of equipment, the stupidity of their mission. It was an amazing story. It went down, it just went down" (Seymour Hersh: Iraq 2005). As the media reveal more atrocities, it appears that there is a swifter mechanism for absorbing it, within and without the media. In this context, rather than reproduce this perennial epistemological mechanism of the citizen who does not know, perhaps it is time to pay attention to the "everyday life of empire" populated with knowing, yet unknowing citizens. At once Christian and corrections officer, healer and "hurtor", this theological-imperialist citizen occupies a distinctly different position, arguably, from that of the premise of democratic citizenship which rests on a time-space imagination of nations bound by territoriality instead of a time-space scale in which transnational locations of home and colony, living room and Baghdad, are interwoven in daily life, daily speech, and daily news.

"The sun is shining, the sky is blue, and this is America"

So said Specialist Charles Graner on the first day of his appearance at the Texas court-martial on Abu Ghraib. "Whatever happens is going to happen, but I still feel it's going to be on the positive side" (Opening statements Monday 2005). The shining sun and the blue sky suggest the security of national citizenship, the full certainty of inviolable, inalienable rights within the America of Graner's imagination, where things never really go wrong, where things always happen in the realm of the known known, and one can always travel back from the bizarre world of the colony back to the secure borders of the home-nation. The political rights of the occupied subject must be measured against this secure knowledge that is an integral part of the free ticket of imperial citizenship.

The civilizational citizen, who is a fictional subject of the all-knowing state which can correct itself without reference to the rest of the world even when an international issue is involved, all too often legitimizes a global sovereign governance, which answers its crises either through pure theological racial suspicion, or through a logic of essentially humanitarian rule and exceptional misdemeanor. Such a citizen-subject – one that has dominated models of propaganda analysis and models of communicating in the public interest – is critical to the linking of knowledge, sanctioned ignorance, and imperial-theological power based on an unquestioned logic of nationalism. This citizen, living under the political eternity of the shining sun and blue skies, is dangerous because they deny blue skies and shining sun, or rather, full political subjectivity and citizenship, to the victims of sovereign power. The specter of the knowing U.S. citizen who may save the world from the militaristic U.S. citizen is a deeply nationalistic fiction that misses the logic of sovereign power, and the normalizing of the state of exception; just as the Christian who will edify the corrections officer is a fiction that excludes the rest of the world as critical mediators of our global policies.

Wartime media has made phenomenal advances and wartime media scholarship now has much productive work ahead. In the preceding pages, I have sought to show how the knowing/unknowing citizen who forms a part of the epistemological underpinning of "communication in the public interest" is a problematic assumption. Inherent in this model of civilized citizenship is the privileging of national consciousness, the subject that can potentially move from ignorant to informed political actor. The ever-deferred moment of political awakening also buries in its epistemological cover the "everyday" sovereign power of the empire, when "doing the job" in a state of exception can normalize even the borderline cases of the exception. The knowing-yet-unknowing citizen as governmental fiction, or as the yet-to-be-awakened subject of propaganda critique, also poses another danger. How can we challenge the new world order with theoretical orientations that operate exclusively within a nationalist framework; in which all authority of constituting power is vested with the citizen-subject of any nation: in this case, that of the U.S.? The centrality granted to the civilized citizen of the empire-masquerading-as-nation is at the cost of political subjectivity to the citizens of the world (including the U.S.) who challenge the sovereign power to wage wars without accountability. This is evident from the way that Abu Ghraib, as norm and exception, was considered America's problem as nation, not as an international issue. Moreover, media analyses that reproduce the nationalist subject of propaganda run the risk of repeating the same communication model of analyses for the brown populations of Vietnam, Panama, Indonesia, Korea, and Iraq. At this point, the question returns to the original paradox of the unknown unknown: the very (im)possibility of knowing the Other through the framework of civilized citizenship.

In conclusion, one could ask: is not anti-imperial citizenship, even within "America" as territory, fashioned by lives and bodies outside "America" as nation? Is not the political subjectivity of anti-imperial citizenship fashioned by the mutilation of bodies and extinction of lives in the non-American world, as in Iraq, Panama, Korea, and Vietnam? Rather than silently rest on the epistemological assumption of a potential national consciousness, perhaps we could begin to record the speech of the citizen who knows no national boundaries. To quote Margaret Blank, mother of Spc Joseph Darby who passed on the Abu Ghraib photographs to his superior officer: "It was really hard on him," said Margaret Blank, Darby's mother. "He didn't want to go against ... his troops. It cut him in half, but he said he could not stand the atrocities that he had stumbled upon. He said he kept thinking, 'What if that was my mom, my grandmother, my brother or my wife?'" (Spc. Joseph Darby 2004). [3] The citizenship that Darby claimed is not based on the civilizational premise of traveling from neoliberal private to neoliberal public interest. Such a citizenship cannot be located within narrow, state-carved territorial boundaries, or those tied down to nationalist consciousness, but instead claims fellow-citizens wherever the empire stretches. Perhaps one day, then, we can say, with and against Graner: The sun is shining, the sky is blue…

Notes

[1] [Note from the editor:] As the author died in 2013, this chapter has not been altered. I want to thank Sujata Moorti for establishing the connection with Usha's family, and Ajit Zacharias for patiently helping me to gather all information I needed.

[2] In my analysis, I primarily include network news archives accessed from the Internet archives of CBS, ABC, NBC, and CNN, over the course of May 2004 – May 2005, as well as direct monitoring of ABC World News and CNN during May 2004.

[3] Although Darby's words do not appear to have a religious resonance, his mother clearly saw his actions as part of the battle of good and evil, as seen in her words when Darby was chosen by ABC World News as one of the "People of the Year,": "I said, 'Your picture is on the paper,' and I said, 'Honey, I'm so proud of you because you did the good thing and good always triumphs over evil, and the truth will always set you free.'"
http://abcnews.go.com/WNT/PersonOfWeek/story?id=365920&page=1.

Works Cited

Agamben, Giorgio. 1995. Homo sacer. Sovereign power and bare life. Stanford, CA: Stanford University Press.

Arendt, Hannah. 1994/1963. Eichmann in Jerusalem. A report on the banality of evil. New York, NY: Penguin.

Asen, Robert. 2004. A discourse theory of citizenship. Quarterly Journal of Speech 90: 189-211.

Balibar, Etienne. 2003. We, the people of Europe? Reflections on transnational citizenship. Princeton, NJ: Princeton University Press.

Barnhurst, Kevin G., and Wartella, Ellen. 1998. Young citizens, American TV newscasts, and the collective memory. Critical Studies in Mass Communication 15: 279-305.

Beaumont, Peter. 2005. Abu Ghraib abuse firms are rewarded, The Observer, January 16.

http://observer.guardian.co.uk/print/0,3858,5104379-102275,00.html (accessed January 17, 2005).

Biesecker, Barbara A. 1998. By way of a long and circuitous route. Propaganda and democracy and/as a lesson in effective history. Critical Studies in Media Communication 15: 450-453.

Booth, Jenny. 2005, Torture? Not if cheerleaders do it, claims lawyer. Times Online, January 10. http://www.timesonline.co.uk/article/0,,7374-1434680,00.html (accessed May 24, 2006).

Bostdorff, Denise M. 2003. George W. Bush's post-September 11 rhetoric of covenant renewal: upholding the faith of the greatest generation. Quarterly Journal of Speech 89: 293-319.

Bush: abuse was "stain" on U.S. 2004. CBS/Associated Press, May 8. http://www.cbsnews.com/stories/2004/05/09/iraq/main616392.shtml (accessed January 17, 2005).

Bush: I have never ordered torture. 2004. CNN, June 23. http://edition.cnn.com/2004/ALLPOLITICS/06/22/prisoner.memos/index.htmlCNN (accessed May 24, 2006).

Bush: prison scandal will not deter U.S. forces. 2004. CNN, May 8. http://www.cnn.com/2004/ALLPOLITICS/05/08/radio.addresses.ap (accessed January 17, 2005).

Cammaerts, Bart, and Van Audenhove, Leo. 2005. Online political debate, unbounded citizenship, and the problematic nature of the transnational public sphere. Political Communication 22: 179-196.

CBS Wins Peabody for Abu Ghraib Report. 2004. MSNBC, April 13. http://www.msnbc.msn.com/id/7418881 (accessed May 17, 2006).

Chomsky, Noam. 2003. Iraq as trial run. Interview with V. K. Ramachandran. Frontline http://www.frontlineonnet.com/fl2007/stories/20030411005701000.htm (accessed October 17, 2005).

Coe, Kevin, Domke, David, Graham, Erica S., John, Sue L., and Pickard, Victor W. 2004. No shades of gray. The binary discourse of George W. Bush and an echoing press. Journal of Communication 54: 234-252.

Danner, Mark. 2004. Torture and Truth. America, Abu Ghraib, and the War on Terror. New York Review of Books, June 10.

—. 2005. We are all torturers now, The New York Times, January 6. http://www.markdanner.com/nyt/010605_torturers.htm (accessed January 17, 2005).

Foucault, Michel. 1972. Power/knowledge: selected interviews and other writings, 1972-1977. New York: Pantheon Books.

Gunn, Joshua. 2004. The rhetoric of exorcism. George W. Bush and the return of political demonology. Western Journal of Communication 68: 1-23.

Herman, Edward, and Chomsky, Noam. 1988. Manufacturing consent. The political economy of the mass media. New York: Pantheon Books.

Kellner, Douglas. 1992. The Persian Gulf TV war. Boulder, CO: Westview Press.

—. 2004. The Media and the Crisis of Democracy in the Age of Bush-2. Communication & Critical/Cultural Studies 1: 29-58.

Lewis, Justin, Maxwell, Richard, and Miller, Toby. 2002. 9-11. Editorial. Television and New Media 3:125-131.

Lule, Jack. 2002. Myth and terror on the editorial page. The New York Times responds to September 11, 2001. Journalism and Mass Communication Quarterly 79(2): 275-293.

McChesney, Robert. 2002. The zillionth time as tragedy. Television and New Media 3: 133-137.

Merskin, Debra. 2003. The construction of Arabs as enemies: post September 11 discourse of George W. Bush. Mass Communication and Society 7: 157-175.

Miller, Toby. 1983. The well-tempered self. Citizenship, culture, and the postmodern subject. Baltimore, MD: Johns Hopkins University Press.

Murphy, Troy A. 2003. Romantic democracy and the rhetoric of heroic citizenship. Communication Quarterly 51: 192-208.

Neilson, Brett. 2002. Bodies of protest: performing citizenship at the 2000 Olympic games. Continuum: Journal of Media and Cultural Studies 16: 13-25.

Ong, Aihwa. 1999. Flexible citizenship. The cultural logics of transnationality. Durham, NC: Duke University Press.

Opening statements Monday in Abu Ghraib trial. 2005. CNN, January 10. http://edition.cnn.com/2005/LAW/01/09/prisoner.abuse.graner.ap/ (accessed January 17, 2005).

Rummy rant wins dubious honor. 2003. Associated Press, December 2. http://www.cbsnews.com/stories/2003/12/02/world/main586352.shtml (accessed January 17, 2005).

Rumsfeld testifies before Senate Armed Services Committee. 2004. The Washington Post, May 7. http://www.washingtonpost.com/ac2/wp-dyn/A8575-2004May7 (accessed January 17, 2005).

Rumsfeld visits Iraq's Abu Ghraib prison. 2004. CNN, May 13. http://www.cnn.com/2004/WORLD/meast/05/13/iraq.abuse (accessed January 17, 2005).

Rush: MPs Just "Blowing Off Steam". 2004. CBS, May 6.

http://www.cbsnews.com/stories/2004/05/06/opinion/meyer/printable6
    16021.shtml (accessed January 17, 2005).
Said, Edward. 1979. Orientalism. New York: Vintage Books.
Sassen, Saskia. 2003. The repositioning of citizenship: emergent subjects
    and spaces for politics. CR: The New Centennial Review 3: 41-66.
Secretary Rumsfeld press conference at NATO headquarters, Brussels,
    Belgium. 2002, June 6. United States Department of Defense news
    transcript of press conference.
    http://www.defense.gov/transcripts/2002/t06062002_t0606sd.html
    (accessed January 17, 2005).
Seymour Hersh: Iraq moving towards open civil war. 2005. Democracy
    Now, May 11.
    http://www.democracynow.org/article.pl?sid=05/05/11/142250
    (accessed May 24, 2005).
Shah, Hemant. 1999. Race, nation and citizenship. Asian Indians and the
    idea of whiteness in the U.S. press, 1906-1923. Howard Journal of
    Communication 10: 249-267.
She's no stranger to grisly images. 2004. CBS, May 10.
    http://www.cbsnews.com/stories/2004/05/10/iraq/main616584.shtml
    (accessed January 17, 2005).
Shohat, Ella, and Stam, Robert. 1994. Unthinking Eurocentrism.
    Multiculturalism and the Media. London and New York: Routledge.
Sontag, Susan. 2004. The photographs are us. Regarding the torture of
    others. New York Times Magazine. May 24.
    http://www.donswaim.com/nytimes.sontag.html (accessed May 17,
    2006).
Spc. Joseph Darby, Iraq prison whistle-blower, followed his conscience.
    2004. ABC, May 7.
    http://abcnews.go.com/WNT/PersonOfWeek/story?id=131827&page=
    1 (accessed January 17, 2005).
Tanner, Adam. 2005. Iraqi victims to testify in Texas Abu Ghraib trial.
    Reuters, January 11.
    http://www.reuters.com/newsArticle.jhtml?type=domesticNews&story
    ID=7292408 (accessed January 17, 2005).
Tapia, Ruby C. 2005. Impregnating images. Visions of race, sex, and
    citizenship in California's teen pregnancy prevention campaign.
    Feminist Media Studies 5: 7-22.
The pictures: Lynndie England. 60 Minutes II.
    http://www.cbsnews.com/stories/2004/05/12/60II/main617121.shtml
    (accessed May 24, 2006).

Watson, Roland. 2005. "Laughing torturer" of Abu Ghraib. The Times Online, January 12. http://www.timesonline.co.uk/article/0,,7374-1436280,00.html (accessed January 17, 2005).

Zaeske, Susan. 2002. Signatures of citizenship: the rhetoric of women's anti-slavery petitions. Quarterly Journal of Speech 88: 147-168.

Zernike, Kate. 2005. Army Reservist's Defense Rests in Abu Ghraib Abuse Case, The New York Times, January 14. Lexis Nexis.

Žižek, Slavoj. 1997. A Leftist Plea for Eurocentrism. Critical Inquiry 24: 988-1009.

—. 2002. Welcome to the Desert of the Real. London and New York: Verso.

—. 2003. "Manufacturing Empire," plenary session, Rethinking Marxism, fifth international conference, University of Massachusetts at Amherst, Massachusetts, November 8, 2003.

—. 2004. Iraq: the Borrowed Kettle. London and New York: Verso.

TORTURE:
ALIBI AND ARCHETYPE IN U.S. NEWS
AND LEGAL WRITING SINCE 2001[1]

STEPHANIE ATHEY

Introduction

Ehab Elmaghraby, a New York restaurant owner and a Muslim immigrant who had lived in the U.S. for 13 years, was apprehended along with hundreds of Muslim and Arab immigrants in the days after September 11, 2001. He was held in the Metropolitan Detention Center of Brooklyn, New York, and he was among many who, after nearly a year in detention, were charged only with financial crimes unrelated to terrorism. He was jailed until 2003 and finally deported. Elmaghraby and fellow inmate Jvail Iqbal filed suit against the U.S. government. Among other things, they charged they were subjected to kicking and punching until they bled and "multiple unnecessary body-cavity searches, including one in which correction officers inserted a flashlight into [Elmaghraby's] rectum, making him bleed" (Bernstein 2006). Theirs was not an isolated case. A Department of Justice review later denounced assaults at the Brooklyn facility during that period, many of them caught on videotape. The Inspector General's 2003 report on the detention center found "widespread abuse of noncitizen detainees." On February 28, 2006, the *New York Times* announced that the U.S. government agreed to pay $300,000 to settle with Elmaghraby.

Rape in detention by corrections officers, described in the *New York Times* as an unnecessary body-cavity search, qualifies as state torture according to the United Nations Convention against Torture. Torture involves acts by agents of the state or persons who with acquiescence, consent or instigation by the state inflict severe pain or suffering, whether physical or mental, on persons in custody. Rape is a routine form of torture, and historically, a "search" is a common alibi for rape. And yet, though a rape in a New York detention center by corrections officers falls well within the definition of state torture, the location, perpetrators, and act itself place it in a universe of similar violations that the United States is accustomed to recognize as "police brutality" or abuse rather than "torture." The use of one term instead of another is more than a matter of euphemism or careful language crafted to evade prosecution. It is also indicative of how U.S. citizens imagine torture, what they have come to believe torture is and what it is not.

Ehab Elmaghraby and Jvail Iqbal and hundreds of other immigrant men rounded up in the first weeks of September 2001 were among the first "war on terror" detainees. They were held in Brooklyn, before detention camps were established in Afghanistan, Guantánamo and beyond, before Iraq. They were among the first to understand that with respect to torture, however "new" or unprecedented this war might be, it would build on old routines of detention and suppression.

I want to use three aspects of Elmaghraby's ordeal to draw attention to key arguments of this chapter. The chapter first considers an archetypal representation of "torture" circulating widely in news and legal argument since 9/11. The unquestioned status and prevalence of this archetype in arguments both for and against the use of torture, I argue, has closed off inquiry into the social nature of torture and its historical continuity. It has helped to limit public understanding and promote a misrecognition of torture, past and present. While Elmaghraby's torture, for instance, meets the UN definition of torture, it falls outside of the circle defined by this archetypal instance. I highlight the representation of torture in these speculative news and legal arguments, examining the archetypal encounter between interrogator and victim that has become iconic, defining and limiting our understanding of torture, terrorist, and terror through its very repetition. Though this iconic depiction is far afield from, say, torture events at Abu Ghraib prison in Iraq or the circumstances alleged in the cases of the 45 men confirmed or suspected to have been murdered in U.S. military custody (Mazzetti 2005), it has been and continues to be mobilized routinely in news writing.[2] This archetype functions, even in nuanced rejections of torture, to narrow our understanding of the systemic and communal nature of torture and to disconnect torture from its history of use in the U.S.: the use of torture in lynching and internal racial repression; its use in U.S. colonial wars and counter-insurgency programs in cold war client states; and its use in policing contexts and prisons. These three lines of American descent are visible in the torture methods at issue in the war on terror today.

The first argument, therefore, details and traces the archetypal view of "torture" found in recent news and law suggesting ways it limits understanding and recognition of "torture," past and present. The second argument concerns the interplay between archetype and alibi, focusing in particular on one official alibi for torture that has proven very effective. More than a justification or rationalization offered before or after the fact, an alibi is often encoded in the very act of torture as one of its necessary elements. The flashlight used in Ehab Elmaghraby's torture is an instructive example of this. Aside from its ability to create pain, humiliation and injury, the flashlight plays another strategic role. A flashlight is a common – and often easily available – tool for use in a "search," and it bears a common sense association with the act of searching. Therefore, when a flashlight is used to rape, it also enacts the alibi in symbolic form; it is simultaneously a tool of torture and a powerful tool of misdirection.

Scholar Elaine Scarry (1985) produced a foundational text in the study of trauma in the 1980s, a treatise on the practice of torture and the symbolic language of pain. Her work has often been made to represent a position from in which language and traumatic violence are opposed, and the suffering of the traumatized individual is relegated to silence and inexpressibility or elevated to the point where the "individual suffering" of torture draws a level of empathy and activism not directed toward purportedly broader institutionalized forms of violence (Dawes 2005; Moyn 2013). However, her work is not so easily compatible with the former readings, and those who indict her for the latter fail to see how that equation of torture with "individual suffering" is a deeper problem of cultural imagination that mars their own work. Here it is apt to point to ways her work suggests why torture and trauma become the occasion for an outpouring of multiple, conflicting narratives as perpetrators, victims and advocates contend over the exact meaning of trauma and the political significance and consequence of pain.

Drawing heavily on Amnesty International documentation from 1975-80 recording torture in Greece, South Vietnam, Brazil, and the Philippines, *The Body in Pain* underscored the theatrical and representational core of torture. The calculated display of weapons, wounds, and techniques to the prisoner, his or her family, or the public, the theatrical rituals of interrogation that accompany physical pain, all these are common symbolic elements and all are important to torture's ends. For Scarry, torture is itself a ritualized language, a system of signs, producing pain and this kind of calculated symbolic content. Those symbols can be made, on the one hand, to tell a story of the torturer's power. On the other hand, they can be made to point to the suffering human body, isolated and destroyed by pain. While Scarry's narrative promotes the latter, torturers promote the former. From the ritual and symbol of torture, they weave a story that ultimately, "converts pain into the fiction of the torturer's power."

Ironically and necessarily, that fiction of power always conveys vulnerability as well. The victims, though in custody, are made to represent an immediate and overwhelming threat to state power. And the state's vulnerability justifies a further display and extension of state power.

In the ritualized language of torture, then, the flashlight is both a visual and conceptual prop, an aspect of the symbolic structure of Elmaghraby's torture. It violates the prisoner but signals the converse, the prisoner's latent violence, the weapon or secret contained in his anus. Armed with a flashlight, the perpetrators may appear as if they truly are committed to nothing more than an especially diligent, thorough technique for searching the body, for seeking out Elmaghraby's violent potential. Perhaps, one might argue, out of an excess of zealousness or professionalism, the "search" went "too far." The flashlight rape offers a clear example of the way in which the very tools, rituals and methods of torture establish their own alibi. While such an alibi may not be so effective as to make torture acceptable, it can serve to misconstrue and rename it. Indeed, that the *New York Times* categorized the rape as an "unnecessary body cavity search" goes a long way to proving this point.

Like the flashlight, the torture alibi is an important and integral part of the performance; it helps accomplish the act. Writing on genocide and other atrocities, Stanley Cohen (2008) has argued that the rationales and rhetoric of denial precede the violence and prepare the way for it. In a similar way, but one harder to see, certain symbolic props and rituals lay the groundwork for torture (but do not in themselves cause it). Simply by being associated with questioning or searching prisoners (e.g. an interrogation booth, a flashlight), these props consistently invoke "interrogation" as the alibi where torture and assault were likely or intended. In 1985, Elaine Scarry articulated "intelligence gathering" or "interrogation" as a powerful false motive for torture. That false motive, she wrote, was an alibi integrated into torture practice at the very level we have been describing. For Scarry, pain accompanied by ritual questioning is a specific type of torture, not a specific type of questioning. It is domination meant to break the prisoners' ties to language, to society, to reality, the better to enlarge state power. The "torture debate" has in no way really tested that alibi of "interrogation," and the archetype further anchors our thinking to it.

The third and final argument of the chapter holds that just as the archetype reinforces the alibi, the archetype also complements a common assertion that recurs throughout the torture debate: that torture is a new and possibly necessary tool in the U.S. arsenal against terror. All sides in the U.S. torture debate have routinely asserted or implied that torture is something alien to the contemporary U.S., not something thoroughly integrated into police work, domestic systems of punishment, or international security relationships (see Rejali 2003, 2007; Human Rights Clinic 2006; Dayan 2007, 2013). No new doctrine, or legal memos, Executive Orders, or Defense Department protocols were necessary to initiate the torture of Elmaghraby or the other men who suffered from "widespread abuse of noncitizen detainees" in September of 2001.

Speculation on torture

As a possibility and practice, torture has been proposed and discussed in the U.S. press since September 2001, first emerging in mid-September in news I call "speculative" as opposed to "investigative." Dozens of feature stories, news analyses, and commentaries debated the utility of torture in the war on terror in the pages of the *New York Times, Wall Street Journal, Washington Post, Newsweek, Time, Atlantic Monthly*, and *New Yorker*. Many features distinguish the speculative writing from investigative reporting, but just a few of the titles that appeared from September 2001 to the end of 2003 will illustrate this point: "How Far Americans Would Go to Fight Terror" - "Seeking a Moral Compass While Chasing Terrorists" - "Security Comes Before Liberty" - "Time to Think about Torture"- "Agonizing Over Torture: Can Deliberate Hurt Be Justified in Times of Terror?" - "No Tortured Dilemma" - "A Nasty Business"- "Should We Torture Qaeda Higher Ups?" - "Making Terrorists Talk: America Doesn't Use Torture to Get Information Out of Terrorists. Perhaps We Just Need to use the Magic Word: Mossad" - "Make Them Talk" - "Interrogation School—30 Techniques…Just Short of Torture; Do They Yield Much?" – "The Torturer's Apprentice" - "Torture, Tough or Lite: If a Terror Suspect Won't Talk, Should He Be Made To?" - "Psychology and Sometimes a Slap: The Man Who Made Prisoners Talk" - "The Dark Art of Interrogation: The Most Effective Way to Gather Intelligence and Thwart Terrorism Can also Be a Direct Route into Morally Repugnant Terrain. A Survey of the Landscape of Persuasion."

What are we to make of the speculative engine that began to turn as early as September 2001? Though scholars assert that modern democracies torture in secret (Asad 2003; Rejali 2007; McCoy 2012), it is clear that since 9/11, "torture" has circulated in the U.S. as a deliberately *open* secret.

Two things are important to note here. First, such speculative commentaries and features on torture have been prolific and sustained, gathering momentum *before* the November 2001 Executive Order on military tribunals signaled the scope of the U.S. administration's intentions toward captives, and they gained critical mass years before the 2004 photos from Abu Ghraib. That is to say, the speculative press was defining torture and imagining its uses well in advance of and alongside the classified torture memos and interrogation protocols quietly being drawn up inside the Executive Branch.

Second, hypothetical torture became a big news story during years when actual torture was not getting reported. It is striking that during the same period in which these speculations on torture occasioned lively response, indications and evidence that torture was already in use were met by near silence. Only a few, perhaps as few as six, investigative pieces in the same papers looked at brutal and illegal measures that characterized the actual practice of apprehending, handling, detaining, transferring or interrogating prisoners.[3] One of the first of the investigative looks at torture was a report on March 11, 2002 in the *Washington Post*, "U.S. Behind Secret Transfer of Terror Suspects." Journalists Rajiv Chandrasekaran and Peter Finn (2002) describe in some detail the cases of eight persons who had been subject to extralegal arrest and rendition to a third country. Their discussion of torture and U.S. responsibility is frank:

> The suspects have been taken to countries, including Egypt and Jordan, whose intelligence services have close ties to the CIA and where they can be subjected to interrogation tactics – including torture and threats to families – that are illegal in the United States, the sources said. In some cases, U.S. intelligence agents remain closely involved in the interrogation, the sources said. "After September 11, these sorts of movements have been occurring all the time," a U.S. diplomat said. "It allows us to get information from terrorists in a way we can't do on U.S. soil."

When the *Washington Post* returned to the topic nine months later, on December 26, 2002, they published a piece about treatment in U.S. custody entitled "U.S. Decries Abuse but Defends Interrogations; 'Stress and Duress' Tactics Used on Terrorism Suspects Held in Secret Overseas Facilities." Writers Dana Priest and Barton Gellman identified U.S. strategies of physical violence and sensory manipulation in custody as well as third-country rendition. The report did not assign the term torture to the detainee treatment it recorded, preferring to examine the term "torture" and to walk around the notion with great care.

This scant handful of early investigative reports bear all the elements of the broader story on U.S. torture that would consume the press after 2004, minus only the nudity, dogs, corpses, and of course the photos.

These early articles contained detailed observations and telling comments from government officials, but nevertheless they vanished without follow-up stories.

What is more, the government's own near-acknowledgement of torture in January of 2004 set off no storm of curiosity. A one-paragraph press release issued on January 16 indicated in colorless language that an investigation into detainee abuse at a "coalition facility" was under way. *The American Journalism Review* counted only four newspapers and three networks that offered cursory reports on the release (Ricchiardi 2004).

When CBS broadcast visual evidence of torture at Abu Ghraib prison in Iraq three months later, in late April of 2004, the investigative press was stirred to action and has since pursued a string of legal memos and executive protocols; it has parsed the language of international conventions and scrutinized arguments made in courts-martial. The press uncovered a trail of command documents that not only created the environment necessary for torture but also attempted to establish zones of impunity.

Obsessed as we have been with one paper trail, we have neglected to investigate another. The speculative news writing on torture has been broadly influential; it struck narrative postures, anointed experts, and lent terminology, propositions and anecdotal evidence that were taken up and repeated in other arenas. In circular fashion, the speculative pieces generated then echoed and publicized what has been termed "the torture debate" taking place in legal reviews and academic publishing throughout 2002, 2003 and beyond. And prevalent in that debate has been a single archetypal depiction of torture.

The torture archetype

Valuable studies of media, terror and violence have demonstrated the power of representational choices to shape public response (Nacos 2002, Taleb 2004, Seaton 2005; Flynn and Salek, 2012). This outpouring of speculative prose that debated torture's desirability has received no critical attention in studies of the media response to 9/11. Nor has it received extended comment in the press's own self-critical reflections on reporting following the Abu Ghraib revelations.

Yet there are patterns worthy of study. For instance, the speculative news writing can be sorted into three uneven groups to highlight common structures and approaches, namely, "Hypothetical," "Historical," and "Heart of Darkness" narratives. The "hypothetical" stories use imagined scenarios to pose the "should we or should we not" question to "specialists." The stories might elicit comment on a ticking time-bomb scenario, or they may discuss results of opinion surveys or student quizzes on torture.[4] The "historical" group ponders torture through two primary models. Not coincidentally, both are campaigns against Muslim populations: Israel's use of torture against Palestinians and France's use of torture against Algerians.[5] The third group of news speculation draws core elements from the "hypothetical" and "historical" stories, fusing them into a larger "Heart of Darkness" narrative. Here, a lone journalist sets forth to explore the practice and practitioners of torture. He exudes a calculated moral ambivalence and exhibits a powerful fascination with the torturer and his "dark arts," "hard questions," "unthinkable choices."[6]

Among many other things, these formulaic structures promote certain views of history, weighing the utility of "torture" by conflating quite distinct land-based occupations and anti-colonial struggles in Palestine and Algeria with a newer, specialized and Islamist strain of terrorist franchise. While ignoring the U.S. historical track record on torture, they strike narrative postures that promote the reader's identification with the would-be torturers, or with the protected citizenry, but not with the victims.

This last is critically important of course; speculative stories on torture must be weighed in light of the cultural and political work they do imagining and projecting a unified community that believes it has a stake in torture. While the most important aspect of these stories may be their attempt to fashion that community, I focus instead on a very simple but pervasive depiction of "torture" in news since 2001.

The depiction of torture in speculative news narratives is important not only because representation is central to the act of torture, but also because representation is central to the perpetuation of torture on a grand scale. Nobel prize-winning novelist James Coetzee (1986) once framed this problem as a moral dilemma; the artist and society must bear witness to torture but with care: "the true challenge is how not to play the game by the rules of the state." Tales of "the dark chamber" can easily assist the state by *spreading* trauma and terror or by infatuating readers with the torturer's power. Representation, in other words, is a moral problem with political consequences.

Writing in the context of torture and testimony in Latin American states, scholar Idelber Avelar notes that human rights documentation demonstrates again and again that representation is a fundamental component of torture. Yet it is narrative representation that concerns Avelar. Narrative in particular is suspect when it comes to torture. Victims rightly show a post-trauma resistance to language (Avelar 2001, 257). The experience of torture withholds a part of itself against the "insult" of interpretation. "The worst insult to the experience of the victims – what Primo Levi called 'the obscenity of interpretation' – [is] the rationalization and supposed comprehension of causes, experience and effects" (Avelar 2001, 260). The victim is rightly suspicious of narrative, since its very coherence and its cause-and-effect chronology all gesture toward meaning and order, betraying the disorder and nihilism of the victim's traumatic experience.

Narration is suspect as well because it opens the unique trauma of torture to simile and metaphor and the circuit of "common nouns": "The torturer's great victory is to define the language in which the atrocity will be named" (Avelar 2001, 262). And yet, because narrative is inescapable though suspect for these many reasons, Avelar argues that political and therapeutic confrontation with torture and trauma demand waging a collective and ongoing "war within language" over the naming of torture, its metaphors, its meaning, and, I would add, its archetypes.

As will become clear, a study in the prevalence of the torture archetype is not a study in trauma or its narrative expression: quite the contrary. While seeming to make "torture" visible, the archetype simultaneously suppresses the historical memory of torture's trauma and enables its perpetuation in the present.

The explicit features of this torture archetype in the speculative news narratives will seem immediately familiar, as if they were representational *prerequisites* that in themselves define torture. The first is a focus on specific *techniques*. The investigative pieces of course pursue these primarily: which techniques were authorized, which out of bounds, which are torture, which so-called "torture lite," etc. But the speculative writing on the utility of torture takes this focus on *technique* and implies its *staging*. The setting is an interrogation, a one-on-one encounter between the subject of questioning and a skilled, goal-oriented professional who inflicts calculated amounts of pain. The pain inflicted is managed by a technique that has a definite beginning and a specific duration, and the pain is produced in a controlled and incremental fashion (that is, one does not murder the subject outright nor begin with the most extreme pain).

Once the scene has been invoked, torture has been named, looked in the face, we know what it is made of, as in Jonathan Alter's 2001 piece, "Time to Think About Torture" or Peter Maas's 2003, "Torture Tough or Lite: If a Terror Suspect Won't Talk, Should He Be Made To?" The scene is so common, so iconic, that one element can imply another: the victim in "the fetid basement cell" or the technique or injury – "the teeth extracted," "limbs broken," can together invoke the torturer and his demands. In a historical piece such as Bruce Hoffman's "A Nasty Business," or a Heart of Darkness feature such as Mark Bowden's "The Dark Art of Interrogation," the struggle between potential torturer and subject is Manichean in tone and drives the structure of the report. The language lyricizes the torturer's dire world of urgency and ethical quandary or the victim's world of pain and isolation, or both.

The dual agonists of the iconic scenario obviously are underscored by the graphics that accompany these articles. The articles by Hoffman and Bowden, for instance, and most of the longer features, carry sidebar illustrations that suggest a single perpetrator – a long shadow leaning in through a cell door – or a single victim, wrists dangling from shackles or a man blindfolded and strapped to a chair beneath a bare light bulb, etc. While at times the news writing may use an example where a single victim is implicitly worked over by many perpetrators, these the story renders as a larger entity: "the Philippine police," or "Jordan." Not only is a team personified as a single entity, but the group nature of the event may be underplayed or erased through passive voice construction that accents the technique not the technicians: "teeth pulled," "limbs broken," etc.

Archetype in anti-torture scholarship

Much of the legal argument as well as the speculative news debating torture in the wake of 9/11 have defined "torture" implicitly through this archetypal interplay between interrogator and subject, torturer and victim. Indeed the "ticking time-bomb scenario," so prevalent in "torture debate" articles by and responding to Alan Dershowitz, Sanford Levinson, Richard Posner and the like, simply recombines features of the archetype. The scenario makes artful enhancements to the motives and circumstances in which the key figures meet. The archetype and the time-bomb, however, are not identical. While the time-bomb scenario recasts the archetype in order to justify torture, even those who reject torture and do so absolutely often portray "torture" in the iconic mold, imagining the same duo locked in the same elemental battle. The key difference is they cast their lot with the victim.

Early instances of this in the modern campaign to end torture are instructive. For instance, Amnesty International's groundbreaking 1973 campaign to abolish torture opened its appeal to the public with selections from a Turkish victim's testimony which closely followed this formula: an isolated victim, a torturer, an array of graphic techniques. Amnesty reassessed its representational strategy a decade later, incorporating an empowered spectator acting to prevent torture, but the point here is the power and recurrence of the archetypal representation of torture (Prokosch 1996).

Elaine Scarry's work in the 1980s drew on the full complexity of Amnesty documentation from the 1970s, not just the rhetoric of the opening appeal. In a fascinating and careful argument based on Amnesty reports as well as literary and philosophical sources, Scarry exposes "interrogation" as an alibi which plays an integral role in the theatrical pantomime of torture. And yet, for Scarry "the structure of torture" is the iconic scenario I have described, her analysis keeps torture structurally bound to the charade of interrogation and the archetypal depiction. Torture is "essentially a two-person event…premised on one-directional injuring" (Scarry 1985, 20). To better delineate its features, she lifts the players out of historical and cultural space and time: "Torture has a structure that is as narrow and consistent as its geographical incidence is widespread" (Scarry 1985, 19). "That structure entails the simultaneous and inseparable occurrence of three events which if described sequentially would occur in the following order: first, the infliction of physical pain; second, the objectification of the eight central attributes of pain, and third, the translation of those attributes into the insignia of the regime" (Scarry 1985, 19). For Scarry, the "one-directional injuring" of torture relies upon the symbolic rituals of "interrogation," but torture is not about eliciting speech and information. Instead it uses speech to reduce the victim's voice either to silence or to an echo of the interrogator's own. The pretense to interrogation is part of the ritual violence.

Defining torture, therefore, through this archetypal exchange between torturer and victim, Scarry concludes torture is an extreme limit, the "condensed case," the "absolute model" of destruction, more exemplary of total destruction than war. An attack on the self, the voice, and social world, torture reverses the process of creative labor, it is civilization deliberately unmade.

Scarry's *The Body in Pain* has been widely influential, and she is cited in one of the most provocative and thorough legal rebuttals to the contemporary, post-9/11, time-bomb debate. In an essay published in the *Virginia Law Review* in December 2005, David Luban (2006) persuasively unravels the time-bomb as a "jejeune" cheat, an "intellectual fraud". His piece offers historical range on attitudes toward cruelty in liberal democracy; he urges us to look away from the mesmerizing time-bomb toward the "torture lawyers of Washington" and the legal apparatus they have attempted to establish for state torture. His piece points to torture as a practice that would require social networks to sustain it, but ironically his understanding of torture keeps pulling him back to the narrow archetypal dyad. Why is torture more repugnant than killing or war? "The answer lies in the relationship between torturer and victim." Luban explains with a stress on the two-ness of torture:

> Torture aims, in other words, to strip away from its victim all the qualities of human dignity that liberalism prizes. It does this by the deliberate actions of a torturer, who inflicts pain one-on-one, up close and personal, in order to break the spirit of the victim – in other words, to tyrannize and dominate the victim. The relationship between them becomes a perverse parody of friendship and intimacy: intimacy transformed into its inverse image, where the torturer focuses on the victim's body with the intensity of a lover, except that every bit of that focus is bent [on] causing pain and tyrannizing the victim's spirit. At bottom all torture is rape, and all rape is tyranny (Luban 2006, 39).

Luban says, "Torture is a microcosm (raised to the highest level of intensity) of the tyrannical political relationships that liberalism hates the most" (Luban 2006, 39). For Scarry, then, torture is the inverse of civilization, human labor and creation, and for Luban, torture is the inverse of the liberal democratic social bond. For Columbia University law professor Jeremy Waldron, torture is the inverse of law itself. In his *Columbia Law Review* article of October 2005, Waldron argues that torture and its prohibition plays an "archetypal function" within law – by which he means a "background function." Torture is an image and exemplum, persistently embodying and communicating a vital standard. That is, torture is a form of brutal violation so fundamental that its prohibition is the basis of all legal prohibitions; it "expresses and epitomizes the spirit...of the entire legal enterprise." The prohibition is "vividly emblematic of our determination to sever the link between law and brutality, between law and terror, and the enterprise of breaking a person's will" (Waldron 2005, 53). As do Scarry and Luban, Waldron chooses examples that stress the interrogational setting of torture, and his language emphasizes the visual character and power of this legal archetype: the prohibition on torture "sums up or makes vivid to us," the point or purpose of law (Waldron 2005, 48).

Scarry, Luban and Waldron all reduce torture to this "basic structure," emblem, or model the better to enlarge it as a theory of pain and civilization, liberal democracy, or law. In warning against it, they lift the practice out of its historical, social, and institutional complexity and continuities. What is more, they install this image of torture as a threshold the U.S. has yet to cross: there is a before and an after to torture. For liberal democracy, permission to torture is a gateway to the new, a fall from innocence, a plunge into the unknown.

Looking beyond the archetype

Of course, all of these authors – journalists, academics and jurists – mobilize an image of "torture" that is already stylized, an image of interrogation, a one-on-one encounter, an archetype that has been presented repeatedly to the public in the news commentary since 2001. What is fascinating is how far afield this iconic depiction is from actual interrogation, let alone torture.

Even non-coercive questioning is not a one-on-one encounter. It involves questioners, translators, military guards, security contractors, and other observers. Nor is torture itself secluded, or a single identifiable act, or a one-on-one practice. Military investigations, military memoirs, detainee statements, and reporting details routinely indicate multiple persons at the scene of physical and psychological violence in custody. This is the case of course when group violence closely approximates recreation: the "High Five Paintball Club" of Camp Nama used prisoners for target practice (Schmitt 2006). Soldiers at Forward Operating Base Mercury in Iraq lined up to strike prisoners knees and shins with a baseball bat and also assembled human pyramids a la Abu Ghraib (Human Rights Watch 2005, Hirsch 2005). Groups of guards at Bagram used severely painful and eventually fatal kneeing in the thigh because they were amused to hear "Allah!" with each strike (Golden 2006).

The torture of sexual assault is also a group undertaking. Masquerading as a "security measure," it is a persistent feature of detention. Such was the case with those first detainees in the war on terror, men like Ehab Elmaghraby. This form of rape follows a pattern of anal "searches" reported by detainees freed from Guantánamo and confirmed by military personnel. They are deemed "unnecessary" because performed on men who had been under guard, their hands shackled far from the anus between "searches" (Rasul 2004,Yee 2005). Interrogator Chris Mackey writes that at Bagram, these "probes" were preceded by the shout "Cavity Search!" meant to further humiliate the individual and intimidate the group (Mackey 2004).

Some released detainees detail weeks and days of interminable "softening up" activities and the unpredictable, violent, and humiliating attentions of MPs to their daily needs – MPs who function in pairs and teams while escorting, "controlling," caging, feeding, attending and supervising prisoners' bathing and bathroom trips, or depriving them of the use of the facilities.

When torture poses as interrogation, it too is a group event. At Baghdad airport, several Navy SEALs and CIA "interrogated" homicide victim Manadel Al-Jamadi in "the Romper Room" "in a rough manner." When transferred to Abu Ghraib, two MPs, CIA officer Mark Swanner, and a translator worked together to lift and steady the battered prisoner into a "Palestinian hanging" position where he died.[7] Indeed the shackling, overhead or otherwise, as well as enforced standing and sleep deprivation, not to mention waterboarding or beatings, all require teamwork: to restrain, lift, position, or revive the prisoner to consciousness.

Challenging the archetype

These investigative news accounts and testimonials challenge the common archetype for torture in powerful ways. For one, isolating a technique, a moment, or "basic structure" that constitutes torture is difficult in these accounts. What is more, though the iconic scenario diverts our thinking from this fact, torture is a group dynamic and occurs in a context marked by complicated group dynamics (Staub 1995). These accounts exist because spectators are present. As soldiers and intelligence services observe prisoners, they also observe each other. Interrogator Chris Mackey, and military reports on "abuse" at Abu Ghraib by Taguba and Fey/Jones, all point to the mystique, envy and admiration with which the workers at Bagram or Abu Ghraib or Camp Nama watched the CIA or Special Operations personnel who moved among them. Electronic surveillance is an ever-present feature of the environment and is multilayered. At Camp Nama in Iraq, Special Ops personnel took care to watch their watchers, monitoring the e-mail and phone communications of their CIA or FBI colleagues (Schmitt 2006). James Yee (2005) remarks that soldiers at Guantánamo talked circumspectly about the semi-clandestine total surveillance environment, referring to the "secret squirrels" who could be watching and listening to a soldier's every move.

More intimate than electronic surveillance are the host of peers, colleagues, and supervisors involved at close range. Interrogator Mackey (2004), writing about his time at Bagram, describes the populated detention camp as a setting organized by rank, by clear division of labor, and by complex sets of mixed agendas. Professional identities are asserted and formed in the context of peer groups that can be cooperative and also always highly competitive. Groups are attuned to their impact on detainees and how that impact might impress each other and their commanders.

These workers are hyperaware of their own specialized task – scheduling, questioning, translating, report writing, report editing and transmission, but they also are hyperaware of negotiating roles among a hierarchy of players – including military police, and multiple contractors, service branches, and intelligence services. The time MPs or MIs spend with prisoners is anything but isolated. Workers respond to the close physical presence of co-workers and to the awareness of other nearby soldiers, civilians and other prisoners. The above examples of violence, detailed in investigative news and military reports, all took place in such communal contexts.

In the face of this it can only seem strange that so many speculative news features, legal and philosophical arguments for and against torture scrub from the scene all onlookers, co-participants, and captives, leaving only the dyad of torturer and tortured in place.

This dyadic view of power or suffering may be a habit of mind and argument borrowed from Western philosophy, Hegelian dialectics, or Enlightenment rhetorics of suffering (Boltanski 1999). A close look at torture debates over U.S. history however, indicates it is rather a deliberate construction produced in concert with an evolving twentieth century "national security imagination."[8] While the origins of this iconic and dyadic formulation are beyond the scope of this argument, discussion of the political and cultural consequences of this archetype are not. First, the archetype narrowly defines torture and encodes an alibi for torture in that very definition. The archetype anchors the definition of torture to the act of interrogation, limiting recognition and analysis of violence that comes in other varieties and settings. Second, despite all evidence to the contrary, the archetype and alibi promote a dubious understanding of torture as a "means" to a single purported "end." In doing so, the archetype forecloses consideration of the multiple functions and effects of torture, such as: securing power, authority, morale or communal identities through ritualized violence; marking out a particular political, racial, religious, ethnic or gender group for domination (by torture of representative members); ensuring allegiance or subjugation of broader populations through fear. Third, the archetype telegraphs a scenario that removes from consideration the institutions, social structures, and communal energies that support the practice. I will consider these three consequences beginning with the last.

Just as the "two-ness" of the archetypal duo closes down avenues of inquiry, simply reintroducing other players opens torture to different paths of analysis and political action. It may be clear that a dyadic view of the "basic structure" of torture does not make a chain of command basic to that structure, although torture certainly is embedded in a chain of command. In fact the dyad closes off from scrutiny all professional, political, social, and economic networks that support the activity. This includes erasure of the supply chain that manufactures and equips state personnel with, say, electric tasers in the first place – tasers like those used by four Special Ops men disciplined for burning captives at Camp Nama and like those exported to our rendition allies annually (Schmitt 2006). In 2003, in the midst of all the speculative debate on the utility of torture in the war on terror, a single story in *US News and World Report* noted more than 60 U.S. companies had obtained the annual approvals to export stun batons, stun guns, *thumb cuffs* and other devices to 39 countries known to torture dissidents (Knight 2003). The 2013 Annual Report to Congress from the Bureau that controls these devices indicated sales of items under the category of "Thumbcuffs, Leg Irons, Shackles" were allowed that year to restricted five nations: Georgia, Iraq, Moldova, the Russian Federation, and Tajikistan. These exports totaled $207,726 or 11.6% of the $1.7 million in exports documented in all Commerce Control List categories.[9] There are other devices, special and mundane, that come from somewhere at a profit: restraint chairs for forced feeding, the trained dogs, shackles, flexicuffs, goggles, hoods.

Torture requires a command structure and an infrastructure and supply chain. So it also requires group support. Torture may produce a fiction of state power, as Scarry has it, yet it produces as well a communal dynamic. Torture forges group or individual identities for perpetrators, supervisors, and bystanders. There is not only the semi-clandestine surveillance of soldiers' and civilians' activities to consider, but also the physical and psychological dynamics of small or large group participation, the camaraderie and energy of people together, responding to, performing for, competing with each other through violence. The "perverse parody of friendship and intimacy" Luban sees enacted in the limited, iconic exchange between a single torturer and a single victim must be revised in the light of this group participation. A view of the group calls attention to the real physical intimacy, energy and eroticism forged among spectators and perpetrators of sexual, psychological and physical violence.[10]

In the same way that perpetrators are not acting alone, victims are not simply or only "isolated in their pain," as Scarry and Luban have it.[11] Victims are assaulted together or forced to hear or witness the terror, trauma and shaming of others. To reorient our thinking and to reckon with torture as a communal assault on groups or aggregates obviously lays open to view the range of functions, effects and ends otherwise obscured by the archetypal depiction. That reorientation opens for consideration the relations between torture and racism, misogyny, religious persecution and other oppressions which have been enacted historically through torture but rendered absent from the "basic structure" of the archetype. The fact that the Abu Ghraib torture photos implied that spectators were anticipated and essential, was as profoundly disturbing to some as the corpses or brutalities depicted. That the Abu Ghraib tortures were community-building, identity-forging events, enacting, drawing or securing lines of racial, gender and religious division through forms of sexual and religious violence, this was captured in some of the writing in 2004 (Carby 2004, Feldman 2004, Sontag 2004, see also Bourke 2005; Cammaerts and Carpentier 2006). But this insight was fleeting and was not applied to torture in the general case. The dyadic view of torture was not remade to accommodate an understanding of torture as a communal rite. It is telling that when the crowded cell block of Abu Ghraib has been memorialized visually as "torture" on book jackets and elsewhere, it has been so through the silhouette of a single hooded man, not the group silhouette of human backs, buttocks and genitals exposed in a human pyramid or a masturbation circle of captives and captors.

Finally, to return to the first point on political and cultural consequences – the archetype's narrow definition of torture encodes its own alibi. Instead of bringing into view the multiple forms of torture and environments in which it takes place, its complex institutional and communal conditions of possibility and its breadth of impact, the archetype deliberately excises these, keeping torture bound to a scenario in which information-gathering is said to be its primary purpose and alibi.

Considering the power and prevalence of the archetype and its grip on the public imagination, perhaps only a momentous conceptual shift could prepare one to look beyond the "interrogation" alibi and fairly consider whether information-gathering is really at stake in torture at all. Reviewing investigative reports and testimonials on torture from the current conflict, it seems clear that torture is not linked necessarily or even primarily to the interrogation booth. To the contrary, some detainees have described actual questioning as a period of respite from the mental and physical violence of "care" in detention (e.g. Rasul 2004). What is more, no matter how far removed from the rituals and symbols of "interrogation," the alibi of "interrogation" persists. All treatment in detention no matter how violent or bizarre becomes a preparation for "interrogation" – so-called "softening up." Nothing occurs that does not in some way refer back to and support the alibi.

Detainee accounts, together with participant memoirs by military personnel and detainees, suggest that torture is not an isolatable "act" or "scene" but a larger more extensive condition, a mode of domination enacted through ritualized interaction and a deliberately transformed experience of time and space. This altered understanding of torture comes into view when reading survivor testimony across many periods and geographical locations, and when reviewing psychological and sociological documents on torture survivors and perpetrators. Nigel Rodley, former UN Special Rapporteur of the UN Commission on Human Rights on Questions Relevant to Torture, locates the origin of torture in detention, specifically, incommunicado detention prolonged for more than one day.

Nonetheless, news and legal scholarship persistently reinforce the mental link between the idea of torture and the pretense of information-gathering, even if only to point out, as does Jeremy Waldron, that it makes for lousy interrogation. Even when used to reject torture, the dyadic view has helped reinforce "intelligence-gathering" as the underlying goal and has continued to assert the interrogator's booth as the place where torture begins only to break free, "metastasize" or "run amok." We have lost Scarry's fundamental insight that this is a false motive, an integrated alibi. Torture masquerades as "interrogation" and has many other guises.

As argued by practitioners themselves, while questioning might devolve into physical and mental assault, it ceases to be effective questioning at precisely that point. It becomes merely assault. Ritual questioning may continue during assaults in order to reinforce the alibi and the personal humiliations. Abusive "questioning" while beating or freezing or hanging or drowning a prisoner is no more related to "information-gathering" than a flashlight in the anus is related to a "search." Questioning prisoners for information is a separate undertaking, requiring different skills (Alexander 2011; Soufan 2011).[12]

In the larger institutional sense, physical and mental violence actually undermines information-gathering. Darius Rejali (2003, 2007) repeatedly makes the point that torture saps energy and resources from modes of investigation that collect, follow and develop information. In his terms, reliance on torture actually "de-skills" the intelligence or police service that uses it. It also completely erodes and destabilizes the justice system from top to bottom, as has been demonstrated so painfully over so many decades in the case of Jon Burge, his accomplices, Cook County, Illinois, and the city of Chicago.[13] In the U.S. national security context one can easily see that the necessary debates over "intelligence-gathering" through torture have taken precedence over valid but neglected intelligence-gathering challenges – e.g. hiring, training and retaining translators, or designing and bringing on-line data management software with adequate search capacity for the FBI. Ten years after 9/11 exposed this fundamental failure in the U.S. intelligence service, the heralded connect-the-dot ware had been not only frequently derailed, but it also failed numerous tests, skyrocketed to over $501 million, and was still not in place (Eggan 2006; Miller 2009; Perera 2012).

Conclusion

Too often in the speculative torture debate, one's willingness to face the "hard questions" and one's commitment to homeland protection have been measured in one's willingness to commit violence, instead of, say, one's willingness to improve investigation. The latter requires willingness to wage battle within a nation's bureaucracies, restructuring Washington's pathways of money and power. One could argue that far "harder" than deciding to torture suspected terrorists is the task of devising and implementing faster and more effective institutional routines for identifying and tracking terror cells; detecting the flows of funding, ammunitions, technology and data that support terrorists; collecting, translating and analyzing relevant communications; projecting possible terror scenarios and devising and funding new policy or practices to prevent those scenarios; and doing all this with speed and accuracy. The archetypal presentation of torture not only narrows our recognition and understanding of torture, but also our understanding of neglected but necessary intelligence-gathering tasks.

One urgent conclusion is that our thinking and discussion about torture needs to move much further out from under the shadow of the interrogator's booth and the spell of the archetype if we are to contend with the many varieties of torture and torture's multiple functions and effects. Idelbar Avelar (2004) suggests we think of torture as *ubiquitous*, instead of an *accident* or *excess*. Put in other terms, having declared a state of war on a racialized, global enemy, violence is the rule of engagement; it is the *medium* of contact. Interrogational-torture is but one ritualized and self-justifying form of that ubiquitous violence. Torture may occur in the interrogation booth, but it does not emanate from it. More critical energy needs to attack the false link between interrogation and torture.

Further, archetype and alibi not only confound the functions and effects of torture but also curtail responsibility for it. To remove suppliers, commanders, participants, multiple victims and spectators from our "basic" representation of torture closes off avenues of thought that lead to theories of complicity, and from these back to ourselves as news consumers, spectators and participants of the debate, not to mention ourselves as beneficiaries of the protection (or profit) said to be generated by the practice. Luc Boltanski's (1999) work on morality, media and politics argues that contemporary media shape positive moral and emotional response to suffering by mobilizing specific rhetorical forms, vignettes that "nourish the imagination and coordinate political response" across populations. The iconic representation of torture I have been discussing might be likened to one such vignette: it features a subject of suffering and an agent of pain, but removes the reflective spectator that Boltanski takes to be crucial in vignettes that enlist a political response. Ervin Staub (1995) has argued that entire societies prepare in advance to commit the violence of torture or genocide. The iconic image circulated in news and legal debate has been a powerful "vignette" on this order, at worst a form of preparation for violence, at best a dead-end for analytical thought and for political response to torture in all the ways I have suggested.

Finally, in its depiction of torture as an isolated exchange cut off from communal dynamics and a history of training, supervision, torture technology and supply, the archetype complements assertions that the use of torture in the U.S. war on terror augurs something exceptional and new. This contention is common among those who advocate torture's use; they depict torture as a new tool to fight "a new kind of war." It is common as well among those who reject torture; they hold that the Bush administration's attempts to legalize the practice signal a new era and bring us to the "gateway by which the demonic and depraved enter into public life" (Waldron 2006).

These persistent assertions are odd, almost absurd, in their neglect or willful denial of this nation's long and intimate history with the practice of torture. Some may certainly see the George W. Bush administration as distinct in its claim to sweeping war powers for the President; his signing statements on anti-torture legislation, supported by the legislature's October 2006 Military Commissions Act, empower the Executive to define and authorize torture at will. But consider: torture has always belonged to the state to define and deploy. We need not look far back in the *New York Times* to find reports of torture used against al-Qaeda suspects, for instance in 1995 and 2000 against World Trade Center and U.S. embassy bombing suspects respectively, who were tortured under the supervision of the FBI, not the CIA (Athey 2008).[14]

In this light it is indeed peculiar that the news writing I have discussed looks repeatedly to Israel and France for a torture track record, not to the U.S. in the Philippines, Latin America, or Vietnam. As with the made-in-America torture devices, we have deliberately practiced, developed and exported U.S. torture know-how for the whole of the twentieth century (Williams 2006; McCoy 2012).

Indeed torture's history of use in lynching and internal racial repression; its use in U.S. colonial wars and counter-insurgency programs in cold war client states; and its use in policing contexts and prisons form three lines of descent that are important for analyzing the practice as it is visible today, given, for example, the sexual, racial, and communal features common to lynching and now evident in the War on Terror prison camps. Since the 1950s, U.S. agencies have developed not only torture techniques, manuals and pedagogy, but also transnational torture relationships and routines of deniability, all of which are evident in current rendition practice. While in 2001 and 2002, journalists and jurists such as Alan Dershowitz purported to broach torture as an unspeakably new idea whose time was right, U.S. police torture was also in the news: Abner Louima's last assailant was being retried and sentenced, and John Conroy continued his lonely, dogged reporting on the ongoing, obstructed prosecution of Chicago's Area 2 police torture team, led by Jon Burge, who brought electroshock tactics from his tour in Vietnam and used them on numerous Chicagoans during the 1970s and 1980s (Conroy 2000, 2001, 2005). In this way, torture in the present reinvents and builds on torture of the past. Torture is not everywhere and always the same, of course. However, personnel, techniques, rituals, rhetorics and routines of denial or justification are passed on, borrowed and adapted for use in new contexts. It did not escape notice that Abu Ghraib's Charles Graner and Ivan Chip Frederick were seasoned guards in maximum security prisons bringing their expertise to bear in Iraq. No memo from the Secretary of Defense or the Office of Legal Counsel was necessary to initiate the flashlight rapes of 9/11 detainees at Brooklyn's Metropolitan Detention Center in September of 2001.

This all is to say that the representation, the imagining, of torture in speculative news and legal writing since 2001 has not only closed off the *social nature* of torture but also *its historical continuity*. Page Dubois (1991) would argue that torture is not a departure from democratic ideals, that it has been at the foundation of Western democratic life since classical Greece. U.S. history provides clear examples of torture as accomplice and tool of civilizing and democratizing efforts at home and abroad.

Despite this fact, a denial of torture's historical role can be communicated even in smart, powerful arguments against the practice. The legal arguments of David Luban and Jeremy Waldron are instructive in this way. Both write in late 2005 and acknowledge the horrors of Abu Ghraib in many ways, but both preserve the sense of newness surrounding the idea of torture in the torture debate. Torture is seen as an abomination that occasionally threatens to obtain legitimacy but one that is and must be suppressed through force of law. They also preserve the sense of state authorized torture as a threshold event, a point beyond which law collapses and a torture culture proliferates, tyranny abounds, and (as Scarry would put it) the world is unmade. In an important way their arguments situate the current debate itself as exceptional, something new in U.S. history, and a challenge to long held principles of law and belief.

In a strong example of this, Slavoj Žižek (2002, 104) has deplored the "torture debate" itself as a dangerous shift in fundamental assumptions:

> Such legitimization of torture as a topic of debate changes the background of ideological presuppositions and options much more radically than its outright advocacy: it changes the entire field while, without this change, outright advocacy remains an idiosyncratic view.

While on the one hand Luban or Waldron or Žižek nod toward torture events in the U.S. past, on the other they reinforce the belief that across that history, our ideological presuppositions have moved decidedly against torture and that torture has been progressively eliminated. As a result, its emergence now – in debate and in practice – is met as something new. My point is that when torture or the idea of torture is preserved or reinforced as something "new" in this way, an exception in the national narrative, torture will not be analyzed as the story of the U.S. past and a practice woven deeply into its cultural ideas about national identity, state power, punishment, and necessary violence. The historical continuities that exist within torture routines suggest we need to look more carefully for the ways certain fundamental "ideological presuppositions" have always been consistent with torture.

This is to say that, perhaps, when we claim liberal democracy has progressively prohibited torture, what we mean to say or ought to say is that we believe we have relegated its practice to certain spaces and client states, certain agencies or prisons, certain populations or "theaters of operation." In this sense, the U.S. has a dual history to consider with regard to torture: a long history of torture and, of equal importance, a long history of tolerance for it. The terms, metaphors and archetypes by which we imagine, define, and foreclose inquiry into torture are surely fundamental to that tolerance.

Notes

[1] I wish to thank Andy Nathan, Lisa Lynch and the Center for the Study of Human Rights at Columbia University for thoughtful comments and support in the development of this essay. Many thanks as well to all the members of the 2005 NEH Seminar on Human Rights in the Era of Globalization for their engaging conversations on the news archive, representation and human rights. The argument concerning the archetype first made here was substantially revised and reoriented around the topic of democracy and the human body, and developed accordingly to include legal arguments, detainee testimony and pop cultural elements of the debate occurring after the 2005 time frame examined here (Athey 2011).

[2] Between 2002 and 2009, at least 98 detainees died while in U.S. custody. According to the military, 34 are suspected or confirmed homicides. Human Rights First identified eleven more cases in which physical abuse or harsh detention resulted in death, bringing its total to forty-five suspected or confirmed homicides in custody. Human Rights First, "Torture: Quick Facts," www.humanrightsfirst.org/us_law/etn/misc/factsheet. (accessed December 7, 2009).

[3] Ricchiardi (2004) counted as few as six investigative pieces from 2001- April 2004 that looked at brutal and illegal measures used in handling US prisoners. See also, Umansky 2006.

[4] For quizzes and surveys, see Argetsinger 2001, McLaughlin 2001. Other pieces in the hypothetical vein are Blake 2001, Winik 2001, Alter 2001, Rutenberg 2001, Dolbee 2001, Bravin 2002, Kantorovich 2002, Maas 2003.

[5] See Chapman 2001, Hoffman 2002, Kaufman 2003, Bennett 2005, and Bowden 2003. In variations on this Israel-and-France pattern, Hoffman discusses potential US techniques in the war on terror in the context of the French campaign in Algeria, and the Sri Lankan's fight against the Muslim Tamil Tigers. Bowden discusses Israel and France and then reviews aspects of England's torture of IRA suspects in the 1970s. Historians have demonstrated the assumptions prevalent in this genre of speculative news are incorrect. Scholarship on France's use of torture in Algeria is representative of the news' departure from the data (Rejali 2007; Lazreg 2010; Hajjar 2011).

[6] E.g. Hoffman 2002. Also "Psychology and Sometimes a Slap," and Bowden 2003, Lelyveld 2005.

[7] With six broken ribs, he was left hanging from wrists shackled behind his back. The cause of death was asphyxiation, "as in a crucifixion," according to Dr. Michael Baden, chief forensic pathologist for the New York State Police. As a CIA official, Swanner has so far avoided penalty or prosecution (Mayer 2005).

[8] This argument is central to my book manuscript, Torture's Echo: Sponsoring violence through rituals of debate.

[9] U.S. Department of Commerce Bureau of Industry and Security: Annual Report to Congress for Fiscal Year 2013, pp. 53-69.

[10] Yee (2005) describes the rituals of the Initial Reaction Force (IRF) at Guantánamo, from initial huddles, chanting and "pumping up" prior to attack on a "resistant" detainee to the adrenalized high-fives and chest-to-chest body slams

afterward. One company exchanged attack counts at shift changes, "How many IRFings did you do today?" (Yee 2005, 71-73).
[11] "Torture isolates and privatizes." "The world of the man or woman in bad pain is a world without relationships or engagements, a world without an exterior. It is a world reduced to a point, a world that makes no sense and in which the human soul finds no home and no response" (Luban 2006, 39).
[12] This is not a fringe view among interrogation practitioners, and many spoke out repeatedly between 2001 and 2005. See Mackey 2004, and discussion by Michael Gelles, Navy Criminal Investigative Service, in Savage 2005. The CIA Kubark manual on intelligence says pain is counterproductive in interrogation, and FBI specialists hold that techniques other than pain, so-called abuse and coercion are likewise "ineffective, counterproductive and unlikely to produce reliable information." Boston Globe, February 25, 2005. See also Dodds 2004.
[13] John Conroy's writing brought the case of Chicago's Commander Jon Burge and the work of his police torture team from 1973 to light and he pursued it over decades of cover up. (Conroy 2000, 2001, 2005). Cook County, the city of Chicago, its numerous survivors and taxpayers have continued to pay a heavy price – financial, judicial and moral. In 2001 Governor George Ryan granted clemency to 163 men on death row because systemic torture and impunity had undermined all certainty attached to their trials and sentencing. He issued four pardons. In 2008 Burge was finally indicted and 7 other prisoners exonerated and released. Burge was sentenced to 4.5 years for perjury and obstruction of justice and collected his pension while in federal prison. In 2011 owing to the work of a survivor, two state legislatures and the Illinois Coalition against the Death Penalty, Illinois repealed the death penalty. Civil suits have named former Mayor Richard M. Daley, the one-time Cook County State's Attorney, a co-conspirator with Burge, and in 2011 a federal judge ruled allegations against Daley could go forward in the case of Michael Tillman. The city and county settled with Tillman for $6 million dollars the night before Daley was to be deposed (Taylor 2010).
[14] The torture of terrorist Abdul Hakim Murad in 1995 has since 9/11 been widely used to demonstrate "torture works," a contention that readily falls apart under scrutiny of his case. He was tortured in the Philippines with FBI collaboration (Athey 2007). In 2000, three of the four defendants brought to trial for the 1998 embassy bombings in Kenya and Tanzania argued they had signed confessions only after physical coercion (Weiser 2000; Weiser 2007; Athey 2007).

Works Cited

Alexander, Matther with John R. Bruning. 2011. How to Break and Terrorist: The U.S. Interrogator Who Used Brains, Not Brutality to Take Down the Deadliest Man. New York: St. Martin's Griffin.

Alter, Jonathan. 2001. Time to think about torture. Newsweek November 5, 45.

Argetsinger, Amy. 2001. At colleges, students are facing a big test. Washington Post September 17: B1.

Asad, Talal. 2003. Reflections on cruelty and torture. Formations of the secular. Palo Alto: Stanford University Press.

Athey, Stephanie. 2008. Reprint. The terrorist we torture: The tale of Abdul Hakim Murad. In On torture. Edited by Tom Hilde. Baltimore: Johns Hopkins University Press. Orinal publication, 2007. South Central Review 24(1): 73-90.

—. 2011. The Torture Device: Debate and Archetype. In Torture: Power, democracy and the human Body. Edited by Shampa Biswas and Zahi Zalloua. Seattle: University of Washington Press.

Avelar, Idelber. 2001. Five theses on torture. Journal of Latin American Cultural Studies 10(3): 253-271.

—. 2004. The letter of violence: Essays on narrative, ethics and politics. New York: Palgrave Macmillan.

Bennett, Drake. 2005. The war in the mind. Psychology and psychiatry have long had and uneasy relationship with the dark art of interrogation . But what, if anything, can psychologists and psychiatrists tell us about the effectiveness, and the effects, of coercive interrogations – and the moral questions they raise. Boston Globe November 27: K1, K5.

Bernstein, Nina. 2006. U.S. is settling detainee's suit in 9/11 sweep. New York Times February 28. http://www.nytimes.com.

Blake, John. 2001. Seeking a moral compass while chasing terrorists: How to react to enemies raises tough issues for people of faith. Atlanta Journal Constitution September 22, 1B.

Boltanski, Luc. 1999. Distant suffering: Media, morality, and politics. New York: Cambridge University Press.

Bourke, Joanna. 2005. Sexy snaps. Index on Censorship 1: 39-45.

Bowden, Mark. 2003. The dark art of interrogation. The most effective way to gather intelligence and thwart terrorism can also be a direct route into morally repugnant terrain. A survey of the landscape of persuasion. Atlantic Monthly October: 51-70.

Bravin, Jess. 2002. Interrogation school tells army recruits how grilling works – 30 techniques in 16 weeks, just short of torture; do they yield much? Wall Street Journal April 26: A1.

Cammaerts, Bart, and Carpentier, Nico. 2006. The Internet and the second Iraqi war: Extending participation and challenging mainstream journalism. Researching media, democracy and participation. Edited by Nico Carpentier, Pille Pruulmann-Venberfeldt, Kaarle

Nordenstreng, Maren Hartmann, Peeter Vihalemm and Bart Cammaerts. Tartu: University of Tartu Press.

Carby, Hazel. 2004. A strange and bitter crop: The spectacle of torture. 11 October. http://www.openDemocracy.net.

Chandrasekaran, Rajiv and Peter Finn. 2002. US behind secret transfer of terror suspects. Washington Post March 11: A1.

Chapman, Steve. 2001. No tortured dilemma. Washington Times November 5: A18.

Coetzee, James M. 1986. Into the dark chamber: The novelist and South Africa. New York Times Book Review January 12: 13.

Cohen, Stanley. 2008. States of denial: Knowing about atrocities and suffering. Reprint edition. Cambridge: Polity Press.

Conroy, John. 2000. Unspeakable acts, ordinary people: Dynamics of torture. New York: Knopf.

—. 2001. Annals of police torture: What price is freedom? Chicago Reader March 2: 1.

—. 2005. Tools of torture: Though he continues to deny it, Jon Burge tortured suspects while he was a Chicago police detective. Now his contemporaries from Vietnam reveal where he may have learned the tricks of his trade. Chicago Reader February 4: 1.

Convention against torture and other cruel, inhuman or degrading treatment or punishment. 2001. In 25+ human rights documents. New York: Columbia University Center for the Study of Human Rights: 71-79.

Dawes, James. 2005. The language of war: Literature and culture in the US from the Civil War to World War II. Cambridge: Harvard University Press.

Dayan, Colin. 2007. The story of cruel and unusual. Cambridge, Massachusetts: MIT Press.

—. 2013. The law is a white dog. How legal rituals make and unmake persons. Reprint edition. Princeton, New Jersey: Princeton University Press.

Dodds, Paisley. 2004. FBI letter alleged abuse. Boston Globe December 7: A1.

Dolbee, Sandi. 2001. Agonizing over torture: Can deliberate hurt be justified in times of terror? San Diego Union-Tribune November 23: D1.

DuBois, Page. 1991. Torture and truth. New York: Routledge.

Eggan, Dan, and Witte, Griff. 2006. The FBI's upgrade that wasn't: $170 million bought an unusable computer system. The Washington Post August 18: A1.

Feldman, Allen. 2004. Abu Ghraib: Ceremonies of nostalgia. 18 October. http://www.openDemocracy.com.

Flynn, Michael, and Salek, Fabiola (eds.) 2012. Screening torture: Media representations of the state of terror and political domination. New York: Columbia University Press.

Foley, John. 2012. FBIs Sentinel project: 5 lessons learned. Information Week. 2 August. http://www.informationweek.com/applications/fbis-sentinel-project-5-lessons-learned/d/d-id/1105637 (accessed July 28, 2014).

Golden, Tim. 2006. Years after two Afghans died, abuse case falters. New York Times February 13: A1, A11.

Hajjar, Lisa. 2010. Bagram: Obama's Gitmo. Middle East Research and Information Project 41(260). http://ns2.merip.org/mer/mer260/bagram-obamas-gitmo vol41/ 260 (accessed July 28, 2014).

Hirsch, Michael. 2005. Truth about torture: A courageous soldier and a determined senator demand clear standards. Newsweek November 7.

Human Rights Clinic of Columbia Law School. 2006. In the shadows of the war on terror: Persistent police brutality and abuse in the United States. A report prepared for the United Nations Human Rights Committee on the occasion of its review of the United States of America's second and third periodic report to the Human Rights Committee May.

Human Rights Watch. 2005. Leadership failure: Firsthand accounts of torture of Iraqi detainees by the US Army 82nd Airborne Division. http://www.hrw.org/en/reports/2005/09/22/leadership-failure (accessed August 2, 2014).

Hoffman, Bruce. 2002. Nasty business. Atlantic Monthly January: 49-52.

Kantorovich, E.V. 2002. Make them talk. Wall Street Journal June 18: A16.

Kaufman, Michael T. 2003. The world: Film studies: What does the Pentagon see in "Battle of Algiers"? New York Times September 7.

Knight, Danielle. 2003. Trade in tools of torture. US News and World Report November 24.

Kooijmans, Pieter H. 1995. Torturers and their masters. In The politics of pain: Torturers and their masters. Edited by Ronald Crelinsten and Alex P. Schmid, San Francisco: Westview Press: 13-17.

Lazreg, Marnia. 2010. Algeria as template: Torture and counterinsurgency war. Global Dialogue 12(1). http://worlddialogue.org/content.php?id=462 (accessed July 28, 2014.)

Lelyveld, Joseph. 2005. Interrogating ourselves. New York Times Magazine, June 12.

http://www.nytimes.com/2005/06/12/magazine/12TORTURE.html (accessed June 15, 2005).

Luban, David. 2006. Liberalism, torture and the ticking bomb. In The torture debate in America. Edited by Karen J. Greenberg. New York: Cambridge University Press: 35-83.

Maas, Peter. 2003. Torture, tough or lite. If a terror suspect won't talk, should he be made to? The New York Times, March 9, Week in Review, 4.

Mackey, Chris (pseudonym). 2004. Interrogator's war: Inside the secret war on Al Qaeda. Boston: Little Brown.

Mayer, Jane. 2005. A deadly interrogation. New Yorker November 15: 44.

Mazzetti, Mark. 2005. U.S. Army says prison deaths are homicides. Los Angeles Times March 26.

McCoy, Alfred W. 2012. Torture and impunity: The U.S. doctrine of coercive interrogation. Madison: University of Wisconsin Press.

McLaughlin, Abraham. 2001. How far Americans would go to fight terror. Christian Science Monitor November 14: 1.

Moyn, Sam. 2013. Torture and taboo: On Elaine Scarry - How the work of a literary critic became the proxy for our preoccupation with the horrors of torture. The Nation February 5 http://www.thenation.com/article/172677/torture-and-taboo-elaine-scarry (accessed July 28, 2014).

Nacos, Brigitte. 2002. Mass-mediated terrorism: The central role of the media in terrorism and counterterrorism. New York: Rowman and Littlefield.

Perera, David. 2012. Sentinel 'finished' but not complete: The system also cost the FBI more than it says, auditors say. FierceGovernmentIT. September 11. http://www.fiercegovernmentit.com/story/sentinel-finished-not-complete/2012-09-11 (accessed June 20, 2014).

Priest, Dana, and Gellman, Barton. 2002. U.S. decries abuse but defends interrogations; "Stress and duress" tactics used on terrorism suspects held in secret overseas facilities. Washington Post December 26: A1.

Prokosch, Eric. 1996. Amnesty International's anti-torture campaigns. In A glimpse of hell: Reports on torture worldwide. New York: Amnesty International/New York University: 26-35.

Psychology and sometimes a slap: The man who made prisoners talk. New York Times December 12, Section 4: 7.

Rasul, Shafiq, Iqbal, Asif, and Ahmed, Rhuhel. 2004. Detention in Afghanistan and Guantánamo Bay. Statement released August 4. http://humanrights.ucdavis.edu/resources/library/documents-and-reports/tipton_report.pdf (accessed August 3, 2014).

Rejali, Darius. 1994. Torture and modernity: Self, society and the state in modern Iran. San Francisco: Westview Press.

—. 2003. Modern torture as a civic marker: Solving a global anxiety with a new political technology. Journal of Human Rights 2(2): 153-171.

—. 2004. Torture's dark allure. Salon.com June 18.

__. 2007. Torture and Democracy. Princeton, New Jersey: Princeton University Press.

Ricchiardi, Sherry. 2004. Missed signals. American Journalism Review August-September.

Rodley, Nigel. 1995. Forward. The Politics of Pain. Torturers and Their Masters. Edited by Ronald Crelinsten and Alex P. Schmid, San Francisco: Westview Press: 13-17.

Rutenberg, Jim. 2001. Torture Seeps Into Discussion by News Media. New York Times November 5: C1.

Ryan, Jason. 2012. A decade and $451 million later: FBI computers just now working together. http://www.abc.go.news.com/Blotter/sentinel-decade-451m-fbi-computers-now-working/story?id+16904032 (accessed July 27, 2014).

Savage, Charlie. 2005. Split seen on interrogation techniques. Boston Globe March 31: A12.

Seaton, Jane. 2005. Carnage and the media. London: Allen Lane.

Scarry, Elaine. 1985. The body in pain: The making and unmaking of the world. New York: Oxford University Press.

Schmitt, Eric, and Marshall, Carolyn. 2006. In secret unit's "black room," a grim portrait of U.S. abuse, http://www.nytimes.com, March 19: 4.

Sontag, Susan. 2004. Regarding the torture of others. New York Times Magazine May 23.

Soufan, Ali H. 2011. The black banners: The inside story of 9/11 and the war against al-qaeda. New York: W.W. Norton.

Staub, Ervin. 1995. Torture: Psychological and cultural origins. In The politics of pain: torturers and their masters. Edited by Ronald Crelinsten and Alex P. Schmid, San Francisco: Westview Press: 99-112.

Taleb, Bashar A. 2004. The bewildered herd: Media coverage of international conflicts and public opinion. Lincoln, NE: iUniverse, Inc.

Taylor, Flint. 2013. Police torture and the death penalty in Illinois: Ten years later. The Nation January 11. http://www.thenation.com/article/172152/police-torture-and-death-penalty-illinois-ten-years-later (accessed June 28, 2014).

U.S. Department of Commerce Bureau of Industry and Security. 2014. The Bureau of Industry and Security annual report to Congress for fiscal year 2013. The Bureau of Industry and Security Web Site. http://www.bis.doc.gov/bis_annual_report_for_fiscal_year_2013_final _secretary_approved_jan_2014.pdf (accessed June 28, 2014).

Waldron, Jeremy. 2005. Torture and positive law: Jurisprudence for the White House. Columbia Law Review 105(6): 1681-1750.

—. 2006. Torture on trial: Morality, law and the utility of torture. Presentation at Columbia Law School, April 14.

Weiser, Benjamin. 2000. Asserting coercion, embassy bombing suspect tries to suppress statements. New York Times, July 13, B3.

—. 2001. US faces tough challenge to statements in terrorism case. New York Times, January 25, B3.

Williams, Kristian. 2006. American methods: Torture and the logic of domination. Cambridge, MA: South End Press.

Winik, Jay. 2001. Security comes before liberty. Wall Street Journal October 23: A26.

Umansky, Eric. 2006. Failures of imagination. Columbia Journalism Review September.

Yee, James. 2005. For God and country: Faith and patriotism under fire. New York: Public Affairs.

Žižek, Slavoj. 2002. From homo sucker to homo sacer. Welcome to the desert of the real. New York: Verso.

PART III:

TRAUMA AND MEMORY

NEWS IMAGES AS LIVED IMAGES: WITNESS, PERFORMANCE, AND THE U.S. FLAG AFTER 9/11[1]

GORDON COONFIELD

Something becomes real – to those who are elsewhere, following it as "news" – by being photographed.
—Sontag 2003, 21

A newspaper is not merely printed. It is circulated and read. Otherwise it is not a newspaper.
—Park 1960, 9

(N)ews is not information but drama. It does not describe the world but portrays an arena of dramatic forces and actions ...
—Carey 1988, 21

A people can become what they display.
—Conquergood 1983, 35

Introduction

This essay invites reflection on the relation between news images – those photographs sought, captured, selected, written about, printed, and distributed in the course of the news process – and cultural performances – those everyday "corporeal forms of reciprocally responsive expression" (Shotter 2002, 444) by which a people can "become what they display" (Conquergood 1983, 35). This essay considers this relation between news images and cultural performances in times of public trauma, when cataclysmic events challenge a cultural collective by calling into question the very conditions underlying its collectivity (Zelizer 2003). In taking up this task of reflection, this essay explores the potential for connecting media studies and performance studies on the interdisciplinary field of Cultural Studies. In order to give some traction to these reflections I want to begin with a story drawn from reportage concerning the U.S. flag.

Displaying the flag

On Monday, 10 September 2001, the Associated Press reported a squabble in the city of Amherst, Massachusetts, concerning the display of 29 U.S. flags in the downtown area. Town veterans agent Rod Raubeson, who had the flags displayed, did so intending to leave them in place from Labor Day in September through Veterans Day in November, and again from Patriots Day in April to Independence Day in July (a period totaling approximately 6 months). However, Town Manager Barry Del Castilho ordered the 29 flags removed from light poles along Main and Pleasant Streets. In a letter to Raubeson, Del Castilho explained displaying the flags on "special occasions" was fine, but the extended display seemed "a bit too much" (Amherst selectmen consider how many American flags 2001). That evening a town meeting was held on the issue. With more than 50 townsfolk in attendance, the Select Board voted to permit the 29 flags to be displayed, but agreed such displays should be restricted to six specific holidays: Patriots Day, Memorial Day, Flag Day, Bunker Hill Day, July 4, Labor Day and Veterans Day (Amherst selectmen limit downtown flags 2001).[2]

The afternoon of Tuesday, September 11, 2001, as the fires continued to burn at the Pentagon and at Ground Zero in New York, Select Board Chairman Carl Seppala helped re-display the 29 flags at half staff. He had voted with the majority against the "excessive" display of the flags the evening before, but in light of the infamous events that took place that morning he conjectured the flags would remain on display "for a very long time" (Attacks bring Quick End to the Dispute 2001).

The impulse to display the flag by Amherst officials was repeated on Main Streets in towns large and small throughout the U.S. (Szaniszlo 2001). Along with the famous Franklin photograph and an image of the flag covering the side of the Pentagon in Washington D.C., newspapers across the U.S. and around the world teemed with news images and reports concerning the U.S. flag. Flags displayed by officials on the usual flag poles at the usual local, state, and federal government locations – an ordinary occurrence – suddenly became newsworthy post-September 11. Newspapers reported and photographed the flag's being displayed over the New York Stock Exchange and the Pentagon, its being waved by everyone from the President at the ruins of the World Trade Center (WTC) at Ground Zero to teens and veterans at busy intersections; it was displayed in the windows of local businesses and private homes, on the trailers of semi trucks, car antennas, over fences, freeway overpasses, and construction sites, on the uniforms of professional athletes, and at entertainment events ranging from the New York City Opera to a Godsmack concert (Fallon and Clegg 2001; Szaniszlo 2001; Passers-by Applaud 2001; English 2001; Reide, Fish, and Read 2001; New Era 2001; Elber 2001; Blum 2001; Morris 2001). Even as the U.S. economy sputtered, the *Wall Street Journal* reported booming flag sales. As manufactures struggled to keep up with the deluge of demand and retailers ran out of anything bearing its famed colors (Achenbaum 2001; Reide, Fish, and Read 2001), local newspapers offered free, full-paged color reproductions which they urged their readers to display as a sign of patriotic fervor (Wickham 2001). It indeed seemed, as one headline put it, that the U.S. was binding its wounds in "red, white, and blue" (Bragg 2001).

Seppela's words were prophetic. Now, more than a decade later, the flag remains widely displayed in a manner that still visually insists we live in a post-September 11 world. Many acts of display continue to draw explicit connections between the flag, patriotic citizenship, and the events of September 11 (Fig. 8-1). As much as the Department of Homeland Security's color-coded threat levels, the U.S. flag is a key feature in the post-September 11 American visual landscape, one whose affective charge intensified in important ways in the aftermath of September 11. As photographer Jonathan Hyman put it, the flag became a potent element in a "new memorial vocabulary" (Hyman 2007).

The story of the flags' display in Amherst depicts the American cultural collective at a liminal moment in its history. On one side of this threshold, we find a sensible and reasonable call for decorum and restraint. The flag's display is constrained if not by laws then certainly by ritual rules and by a sense of decorum regarding the appropriate time and place, as well as sentiments about who should participate in such displays.[3] Except for a slow news day when any dispute will suffice, this incident would hardly seem newsworthy. On the other side of the threshold, the same flags and the same controversy come to participate in a conscious excess of display. The rules are loosened: anytime is the right time, any visible surface or conspicuous place is the right place, and it is not only appropriate but more or less expected that everyone considering themselves part of the collective will display a flag anywhere he or she can as a sign of a particular kind of belonging that we have dubbed "patriotism." The very decorum and restraint of the day before become conspicuously unpatriotic sensibilities. And the expression of such sentiments becomes profoundly newsworthy.

This story demonstrates the liminal nature of September 11 in the life of a collective and is thus an opportunity to think about what changed. It is also an opportunity to consider the relation between cultural performances like the displaying of the flag and the news images that made these displays a prominent element of the post-September 11 visual landscape. Of course numbers never tell the whole story, but according to a search of the LexisNexis U.S. news database, in the first 8 months of 2001 there were 933 mentions of the U.S. flag in newspapers from the four major regions of the U.S. The number more than doubled in the last 20 days of September, 2001. In the remaining months between September 11 and December 31, there were 4,060 mentions of the flag.[4] The post-September 11 run on U.S. flags and practically anything emblazoned with the flag or bearing its colors was also widely reported. An article in the *Boston Globe* reported sales of flags more than doubled from $40 million in 2000 to $100 million in 2002 (Kerber 2003). While the article reports a "leveling off" of consumer demand, the National Retailers Federation continues to report increasing percentages of Americans who say they own or plan to purchase flags and other patriotic merchandise each year.[5]

There are two very simple explanations for this massive upsurge in displays of the U.S. flag. First, one might conclude that news coverage simply reported on displays of the flag that were already occurring, and have been occurring for a long time before September 11. This explanation is unsatisfactory when we consider that news media actively encouraged such displays both in the tenor of their reportage and in their editorial exhortations to readers to display the full-page color images of the flag printed in their pages for that very purpose. Or one might conclude the reportage somehow simply caused the increase in displays, that Americans just mimicked what they saw in their news. This, too, seems unsatisfactory if we consider that many of the public displays of the flag – at the WTC site, over the Pentagon, and even those reportedly occurring in public places like freeway overpasses, at busy intersections, and on public utility vehicles – appear designed to garner public and media attention – and often in novel ways – rather than mindlessly copy existing news coverage.

Rather than resort to either of these overly simplistic explanations, I want to traverse the ground of this story by taking a number of different but intersecting paths. The first considers how analyses of news images have approached the subject of September 11. This section is particularly concerned with a critique of the structure of witnessing in relation to images and events. The second traverses this ground by considering what performance studies might offer. It considers displays of the flag as cultural performances and considers the relation between performer, audience, performance, and news representation. The conclusion reflects on the relation between news and terror, image and performance within what Gardiner (2004, 230) calls the "problematic" of everyday life.

Fig. 8-1: An American flag (approximately 4m x 6m/ 12ft. x 18ft.) attached to a
sound wall on PA State Route 202 near King of Prussia, PA (USA). Photograph by
the author (5 June 2006).

News images and acts of witness

Barbie Zelizer (2003, 49) has argued that journalistic images bring
about healing when the cultural collective has experienced public trauma:
a cataclysmic event that "rattle(s) default notions of what it means morally
to remain members of a collective." Because of their "elegiac" nature,
news images call upon those who view them to bear witness to the events,
to believe the unbelievable and make sense of the senseless. For this
reason they figure prominently in the constitution of a "post-traumatic
space" in which the senselessness of suffering can be rendered sensible
and the collectivity can begin the difficult task of healing and rebuilding
itself (Zelizer 2003, 49). The movement to a post-traumatic social space
can be read in the rapid shift in news images: from coverage of the disaster
itself (primarily NYC, but also the Pentagon and to a far more limited
extent to the crash site near Shanksville, PA); to individuals' "bearing
witness" to the disaster (responses and reactions); and finally to the
aftermath and the work of sifting through the wreckage in order to rebuild.

According to Zelizer, these shifts in representational content both mirrored and aided in the process of social healing.

If this is healing, then events since September 11, 2001 indicate the bones of domestic tranquility have knit poorly indeed. As Zelizer notes, the "templates" upon which journalists drew to frame September 11 – the 1945 liberation of Nazi concentration camps by U.S. forces – were in part responsible. By enabling the appropriation of the moral authority of victim-hood, these templates simultaneously constituted a post-traumatic space that enabled moral outrage to supplant any reflection on the status of America as a cultural collective or the conditions underlying that collectivity and the ways these impact the wider world. They pushed the nostrum of "just war," a poor and dangerously addictive substitute for the more laborious but profoundly more ethical rehabilitation process in which the collective might have engaged. Zelizer (2003, 66) concludes the "uncritical acceptance" of this framing of traumatic events has made the cultural collective "complacent about seeing less when we should be seeing more." I suspect this not "seeing" references what Shepperson and Tomasseli (2002, 153) describe as the "myopic and self-destructive policy of a country that, though in the world, conducts itself separately from it, mostly against it, and then wonders at the consequences". The simultaneous rise of American exceptionalism and the failure of this collective to genuinely contemplate George W. Bush's disingenuous question: "Why do they hate us?"

Such conclusions lead to questions about *how* news images are thought to accomplish what they do: how are they thought to relate to the abstract socio-cultural matrix of the "imagined community" that feels itself traumatized by events most of its members only grasped as news? If the overwhelming majority of those comprising the collective were "elsewhere," then as Sontag (2003) suggests, to a large extent the events of September 11 were "real" for that collective insofar as they were represented in news media. Sontag suggests photographs of such traumatic events not only make them real, they also serve as the "basic unit" of collective memory. "In an era of information overload, the photograph provides a quick way of apprehending something and a compact form for memorizing it" (Sontag 2003, 22). In our busy cognitive lives as media consumers, lives made so by the very advertising- and profit-driven media that make news, the "shocking" news image becomes the "quotation or maxim or proverb" of our times (Sontag 2003, 22-23). News images bear witness to events and in so doing shape our ability to respond. Whether acts of witness are thought to be "mundane" or "extraordinary" (Rentschler 2004, 298), it is clear that seeing media depictions of traumatic events (whether it is merely seeing or not) answers the question of how news images have their affectivity.

I am not concerned with the reality or not of events outside the news process, or of the possibility or desirability of judging between true and false representations of those events. Simulacra or not, the question of how the deluge of images of September 11 did (and do) what they are purported to have done, invites further consideration. For underlying claims such as those of Zelizer (2002) and Sontag (2003) about the ritual power of "image as witness" are some assumptions about the news process, assumptions which subordinate understandings of images and their effects to those attributed to texts. What is often implied in discussions of news images was made explicit in sociologist Robert Park's (1960, 9) definition of a newspaper: "A newspaper is not merely printed. It is circulated and read. Otherwise it is not a newspaper". In this view a newspaper's affectivity lies not in its being produced, even if it is to the "conditions of production" that understandings of the news process overwhelmingly direct their attention. Affectivity comes from its being consumed ("read"). Here, reading is a presumably transparent activity in which the ability to decipher the marks on a page (a narrow definition of literacy) equates to understanding, from which naturally follows any effect of significance.

Similarly, explanations of the affectivity of news images presume that people are affected simply because they see them. Echoing Park, we might say a news image is not merely photographed. If it is to be a news image it must be circulated and "read." But in a sense, for an image to be a news image, it must *not* require reading. Barthes explains that the photographic message involves a necessary reduction of the scene it represents, but a reduction without transformation. As a "perfect analogon," the photograph is a "continuous" or "codeless" message (Barthes 1977, 17). Text – dateline, photo credits, sometimes a brief indication of who is whom – may "anchor" that message (Barthes 1977, 39). But these anchors remarkably constitute the only direct acknowledgement of the image or of its "conditions of production." Rarely does one see reference in a hard news story to the images that accompany that story. That is what tabloids do. There is the rare exception, that special case in which the image *is* the story (the Abu Ghraib prisoner-abuse scandal). But more frequently, the image is para-textual, with the text remaining largely indifferent to the image appearing at its side. This indifference of the text toward the image (and, let's be fair, vice versa) along with the general absence of professional standards regarding the handling of news images (Zelizer 2003) indicates that news images are expected to display their significance "on the surface." As Sontag (2003, 24) puts it, this naïve view takes the photograph to be "a trace of something." It is made to be seen – and in being seen understood – with any "effects" flowing directly and unproblematically from the fact.

In another sense, it is not necessarily the content of an image so much as that which envelops it that achieves effect. In Zelizer's argument, the form/frame of Nazi prison camp liberation images is clearly taken to pre-exist historically and logically the specific content of September 11 images. It thus confers upon the contents and the events to which they are held to correspond with a structure of significance that orients the taker of the photograph and the maker of the news to the world of events. Where this structured orientation is characterized as witnessing, to read is by extension to adopt the orientation that frames the image's contents and the event it captures. Sontag offers the Kuleshov-effect as a figure for how news images are interpreted: we base our interpretations on what the photographer seems to say or should have said in the photograph by "splicing" in what we know of the "drama" in which the image's subject plays a part (2003, 29-30). Although external to it, these spliced scenes can trump the image's contents. Much in the way Kuleshov's test subjects interpreted a still subject's "performance" differently based on the scenes with which it was juxtapositioned, the drama changes how we interpret an image's contents, altering it "according to memory's needs" (2003, 30). Since in Sontag's account the knowledge of those who grasp the drama as news depends almost entirely on the words that envelop the images we see, it is again in that which envelops the image that cultural force resides.

There is a certain symmetry at work in these accounts between how an image's meanings are said to be structured and the effects it is purported to have on those who see it. The appearance alone of the image before a reader seems sufficient to explain its effect. The argument might be expressed in the equation: appearance=effect. While both Barthes and Sontag seem occasionally to suggest the news image stands in an untroubled, unmediated relation to that which is "brought before the lens" (Sontag 2003, 24; Barthes 1977, 17), it should be noted this appearance-effect is neither simple nor direct; as Sontag notes, news images are "not simply anything" (2003, 26). Barthes (1977, 17) describes the connotative counterpart accompanying codeless images, the code that indicates "the manner in which the society to a certain extent communicates what it thinks" of the photographic message. Zelizer posits roles for the photographers who take the pictures, the journalists who "anchor" them with text, and the news editors who oversee these and other facets of their framing, all of whom engage in the mediation of effect. However mediated an image's effects, clearly the act of seeing is posited as symmetrical with the assumption Park makes about reading: the fact of a story having been read and an image having been seen is presumed to delineate an "effect" so uniform and predictable as to pass out of consideration.

In these conceptions of image as witness, there is a conflation of the photographer and the audience. Zelizer (2002, 698) defines bearing witness as "an act of witnessing that enables people to take responsibility for what they see." This act enables individuals to move beyond an individual response to a collective response to the significance of the event. Photos, then, "offer a vehicle" for individuals to see and overcome their disbelief, an effect that applies to both "the making of photographs" and their "usage over time" (Zelizer 2002, 699). In a similar vein, throughout *Regarding the Pain of Others*, Sontag (2003, 18) passes seamlessly between meditations on the "modern condition" of "being a spectator" via images of suffering and the photographer's status as "witness" to those calamities as expressed in their photographs (Sontag 2003, 29). As Peters (2001) observes, this constitutes a category mistake that confuses the "active" witness of the photographer watching a group of firemen raise a flag over the WTC ruins through his viewfinder, standing in the same debris, feeling the same sun, and breathing the same carcinogenic dust as his subjects, and the millions of "passive" witnesses who saw the photograph on the front page of their local papers or reproduced on a t-shirt.

Peters posits four types of relations to events that helps clarify my point: being there in time and space (first-hand observer); being there in time but not space (audience of a live television broadcast); being there in space but not time (visitors to "the pit"); and absence in both time and space (viewing a news image or video recording of the event elsewhere). As Peters notes, only the first three sustain acts of witness. The latter marks "the profane zone in which the attitude of witnessing is hardest to sustain" (Peters 2001, 720). Conflating the difference, like conflating photographers with readers, requires a dubious suspension of disbelief – whatever our faith in the media.

Finally, for all its efforts to advance our understanding of the unique role of images in times of public trauma, the structure of witness remains committed to a logic of communication as transportation. That is, the notion of witness continues to be haunted by what both Carey (1988) and Hall (1993) described as the transmission model of communication. Carey (1988, 21) asserted that the news was not information but the "portrayal of an arena of dramatic actions and forces." Opposed to "a particular notion of content as a preformed and fixed meaning or message which can be analyzed in terms of transmission from sender to receiver," Hall (1993, 253) offered the encoding-decoding model as a way to account for the audience's role in the communication process. He did so by elaborating a critical "moment" heretofore reduced to "effects" or "uses" by the transmission model. Before a news image can "have an 'effect,' satisfy a 'need,' or be put to a use, it must first be appropriated as a meaningful discourse and be meaningfully decoded" (1993, 93). As opposed to the assumption that "all communication is perfect communication" (Hall in Angus, et al. 1994, 254), with success or failure judged against the producer's intentions as they mark the message produced, Hall's model theorizes the possibility of discontinuity between encoding and decoding. He posited, in other words, that the "codes of encoding" and the "codes of decoding" are discontinuous, potentially non-symmetrical moments. Decodings are not merely cognitive in nature. They must be connected to understandings and the codes through which meanings are accessed, but also to those material practices and relations of power by which predominant meanings are impressed, negotiated, or resisted. Such connections constitute what Hall (1993, 95) describes as "the articulation of language" – and here I would add images, rather than subsume them into language – "on real relations and conditions."

Studies of the place of news images in times of public trauma assume and imply what Hall's model makes explicit and urges us to elaborate: something must *happen* after the newspaper is read and recycled, after the magazine is discarded, or the telecast ended. If we take literally Carey's assertion that news is not information but drama, and Hall's insistence that we attend with the same care to the real relations and conditions of decoding as we have to encoding, then we must open that "black box" of cultural processes that result in the kind of healing in which news images are said to play a significant part.

News images as lived images

The kinds of cultural phenomena to which conceptions of performance are drawn are seldom the mass produced, packaged, and distributed phenomena which media make and audiences consume. Rather, performance gestures in a different direction: to the theater, drama, sacred or secular religious rituals, and to the punctuation of the everyday by lived cultural roles and rituals that are often beneath the notice of the papers, magazines, and broadcasts of record – except when they can be exploited for news value. Benjamin's (1968) distinction in "Art in the Age of Mechanical Reproduction" between performance for an audience and performance for "a mechanical contrivance" might also indicate something of a disciplinary rift between the interests of media studies and those of performance studies. Whether we agree or not that exhibition value has come to trump cultural value, or that being at a theatrical performance differs in precisely Benjamin's terms from watching the recorded version broadcast on television, we nevertheless acknowledge a difference.

I am fully content to leave that difference untroubled for the purposes of this essay, because the distinction seems irrelevant to recognizing that mass mediated images filter into everyday life, that "news images" can be "lived images."[6] As Victor Turner noted: "there was a lot of Perry Mason in Watergate!" (1979). In other words, there is a certain convergence between the social drama of the news and cultural performances that constitute the material existence of everyday life. For example, one need not have been in New York City in the days following September 11 to engage in performances that took media images as a script for setting up impromptu shrines to express grief and commemorate lost lives. Experiencing those shrines that appeared around Manhattan through news images does not make those shrines built elsewhere any less real or less meaningful. Yet they are performances taken up with respect to images in response to the passive witness the audience constitutes.

Although performance is an "essentially contested concept" (Carlson 1996, 1), the definition I offer here is designed not to be contentious, but rather to synthesize some of the literature on performance associated with anthropology (Turner 1979; Bauman 1974), communication (Conquergood 1983; 2002), sociology (Goffman 1959), cultural studies (Pollock 1998), philosophy (Butler 2004), and theater (Schechner 1973b).

A performance is embodied. While it is perhaps better understood as the body one *does* than the body one *has* or *is* (Butler 2004), as Stern and Henderson (1993, 3) note, performances involve "live bodies." In other words, a performance requires the presence of a body for its accomplishment. Whether the performance is for an audience or, as Benjamin put it, for "a mechanical contrivance," the body of the performer is present to the act. Most (though certainly not all) work in performance studies focuses on acts for which performer and audience are co-present. While Chvasta (2004) insists the body need not be valorized at the expense of texts, it is nonetheless important to acknowledge the necessity of embodiment as a significant component of performance, even in online or other technologically-mediated environments. Embodiment, then, constitutes the presencing or "presentation" of selves to others in communicative interaction (Goffman 1967).

A performance is expressive. Perhaps the most succinct articulation of this aspect of performance comes from Richard Schechner's (1973a, 3) assertion that "performance is a kind of communicative behavior." If so, it is communicative in a particular sense. A performance is not a passive conduit for the transmission of informational messages, nor is a performance the passive or neutral reflection of a script. Rather, performance is simultaneously a way of being in and a way of knowing the world (Conquergood 2002; Chvasta 2004). It is constitutive of human experience and expression. Carey describes the acts by which we produce, maintain, appropriate, and transform our social realities as a "miracle we perform daily and hourly" (1988, 29). It is in this sense that Victor Turner's aphorism – performance is "making, not faking" (cited in Conquergood 1983) – can be understood. To perform is neither simply to mimic or "fake" oneself, though one can perform to deceive (Goffman 1959). Even (especially) when one is being deceptive, to perform requires at least tacit knowledge and acceptance of the "social text" (Conquergood 1983, 30) that scripts everyday performances and belief in the role one thus plays (Goffman 1959). As an expressive activity, performance is thus imbued with a communicative impulse, one that invokes and implies others. Even if the audience is oneself, to perform is to be, to experience and to communicate with others.

A performance is enveloped in time, space, and culture. Kapchan (1995, 479) explains that performances "situate actors in time and space." But a performance is enveloped or situated in other, no less significant ways. Butler (2004) suggests the body is a "situation" that is enveloped in interpretations and other acts, all of which comprise the scene within which the project of gender is undertaken. Both Goffman and Bateson (1974) describe interaction frames as the social-semiotic and hermeneutic envelopes to which both performers and audiences have recourse as they interpret and respond to a situation. This does not mean that a performance is a reflex-like reaction to environmental cues, for context and performance are mutually dependent and mutually constitutive. Goffman (1959) explains that the situation with respect to which a performance occurs simultaneously frames the conduct's significance and is modified by that conduct. Conquergood (1983, 31, original emphasis) similarly emphasizes the significance of scene to the sense-making aspects of performance: "the expressive and consequential force of an act cannot be experienced or understood apart from the *scene* of its enactment." Thus, performances are complexly enveloped historically, geographically, and culturally, as well as spatio-temporally.

A performance is an enactment. Whatever a performance's effect, whether a performance "excites emotions" or "arouses us to action," whether "ecstatic, therapeutic, confrontational," or "instructive," a performance is an enactment (Stern and Henderson 1993, 4). Describing performances as aesthetic practices, Kapchan (1995) emphasizes their enacted nature as "patterns of behavior, ways of speaking, manners of bodily comportment." Insofar as performances "carry something into effect," their study concerns the processes whereby different phenomena are "enacted" (Kapchan 1995, 479). Butler (1993, 234) similarly emphasizes across her work the notion that gender, for example, is a "bounded 'act,'" a project of doing and becoming rather than of being. In expressive enactments a performance ultimately elicits and resonates with other expressive acts carried on in other bodies within a scene or situation.

Returning to the image of the flag (Fig. 8-1), we might not think of its display as an embodied, expressive, enveloped enactment. But this flag did not arrive spontaneously on the sound wall of Highway 202. It has even been purposefully altered from its conventional form by the addition of white text on a black field ("9.11.2001") to the black right- and left-hand borders. Both the flag and the sound wall on which it hangs had to be prepared in order for the flag to remain securely in place. It was positioned in a particular location so it would be seen by passersby in both the North and South bound lanes. It even remains displayed in violation of Pennsylvania Department of Transportation safety regulations. So at the very least a small group of individuals must have made and carried out a plan. We can infer the desire to communicate, not only by the fact the flag was carefully displayed, but by the fact it was displayed in a conspicuous space, one that is by federal and state law kept free of the clutter of any messages not immediately relevant to the safe flow of traffic. The text can be read as a command – to remember September 11 – as well as an insistence on the articulation of patriotism and national pride to that remembering. Every North and South bound passenger on this section of highway comprises the performance's audience. The performance is enveloped. Its display persists in time beyond the initial work of mounting the flag to the sound wall. It unfolds in a very special space, one that is relatively pristine in terms of other performances, but one that would be dangerous and difficult to reach for those who mounted the display. The acts involved are perhaps too numerous and complicated to speculate, but we know they bundle together and contract in the flag's persistent presence. The space of State Route 202 is momentarily for a short stretch redefined by that display as those passing through that space participate by engaging in acts of looking, speculation, and feeling. This display is enveloped in a situation that it invokes by enacting cultural memory as well as the affects and meanings articulated to its primary subject.

This display of the flag shares many of the features Kennerly (2002) considers in her work on roadside shrines. Like roadside shrines, displays of the flag are "an increasingly popular cultural practice" that marks "several interconnected layers of performance" (Kennerly 2002, 232). Kennerly (2002, 233) explains that "roadside shrines are constructed in moments of performance, leave traces that bear witness to those past performances, and invite future performances." At the least, then, there are performances related to the displaying of this flag and the untold number of performances which occur in others' responsiveness to the display. However, this bearing witness Kennerly describes concerns more than this particular display-performance. In a sense, the display is itself a bearing witness ("9.11.2001") that is complexly layered. Whether or not those involved in the display were temporally and spatially present at either New York City, Washington, DC, or Shankesville, Pennsylvania on 11 September 2001, the many news images of the destruction wrought in these spaces (by still other performances of martyrdom, of murder, of destruction) are layered in as well. They resonate with and help to shape even first-hand experiences. So, too, are the many images and accounts of other displays of the flag that make explicit connections between American identity, patriotism, the flag, and the events of September 11.

It is in this sense that *news images* become *lived images*: the passive witness of viewing live coverage (temporal presence, spatial absence) and the spectatorship of looking at news images in print (temporal-spatial absence) are refashioned as scripts for the complexly layered performances of displayers and audiences and the enfolding situation. News images partly constitute this situation. The display – like many others that may or may not have made the news – is a "restoration" of that behavior. However, this freeway display is not merely mimicking these news images or other performances, for as Roach (2003, 125) notes, restored behavior is paradoxical. While there is an element of repetition, "no action or sequence of actions may be performed exactly the same way twice; they must be reinvented or recreated at each appearance." In the case of roadside shrines and other performances that persist in time and space, this display has the power to restore acts that are temporally-spatially persistent in a way that many kinds of performance are not. Rather than being neatly bounded by a clear beginning and ending, displays of the flag are perdurable.

Not only the layer of displayer-performances but also audience-performances needs to be taken into account. To consider how the layer of audiencing might be situated, I want to modify Peters' (2001) schematization of witness. By distinguishing presence/absence, space/time, Peters creates four possibilities: present in time and space; present in time/absent in space; absent in time/present in space; and absent in time and space. In the case of many performances – perhaps most – the audience and performer are co-present in both time and space. By definition, attending a play or a bar mitzvah means being present in the time and space in which these occur. They typically have well-defined beginnings and endings.

Second, there are also performances for which the performer and audience are co-present in time, but not space. Similar to the condition of liveness Peters discusses, these would constitute the performance of a live newscast by a television reporter. Performances of the sort Chvasta (2004) analyzes, in which an act (in this case a rape) is accomplished through computer commands in an online MOO (a text-based, object-oriented multi-user domain), would also be acts for which performer and audience are co-present in time but not space. Such performances are effected through the technological mediation of space.

Third are performances for which performer and audience share a space but at different times. With roadside shrines, the maker of the shrine enacts something that remains for those who happen upon it. They share a space but under conditions of temporal discontinuity. Displays of the U.S. flag similarly require individuals to share the space of the display, though not necessarily at the same time. Such aesthetic acts of memorialization are perdurable: they necessarily inhere in matters of expression, making them performative. These persist in time and redefine space to evokes other acts of memory. Bolt (2004, 3, emphasis in original) argues convincingly that by way of the "life" a painting takes on in the process of the work of painting, it "performs rather than merely represents some other *thing.*" By inhering in expressive materials that enable their persistence in space such performance-displays mediate time.

Lastly, there is the "null" category for which the audience and the performer share neither space nor time. Benjamin's famous example serves as a paradigmatic case, for in film time and space are technologically mediated by means of editing and framing. The performer is present to the camera and the film crew on the set, but framing and editing render space and time malleable and enable their reorganization in myriad ways. The actor's performance as witnessed by the audience may be compiled from dozens of takes shot from multiple cameras positions at different locations. This troubles our ability to grasp it as a performance. The many instances of performance artists' appropriating the modes of mass culture may still be performances (Auslander 1989). However, as Peters (2001, 720) explains, this is the "condition of recording." Peters' conclusion applies equally well to performance and witness: absence in time and space constitutes "the profane zone" in which both are "hardest to sustain."

Conclusion

What happens when the telecast is ended or the newspaper recycled? After seeing images of the devastation of September 11, many of those who displayed flags, created memorials, or flocked to the ruins of the World Trade Center said the same thing: they wanted to "do something." We might conclude that a great deal happens when the image fades: someone does something. Such acts are embodied and expressive, enveloped in situations whose variability and complexity we have yet adequately to consider. The performances that have made the U.S. flag an indelible part of the post-September 11 visual landscape persist in forms that mediate time by taking residence in matters of expression. If we allow that displays of the U.S. flag are performances, we must also allow for the possibility that those who see news images do more than simply see. For the act of seeing is a complex and uncertain one, discontinuous from acts of image-making, and we must allow that those who mobilize codes of seeing may move out of that profane zone of spectation and "do something."

Terror can be understood as a trauma inflicted not only on individuals' bodies or property, and not only on cultural collectives. For trauma to be terrorizing it must damage the very fabric of everyday life: it must wound the unattended, unreflective moments within which reflection and attention, even cultural life as such are made constantly to unfold. In this it shares with news a special relationship. News – especially when it involves photographs – is a predatory capturing or seizing of something in events as well as of public attention. It endeavors to freeze a moment, to cut singular events from the innumerable flow of instants; capture, magnify, and display them in such a way that the collectivity is compelled to attend to those moments. Terror is a violent and visceral seizing of attention (and of the news). While the acts of capture in which the news engages are meant to seize on the potential of any moment to be worthy of the collective attention, acts of terror are efforts to disrupt the plane of everyday life by showing the vulnerability inherent in every moment and element in and of which the everyday is composed. News cautions us that our habits of inattention may cause us to miss something of collective significance; terror teaches us that inattention may cost us our very lives.

I see in the endless, perdurable repetition of displays of the flag an effort to mark a territory, to reconstitute the terrain of the everyday which terror disrupted. American culture has and continues to follow a prescription for healing that involves binding its wounds in a kind of patriotic fervor that the U.S. flag symbolizes. And it is indeed becoming what it displays: a cultural collective bent on unity at the expense of difference and security by any means. But perhaps members of this collective need not be as hapless and passive as either terror or the news makes them seem. In order to be a fully ritual view, the drama of events and the drama of making the news must be considered alongside the codes of reading and seeing and the dramatic actions and forces the mobilization of such codes unleashes. The virtual connections within this complexly and discontinuously layered multiplicity – at once local and global – must be mapped in the hope of becoming something else.

Notes

[1] I would like to thank Daniel Makagon and Marcy Chvasta for formative conversations about performance; John Huxford for helping me develop aspects of the argument; and Heidi Rose for both suggesting readings and generously reading and commenting on a draft of this essay. A previous version was presented at the 5th Annual Cultural Studies Association (U.S.) Conference at George Mason University.
[2] Newspaper articles referred to here and in subsequent paragraphs were accessed electronically via the LexisNexis U.S. news database (http://lexisnexis.com). July 24, 2006.
[3] For further discussion of shifts in decorum regarding rituals and rules for displaying the U.S. flag, especially some of the novel uses to which such rituals are put, see Coonfield and Huxford, 2009.

[4] This search was conducted August 5, 2006. The breakdown by region is as follows. For the search ranging between January 1 and September 10, 2001: 190 Midwest; 219 Northeast; 335 Southeast; 189 Western. Between Sept. 11 and December 31, 2001: 708 Midwest; 989 Northeast; 1207 Southeast; 1156 Western.
[5] See National Retailers Federation (NRF) press releases relating to the "NRF July 4th 2003 Consumer Intentions and Actions Survey," the "NRF July 4th 2004 Consumer Intentions and Actions Survey," and the "NRF 2006 Independence Day Consumer Intentions and Actions Survey." Available http://www.nrf.com/content/default.asp?folder=press/holiday&file=main.htm (Downloaded: 22 August 2006).
[6] I consider Benjamin's discussion of the distinction between acting before an audience and acting before a camera in the context of performance and mediation in Coonfield and Rose (2012).

Works Cited

Achenbaum, Emily. 2001. Symbol of security; area residents, firms buying up all U.S. flags in local stores. Buffalo News September 14, Business section.

Amherst selectmen consider how many American flags to fly on Main Street. 2001. The Associated Press state and local wire September 10, State and Regional.

Amherst selectmen limit downtown flags to six holidays. 2001. The Associated Press state and local wire September 11, State and Regional.

Angus, Ian, Cruz, Jon, Der Derian, James, Jhally, Sut, Lewis, Justin, and Schwichtenberg, Cathy. 1994. Reflections upon the Encoding/ Decoding model. An interview with Stuart Hall. In Viewing, reading, listening. Audiences and cultural reception. Edited by Jon Cruz and Justin Lewis. Boulder: Westview Press.

Attacks bring Quick End to the Dispute over Downtown Flag Display. 2001. The Associated Press state and local wire September 12, State and Regional.

Auslander, Philip. 1989. Going with the Flow. Performance Art and Mass Culture. TDR 32: 119-136.

Barthes, Roland. 1977. Image-Music-Text. New York: Hill and Wang.

Bateson, Gregory. 1974. Steps to an ecology of mind. New York: Ballantine Books.

Bauman, Richard. 1974. Verbal art as performance. American anthropologist 77: 290-311.

Blum, Ronald. NY City Opera opens with subdued doubleheader of
"Dutchman" & "Mikado"; An AP Arts and Entertainment review. The
Associated Press State & Local Wire September 16.

Bolt, Barbara. 2004. Art Beyond Representation: The Performative Power
of the Image. New York: Leatris.

Bragg, Rick. 2001. After the attacks: the flag; U.S. binds wounds in red,
white and blue. The New York Times September 17, Section A.

Butler, Judith. 2004. Variations on sex and gender: Beauvoir, Wittig,
Foucault. In The Judith Butler Reader. Edited by Sara Salhi. New
York: Blackwell.

Carey, James. 1988. Communication as Culture. Essays on Media and
Society. New York: Routledge.

Carlson, Marvin. 1996. Performance studies: a critical introduction. New
York: Routledge.

Conquergood, Dwight. 1983. Communication as performance.
Dramaturgical dimensions of everyday life. In The Jensen lectures.
Contemporary communication Studies. Edited by John Sisco. Tampa:
University of South Florida.

—. 2002. Performance studies. Interventions and radical research. The
Drama Review 46: 145-156.

Coonfield, Gordon and John Huxford. 2009. News Images as Lived
Images: Media Ritual, Cultural Performance, and Public Trauma.
Critical Studies in Media Communication 26: 457-479.

Coonfield, Gordon and Heidi Rose. 2012. What is Called Presence. Text
and Performance Quarterly 32: 192-208.

Chvasta, Marcy R. 2004. Screening bodies: Performance and technology.
Performance/Text/Technology 1.
http://www.cyberdiva.org/PTT/ Marcy.html (accessed April 10, 2006).

Elber, Lynn. 2001. Muted late-night shows return to air after terrorist
attacks. Associate Press State & Local Wire September 18.

English, Bella. 2001. Facing terror/ moment of unity/ National spirit. The
Boston Globe September 14, National/Foreign section.

Fallon, Scott, and Clegg, Jeannine. 2001. Stock market ready to open. The
Bergen County Record September 17, News.

Gardiner 2004. Everyday Utopianism: Lefebvre and his Critics. Cultural
Studies 28: 228-254.

Goffman, Erving. 1959. The presentation of self in everyday life. Garden
City, NY: Anchor books/Doubleday.

—. 1967. Interaction ritual. New York: Pantheon Books.

Grossberg, Lawrence. 1997. Bringing it all back home. Essays on cultural
studies. New York: Routledge.

Hall, Stuart. 1993. Encoding, Decoding. In The cultural studies reader. Edited by Simon During. New York: Routledge.

Hymman, Jonathan. 2007. The Public Face of 9/11: Memory and Portraiture in the Landscape. The Journal of American History 94: 183-192.

Kapchan, Deborah. 1995. Performance. Journal of American Folklore 108: 479-508.

Kerber, Ross. 2003. Flagging desire for Americana sales of patriotic products are lagging well below 2002's record-breaking levels. The Boston Globe July 4, Business section.

Kennerly, Rebecca. 2002. Getting messy. In the field and at the crossroads with roadside shrines. Text and Performance Quarterly 22: 229-260.

Morris, Jeanne. 2001. An unGodsmackly concert. New Hampshire Sunday News, September 16, Section B.

New Era begins sewing stars and stripes on baseball caps. 2001. The Associated Press State & Local Wire September 14.

Park, Robert. 1960. A natural history of the newspaper. In Mass Communications: A Book of Readings. Edited by Wilbur Schramm. Urbana: University of Illinois Press.

Passers-by Applaud Flag-displaying trucker. 2001. The Post-Standard, September 14, Local section.

Peters, John Durham. 2001. Witnessing. Media, Culture & Society 23: 707-723.

Pollock, Della. 1998. Introduction to Exceptional spaces. Essays in performance and history. Chapel Hill; London: University of North Carolina Press.

Riede, Paul, Fish, Mike, and Read, Jim. 2001. Hundreds buy flags to display solidarity. The Post-Standard September 14, News section.

Rentschler, Carrie. 2004. Witnessing: US citizenship and the vicarious experience of suffering. Media, Culture & Society 26: 296-304.

Roach, Joseph. 2003. Culture and performance in the circum-Atlantic world. In Performance studies. Edited by Erin Striff. New York: Palgrave/Macmillan.

Schechner, Richard. 1973a. Introduction. TDR 17: 3-4.

—. 1973b. Performance, theater, drama, script. TDR 17: 5-36.

Shepperson, Arnold, and Tomaselli, Keyan. 2002. What relevance cultural studies post-September 11? Critical Studies-Cultural Methodologies 2: 153-156.

Sontag, Susan. 2003. Regarding the pain of others. New York: Farrar, Straus and Giroux.

Stern, Carol Simpson, and Henderson, Bruce. 1993. Performance: Texts and contexts. New York: Longman.

Szaniszlo, Marie. 2001. Attack on America; flags are just everywhere; Boson puts patriotism on display. The Boston Herald September 15, News.

Turner, Victor. 1979. Dramatic ritual/ritual drama. Performative and reflexive anthropology. Kenyon Review 84: 80-93.

Wickham, Shawne K. 2001. Manchester's Muslims call attacks "barbaric"; American flag poster available on back page. The Union Leader, September 15, Section A.

Zelizer, Barbie. 2002. Finding aids to the past: bearing personal witness to traumatic public events. Media, Culture & Society 24: 697-714.

—. 2003. Photography, journalism, and trauma. In Journalism after September 11. Edited by Barbie Zelizer and Stuart Allan. London, New York: Routledge.

AMERICAN INFANTS: COPING WITH TRAUMA AND BECOMING HISTORICAL IN *A HOME AT THE END OF THE WORLD* AND *AMERICAN PASTORAL*

VINCENT STEPHENS

Introduction

Childhood is a national focal point for properly socializing future citizens. Vernacular notions of children as "the future" and the nation's most "precious resources" inform the ways schools, churches, and families initiate children into citizenship and nationhood. In the contemporary U.S.A. there is a palpable national investment in securing the potential "resources" children offer and the implied "future" they represent, through modes that often reproduce conservative logics of assimilation. Replicating social attitudes and behaviors that perpetuate social uniformity in its young obscures the potential for more complete and progressive modes of citizenship formation. Depictions of children in fictional literature are a fruitful source for exploring examples of youth citizen initiation. These representations can stimulate imagination and illustrate possibilities that point to a genuinely new national future rather than a static reproduction of the status quo. My essay explores key characters in Michael Cunningham's *A Home at the End of the World* and Philip Roth's *American Pastoral* to illustrate how adult negotiations of traumatized citizenship are integral to how children incorporate social difference and disruption into their sense of national identity.[1] The essay is chiefly concerned with ways of reconsidering social principles rather than direct policy reform.

U.S. public institutions tend to emphasize homogeneity and assimilation as national ideals. Implicit in these ideals, rooted in post-WWII, is the notion that cultural homogeneity/assimilation is the most desirable path to achieving social access and equality. In terms of American children's education, Valerie Lehr has noted how integral the traditional heterosexual nuclear family structure and "proper" gender roles are to psychological and moral development literature. Indeed, such literature tends to emphasize these as keys to an "orderly society." She has appropriately noted how such theories and the related social attitudes fail to consider how children/youth can be helped to recognize and face conflicts they will experience as they try to develop a sense of identity (Lehr 1999, 149). Building from Lehr, I would argue even further that such restrictive narratives maintain an artificial and traumatizing "order" that fails to adequately prepare children for engaging with the very inequities, tensions and dissatisfaction that have haunted adult citizens negotiating postwar American life.

In the "War on Terror" era, the Bush administration introduced a host of initiatives intended to regulate information, communication and bodies. Whereas such efforts focus on "external threats", there is an internal war conservatives have waged in an effort to codify normalcy in the intimate realms of family, childcare, and kinship. President Bush's proposed Federal Marriage Amendment, the series of anti-gay/lesbian initiatives passed in eleven states during the 2004 presidential election, and related measures intended to restrict queer citizens' access to civil protections are explicit attempts to restrict the permissible intimacies within the modern "American Way of Life" (Wildman 2004, 26-27).[2] Such measures are the historical byproduct of explicitly anti-gay and lesbian conservative organizing rooted in the late 70s political emergence of evangelical fundamentalist movements loosely defined as the Christian Right (Herman 1997; Lassiter 2008). The contemporary investment in American nationalism makes uniform notions of authentic "American" kinship profoundly relevant to social politics. The postwar nationalistic focus on assimilation is a broad paradigm that has fostered organized attempts to narrow the constitution of legally protected and culturally affirmed social identities.

In the immediate postwar era, the assimilation ideal enabled Americans to distinguish themselves from other nations by defining an "American Way of Life" as one characterized by a firm belief in democracy, the embrace of free enterprise and a commonsense reliance on Judeo-Christian theologies as the basis for cultural morality (Foner 1998, 236-47). Racially and religiously stigmatized groups – particularly African-Americans, Catholics, Jewish Americans and "white ethnics" – were among those groups who approached the period with the greatest optimism (Chafe 1982, 69-71; Hertzberg 1997, 290).[3] However, the promises of access and equality were stalled for many socially excluded groups until the mid-to-late 50s social movements that culminated in the Civil Rights and New Left movements. America asserted its political and militaristic world supremacy in WWII and the Vietnam War with differing degrees of success. These wars can also be understood as crucial benchmarks for assessing the underlying cultural logics of the postwar "American Way of Life." Anxieties about the stability of a distinctly American life, amidst an era of mass immigration, and the ability of U.S. democracy, and national values, to righteously assert themselves globally are central to the U.S.' delayed intervention into WWII and aggressive Vietnam interference.

The democracy-centered discourse that emerged from America's defeat of Nazism centered on a contrast between democratic freedom and diversity, and communist oppression. The paradox of America's victory is that despite substantial evidence of the European genocide, the U.S. intervened after millions had been killed and extensive political maneuvering. President Roosevelt struggled to balance his personal awareness of the Holocaust with political perceptions of him as biased toward Jewish interests, and public anti-immigrant sentiments rooted in fears of an immigrant "flood" (Diner 2004, 212-13; Hertzberg 1997, 280). Immigration quotas quietly increased from 1938-41, which Hertzberg defines as Roosevelt's "act of conscience," but it was an act devoid of "political trouble"; in December 1942 Roosevelt declared that the Nazis would be punished as war criminals but also, "reassured Congress . . . that he had no plans for proposing the lifting of immigration restrictions" (Hertzberg 1997, 284). The administration also initially declined to use money or supplies to bribe the Nazis, which changed in 1944 when Roosevelt established the War Refugee Board (Hertzberg 1997, 286-87). An extensive cultural investment in a national purity and way of life, untainted by foreign cultures, informed the United States' initially neutral WWII stance. Postwar the United States employed its eradication of the Holocaust and freeing of imprisoned European Jews as a symbol of American morality anchored in the nation's unique diversity. The penalty of this renewed nationalism was explicit pressure on "ethnic" Americans to succumb to majority culture and minimize difference. American Jews were among the groups restricted by the new nationalism and they largely dissembled, for they had little room to question America and resist assimilation since they, ". . . needed to feel that they were part of America, that they were among the victors. Possible American complicity by inaction in the murder of the Jews of Europe could not be discussed. If such an accusation were true, America's Jews would have had to continue to think of themselves as deeply alien" (Hertzberg 1997, 291). Though the postwar period fostered a new era of social access for American Jews, hope for national accountability and a genuine national investment in diversity linger.

Lingering postwar fears of a missed opportunity to thwart communism were also central to the U.S. intervention into Vietnam. According to Randall Bennett Woods, "With the onslaught of Cold war, realpolitikers preoccupied with markets and bases joined with liberal idealists who wanted to spread the blessings of freedom, democracy, and a mixed economy to the rest of the world. In turn, they joined together to call for an all-out effort to defeat the forces of international communism" (Woods 2005, 222). Vietnam is especially significant to the study of postwar American culture because it catalyzed questions about the way of life implied by the militaristic assertion of democracy. The New Left movement protested the war but also posed a larger critique of the restrictive ideas about racial hierarchy, gender propriety and family structures central to the national culture. As Woods notes, ". . . the antiwar movement included left-wing students and intellectuals, many of whom had been active in the civil rights movement and who saw the war as an expression of an essentially corrupt political and economic system" (Woods 2005, 236). By assessing the essential paradox of a culture premised on equality and freedom yet characterized by patterns of social and economic inequality the movement ultimately questioned whether the "American Way of Life," fostered by democracy and capitalism, was a lifestyle worth spreading. The emergence of youth-oriented communitarianism and the broad countercultural "rejection of traditional sexual mores and family structures" during the era were not entirely successful or enduring (Woods 2005, 261-62). However their emergence, alongside the increasingly prominent second-wave feminist, and gay and lesbian liberation movements embodied the search for new American ways of living in the intimate realms of sexuality, gender, and family. The tensions between American postwar ideals of freedom and institutional oppression constitute the core of postwar traumatized citizenship, particularly for racial and sexual outsiders excluded from an imagined cultural mainstream.

Stymied optimism

The subtext of the postwar assimilation narrative was the continuation of structural inequities such as lower pay scales for women (Evans 2001, 191-94), racial segregation and the proliferation of White Anglo-Saxon Protestant (WASP) identity as the core American power elite (Brookhiser 1991; Christopher 1989; Robertiello and Hoguet 1987; Kaufmann 2004).[4] African-Americans did not gain access to legal and social inclusion until the Civil Rights era, and feminist groups reached their acme in the late 60s/early 70s. In contrast the racialization of "white ethnics" fostered greater social access to American life for Catholics and Jewish Americans who, in the face of Hitler's attempted "Final Solution", had perhaps the greatest incentive to embrace the "American Way of Life" (Martin 1978, 3; Diner 2004, 6; Sarna 2004, 274; Moore 2004, xi; Shapiro 1992, xv).[5] Despite overt racial and gender discrimination, the looming possibility of racial conformity was an alluring conceit for groups who could integrate themselves into a white-dominated culture. However, the implied "authenticity" of WASP identity, and related social privileges/advantages complicated the potential for Jewish Americans to fully inhabit their newfound access to white privilege in America (Foner 1998, 239).[6] The negotiation of white privilege with religious and ethnic "difference" of Judaism has remained a trope of post-WWII Jewish American arts and letters (Hertzberg 1997, 291-93).[7]

Within the postwar era, legalized discrimination and inequality based on racial/ethnic and gender differences co-existed with the new era of freedom. The white and patriarchal biases of the new citizenship ideal were grounded in heteronormative relations supported by multiple logics that stigmatized sexual diversity and gender transgression. The cultural reliance on fixed gender roles, Judeo-Christian fundamentalism, and irrational fears of "inverts" susceptible to Communist blackmail and thus national security threats were among the justifications for socially excluding and legally persecuting "sexual deviants" (Johnson 2004, 9). Gender propriety also fostered social suspicion toward professional and/or unmarried women as non-normative (Evans 2001, 192).

The social identity movements that arose in the 1950s onward were grounded in social responses to micro and macro levels of stigma, exclusion, and inequality that traumatized, and mobilized, generations of social outsiders. The social sphere is a particularly salient mode of transformation and identity formation within the dialectical relationship of the social with the legal, economic and political spheres. The major postwar social movements, the Black Freedom Movement and the New Left it inspired, were largely organized around a uniquely American postwar traumatic moment (Foner 1998, 288). Notably, these subcultures awakened to the postwar nation's failure to embrace and incorporate the democratic ideals it proclaimed as the cores of U.S. citizenship. The defeat of widespread fascism and assertion of U.S. military power bolstered America's world profile but failed to reform internal constraints until citizen-led movements revealed and attempted to reverse the traumas of failed citizenship. The ongoing relevance of these landmark movements is undervalued in contemporary America because they disrupted postwar narratives of nationalistic unity – values American public institutions continue to idealize and advocate.

The epistemology of traumatic citizenship

There is a vast epistemological value of discussing modern American history in terms of how citizens have responded to citizenship trauma by resisting and transforming such historical traumas into ethical democratic social practices. Engaging with responses to trauma is particularly germane at a time when American institutions continue to perpetuate narratives of homogeneity that de-emphasize the nation's ongoing struggles with social difference in favor of broad unifying narratives emphasizing Americanness in an anti-terrorism, pro-empire global context. Economic and political marginalization are quantifiable dimensions of American experience; however the profound role of social exclusion as a suppressive "structure of feeling" is less palpable. If history is not merely comprised of Great Events we must begin to account for how history is translated in the most intimate of social spaces – homes, schools, places of worship, etc.[8] These intimate spaces make the concept of the world and the possibilities of citizenship accessible from our earliest stages of learning. A fear of social transformation – the way people understand themselves and relate as a society and as citizens is central to the political suspicion and social disapproval movements experienced at their most disruptive moments. Though racial and ethnic social movements still struggle for social recognition, certain leaders and movements have attained iconicity.

It is arguable that second and third wave feminism and sexual liberation movements have rarely entered into mainstream discourse as "positive" movements "suitable" for translating to children. One suspects that the questions various factions within these movements have raised about sexual diversity, gender roles, sexual orientation and family structures could complicate and challenge the discourses of intimate spaces. National trends such as the gendered division of labor and valorization of the nuclear family would require serious reconsideration. Articulating the vulnerabilities of women and sexual minorities to explicit forms of violation and discrimination are challenging and vital because these are not in the past tense but central to American life in covert forms. Addressing the ways that racism, sexism, gender- and homophobia inform the social experiences of Americans is a challenging conversation to have with children in intimate settings. Such conversations require adults to interrogate national history in ways that might disrupt their own sense of citizenship. These disruptive practices are essential knowledge for children. Shielding children – future citizens – from the richness and relevance of trauma-fueled movements undermines the way these movements fully enacted democratic principles and fails to prepare children for engaging with and valuing "difference." Historical distortions also stifle children's potential to use social experience in transformative ways – the key component to imagining other forms of living and relating beyond narrowly racialized and heteronormative forms. "Ethnic" children, female children, gender disruptive children and those raised in non-traditional households need knowledge of the movements which affirmed the right of cultural outsiders to civic access and social inclusion to develop a sense of personal identity and national belonging. The novels my chapter examines illuminate ways to engage with the vitality of social trauma as an episteme.

Two tales of sexual and familial ethics

Contemporary American literature is one of the vital spaces for reflecting on the psychological and cultural toll of sublimating traumas of difference for acceptance, and the possibilities modeled by characters who use trauma and difference to transform social relations. As a cultural genre, novels are a potent archive of the diverse ways humans conceptualize cultural negotiations of everyday lives framed by political and militaristic unrest. The most lucid and influential depictions of the quotidian can stimulate complex intellectual and political engagement with a range of social possibilities. My chapter contrasts the depictions of children of the American future in *American Pastoral* and Michael Cunningham's *A Home at the End of the World*. The potential of children to perpetuate U.S. citizenship ideals is one of the core themes of both novels. *Pastoral* illustrates how a postwar couple's disengagement from the complexity of American ethnic and religious conflict distorts their daughter's ability to develop a critical perspective. Essentially forced to choose between absolute conformity and free form radicalism she resorts to a dangerous and near parodically depicted kind of protest. *Home*'s narrative traces the experiences of adults traumatized by death, sexual difference and familial dysfunction. The characters' transgressions of heteronormative sex and gender roles reshapes their sense of identity and fuels the creation of unconventional family forms that incorporate sex, friendship, romance, and parenting in innovative ways. Comparing the two novels illuminates both the appeal of assimilation to the historically traumatized and its limitations, and the unique potential of transforming trauma. Comparison also illustrates how progressive citizenship lies in active responses to historical conditions and changes in behavior rather than the embrace of received narratives that anchor national memory.

In *Pastoral* Roth's perennial alter ego/brain Nathan Zuckerman runs into a neighborhood hero from his childhood, Seymour "Swede" Levov, at a baseball game in New York in 1985.[9] Levov asks Zuckerman to help him write a tribute for his father Lou's funeral. During Zuckerman's initial encounter with Seymour, his blank, inoffensive demeanor amazes him. Zuckerman recalls how the Swede was a Nordic-looking heroic, high school jock, who embodied the image of the 40s "All-American" and as a Jew suggested the possibility of Jewish assimilation in postwar America. Levov enlisted in the army at the tail end of the war and upon his return declined a baseball career to work at the family's glove-making business. Levov also married Dawn, an Irish Catholic former Miss New Jersey 1945 who competed in the Miss America Pageant. Seymour and Dawn moved to a suburban enclave, Rimrock, New Jersey and had a daughter, Merry. At a 1995 class reunion Zuckerman learns from Seymour's younger brother Jerry that Seymour passed away as a result of prostate cancer. Jerry further informs him that Seymour's life was disrupted in 1968 when Merry became known as the "Rimrock bomber" after she bombed the local post station, killing a local doctor, and disappeared. The remainder of the novel is Zuckerman's speculative narration of Seymour's life as he copes with Merry's disappearance. As Derek Royal notes, *Pastoral* is Zuckerman's fiction, a "literary act," "not the *actual* life of the Swede" which Zuckerman admits (Royal 2001, 6; Roth 1997, 55). Royal posits the novel as a rumination on the "process and the power of reimagining lives", which extends Roth's continual self-examination of how "remembering (or reimagining) reality is the way in which we make sense of our lives, a process similar to narrative in ordering and creating the self" (Royal 2001, 6). Parrish also notes how in *Pastoral* "Roth rewrites Zuckerman's story as a way of rewriting all of his previous Zuckerman stories" and his "reappearance in *American Pastoral* signals Roth's re-evaluation of the fictional stance toward identity – whether understood as cultural identity or individual identity – codified in *The Counterlife*" (Parrish 2000, 86). Through Roth's postmodern concern with *process,* he (or rather Zuckerman) still raises important questions about how U.S. citizens negotiate national *history* and *identity*.

Bobby, Jonathan, Alice and Clare express their internal perceptions in first person voice in *Home*'s chapters. Spanning the mid-1960s to 1990, *Home* traces the way emotional dissatisfaction and displacement informs relationships and personal identity. Bobby Morrow grows up in Cleveland under the influence of his hippie brother Carlton. Carlton's death puts Bobby into an extended fugue state during his childhood. As a middle-school student he befriends the introverted Jonathan Glover, the only child of Alice, a frustrated housewife, and Ned, an emotionally distant theater owner. Bobby inspires a newfound confidence in Jonathan, who grows increasingly distant from Alice. Alice is initially skeptical of Bobby but he intuitively senses Alice's frustrations and introduces her to marijuana and progressive 60s music, which provides her with something apart from domestic chores. Jonathan begins to explore his homosexuality with Bobby but grows increasingly uncomfortable with the closeness among he, Alice and Bobby and leaves for New York to attend college. Bobby, whose mother and father have passed away, remains in Cleveland as a baker and adopts the Glovers as his *de-facto* family. When Ned and Alice decide to move to Arizona they encourage Bobby to develop his independence. Bobby moves to New York to live with Jonathan and his roommate Clare, a 40-something costume jeweler with a long-term lesbian relationship and divorce in her past. As Bobby and Jonathan reacquaint themselves, Clare grows fixated on the attractive, but sexually ambiguous Bobby. While Jonathan dates an elusive bartender named Erich, Clare seduces Bobby and they develop a sexual relationship. Jonathan grows frustrated with their arrangement and abruptly moves to Arizona, which creates tension between Bobby and Clare. When Ned dies, Bobby and Clare fly to Arizona, where Clare reveals she is pregnant. The trio returns to the East and purchases a home in Woodstock, using Clare's trust fund. There they raise Bobby and Clare's biological daughter Rebecca and run a café. Clare ultimately seeks a more traditional arrangement. When the HIV-positive Erich moves in, she eventually leaves with Rebecca to live with her mother. At the novel's end Alice finds contentment in Arizona, and Jonathan and Bobby devote themselves to running the restaurant and nurse Erich, who passes away.

Negotiating alien/nation status

My analysis of the novels primarily focuses on Seymour and Merry, and Bobby and Rebecca to illuminate the limits and possibilities of citizenship within families. The desire to avoid the "white ethnic" alienation which could stem from questioning the U.S. WWII intervention, and the consequential affirmation of postwar opportunities for acceptance taints the Levovs' political engagement. In *Pastoral* a third-generation Jewish man, Seymour, and his Irish-Catholic wife Dawn envision the ideal American life as one where religious and ethnic specificity disappear under the imaginary of "American." In their conception of the nation they never envision that raising a daughter would require them to engage with Americanness as an ongoing construction that raises new questions, challenges and possibilities for each generation. The Levovs perfunctorily oppose Vietnam but adamantly oppose Merry's anti-Vietnam activism because it disrupts their contented, assimilationist way of life. When Merry bombs a post-office to protest Vietnam their postwar optimism quickly tempers. The bombing ignites an array of missed opportunities for the Levovs to trump assimilation with a more nuanced sense of how ethnic Americans can *define* rather than *occupy* American identity. There are wildly varying critical opinions on Roth's ideological perspective in *Pastoral*.[10] Perhaps one of the novel's greatest virtues lies less in its political peculiarities than the questions it raises about whether assimilation is desirable and what are the ethical responsibilities of citizens who purport to integrate themselves and their loved ones into the historical morass of postwar America. The lingering collision of WWII ghosts with Vietnam inspires a deep dissemblance away from national critique. To overtly critique Vietnam and champion critical inquiry is to assess the motives of militaristic intervention and the national ways of life it fosters. Feigning contentment enables the family to disengage from the cultural questions linking the wars as deeply political rather than altruistic wars.

In contrast to postwar optimism, the fluid relationships of *Home* grow out of the experiences of characters who mature during the late 60s counterculture era. In *Home,* Bobby's biological family life was a traumatic space decimated over the course of his young life – Carlton accidentally walked through a glass sliding door when Bobby was a child; his mother passed away during his teen years and his father accidentally burned himself to death via cigarette when Bobby was a young adult (Cunningham 1990, 65, 76, 104). At each instance Bobby was traumatized and lapsed into a near fugue state.[11] Whereas Seymour's gradual family dissolution paralyzed him, Bobby's pain transformed him. For Bobby, life transcended the corporeal and material: thus for him death and loss were not permanent endings but natural extensions of life where people were constituted by memory and impact rather than physical presence.[12] Bobby's coping with death and his disjuncture with traditional sex and gender expectations enabled him to transform trauma into an alternative sense of kinship. He embodied a notion Ann Cvetkovich has theorized, notably, "how trauma can be a foundation for creating counterpublic spheres rather than evacuating them" (Cvetkovich 2003, 15). The counterpublic Bobby represented on the micro-level of his friends embodied hippie idealism but did not overtly adhere to a political model, a freedom that allowed him to avoid the indulgences and excesses of some hippie culture while fulfilling its freedom-oriented ideals. Bobby modeled a central aspect of Cvetkovich's inquiry into, "how affective experience that falls outside of institutionalized or stable forms of identity or politics can form the basis of public culture" (Cvetkovich 2003, 17). David J. Jarraway eloquently addressed the counterpublic "poetry" of *Home*'s characters when he noted how, "The monolithic notions of familial loyalty, marital monogamy, and passional privacy – the unmovable mountains if not the unshakable bedrock of mainstream, heterosexual culture – these notions would all appear to dissolve in the sheer "poetry" of Jonathan and Bobby and Clare's extraordinarily unconventional lives" (Jarraway 1996, 380).

Cunningham has noted how the novel was written during the first ten years of the AIDS epidemic and grew out of his experience as a teenage observer of 60s counterculture and a witness to AIDS (Canning 2003, 92). Transcendence and alternate visions of living were inherent to the novel's design. According to Cunningham:

> Anybody who lived through and came out the other end of the period had a certain sense that the world was going to profoundly change. I was foolish enough to imagine that we were going to win, that women and gay people and people of color were going to triumph. And in some disorganized way, that we would actually defeat death itself. When you're a seventeen-year-old on acid in 1968 that doesn't seem wholly out of the question. And obviously that didn't happen and things have changed in ways we never imagined (Cunningham in Gambone 1999, 147).

The lingering hope for transcendence from systematic oppression seems to have inspired the possibilities Bobby represented. After Bobby eventually joins Clare and Jonathan an array of "chosen family" forms sustains them (Weston 1991). Bobby and Jonathan maintain their ambiguous brother/companion relationship and Bobby serves as a lover and child to Clare. Jonathan variously functions as a platonic husband for Clare and an "uncle" for Bobby. When the trio moves to Woodstock co-parenting and mixing gender roles is integral to raising Rebecca. The family's incorporation of Alice as a virtual grandmother to Rebecca and their embrace of Erich into the family defied the "blood" ties implicit to "family." *Home*'s characters suggest that idealized nuclear families and well-worn mythologies of assimilation and tolerance are inadequate for the new questions counterculture politics asked about U.S. citizenship. *Home* only mildly alludes to the specific Vietnam context of hippiedom but the characters' domestic and sexual interrogations emerge from a war-inspired clash of cultural values. The domestic alienation *Home*'s characters experience is a multi-generational microcosm of broader counterculture questions about the national ways of life fostered by a militarized national culture. *Home*'s characters struggle to confront and interrogate the limits of prefabricated gender and sex roles, which subtly reflects the psychic hegemony of the cultural enforcement and naturalization of these roles and lifeways. The fluid family *Home* presents is a literary concoction but not a simple contrived utopian construct. Rather, Cunningham imagines a series of workable structures that use complex notions of sex, love, friendship, and parenting as metaphors for re-imagining U.S. citizenship as a process of critique and creation.

Both novels present the fallout from the nuclear family ideal or "broken homes" in different war-torn (WWII and Vietnam) eras. The Levovs idealize home as a haven from the world. Merry's internal questioning and external terrorist acts destabilize the family but this is only one of several transgressions, including Seymour and Dawn's extramarital affairs. "Home" is broken because the Levovs betray postwar ideals, of assimilation and mobility, they have never interrogated. *Home*'s characters openly confront the limits and failures of traditional family. The Morrow family's deaths, Alice's marital dissatisfaction, and Jonathan's struggles with his sexuality are the impetus for the characters to rethink the stability they have been socialized to anticipate. Broken homes herald new horizons for the characters, whereas family trauma destroys the Levovs.

In the contemporary "family values" political climate, fragmented families serve as a particularly volatile metaphor for the breakdown of families, and by implication, American society. As extreme as this conservative formulation may be its persuasiveness lies in the iconization of the white, gender normative, heterosexual, nuclear middle-class family and the lack of more complex visions of kinship. Judith Stacey has thoroughly critiqued the 1990s' "aura of false consensus on family values that permeates our culture" (Stacey 1996, 13).[13] More recently Kathleen M. Sands argues that family values function as "civil religion" and derive their authority from the invisible hegemony of Judeo-Christian notions and the implied opposition between religion and secularism. She defines family values as an inadequate civic ethos that fails to advance American culture toward its best ideals (Sands 2000, 12-13). Complementing Sands' critique are Jakobsen and Pellegrini, who interrogate the commonsense notion that morality is inherently religious and primarily defined by regulation, and describe ways that sexuality can be a, "vital resource for remaking the social and saving our lives" (Jakobsen and Pellegrini 2004, 11, 156). The potential of sex and sexuality as political and ethically transformative has been well established by scholars on gay and lesbian and queer social ethics (Ball 2003; Blasius 1994; Hoagland 1988; Seidman 1993; Warner 1999). Further, an array of scholars has explored how diverse modes of queer kinship have complicated the notion of family and kinship, usually in sociological contexts (LeVay and Nonas 1995; Murray 1996; Nardi 1999; Nimmons 2002; Stacey 1996; Weston 1991). A central task of this chapter is to explore the social and ethical import of this important ethical and kinship-oriented work to contemporary social politics. A renewed engagement with social and ethical transformation is essential to moving beyond liberals' reliance on classic rationality and what Carlos A. Ball defines as "moral bracketing. " Ball describes gay rights movements' historic avoidance of engaging with morality in favor of "morally neutral (and largely liberal) arguments based on considerations of privacy, equality and tolerance" and classifies this recalcitrance as a form of "moral bracketing" – "the strict separation of moral, philosophical, and religious views (or what philosophers call questions of the good) from considerations of justice (or what philosophers call questions of the right)" (Ball 2003, 1).[14] Infusing progressive politics in the language of moral and ethics is a preliminary step for forging relevant and effective politics. Coldly "rational" perspectives that avoid ethical and moral discourse are out-of-sync with the contemporary moral and social turn in politics, and forging ahead with new progressive strategies is crucial to discerning possibilities of citizenship in contemporary American life. Lauren Berlant has defined the political shift toward social politics as the "intimate public" sphere. The remainder of the chapter places the novels in the context of Berlant's formulation.

Infantile citizenships

The emergence of *Pastoral* and *Home's* critique of ethnic erasure and sexual transgression in the 1990s directly parallels the emergence of the "intimate public sphere." Berlant argues that, " . . . the intimate public sphere of the U. S. present tense renders citizenship as a condition of social membership produced by personal acts and values, especially acts originating in or directed toward the family sphere" (Berlant 1997, 5). Ultimately within the paradigm, politicians and mass media discourage citizens from engaging with historically mediated economic and social discrimination because they lack the titillation of emotion-driven social issues.

In conjunction with the erasure of history and the downplaying of structures emerges what she defines as the new ideal citizen – the American infant. According to Berlant:

> . . . the nation's value is figured not on behalf of an actually existing and laboring adult, but of a future American, both incipient and pre-historical: especially invested with this hope are the American fetus and the American child. What constitutes their national supericonicity is an image of an American, perhaps the last living American, not yet bruised by history: not yet caught up in the processes of secularization and sexualization; not yet caught in the confusing and exciting identity exchanges made possible by mass consumption and ethnic, racial, and sexual mixing; not yet tainted by money or war. . . This national icon is still innocent of knowledge, agency, and accountability and thus ethical claims on the adult political agents who write laws, make culture, administer resources, control things.
>
> But most important, the fetal/infantile person is a *stand-in* for a complicated and contradictory set of anxieties and desires about national identity (Berlant 1997, 8).[15]

It is in this territory – the complicated and contradictory – that both novels' infant and infant-like characters raise useful questions about families and citizenship.

Berlant's notion of the infantile citizen is particularly relevant to *Pastoral* because Roth indirectly challenges the validity of the infantile model through Merry. Seymour and Dawn attempted to raise the very kind of ideal citizen Berlant formulates – one devoid of political subjectivity or social awareness. Merry resisted her parents' efforts but had no force to temper and redirect her anger. If Roth acutely parodies the extremes of misguided radicalism, he also skewers the notion of a U.S. citizen immune or indifferent to the histories that have made U.S. citizenship so contentious. Merry's descent is not exclusively the result of radical leftist ideology gone awry; rather it is the by-product of a particularly modern American postwar mentality – translated in families and supported by societal institutions – that attempts to pretend there is no need for change, disruption, questioning or subversion. Such a perceptive lens devalues and demoralizes informed citizenship as threatening rather than progressive. Questioning, challenging, and protesting are the very gestures postwar social movements enacted to advance U.S. citizenship. These challenges to the balance of social power could not be ignored, hence conservative appropriations of Reagan era activism in the form of "a nationalist politics of intimacy, which it contrasts to threatening practices of nonfamilial sexuality and by implication, other forms of racial and economic alterity"

(Berlant 1997, 7). *Pastoral*'s strongest political thread is its implied critique of citizenship as "a category of feeling irrelevant to practices of hegemony or sociality in everyday life" (Berlant 1997, 11).

Home brilliantly subverts Berlant's theory by illustrating the transformative possibilities of intimacy and the potential for progressive citizenship within social structures like families and friendships. *Home*'s characters are rarely political in the traditional sense; rather their social interactions operate stealthily. The seemingly naïve and docile infant Bobby best exemplifies the stealth model in his deft reconfigurations of his personal trauma into communality. Cunningham has sketched *Home*'s characters in subtle ways that can easily obscure the radical structures of their lives. The complex sexual and familial boundaries of Bobby and Jonathan's relationship, Jonathan's questioning of how relationships constrain "love," Alice's conscious critiques of her traditional American family life, and Bobby, Jonathan and Clare's collective subversion/conflation of gender roles in raising Rebecca are poignant sociopolitical challenges to family, sexuality and gender enveloped in a deceptively utopian narrative. In *Home*, intimate spaces and relationships embody social radicalism in a functional manner. Berlant's infant ideal is a particularly useful framework for discussing child and adult behaviors in the novels. I begin my discussion by describing the novels' infant citizens – Merry, who acts as a baby anarchist, and Rebecca, an actual baby. I also explore the poignant role of families in initiating the children into national citizenship through exploring the adult infants Bobby and Seymour. I conclude by discussing the ethical implications of family structures.

Adult infants and their children

In *Pastoral* a *spoiled adult infant*, (Seymour) begets a *disruptive infant* (Merry). Seymour, the "All-American" proverbial winner fails to nurture Merry, a social outsider, and the winner's assimilationist dreams literally explode. In *Home*, a *signifying/defiant adult infant* (Bobby) begets a *progressive infant* (Rebecca). *Home*'s sexual outsiders raise Rebecca in an improvised family environment that nurtures a child who seems poised to reconcile structure with possibility.

Seymour's childrearing of his half-Jewish/half-Catholic daughter, Merry, functions as a cautionary tale about infantile citizens. Seymour fails to acknowledge how he is implicated in the lament that after three generations of growth "with the fourth it had all come to nothing. The total vandalization of their world" (Roth 1997, 237). Roth illustrates what is lost when generational progress is actually generational *forgetting*. Merry is a *disruptive infant* raised by dedicated conformists. Everything she knows about being a citizen is warped. The dominant message her parents convey is that geniality is more important than articulating boundaries, and correcting imperfection is less important than questioning what *defines* perfection.

When Seymour first asks for his father Lou's approval of his *shiksa* wife, Lou interrogates Dawn and demands they determine the child's religious heritage. Though Dawn feigns indifference to Catholicism and promises not to baptize Merry, they secretly do (Roth 1997, 389, 396). Better she lives as a quasi-Catholic than a full-fledged Jew or anything concrete – her parents' refusal to provide Merry with an identity to engage with is central to her anger. No matter how hard the Levovs try to blend in half-Jewish, overweight, stuttering Merry will never be "normal" like her former beauty pageant mother and star athlete father. She is perpetually inadequate because she is physically and verbally noticeable – the opposite of the assimilated body. When Seymour confronts a dirty, starving Jainist-identified Merry at the novel's end she has lost weight and stopped stuttering and he sees that "Everything she could not achieve with a speech therapist and a psychiatrist and a stuttering diary she had beautifully realized by going mad" (Roth 1997, 246). Merry's ultimate subversion is her public engagement. Her confrontational instincts defy Seymour's long held goal of invisibility. As a high school sophomore Seymour has privatized, capitalistic nuclear family dreams, "At school he'd find himself thinking about which girl in each of his classes to marry and take to live with him . . . he would imagine himself going home after work to that house back of the trees and seeing his daughter there, his little daughter high up in the air on the swing he'd built for her. Though he was only a high school sophomore, he could imagine a daughter of his own running to kiss him, see her flinging herself at him, see himself carrying her on his shoulders . . ." (Roth 1997, 190). Young adulthood did not temper this fantasy as he, "was fully charged up with purpose long, long before anyone else he knew, with a grown man's aims and ambitions, someone who excitedly foresaw, in perfect detail, the outcome of his story" (Roth 1997, 192).

Several benchmark family and school moments define Merry's growth into anarchy. First, narrator Zuckerman recalls an episode where Merry demands to be kissed like her father kisses her mother. Seymour, raised to follow orders and avoid confrontation relents and kisses Merry. In this scenario the adult without boundaries is more problematic than the precocious child. By appeasing Merry, Seymour protects himself from making a moral decision rather than providing her with a reasonable sense of propriety (Roth 1997, 91, 240). Responsibility and ethical propriety materialize as value neutral negotiations, misguided notions that prove fatal for Merry and haunt Seymour.

Second, Dawn and Seymour enroll Merry in a series of corrective activities, such as speech therapy, to normalize her (Roth 1997, 95-96). Merry publicly embarrasses her parents, especially Dawn, because she presents an ambiguous and challenging new ethnic and social position for them. She is born an outsider and has a limited drive for the assimilation her parents crave.

Third, in middle school Merry questions her teacher on an assignment and is informed by her teacher that she has "a stubborn streak" (Roth 1997, 248). Her parents never question the teacher's judgment but view Merry's probing intelligence as charming. As a teenager her classmates also call her Ho Chi Levov because she is overweight and enraged by Vietnam (Roth 1997, 100). The Levovs never fully engage Merry's initial humanistic passion. As she struggles to understand the cruelty of Vietnam, any semblance of her parents' maturation under wartime circumstances are absent, and she is left alone and directionless to process without support.

Fourth, when Merry openly critiques America, her second generation grandfather encourages her to write letters rather than propose outright destruction, and her third generation father distantly moderates (Roth 1997, 285-91). Lou and Seymour never reveal themselves to her; Lou attempts to reason with her but abstracts the personal toll of war, and Seymour disengages entirely. Presuming a direct causal relationship between parents' child raising intentions and a child's behavior is aimless. However, these benchmark episodes reiterate how her lack of definition and guidance inspire a destructive intelligence ungrounded in any sense of self beyond her assimilationist family. She is culturally anomalous in relation to her family's aspiration. Seymour wonders, "Who had enlisted her and lured her into this?" since she was "Blessed with a loving and ethical and prosperous family" (Roth 1997, 248). The Levovs' inability to nurture and engage Merry as a person rather than a symbol reveals the ugly side of postwar assimilationist dreams – an unbalanced, indiscrete child raised to believe there are no boundaries or limits by people still trapped by historic stigmas they can never transcend and will never question. Rather than questioning their stake in a nation with an ambiguous history toward religious and ethnic difference, the Levovs are vigorously complicit. The postwar era symbolically and materially afforded them a new sense of belonging but a lingering psychic insecurity about social acceptance inspires a policing of social propriety and suspicion toward disruption. At an early 70s dinner party toward the end of *Pastoral*, Seymour's obstinate, self-righteous second generation Jewish father laments the indecency of *Deep Throat* (1972), a response echoed by Bill Orcutt a blueblood architect whom Seymour has discovered as Dawn's secret paramour. In response a stereotypically "obnoxious" literature professor, Marcia Umanoff, proclaims, "Without transgression there is no knowledge" (Roth 1997, 360). Predictably the houseguests are befuddled by her response.

In *Home,* Bobby's co-parenting of daughter Rebecca is less about the literal childrearing than the traumatic experiences that precede his parenting. Having witnessed the deaths of his immediately family, the domestic disappointment of his adoptive mother Alice, and Jonathan and Clare's struggles with sexuality and love he is leery of the assumed stability and health of the American nuclear family. When he, Jonathan and Clare move to a hamlet in Woodstock to raise Rebecca they lay a crucial groundwork for the future citizen or *progressive infant*. Futurity is a key theme of *Home,* and Rebecca is its symbolic and material manifestation.

The contrast between Bobby and Clare's raising of Rebecca reflects their personae in significant ways. Clare, who grows increasingly frustrated with the living arrangement, comes to terms with her identity as a bohemian poser and a 40-something woman who has always rejected traditional domesticity but craves it. Clare is in love with Jonathan, who is gay, and Bobby who is too consumed with fulfilling everyone's emotional needs and desires to commit solely to her. Clare wants to prevent Rebecca from following her path and takes on a fiercely protective, rather than nurturing stance. Clare says:

> I found that I loved her without a true sense of charity or goodwill. It was a howling, floodlit love; a frightening thing. I would shield her from a speeding car but I'd curse her as I did it, like a prisoner cursing the executioner (Cunningham 1990, 274).

Clare's investment in protection and sheltering makes parenthood a terrifying prospect. She wants to protect Rebecca. But the notion of nurturing is more frightening because it is unfamiliar and must be created. Such a reactionary stance reproduces an investment in what seems safe, stable and secure – traditional family structures – but often leaves people feeling dissatisfied. Clare imagines for Rebecca that:

> Someday she'd pay a fortune to therapists for their help in solving the mystery of my personality. There would be plenty of material – a mother living with two men, intricately in love with both of men. An undecided,

disorganized woman who fell out of every conventional arrangement. Who dragged her own childhood along with her into her forties (Cunningham 1990, 274).

However Rebecca seems well adjusted – the unconventional trio is all she has ever known and appears natural. This is an important contrast with Clare, who grew up in a traditional but dysfunctional nuclear family. Unable to reconcile either situation, Clare's default response is protection; her response seems more about self-protection and assurance than Rebecca. The "undecided" comment is her moment of truth – her self-confessed discomfort with the ambiguity of living in Woodstock.

In contrast, Bobby always approaches their lives as ambiguous. As they move in he declares, "We are forces of order, come from the city with talents and tools and our belief in a generous future," a metaphor for his role as an improviser (Cunningham 1990, 264). Similarly, when Clare confronts him about his frustrating emotional availability he responds, "I am part of the living and part of the dead. I am living for more people than just myself" (Cunningham 1990, 272). Lest this sound too airy Clare appreciates his parenting noting:

> Bobby loved our daughter but was not tormented by her vulnerable, noisy existence. . . . He had that religious quality. He was soft-hearted and intensely focused. He was not deeply interested in the flesh. Sometimes when he held Rebecca I knew how he saw her – as a citizen in his future world. He respected her for swelling the population but did not agonize over particulars of her fate. In his eyes, she was part of a movement (Cunningham 1990, 276).

Clare has a pragmatic, immediate investment in the tangible, structured and safe paralleling broader cultural investments in linearity and inherited structures. Bobby sees the future as something more ambiguous, depending on how people transform rather than adhere to prefabricated rules. He models an improvisational foundation for Rebecca where engaging with danger, vulnerability and the unexpected are more useful tools than reliance on abstractions like "shelter and protection." Bobby sees Rebecca as not merely his child but a citizen who will have to engage with and become a part of a broader society – not shelter herself from it. These philosophical differences lead Clare to abandon Woodstock when she realizes the limits of her bohemian pose.

Regarding the actual child, the characters describe her as the opposite of Merry: balanced. Clare comments:

> She needed, and with growing vehemence, resented my protection. I only needed her safety but I needed it completely, all the time. . . .She wept if I watched her too closely, and wept if she realized that for a moment I'd forgotten to watch her at all (Cunningham 1990, 278).

If Clare is too protective and Bobby too abstract, Rebecca balances their seeming excesses – she is a baby with palpable subjectivity. Bobby describes Rebecca's temperament and physicality noting, "Already, at eleven months, she has a nature. She is prone to contemplation. She resists both laughter and sorrow until they overwhelm her, and then she gives herself up completely" (Cunningham 1990, 265). Clare notes how, "It seemed that every day she developed a new gesture or response that carried her much closer to her own eventual personality. From hour to hour she kept turning more fully into somebody" (Cunningham 1990, 276). Bobby and Clare most favorably describe Rebecca's relationship with co-parent Jonathan. Bobby notes how, "Of all her qualities, Jonathan is most in love with her capacity for amazement" (Cunningham 1990, 265-66).

Adults who seemingly disengage from their surrounding environments can be loosely interpreted as adult infants. By definition they represent innocence or, more troublingly, an aversion to "knowledge, agency, and accountability" (Berlant 1997, 8). One of the most striking and significant aspects *Pastoral* and *Home* share are their depictions of Bobby and Seymour in terms that allude to infant-like behavior. Seymour represents the infant as passive, dependent, selfish and helpless. In essence he is what I term a *spoiled infant* who refuses to grow up. Like Berlant's idealized infant he is content to passively embrace national mythologies – particularly American assimilation as a form of erasure and the private, nuclear family as a protective space from broader political and social realities. Though Seymour inherits the family business, he never builds from his heritage or develops what Jeffrey Rubin-Dorsky defines as, "a new, unpredicted yet vital phase of Jewish history," *American Jewish* identity. According to Rubin-Dorsky, "in America Jews can be deeply committed to the values, aspirations, and meanings embodied in Jewish history while at the same time remaining loyal to American institutions that ensure democratic freedoms" (Rubin-Dorsky 2001, 79-80). Driven by a linear view of assimilation, Seymour, being an "American who happens to be Jewish", subsumes *American Jewish* identity. Where the Levovs raised their eyebrows at the value of transgression, Bobby would raise his glass.

Bobby represents the wonder, optimism and possibility of the pre-socialized infant. However he transforms the vacuousness of infancy to a mode of creation and transformation. In this respect Bobby is a rebel disguised as an innocent – or what I term a *signifying/defiant infant* (Gates 1988, 51).[16] Throughout the novel, characters refer to Bobby as an infant, including Jonathan's initial description of Bobby's face as "nakedly fretful as a baby's" and Clare, who labels him "half child, an innocent" (Cunningham 1990, 47, 166). However, as characters familiarize themselves with him they realize he is smart, subversive and purposeful. Bobby emotionally grasps pre-conceived expectations and improvises around these to create new knowledges, which is an ethically-motivated choice that opens new possibilities for his community.

Social ethics and kinship: conclusion

If the post-WWII period catalyzed a racial and ethnic redefinition of who comprises the American family, the Vietnam inspired 1960s counterculture publicly questioned the ability of traditional nuclear families, as a way of life, to provide fulfillment and advance citizenship ideals. The quest for increased social access and recognition which fueled these pivotal social movements endures in a context of reified American nationalism. In *Pastoral,* Roth suggests the counterculture had a necessary political spirit but lacked a sustainable social vision. Within *Home,* counterculture politics broadly motivate Bobby but it is through sexuality, friendship and family – rather than overt politics – that an alternative social logic emerges. The highly visible, nationalistic unity rhetoric of the postwar era obscured deep cultural divisions under the guise of increased social access and the promotion of national ways of life. Implicit in this rhetoric was the inference of social equality and psychic reconciliation with patterns of discrimination. Vietnam awakened these dormant inconsistencies via a broad political critique largely defined by a cultural rejection of enforced social roles. The cultural tensions which emerged during the era spanning the postwar and Vietnam eras spurred a range of questions that have altered the contours of national intimacies.

The *Home* and *Pastoral* comparison is historically useful because Seymour grows into adulthood in an era when religious and "ethnic" identity are perceived as declining barriers. But the actual transformative work to reduce these prejudices is an active process, not simply a mythology to be fulfilled. Seymour's focus on individualism stymies his sense of how to achieve an identity that queers "American" identity by challenging WASP assimilation as the national racial, ethnic and religious core. Merry, whom Seymour's brother Jerry refers to as a symbol of Seymour and Dawn's social experiment, is a fragmented, dislocated, and ultimately destructive citizen who inherits staid narratives of assimilation rather than possibilities for developing the new modes of citizenship her parents bypass on their assimilation excursion (Roth 1997, 272-81) The symbolism is chilling because it represents the reproduction of generations of dissatisfied citizens encouraged to suppress difference for the sake of citizenship that negates their particularity.

Even though race and ethnicity are easily perceived as more salient categories of discrimination than gender and sexual difference, less attention has been focused on how queer social practices model valuable forms of community and culture building that redefine possibilities of citizenship. Bobby and Seymour's differences illuminate tensions between two familial modes battling for acceptance in the intimate public sphere. There is an imagined apolitical, de-ethnicized, private American nuclear family insulated from history because of the "order" and "stability" it inherently offers. In contrast are more exploratory, public/communal formations that employ community, multiplicity and flexibility as the basis for progressive citizenship. The legal vulnerabilities and social stigmas non-traditional kinship systems face are realistic barriers. But their value lies in the ways "choice" challenges and reconstructs kinship and family on personal and affirming terms which represent a larger potential for active resistance to intimate traumas.

The subversion of gender roles and the emphasis on community over blood defines *Home*'s progressive family. The ways Alice functions as an adoptive mother for Bobby and grandmother to Rebecca and Erich's presence exemplify the way queer communities have nurtured each other during the AIDS crisis, illustrating how family and home function as elastic concepts. *Home*'s queer family ultimately illustrates the possibility for ethical living beyond nuclear family structures. The intricacies of *Home*'s family configurations, and Rebecca the individual character, are less important than the provocative and pragmatic social possibilities they present.

In the neoconservative climate of the last four decades there remains a need for sexual minorities and the unique kinship systems they create/inhabit to gain access to the public sphere. In the face of an imagined and idealized national uniformity, such kinship systems are an essential tool to gaining political footing in the intimate public sphere. Their identities and values are not merely alternatives to nuclear families, but formations stemming from vital historical disruptions that have gradually redefined sexuality, gender roles and family structures. Liberal politics has abandoned the counterculture ethos for political moderation, thus the value of progressive *social* formations is obscured. Comparing

Pastoral and *Home* illustrates how a wider range of kinship systems are essential because they complement key postwar movements that have redefined the potential of citizenship. Social conceptions of family need to transition from generic structures that create bodies to occupy, consume and reproduce to a space that can operate independently of traditional generationality. Re-imagining family as an ethical space where adults nurture children as future citizens, rather than generational receptacles, could enable a transition in cultural discourse toward a more nuanced recognition of *how* children are engaged. Such transitioning could also open up a critical space for progressives to articulate the ethical value of child rearing where transgression is a social necessity that enriches and prepares young citizens for the unresolved historical tensions and conflicts they have inherited and must negotiate. Now is the future our children are building, what tools are societies supplying?

Notes

[1] Cunningham, Michael. [1990] 1998. *A home at the end of the world*. New York: Picador. Originally published in 1990, my chapter refers to the 1998 Picador USA Paperback Edition. Roth, Philip. 1997. *American pastoral*. New York: Vintage International. Hereafter cited in the text as *Pastoral* and *Home*.

[2] In a February 24, 2004 speech President Bush announced his support for a proposed Federal Marriage Amendment which would define marriage exclusively as a union between a man and a woman. In 2004 and 2006 voting sessions the Amendment has twice failed to receive the necessary votes to become law from the U.S. Senate and House of Representatives. A combination of judicial decisions and ballot measures has subsequently extended marriage rights to same-sex couples. According to the Human Rights Campaign, as of July 9, 2014 19 states and the District of Columbia have legalized same-sex marriage. For more information visit: http://www.hrc.org/campaigns/marriage-center. President Obama and Vice-President Joe Biden became the first sitting White House administration to publicly endorse same-sex marriage, and marriage equality was included in the 2012 Democratic Party's official platform.

[3] Chafe cites Northern migration, increased economic opportunities, and army integration as key WWII era shifts that created hope for a better life among blacks but notes how the dynamic of "some improvement together with daily reminders of ongoing oppression" "galvanized anger and transformed it into political and social activism" (Chafe 1982, 69-71). Hertzberg defines, ". . . Catholics, Negroes and Jews" and the "three major outsiders in American Society . . ." based on popular depictions in wartime American films (Hertzberg 1997, 290).

[4] Brookhiser's (1991, 14-15; 147-51) polemic asserts, "The WASP character is the American character" and attempts to argue the reassertion of values WASP will reverse what he perceives as social and cultural decline; Christopher (1989, 19)

discusses ways "white ethnics" (Greeks, Italians, Jews, Slavic Americans) have historically downplayed their ethnic heritage to integrate themselves into elite positions; Robertuello and Hoguet (1987, 153-176) present a series of case studies detailing how individual Jews, Italian-Americans, African Americans and WASPs have struggled to attain esteem in a WASP dominated culture; Kaufmann (2004, 177) traces the rise of Anglo-American dominance and maps out its decline in the post-WWII era when he notes the national shift toward incarnating the, "liberal ideal of the transethnic, civic nation."

[5] For examples of discussions regarding the post-WWII era as a defining moment that made U. S. Jews "the most numerous, prosperous, and secure Jewry in the world," see Bernard Martin, ed. 1978. *Movements and issues in American Judaism: An analysis and sourcebook for developments since 1945.* Westport, Connecticut: Greenwood Press; 3, see p. 6 in Diner, 2004, Introduction; p. 274 in Sarna, Jonathan D. 2004. *American Judaism: A history.* New Haven and London: Yale University Press; p. xi in Moore, Deborah Dash. 2004. Preface to *G. I. Jews: How world war II changed a generation.* Cambridge, Mass. and London: The Belknap Press of Harvard University Press; p. xv. Shapiro, Edward S. 1992. Preface to *A time for healing: American Jewry since world war II* (Baltimore and London: The Johns Hopkins University Press.

[6] Foner (1998) briefly describes postwar white racialization noting how, ". . . the war made millions of ethnic Americans, especially the Jewish and Catholic children of the new immigrants, feel fully American for the first time. If the pluralism of the CIO and the Popular Front had begun the process of forging the new immigrants into a white working class, the war greatly accelerated the process."

[7] Hertzberg (1997, 292) notes how, "During and immediately after the war many younger Jewish intellectuals, who had been born and raised in the immigrants' ghettos, were eager to accept what the new American nationalism seemed to offer: minorities would be allowed into society if they adopted the manners and culture of Protestant Christians, of if they became 'universal men.' This 'bargain' was accepted, with variations, by two brilliant young Jewish writers of the war years, Arthur Miller and Saul Bellow."

[8] I employ this term from de Certeau, Michel, trans. 1988. *The Writing of History.* New York: Columbia University Press.

[9] Most writers have referred to Zuckerman as Roth's alter ego, however Norman Podhoretz has suggested Zuckerman is Roth's "alter brain," see 2000. "Bellow at 85, Roth at 67." *Commentary,* July-August, 36; Roth, *Pastoral*, 20.

[10] Rubin-Dorsky (2001, 96) responded to narrow critical attempts to reduce *Pastoral* to an anti-60s screed, "Unfortunately, in the hands of ideological critics of both persuasions, *American Pastoral* instead became a critique of the hedonistic, undisciplined 1960s-to the chagrin of Todd Gitlin on the left, to the delight of Norman Pohoretz on the right . . . They were both wrong." Parrish (2000, 85) also noted, "Roth's postmodern definition of self makes it difficult for his reader to assert with any confidence that his books endorse a particular point of view or cultural position."

[11] Alice described Bobby's response to Burt Morrow's death as, "He did not move. He stood on the lawn beside a black-coated fireman. As Ned and I ran to him, Bobby watched us with his old numbed uncomprehending expression; that foreigner's look" (Cunningham 1990, 104); Jonathan commented on Bobby's response to the Morrow gravesites during a stop in Cleveland, "Bobby gazed at the stones with a simple and almost impersonal respect, like a tourist visiting a shrine. By now his mourning was over and he'd fallen away from the ongoing process of his family's demise" and "If he was not quite somber, he had grown more blank – it was his old response to sorrow . . . Bobby could withdraw from the surface of his skin." "In these vacant states he said and did nothing different. His speech and actions continued unimpaired. But something in him departed, the living snap went out, and he took on a slumbering quality that might have been mistaken for stupidity by someone who knew him less" (Cunningham 1990, 251, 252).

[12] "It came to me that death itself could be a more distant form of participation in the continuing history of the world. Death could be like this, a simultaneous presence and absence while your friends continued to chat among the lamps and furniture about someone who was no longer you" (Cunningham 1990, 152); "Although we think of the dead inhabiting the past, I now believe they exist in an unending present. There is no hope of better things to come. There is no memory of the human progress that led to each moment" (Cunningham 1990, 214).

[13] Stacey interrogates the politics of "family values" rhetoric in the chapters "The Neo-Family-Values Campaign," 52-82 and "Virtual Social Science and the Politics of family Values," 83-104 in 1996. *In the name of the family: Rethinking family values in the postmodern age*. Boston: Beacon Press.

[14] Ball's (2003, 11) discussion distinguishes moral evaluations from judgments and defines morality as a politically urgent stance for gays and lesbians who, "have learned to use their same-gender sexuality as a source for both building lives of self-respect and pride for organizing politically to seek social change." He describes elements of "A Gay and Lesbian Sexual Ethic," 204-17.

[15] Janet R. Jakobsen and Ann Pellegrini have expressed related ideas about the constrained national discourse on the role of family, see p. 56 in Jakobsen, Janet R. 2002. "Can Homosexuals End Western Civilization As we Know It?: Family Values in a Global Economy." *Queer Globalizations: Citizenship and the Afterlife of Colonialism*, edited by Arnaldo Cruz-Malavé and Martin F. Manalansan IV. New York and London: New York University Press; see p. 137 in Pellegrini, Ann. 2002. "Consuming Lifestyle: Commodity Capitalism and Transformations in Gay Identity" in *Queer Globalizations: Citizenship and the Afterlife of Colonialism*, edited by Arnaldo Cruz-Malavé and Martin F. Manalansan IV. New York and London: New York University Press.

[16] I apply Henry Louis Gates' definition of signifying as figurative, implicative speech to Bobby, see p. 51 in 1988. *The signifying monkey: A theory of African-American criticism*. New York: Oxford University Press, 1988.

Works Cited

Ball, Carlos A. 2003. The morality of gay rights. An exploration in political philosophy. New York: Routledge.

Berlant, Lauren. 1997. The Queen of America Goes to Washington City. Essays on Sex and Citizenship. Durham: Duke University Press.

Blasius, Mark. 1994. Gay and lesbian politics. Sexuality and the emergence of a new ethic. Philadelphia: Temple University Press.

Brookhiser, Richard. 1991. The way of the WASP. How it made America, and how it can save it, so to speak. New York: Free Press.

Canning, Richard. 2003, Hear us out. Conversations with gay novelists. New York: Columbia University Press.

Chafe, William H. 1982. The Civil Rights Revolution, 1945-1960. The Gods Bring Threads to Webs Begun. In Reshaping America: Society and institutions, 1945-1960. Edited by Robert H. Bremner and Gary W. Richard. Columbus, OH: Ohio State University Press.

Christopher, Robert C. 1989. Crashing the gates. The De-WASPing of America's power elite. New York: Simon and Schuster.

Cvetkovich, Ann. 2003. An archive of feelings. Trauma, sexuality, and lesbian public cultures. Durham: Duke University Press.

Diner, Hasia R. 2004. The Jews of the United States, 1654 to 2000. Berkeley, Los Angeles, London: University of California Press.

Evans, Sarah. 2001. Sources of the Second Wave: The Rebirth of Feminism. In Long time gone. Sixties America then and now. Edited by Alexander Bloom. Oxford: Oxford University Press.

Foner, Eric. 1998. The story of American freedom. New York: W. W. Norton.

Gambone, Philip. 1999. Something inside. Conversations with gay fiction writers. Madison, Wisconsin: University of Wisconsin Press.

Herman, Didi. 1997. The Antigay Agenda. Orthodox Vision and the Christian Right. Chicago: The University of Chicago Press.

Hertzberg, Arthur. 1997. The Jews in America. Four centuries of an uneasy encounter. A history. New York: Columbia University Press.

Hoagland, Sarah Lucia. 1988. Lesbian ethics. Toward new value. Palo Alto, CA: Institute of Lesbian Studies.

Jakobsen, Janet, and Pellegrini, Ann. 2003. Love the sin. Sexual regulation and the limits of tolerance. New York: New York University Press.

Jarraway, David R. 1996. "The Novel that Took The Place of a Poem": Wallace Stevens and Queer Discourse. English Studies in Canada 22: 377-97.

Kaufmann, Eric P. 2004. The rise and fall of Anglo-America. Cambridge, Mass: Harvard University Press.

Lassiter, Matthew D. 2008. Inventing Family Values. Rightward Bound: Making America Conservative in the 1970s. Edited by Bruce J. Schulman and Julian E. Zelizer. Cambridge, Mass.: Harvard University Press.

Lehr, Valerie. 1999. Queer family values. Debunking the myth of the nuclear family. Philadelphia: Temple University Press.

LeVay, Simon, and Nonas, Elisabeth. 1995. City of friends. A portrait of the gay and lesbian community in America. Cambridge, Mass: MIT Press.

Murray, Stephen O. 1996. American gay. Chicago: The University of Chicago Press.

Nardi, Peter M. 1999. Gay men's friendships. Invincible communities. Chicago: University of Chicago Press.

Nimmons, David. 2002. The soul beneath the skin. The unseen hearts and habits of gay me. New York: St. Martin's Press.

Parrish, Timothy L. 2000. The End of Identity. Philip Roth's American Pastoral. SHOFAR 19: 84-99.

Robertiello, Richard C., and Hoguet, Diana. 1987. The WASP mystique. New York: Donald I. Fine, Inc.

Royal, Derek Parker. 2001. Fictional Realms of Possibility: Reimagining the Ethnic Subject in Philip Roth's American Pastoral. Studies in American Jewish Literature: 1-16.

Rubin-Dorsky, Jeffrey. 2001. Philip Roth and American Jewish Identity: The Question of Authenticity. American Literary History 13: 79-107.

Sands, Kathleen M. 2000. God forbid. Religion and sex in American public life. New York: Oxford Press.

Seidman, Steven. 1993. Romantic longings. Love in America, 1830-1980. New York: Routledge.

Warner, Michael. 1999. The trouble with normal. Sex, politics and the ethics of queer life. New York: Free Press.

Weston, Kath. 1991. Families we choose. Lesbians, gays, kinship. New York: Columbia University Press.

Wildman, Sarah. 2004. Bushwhacked Again. The Advocate December 7: 26-27.

Woods, Randall Bennett. 2005. Quest for identity. America since 1945. Cambridge: Cambridge University Press.

LIFE AND DEATH IN THE SHADOW OF THE A-BOMB: SOVEREIGNTY AND MEMORY ON THE 60TH ANNIVERSARY OF HIROSHIMA AND NAGASAKI

MARC LAFLEUR

Introduction: Everyday spectacles and permanent war

The public secret of the bomb in America is out, but do not tell anyone, for its secrecy is part of the appeal. Across the country nuclear weapons have made a comeback as memorials, museums and tourist excursions. In July of 2005 I was in the midst of a period of fieldwork on the nuclear public sphere in America, investigating the public sites of the nuclear secret and the ways in which these places both affected the body and the body politic in the America.[1] Unlike with Vietnam where the United States was unable to turn its own suffering easily into spectacle, World War Two, the Cold War, and atomic and nuclear weapons specifically, are increasingly the subject of nationalistic memorial enterprise (Rogin 1990; Masco 2006). These impulses, presented under the rubric of clear and moral victory, national heroism and patriotism, national security, and the saving of American lives and, perhaps more importantly, the American way of life are themselves not free from the ambiguities and doubts which haunt America's Vietnam War memories (Berlant 1997; Sturken 1997). Increasingly, as the memorial and "exhibitionary complex" (Bennett 1988) around atomic and nuclear weapons expands, so do fault lines and traumas emerge (Gerster 2013).

It was in Los Alamos, New Mexico, in 1943, where the heart of the Manhattan District project – the codename for America's top secret effort to build the first atomic bomb – was established. The summer of 2005 marked a temporal moment when the still open wounds of history and the underlying cultural politics of memorializing such traumas were fleetingly revealed. That summer was, of course, the sixtieth anniversary of both the development and employment of atomic weapons in New Mexico and Japan, respectively. Whereas elsewhere the sixtieth anniversary of the bombings of Hiroshima and Nagasaki were met with somber memorializations, in New Mexico the commemorative urge took on an altogether different character. In New Mexico, that summer's commemorative events focused upon the bomb as a scientific and technological accomplishment rather than as a weapon of war with a distinct and highly contested historical significance. In this chapter, I describe two events from that anniversary summer of 2005 to examine the ways in which the commemorative impulse in America around atomic and nuclear weapons reveals something about the broader cultural politics of war and trauma in the public sphere. In the two events, it is the bomb itself that was celebrated, a technological fetishism steeped in the fantasies of the victorious and righteous nation. The first event, held at the Bradbury Museum of Science in July of that year, centers around a ceremony held to introduce one of the museum's new exhibits. The museum is part of the Los Alamos National Laboratory in New Mexico, the place where the physicist Robert Oppenheimer and the team of scientists and engineers that made up the Manhattan Project first invented the atomic bomb and where much of the nation's most advanced nuclear weapons research and development continues to this day. The second anecdote focuses on an event, also from July 2005, held at the National Atomic Museum, a Smithsonian affiliated museum located in Albuquerque, New Mexico, in commemoration of the Trinity test, the world's first nuclear explosion.

Traumas, because of their perpetually unresolved status, repeat themselves. Returning in the always inadequate desire for completion or satiation, they cycle back and forth in endless repetitions of presence and absence (Freud 2003; Caruth 1996). That the trauma of the bomb had returned to haunt America once again was not new or particularly surprising. The unresolved nature of America's relationship with atomic and nuclear weapons virtually guarantees periodic traumatic eruptions. The landscape of nuclear weapons is one marked by the lacunae between the ways in which they are positioned as ultimate defense of justice and freedom, and the human, environmental, and political violence of their production (Kuletz 1998). This is due in large part to the veil of secrecy under which these weapons have been produced and the patina of national security and moral certainty in which they have been justified (Gusterson 1996; Masco 1999; Lifton and Mitchell 1995). Anniversaries, over-endowed with memorial fervor, are particularly susceptible to such outbreaks, as we saw in 1995 with the controversy over the display of the Enola Gay at the Smithsonian.

The Enola Gay controversy at the Smithsonian provided a temporary opening in the arena of the public sphere for the trauma of America's destruction of Hiroshima and Nagasaki to be addressed. And while this arena was just as hurriedly shut down, the anniversary was marked not by the exaltation of victory but by multiple lines of fracture and distrust. At that time, the intensity of the debate made it clear that the atomic bombings of Hiroshima and Nagasaki were still far from achieving the status as unambiguous signifiers of morally just acts of war that the military, veteran's groups and succeeding Presidential administrations would like (Bird and Lifschuz 1998; Linenthal and Englehardt 1996). This seems less clear in the present day. In the almost two decades that have passed since the fiftieth anniversary in 1995 the context for the memorializations of war and weaponry have shifted from the euphoria of the immediate Cold War period, where talk of a "peace dividend" trumped that of increased military spending, to the contemporary era which finds the United States caught up in a so-called "global war on terror" (and its failures). And so, whereas during the Smithsonian controversy dueling critics debated questions of whether the United States needed to drop the bomb at all, after the whitewashing of history and issues surrounding the politics of displaying machineries of war, in terms both pro and con the impact of the bomb, the environment has significantly changed. The context, tenor, impact and significance of the sixtieth anniversary memorial events I will discuss below both encompasses and meaningfully exceeds those governing the fiftieth anniversary in 1995.

I argue that in these two events the ongoing merging of war and the everyday, the society of the spectacle with the permanent state of exception can be seen (Hardt and Negri 2000). This article attempts to track, through an analysis of these commemorative events, the intersection of biopolitics and the condition of permanent war both in the United States and more widely, as these political forms both utilize and significantly exceed the formations of the nation-state. It is an attempt to examine the ways in which war, sovereignty, trauma and affect intersect and co-articulate one another in the shared politics of intimate spectatorship. But also to recognize the moments of aporia and paradox that they reveal or produce in their intersection. Specifically, I argue that these commemorative events foster a new biopolitical understanding of war and its weapons as technologies productive of life. In doing so, I contend, all the known axioms and tonalities of war have become largely irrelevant. As they merge with and disappear into the ether of the permanent sovereign exception, wars, their atrocities, and their catastrophes, become obscured and disappear, relegated to fleeting pit-stops of the spectacular around which to gather and make-believe politics and community. And yet in promoting life, the biopolitical forces at work behind these commemorative events do not produce life so much as cast it into what Giorgio Agamben has termed "a zone of indistinction" (1998, 4).

This chapter, then, is largely an initial attempt to expose and to explain some of these theoretical concepts through ethnography and examples from everyday culture. It does so, hoping that through concrete examples we can come to a better, more refined understanding of trauma, biopolitical sovereignty and permanent war. Moreover, it hopes to broaden the conversations on war and violence to encompass the everyday and the banal, the unspectacular spectacles of everyday life, in tourism, recreation, and memorialization. And so it is ultimately a text about the multiply encoded and overlapping plateaus of violence embedded in the permanent state of war and state of exception that is the everyday; an attempt to bring the hidden and camouflaged into relief so as to better formulate the shape and tenor of a politics of potential and hope.

Figure 10-1: "Where's Little Boy?" Photo by the author

Little Boy Revisited

If you visited the Bradbury Museum, in Los Alamos, New Mexico, between 2001 and the summer of 2005 you might have noticed that one of the museum's most prominent displays was missing (see Figure 10-1). The empty space was maintained, however, like a shrine, with railings enclosing the space where it should have been and a small sign explaining why it was missing. The item in question was a version of the Little Boy bomb, the bomb that had been dropped on Hiroshima, Japan, leading to the immediate deaths of approximately 150,000 people on August 6, 1945.

Figure 10-2: "It's a Boy!" Photo by the author

The reason it was missing was "security." After September 11, 2001, the laboratory reassessed all of its security procedures and protocols and one day lab security personnel entered the museum and told museum staff that the Little Boy bombshell that they had on display and which is consistently ranked by visitors as one of the primary reasons they come to the museum was a security risk and had to be removed. The lab's security staff had determined that since the Little Boy on display was in fact a real bombshell, whose internal mechanics had simply been stripped prior to its being turned over to the museum, terrorists could enter the museum with an x-ray machine and discover the basic structures of an atomic bomb.[2] The fact that the entire plans, in detail, for the Little Boy had been available in books and on the Internet for some decades did not seem to matter.

In July 2005 the museum was to receive a new Little Boy replica that they had had built specially for them. The new replica was not a security threat. This new replica was cause for some excitement around the museum for two reasons. First, because one of their most popular exhibits was being restored to them, and second, because the new Little Boy had been painstakingly researched and built to be an exact copy of the bomb dropped on Hiroshima, right down to the placement of screws and the shade of green it was painted. In order to mark the occasion, museum staff began to plan an event that would feature the unveiling of the new exhibit.

That summer I received an invitation (see Figure 10-2) to the event that announced on its front cover: "It's a Boy!" The "boy" in question was, of course, "Little Boy". The invitation was to a ceremony being held at the Bradbury Museum of Science, to mark the unveiling of their new Little Boy replica.

I gathered much of this information after the fact because, I must confess, the return of this exhibit did not strike me as a particularly interesting or important event until the day I received an invitation. Framed in shades of blue, the invitation requested the pleasure of my company to celebrate their new addition.

On the appointed day in July about one hundred people gathered at the museum after hours for the unveiling. The bomb, over which was draped a large sheet, was back in its place on the museum floor. The museum director gave a short introduction and pointed to some dignitaries in the crowd, including the man who had been the flight navigator on the Nagasaki bombing run. The sheet was drawn off to applause and exclaim. The mood was celebratory and jubilant. Many in the crowd gathered around the bomb in momentary awe. One person placed his baby atop the bomb and moved it as if it was dancing. In the speeches, no mention of Hiroshima was ever made.

Spectatorship and indistinction

In America sites of disaster and wound constitute a "pathological" public sphere which encompasses the new nodes around which private desire and public space intersect (Warner 1992; Foster 1996; Seltzer 1998). These sites also constitute the fleeting and emptied out moments of politics siphoned through shock, sympathy and schadenfreude. Most often these sites are organized around a collision between bodies and machinic technologies – of war, transportation, industry – and speak to a set of interrelated anxieties about modernity: technoscientific dominance over everyday sociality, individual powerlessness to effect change, and excessively mediatized affective regimes to name just a few. As Seltzer (1998, 253) describes:

The pathological public sphere takes the form of a fascination with the shock of contact between bodies and technologies: a shock of contact that encodes, in turn, a breakdown in the distinction between the individual and the mass, between private and public registers...One discovers again and again the excitations in the opening of private and bodily and psychic interiors: the exhibition and witnessing, the endlessly reproducible display of wounded bodies and wounded minds in public.

Viewpoints wherein disaster, wounds and catastrophes to human bodies are placed on spectacular display then come to act as one of the few nodes of striation in an otherwise smooth and eviscerated social-political sphere (Deleuze and Guattari 1987). They are gathering points in the new public sphere, places where a "we" can form, however temporarily, in the bloody haze of one more disaster your body has averted. This "mass witness", as Michael Warner (1992) calls it, constitutes itself in the momentary and shocking pleasure garnered from witnessing injury and disaster – the bigger the better. Traumatic witnessing lubricates the mass witness into a single politicized body, as Foster explains:

Here again in its guise as witness the mass subject reveals its sadomasochistic aspect for this subject is often split in relation to a disaster: even as he or she may mourn the victims, even identify with them masochistically, he or she may also be thrilled, sadistically, that there are victims of whom he or she is not one. (There is a triumphalism of the survivor that the trauma of the witness does not cancel out). Paradoxically, perhaps, this sadomasochistic aspect helps the mass subject cohere as a collectivity (Foster 1996, 52-54).

But the trauma witnessed is also the trauma experienced, and the "we" that is formed constitutes itself in the negative, spectral spaces of the "not us". Traumatic witnessing constitutes a mass body only by erasing its own, the body returns only in the gory collision of flesh and machines. "The transitive pleasure of witnessing/injuring makes available our translation into the disembodied publicity of the mass subject. By injuring a mass body – preferably a really mass body, somewhere – we constitute ourselves as noncorporeal mass witness" (Warner 1992, 250). It is this abstraction embedded within this kind of spectatorship, the bodily loss that it necessarily entails, that is important for us to remember.

So let us return for a few moments to the ceremony surrounding Little Boy. That the bomb constitutes such a site of wound and catastrophe is in some ways clear. To stand in the shadow of the bomb is to be caught in a moment of stasis, where the proliferating circulation of everyday narratives of consumption, inadequacy and utopian hope, among others, stops short and is briefly dispelled. The social bond of victory, exhibited by the intact bodies of the audience, fosters a shallow yet nonetheless gripping sense of fraternity. The exhibited A-bomb catches the spectator in the simultaneous impact of fear and awe, sympathy and righteousness, between the sovereign's ability to secure and protect its citizens and its ultimate power to destroy them.

But nonetheless, as a site of catastrophe and wound it is, despite the evidence, decidedly ambiguous. For although Little Boy inevitably refers to the destruction that it wrought, here it was returned intact, as if resurrected. The disaster that it implies is wholly absent from the ceremony of its return and the context of its display, almost as if it did not occur. Almost. Little Boy represents a site of catastrophe, but catastrophe deferred, distanced and rubbed out. But this does not mean that the traumatic/pleasurable element embedded in witnessing the Little Boy ceremony is wholly absent either. Rather it is both present and absent simultaneously, or in other words virtual. The virtual, "where futurity combines, unmediated, with pastness, where outsides are infolded and sadness is happy" marks the spectrality of traumatic witnessing, in this case demonstrating not just the maintenance of a connection to the past but of a traumatic that is productive of a future as well (Massumi 2002, 30).

It is this quality of virtuality that prevents the Little Boy ceremony from slipping completely into the dreamworld of spectacular sovereignty. For it is this virtual element, this direct pipeline between the past and the future, that will not allow Little Boy to ever be completely severed from its history, from the tens of thousands of dead and wounded. This inbuilt virtuality can be understood as haunting, a traumatic reminder never fully revealed or understood, yet nonetheless persistent. Paradoxically it is also this element –the haunting traces of past catastrophe – which maintains the attention of the mass witness, no matter how deferred. So the traumatic return of Little Boy as exhibit compounds the trauma of the Hiroshima bombing itself, each doubling up and spilling over onto the other. The exhibit of the bomb's replica, in the virtuality of its relation to the original event, builds upon and adds to this trauma, pushing it to excess, it itself refers to the absent original Little Boy, pointing to the catastrophe of the original only in its now doubled absence.

A further complication. The characteristics of death and wound which accompany Little Boy, if only as a deferred or virtual-present absence, are in this ceremony the subject of a further and particularly disturbing distancing mechanism. The ceremony introduces us to the bomb via a metaphor of birth. Here Little Boy returns anew, whole and perfect. Even the creepy playfulness of naming the original bomb after President

Roosevelt (Fat Man, the Nagasaki bomb, was named after English Prime Minister Winston Churchill) is dispelled in favor of a fully anthropomorphized death-machine. To produce a birth announcement for an atomic bomb is much more than to wage war in the name of preserving life, a paradoxical rationalization that has always been used by militaries. This bomb's circuitry – despite its magnificent, almost artisanal, attention to detail – is not wired for war or, more specifically, for death at all, at least not in the ways in which we have previously experienced and known them. So it is a death machine, or at least a replica (the differences between the two quickly recede into indistinction at this point), presented under the banner of life. Not just in the name or service of life but as life itself. Little Boy, reborn, represents the aspired to and well-disciplined life, the product of hard work and dedication to life lived in the service and obedience of the nation.

The politico-cultural symbolic which frames and contextualizes the bomb is one of life rather than death. And so the bomb is revealed less as a material weapon of war than as biopolitical tool that, perhaps paradoxically, urges toward life. Little Boy re-emerges on the museum floor apparently cleansed of its catastrophe. This cleansing is itself a product of the regularization and normalization tendencies intrinsic to the biopolitical (Foucault 2003). Restored, it is the body of the bomb – Little Boy – that has become the focus of biopolitical concern – that intimate intrusion of the state – and the sympathetic relationship between the museum audience and the bomb encompasses their body in that biopolitical concern as well. But it does not shed its deathly past completely; instead it is held in reserve, inevitably hinting at this potential all the while seducing its audience. And so the bomb ingratiates itself, embedding itself in the body – a life form – as an ambiguous icon, of control, security, national membership, but also as a persistent kernel of fear. In the aftermath of the ceremony the crowd that day gathered around the bomb, celebrated its return, and appeared to subscribe to the promises embedded within it.

The mounting paradoxes are not the result of a disordered cultural arena or technologies of power thrown into chaotic reaction by the zigzag forms of contemporary culture. Rather, they are indicative of what Agamben calls the "zone of indistinction" into which eventually all features of political life gobbled up in the sovereign exception become permanent (Agamben 1998). "Since 'there is no rule applicable to chaos,'" he writes, "chaos must first be included in the juridical order through the creation of a zone of indistinction between outside and inside, chaos and the normal situation – the state of exception...As such the state of exception is fundamentally unlocalizable" (Agamben 1998, 19). This "zone", which is necessarily and despite its name a non-place, exists only as a negative relationship, a ban which acts to connect the sovereign exception to its biopolitical essence: "bare life", life that can be killed but not sacrificed. In this case the sacrifice of Little Boy is recognized, life itself is promoted in the name of the bomb, yet what kind of life may be lived under the promises and threats embedded within?

Yet, let us return for the moment to the concept of indistinction and the overlapping and contradicting traumas of the Little Boy event. Here the distinctions between life and death, between war and peace are relegated into meaninglessness, and so with them those between soldier and civilian, battlefield and sanctuary and, finally, between violence and harmony. The Little Boy unveiling, from this perspective, emerges as one of the banal yet essential nodes that both produces and maintains indistinction which is necessarily a zone defined by the permanence of violence, by the permanence of war. Not only has war become a permanent feature of everyday life, slipping into and out of tangibility, it lubricates and fosters a dysfunctional and in itself violent foundation for human interaction such as the traumatic mass witnessing discussed earlier. As Hardt and Negri (2004, 12) lament: "Today, however, war tends to extend even farther, becoming a permanent social relation".

Fat Man revisited

On July 16, 1945 the scientists and the engineers of the Manhattan Project detonated what they called the "gadget" in the desert of southern New Mexico at a place called the Trinity Site. It was the world's first nuclear explosion. Three weeks later, the gadget, now re-named Fat Man, was dropped on Nagasaki, Japan, instantaneously killing approximately 75,000 people and leading to the deaths of many more in subsequent weeks, months and years. This past summer, on the weekend of July 15 and 16, 2005, the National Atomic Museum in Albuquerque, New Mexico held an event called "The Blast from the Past" to commemorate the 60th anniversary of Trinity, the original nuclear test. Blast from the Past was a two-day affair consisting of a gala event at the museum on the Friday night and then a group trip to the Trinity Site early the next morning.

Anti-nuclear activists, alerted to "Blast from the Past", protested outside the Friday evening event, calling attention to what they felt was being ignored inside the museum by setting up pictures of the dead and wounded from Hiroshima and Nagasaki on the sidewalks surrounding the museum. One group managed even to get tickets to the event and invited a survivor of the Hiroshima bombing, Shigeko Sasamori, to accompany them. The activist group felt very strongly that a misleading historical narrative was being promoted by the event, one which celebrated the bomb as a technological and industrial marvel while erasing its role as a military weapon and the death and destruction it ultimately caused.

In a newspaper article published on July 16, 2005, the director of the National Atomic Museum was quoted as saying that protesters had misinterpreted the "Blast from the Past" event by calling it a "celebration". It was, he argued, not a celebration but a sober commemoration and contemplation of the Trinity Test and the Manhattan Project.[3] Protesters could be forgiven their misinterpretation, however. That day dozens of participants of "Blast from the Past" had toured the Trinity Site wearing matching backpacks emblazoned – part of the museum's loot bag for the event's participants – with a stylized mushroom cloud (see Figure 10-3). The previous evening's events at the National Atomic Museum had included a vintage military vehicle display as well as a 1940's inspired fashion show to "recreate a sense of the times."[4] Wine bottles scattered on tables throughout the event had been corked with specially made "Fat Man" and "Enola Gay"[5] pewter corks. Moreover, in the spirit of recreating the intense "urgency" and "secrecy" that marked the Manhattan Project all attendees were ushered into the event through the back door of the museum and issued with a dossier labeled "Top Secret", within which was contained a replica Manhattan Project ID badge as well as documents outlining the guest's "mission" for the evening. While that night's program at the museum concluded with a discussion panel that briefly addressed the Second World War, the tone of the evening remained a euphoric look back into a highly manipulated yet nevertheless perceived golden-era of the American past.

During the panel discussion that concluded the gala evening at the museum, Ms. Sasamori rose and addressed the assembled crowd and conveyed her experience of the bombing and her wishes for peace. At the moment of her declaration of identity there was a shiver of unease. When a trace of the real, a survivor, invades the carefully wrought and fragile architectures of the simulacra, it begins to ever so slightly crack and fissure. The debate over Hiroshima changes when it cannot just be waged in the abstract, between citizens of the righteous/guilty nation. Trauma is allowed to return and the sudden quietness of the room is evidence of how it was playing across the bodies of those present, the topic no longer just intellectual but now sensual. Nonetheless, it is difficult to assess the impact of Shigeko Sasamori's comments that night but it seemed as though they were not what participants in the midst of the museum's party really wanted to hear or contemplate. By the next morning it seems the threat has been assimilated, the rupture recuperated, or to put it more accurately, an answer has been formulated, a recuperation has been mounted, no matter that it is destined to fail, it will hold for a while, maintaining stasis until something better comes along.

Shigeko Sasamori was thirteen when the bomb exploded over her hometown of Hiroshima on August 6, 1945.[6] She is thought to be the person closest to the epicenter of the blast who survived. That morning, as she tells it, school had been cancelled and instead students were assigned to municipal work groups. She was with her friend, on their way to work that morning, when a solitary plane flew over the city. In the explosion moments later her friend was killed immediately. Ms. Sasamori's body was taken to a park with other dead and wounded and was left there to die. She was unrecognizable, her arms were fused to her body and she had burns to eighty percent of her body. She did not, of course, die. Some days later her parents found her in the park and, although she was physically unrecognizable, were able to identify her through her cries for help. Eventually she was selected as one of the "Hiroshima Maidens", the group of badly injured women taken to the United States for advanced treatment and therapy under the sponsorship of Norman Cousins. Today, Shigeko Sasamori's body still visibly bears the scars of that day's events. Her hands are contorted and permanently contracted in such a way that prevents her from full dexterity. Her face bears the signs of multiple and uneven skin grafts and surgeries and is characterized by the tightness that is the result of being badly burned.

The next day as "Blast from the Past" participants wandered the grounds that make up the Trinity Site I began to ask people how they felt about Ms. Sasamori or what she had said the night before. My interviews that started that day proved disappointing and were not eliciting enthusiastic or even thoughtful response. This was the case until I was told that perhaps the reason why I was not getting the responses I thought I might was because my question was invalid. I was talking to two women from California. They were there with their husbands and "Blast from the Past" was a part of their holiday. I asked them what they meant and here is what they said to me. My question was not valid, they said, because she was not real. They must have seen the confusion on my face: "She was not really a Hiroshima survivor. She was a fake, an imposter, an actor, a stunt put on for effect by the activists."

When circulation comes to a jarring halt we are left hanging in the sudden absence of meaning and an excess of the bodily sensation of paradox. And then just as abruptly meaning floods back in to fill the gap, threatened by the potentiality embedded in the lack of the rational. It was her skin, they told me, which tipped them off. "Seventy-three year-olds don't have skin that smooth."

Figure 10-3: "Blast from the Past." Photo by the author

Spectacular anesthesia

The two women's declaration speaks with authority on the question of the Real, positively identifying Ms. Sasamori's lack of authenticity. The declaration is jarring, however, as it posits her unreality as opposed to the context in which the women were in, the historical fantasy that was "Blast from the Past." Let me be clear, I do not posit a Real that is simply made inaccessible by spectacle. Rather, it is spectacle in association with the exception that fosters or ignites, to an unparalleled degree, a proliferation of possible realities which create the conditions such that the two women tourists are able to make such a declaration with confidence in its accuracy. "Blast from the Past" like much in the nuclear public sphere executes a nifty political trick, manufacturing consent for nuclear weapons by encouraging nostalgic and patriotic memorializations of the era of their production. It is able to do so, I argue, by hooking itself into the mechanisms of the sovereign exception. By producing greater and greater indistinction, these memorializations wholly divorce the weapons and their iconic status from the catastrophes of their use. Thus "Blast from the Past" billed itself as a commemoration of the Trinity nuclear test, as if the test itself did not directly lead to the Nagasaki bombing. As with "Blast from the Past", so with the two women. The bombing of Japan had nothing to do with the event, with Trinity or with themselves and its intrusion into their space could not possibly be accurate.

What seems clear is that through the denial the women construct or demarcate a shared space of intimacy, one that seeks to extend, via virtual prostheses, to the mass body of America (an always minority yet nevertheless hegemonic body) (Warner 1992). This is an intimacy which recreates and reinforces the intimacy which the Trinity Site itself fosters, that of the nation-state's embrace. There is something uncanny about visiting a site in which there is in fact very little to see. It calls to mind, as Taussig (1999) reminds us, Robert Musil's comment that the most notable thing about monuments is their "lack of strikingness". But the emptiness of the Trinity Site almost paradoxically brims with potential fullness and an excess of meaning. Scuffing the dirt with the toes of their shoes, visitors half-expect to uncover something previously hidden and perhaps dangerous. But that is what excites. The secret hangs heavily over the Trinity Site, and it is easy to imagine that one is among the privileged few being let in on it. As if the state were whispering in our ear alone: "I'm going to let you in on something..." Intimacy and fantasy, as Berlant (2000) writes, are bedfellows, relying upon each other to maintain normalcy or what she calls the "unproblematic."

It is only when a perceived or imagined sense of intimacy comes under scrutiny, "when states, populations, or persons sense that their definition of the real is under threat; when the normative relays between personal and collective ethics become frayed and exposed ; and when the traditional sites of pleasure and profit seem to get "taken away" by the political actions of subordinated groups, a sense of anxiety will be pervasively felt about how to determine responsibility for the disruption of hegemonic comfort" (Berlant 2000, 7). Ms. Sasamori did not just call into question the suitability of the "Blast from the Past" event, but cast its underlying project, the buttressing of American identity itself, into a state of unease and panic. Deftly, and with one stroke of denial and an emphatic re-embrace of fantasy the two women had explained away the trauma that had momentarily interrupted not just the smooth unfolding of their holiday but the very illusion of the good life to which they subscribed themselves with such effort.

Again, as we saw with Little Boy, it is an intimacy which is cast not simply in the common experience of the spectacle of the catastrophe, but the catastrophe which is then deferred, parried and denied. The seeming paradox of this intimacy is that instead of opening up the body to the affective trace of trauma, a trace which according to Berlant (2000) is always sensual, it functions by reinforcing the shell of anesthesia that chokes off the senses from the world around it. Instead of jolting the senses, and jump-starting the body, however artificially, this intimacy tries to shore up the (mass) body by deadening its senses in ever greater attempts to elude the haunting knocks of the traumatic real. This is what Walter Benjamin was afraid of when he formulated his theories of shock and the aestheticization of the political (1968, 1978). In the modern world with its infinite possibilities of both physical and psychic trauma, the synaesthetic system – the human nervous system and the environment to which it responds – becomes transformed, changing its machinery from the sensory to the protective. No longer is the apparatus of human perception open to world. The gateways of the body close, shielding itself from the excesses of the modern world perceived as a series of threats and hazards. The circuitry of the body's senses reverse course in such a situation, attempting to "deaden" or mute themselves from the outside world.

Modern anesthesia removes the subject from a position of judgment and decision by immersion into a apparently limitless ether of the image and the commodity. The aestheticization of the political results in the anaesthetizing of the body. Biopolitical sovereignty controls through reducing the subject to the present tense in which desire plays off against disaster, with consumption acting as the fleeting narcotic easing the fear that haunts sovereignty's ersatz management – that which is unknown, unstable, unpredictable, and beyond one's control (Massumi 1993). In transforming the unknown into a source of fear rather than excitement or anticipation, biopolitics as a mobile system of sovereignty based upon stasis and enclosed management reveals its genius, for it is at this moment that power's almost complete implantation or location within the body is demonstrated. So it is through the production of anaesthetized bodies that sovereignty – through an untempered violence embedded within it –

pushes the state of exception into permanence and maintains it there. Anesthesia and the state of exception rely upon one another, there cannot be one without the other.

The technoaesthetics of these compensatory realities foster social relationships, communal action and interaction, and communication via sophisticated yet thoroughly de-politicized simulations that render the need or desire for human engagement null. Anesthesia is accomplished via a concurrent starvation and deluge of the senses. "The dialectical reversal, whereby aesthetics changes from a cognitive mode of being in touch with reality to a way of blocking out reality, destroys the human organism's power to respond politically even when self-preservation is at stake: so someone who is past experiencing is no longer capable of telling…proven friend…from mortal enemy (Buck Morss 1992, 18). And so "Blast from the Past" and the Trinity Site become extensions of this kind of virtual reality, an almost static "presence-effect", highly aestheticized and anesthetizing. The perception of intimacy created between the two women, and perhaps more broadly between many of the participants, is revealed as a function of marshaled forces of patriotic, always amnesiac, affect. A negative solidarity that slips right into the maintenance of the foundations of the fantasy that is America.

But it is not just the anesthesia of modern life lived under the umbrella of spectacle and simulation that frames the women's denial of the experience of Ms. Sasamori. A radical new calculus of life and death bubbles to the surface, revealing its hidden structure – as it did during the "birth ceremony" for Little Boy-for just a moment. This is the life/death of Agamben's zone of indistinction. Not just the unfeelingness of the anesthesia, or the excessive spectacles of victorious war waged in the name of saving lives, Ms. Sasamori becomes something both more and less than what Agamben has called "bare life" (1998). In other words, Ms. Sasamori is only included in the political order of reality through exclusion or ban from that order, she exists only in the negative relation of her prohibition. Agamben (1999) suggests a revision of Foucault's equation of the sovereign decision as resting between the making live and the letting die, he insists, rather, that sovereign power is now oriented towards the "making survive". And yet Sasamori, already reduced and defined by her simply having survived the unsurvivable, understood not as fully human but simply as biologically tenacious, is denied even this status by the tourist's rejection. In this sense she is no longer that which survives but something – if at all possible – even less, no longer that which just survives, no longer bare life even! The material trace of her body descends in some ways past indistinction into nothingness. By denying the troublesome trace of the event, its living victims, the event cannot sustain itself. Without victims, without a trace, without history, then, the atomic bombing of Japan and its victims, alive and dead, disappear into the ether of indistinction.

But the two women's erasure of Ms. Sasamori and of the entire history she represents does not come immediately or without considerable effort. While she is cast into the status of bare life, she also greatly exceeds that condition, she is permanently caught between those forces which would attempt to maintain her as nothing more than that which survives, and her own body which testifies to the contrary. There is something else as well. There is inevitably a strange blowback effect, in that by denying that death haunts the event in which they are participating and in denying the status of victim to Ms. Sasamori, the two women cast aside much of what makes them alive, their sensual attachment to the world, their ability to empathize and feel compassion, their willingness to recognize and go with the lines of intensity –from which an ethics can be constructed – emanating from their bodies. Instead they rationalize and they explain, they deny and sink further into the logics of the spectacle. Bare life, the status into which they have doubly cast Ms. Sasamori, returns, as in a feedback loop, to encompass them as well.

But what cannot be denied is the ripple of trauma that played through the crowd, the night before, when Ms. Sasamori stood up to speak. It is this that represents the more important rupture for our purposes, over and above even the bombing itself. The crack that was opened up by trace of the traumatic which the two women, perhaps more acutely than others, but perhaps not, worked so hard to sooth and knit back together via their exclusion of her from their cognitive-political order must necessarily return. As with all traumas it cannot ever be fully assimilated and so returns to haunt its subject repeatedly (Caruth 1996). This haunting return of the traumatic can also be read as a potential for new articulations.

Conclusion: Traumatic insurgencies

The virtual public spheres that have begun to form around sites of atomic nostalgia in America momentarily concentrate and provide fleeting glimpses of the ways in which modernity's ghosts have begun to capture and refashion the body. The traumas of the bodily impact with machinic technologies of war are made all the more complicated by the re-presentation of these impacts as banal and emptied out tourist experiences or museum visits. This is the new landscape of the bomb in which time and place become slippery and bodies mingle openly with the haunting phantoms of modernity. Here the weight of historical traumas add up and spill into the present day as if they just happened. Present day traumas reach out and haul those in the past out of retirement. Technologies of spectacle in conjunction with the proliferation of the permanent war and the total violence of the sovereign state of exception, which become visible here, conspire to defer, to numb to deaden. These forces permeate the body and are articulated as forms of memory, experience, belonging, emotion, and ethics. In such a context, life and death, as we think of them, are cast into disarray; no longer tethered concretely they drift, are subject to capture and release, interpretation and reinterpretation. Life, it seems, is increasingly forced to live in the space of death, while death itself is forcibly erased from the sphere of life. Most importantly the fundamental link between life and death and conceptions of ethics and justice are progressively eroded. As war progressively disappears into the no-place of permanence and the forces of indistinction swallow any attempts to mark out or measure resistance, the political horizon seems increasingly bleak. Yet, embedded in these forms exist moments of potential that can and must be articulated and expanded upon.

War has already exceeded the boundaries of meaning by which we have understood it, and consequently so has so much of war's violence, that which could not be calculated in traditional charts of war's truths. It is imperative now that we compose a new vocabulary of war, one which mimics and can thus highlight the very terrain war occupies: the everyday, the virtual, the banal, the immanent. The events narrated in this chapter can, in one sense, be understood as on the edges of the edges of war, so peripheral they seem to be to the so-called realities of war. But there is another way that they can be read and understood, rather than as marginal events which barely register in the grand scheme of importance they can instead be understood as singular centers of war, not connected in a hierarchy of war's visible effects but rather connected relationally via process. The difference is that understood this way they are harder to dismiss and instead of fighting against the boundaryless, permanence of war by imposing ill-fitting architectures of hierarchy, the horizons of war begin to reveal themselves to us episodically and in all their multiplicity. Rather than disappearing under the radar, they begin to stand out.

Traumatic eruptions of sympathy, relief, pleasure or horror into the public sphere, in response to the death and wounding of the Other, demarcate contemporary cultural politics as an arena marked by violence. But they serve another important function. Embedded within these ruptures is a source of potential. Traumas when they erupt onto the surface of things alert us not to the new but to what was always already there.

Traumatic moments, if recognized as such, act to puncture the veneers of the "society of the spectacle." They illuminate a particular cast of features and a terrain. The Bradbury museum's ceremony in honor of the return of Little Boy and "Blast from the Past" act as signals or alarm by placing the zone of indistinction on display.

What trauma taps into the before it is deferred is an autonomous streak in the body (Massumi 2002). This is an insurgent force in the body which defies attempts to regulate and dampen it. In contrast, to capture this streak – which we can call vitality, intensity, affect – points toward emergence, potentiality and change. Emergence signals its own ethics and justice, one that eludes the forces of system and control by refusing to replicate their forms. The two stories I have told today speak to the ways in which life and death have come to articulate one another in new and complex ways. The contemporary shadows of World War Two reveal the confusion of death with life, and the increasing prevalence of bare life and of bodies anaesthetized to the world around them. But on the edges of this encompassing virtuality are always moments of potential, and it is only by latching on to them, pushing them to excess, and to ever greater levels of intensification, that this potential may harnessed.

Notes

[1] This fieldwork was made possible by a generous grant from the Wenner Gren Foundation for Anthropological Research.
[2] Interview Notes, June-July 2005.
[3] Journal Santa Fe, Sunday July 17, 2005. P4.
[4] Personal communication with museum staff member.
[5] The "Enola Gay" was the name of the plane which dropped the atomic bomb on Hiroshima, Japan. The pilot, Paul Tibbetts, named the plane after his mother.
[6] All information concerning Ms. Sasamori is based on personal interviews conducted with her in March 2005 and again in July 2005.

Works Cited

Agamben, Giorgio. 1998. Homo Sacer. Sovereign power and bare life. Stanford: Stanford University Press.
—. 1999. Remnants of Auschwitz. The Witness and the Archive. New York: Zone Books Ltd.
Benjamin, Walter. 1968. The Work of Art in the Age of Mechanical Reproduction. In Illuminations. Edited by Hannah Arendt. New York: Schocken Books.

—. 1978. On Some Motifs in Baudelaire. In Reflections. Edited by Peter Demetz. New York: Schocken Books.

Bennett, Tony. 1988. The Exhibitionary Complex. New Formations 4: 75-102.

Berlant, Lauren. 1997. The Queen of America Goes to Washington. Essays on sex and citizenship. Durham: Duke University Press.

—. 2000. Introduction to Intimacy. In: Intimacy. Edited by Lauren Berlant. Chicago: The University of Chicago Press.

Bird, Kai, and Lifscultz, Lawrence (eds.). 1998. Hirsohima's Shadow. Stony Creek, CT: Pamphleteer's Press.

Buck-Morss, Susan. 1992. Aesthetics and Anaesthetics. Walter Benjamin's Artwork Essay Reconsidered. October 62: 3-41.

Caruth, Cathy. 1996. Unclaimed Experience. Trauma, narrative and history. Baltimore: John's Hopkins University Press.

Debord, Guy. 1994. The Society of the Spectacle. New York: Zone Books.

Deleuze, Gilles, and Guattari, Felix. 1987. A Thousand Plateaus. Capitalism and schizophrenia. (Brian Massumi, trans.) Minneapolis and London: University of Minnesota Press.

Foster, Hal. 1996. Death in America. October 75: 36-59.

Foucault, Michel. 2003. Society Must be Defended. Lectures at the College de France 1975-1976. New York: Picador.

Freud, Sigmund. 2003. Beyond the Pleasure Principle and Other Writings. (John Reddick, trans.). New York and London: Penguin.

Gerster, Robin. 2013. The Bomb in the Museum: Nuclear Technology and the Human Element. Museum & Society 11(3): 207-218.

Gusterson, Hugh. 1996. Nuclear Rites: A Weapons Laboratory at the End of the Cold War. Berkeley: University of California Press.

Kuletz, Valerie. 1998. The Tainted Desert. Environmental Ruin in the American West. New York and London: Routledge

Masco, Joseph. 2006. 5:29:45 AM. In Museum Frictions: Public Cultures/Global Transformations. Edited by Ivan Karp. Durham: Duke University Press.

Hardt, Michael, and Negri, Antonio. 2000. Empire. Cambridge MA and London: Harvard University Press.

—. 2004. Multitude. War and democracy in the age of empire. New York and London: Penguin Press.

Lifton, Robert Jay, and Mitchell, Greg. 1995. Hiroshima in America. Fifty years of denial. New York: Putnam's Sons.

Linenthal, Edward, and Englehardt, Tom (eds.). 1996. History Wars. The Enola Gay and Other Battles for the American Past. New York: Metropolitan Books/Holt.

Masco, Joseph. 1999. States of Insecurity: Plutonium and post-Cold War Anxiety in New Mexico, 1992-1996. In Cultures of insecurity: States, Communities and the production of Danger. Edited by Jutta Weldes, Mark Laffey, Hugh Gusterson and Raymond Duvall. Minneapolis, University of Minnesota Press: 203-231.
Massumi, Brian. 1993. Everywhere you want to be. In The Politics of Everyday Fear. Edited by Brian Massumi. Minneapolis and London: University of Minnesota Press.
—. 2002. Parables for the Virtual: Movement, Affect, Sensation. Durham, NC and London: Duke University Press.
Rogin, Michael. 1990. Make My Day. Spectacle as Amnesia in Imperial Politics. Representations 29(Winter): 99-123.
Seltzer, Mark. 1998. Serial Killers. Death and Life in America's Wound Culture. New York and London: Routledge.
Sturken, Marita. 1997. Tangled Memories: The Vietnam War, the AIDS Epidemic and the Politics of Remembering. Berkeley: University of California Press.
Taussig, Michael. 1999. Defacement. Public secrecy and the labor of the negative. Stanford: Stanford University Press.
Warner, Michael. 1992. The Mass Public and the Mass Subject. In Habermas and The Public Sphere. Edited by C. Calhoun. Cambridge: MIT Press.

INTERSECTING TRAUMAS: THE HOLOCAUST, THE PALESTINIAN OCCUPATION, AND THE WORK OF ISRAELI JOURNALIST AMIRA HASS

TINA WASSERMAN

Introduction

For the past twenty-five years the subject of Israeli journalist Amira Hass' work has been the Palestinian occupation, but a broader view of her writing reveals that it also moves across a plurality of histories and is, in fact, informed by multiple markings of family, place and time. Such movements and markings encompass her own migrations across contested spaces – that is, between the Palestinian Territories and Israel – but also, as the daughter of Holocaust survivors and war refugees, they encompass intergenerational and global migrations between Europe and the Middle East. Her life and work also bridge chronologies of time bearing the corrosive effects of both her parents' catastrophic European past as well as the violence and confusion of the current struggle between the Palestinians and the Israelis.

Hass' primary goal in her writing is to bring a view forward from behind the occupation – one that is often distorted or hidden behind closures and checkpoints – of places in the Palestinian Territories that are misunderstood in the popular Israeli imagination, as the Gaza Strip is, for example, when it is described as an area that is "savage, violent and hostile to Jews" (Hass 1996, 4). She has brought this masked view to the foreground by covering the occupation for the Israeli newspaper *Ha'aretz,* beginning in 1989 with reporting on the Gaza Strip. She has produced two books as well: one on Gaza, where she lived for three years beginning in 1993, and another on Ramallah, where she has lived since 1997. In 2009 she contributed the introduction and afterword to the Holocaust memoir, *Diary of Bergen-Belsen* written by her mother, Hanna Lévy-Hass.

Hass' commitment to reporting on the Israeli–Palestinian conflict, with her distinct focus from inside the occupation, has carried her across decades, though two intifadas (one between 1987-1991, the other between 2000-2005) and countless other crises including, the building of the Israeli West Bank barrier, the intra-Palestinian conflict between Fatah and Hamas, and most recently, the escalating violence that followed the horrific murders of four teenagers – three Israelis and one Palestinian – in the summer of 2014.

Hass has compared Israel's occupation of the Palestinian Territories to other global and historical struggles: "If we wrote about South Africa, everyone would understand," she says in *Between the Lines*, a documentary made about her in 2001 by Israeli filmmaker Yifat Kedar. Importantly, however, her objective is not to privilege one people over another, but to reveal the debilitating and caustic effects of the occupation, of "democracy for some, dispossession for others," precisely for the welfare and survival of *both* the Palestinians and Israelis (Hass 1996, 7). But she is often misinterpreted. Some Israelis and supporters of Israel see her writing about the occupation as only sympathetic to the Palestinians and hostile to Israel. But there is a kind of blindness in placing Hass solely on one side of such an intensely polarized conflict; a conflict, moreover, that is often inflamed by rigid dichotomies, as those, for example, between "self" and "enemy." Indeed, Hass' writing is really meant as an alarm and her target is nothing less than the illogic of the occupation and its terrible consequences for both Palestinians and Israelis: for Palestinians, generations of dispossession, military occupation, and control by Israel, and for Israelis, the anger and violence such control engenders.

Because Hass is quick to reveal inequalities and injustices on either side of the conflict, she is just as likely to be criticized by Palestinians as she is by Israelis. In the past, she has written, for example, about the Palestinians, that in the "structural limitations of a clan-based society" it has, in fact, "been proven difficult to develop a tradition of open debate, and whoever has dared to speak out has suffered for it" (Hass 2003, 113). Hass has also openly criticized the past leadership of the Palestinian Authority who, she wrote, "proved weak at the negotiating table, yet hungry to maintain power" (Hass 1996, 347). And she has revealed inequalities around the social hierarchy within the Palestinian community inside the Gaza strip when she points to the privileged status of the "muwataneen," the original Arab inhabitants of the Gaza Strip who make up one-third of the Gazan population and still own property in addition to some of the only grassy areas of the Strip. Refugees who originated from outside the Strip, on the other hand, make up the other two-thirds of the population, and while many live in eight poverty-stricken refugee camps, they are not allowed access to these limited, but Arab-owned, areas of greenery. In 2008, following the split between the Fatah government of the West Bank and the Hamas led administration in Gaza, tolerance for Hass' statements took a darker turn when, after travelling to Gaza in a protest boat, her vocal criticism of Hamas was met with threats against her life, thus forcing her to flee Gaza.

The real strength of Hass' work, of course, is that in its unflinching style of observation on the ground she has chronicled much of the tragic and absurd consequences of the occupation. Throughout her writing we encounter the corrosive illogic of the occupation as she documents shifting checkpoints, puzzling roadblocks and closures, intermittent, often confusing curfews, misunderstood directions by "baby-faced soldiers barking illogical orders in broken Arabic" and much more (Hass 1996, 32).

Then under Israeli control, one resident of Gaza explained to Hass the feelings of entrapment and control when he said, "the only thing that's missing here in Gaza is the morning roll call" (Hass 1996, 233). The tight rein of control that Israel has over Palestinian lives is evident in a very disturbing scene from Kedar's 2001 documentary when Hass travels to Hebron, a city in the West Bank where both Arabs and Jews live. Hebron itself is partitioned into sections: section H1 is under Palestinian control, whereas section H2, the old city where thousands of Palestinians live along with a small minority of Jewish settlers, is under Israeli control. On the day Hass travels there, the Arab market in the old city has been closed and a curfew has been enforced on all the Arab residents due to tension with the settlers. A Palestinian civil rights activist who received a special permit from the Israeli Army accompanies Hass. "Hebron is under curfew," she states,

> the Jews roam freely while the Palestinians are locked up in their homes. And here I am, privileged to be walking around freely because I am Jewish. It's hard for me to think about all of the people confined in their homes; watching me from their windows walking around freely (Kedar, 2001).

As they walk through the empty, shuttered streets of the Arab section, an Israeli soldier stops them and asks: "Are you Israelis?" Hass retorts, "Would we be here if we weren't asked that ten times already?" The soldier laughs. Later another soldier asks Hass' Palestinian colleague for his identification papers. His presence outdoors is finally challenged when they come upon a group of Jewish settlers. At first mistaken for an Israeli soldier, he is later taunted and told to leave when he is discovered to be Arab. "What's that Arab doing here?" a settler asks. When Hass' colleague produces a permit, another settler rejoins, "Take your permit to the grave. Get this Arab out of here." A young boy further taunts: "You have a permit to the graveyard."

Other curfews have led to more ominous outcomes as, for example, again when Gaza was under Israeli control, a child was mistakenly killed while she purchased milk during what the Palestinians understood as a forty-five minute lift from an ongoing curfew. Indeed a large part of the occupations' lethal legacy is the degree to which Palestinians endure porous, sometimes bewildering, often arbitrary and absurd rules. Crossing checkpoints, borders, roadblocks, and blockades entail the same measure of confusion and frustration as curfews.

Throughout Kedar's documentary, we witness Hass continually challenging the opaque, often cryptic decisions made involving who may pass where and when. In one scene Hass drives to a checkpoint with a Palestinian companion to drop him off at his job inside Palestinian territory, but the Israeli Army has moved the checkpoint hundreds of meters back into Palestinian Territory making it officially – for the moment anyway – Israel. A soldier stops her car and asks her companion for his "crossing permit." But his business was originally in Palestinian territory so Hass asks, "Why does he need a permit? Her companion continues, "I didn't move into Israel. You moved in on me." Later, after Hass exposes the situation in an article for the paper, the army returns the checkpoint to its original location, but why they moved the roadblock in the first place was never explained.

Home demolishment also accounts for bitterness and frustration. While the Israeli army has destroyed many Palestinian homes with the explanation that they belong to men accused of acts of terrorism, other homes are simply destroyed because they are deemed "illegal." Many homes built in Area C of the West Bank, (an area controlled by Israeli security) for example, were demolished in the 1990s because they were constructed without Israeli building permits. A Palestinian man recounts to Hass the overwhelmingly destructive power of the equipment used to destroy his home: "it wasn't a tractor," he says, "it was a building that moves" (Hass 2003, 119).

Perhaps strangest and most spectral aspect of the occupation is the fact that Palestinians live as refugees, but do so within their country of origin. "The pain of being uprooted" Hass writes of a Gazan friend, is "exacerbated by the proximity of her village, Burayr." Her friend explains: "The village is right there before our eyes, but we can't go and see it" (Hass 1996, 159). Whereas most refugees fleeing tragic consequences eventually – for better or worse – leave the site of trauma and start over elsewhere in the world, Palestinians continue to live, across generations, where they began. Hass writes:

> As in the West Bank, the people in Gaza became refugees in their own country – some living as close as fifteen miles from the ruins of their homes – and many people say that is harder than being a refugee in a foreign country (Hass 1996, 157).

The sense of itinerancy, Hass explains, is perhaps more deeply felt in the Palestinian community in Gaza than the West Bank because of its own particular history. While Egypt refused to annex the Gaza Strip after the 1948 war and before the post-1967 Israeli occupation, Jordan made the Palestinians of the West Bank citizens in 1950. For this reason, Gaza, Hass writes, has "preserved its refugee character and its people's permanent sense of rootlessness" (Hass 1996, 157).

As an Israeli journalist, Hass has acquired a uniquely profound understanding of the conditions of occupation by placing herself at its center thereby trading a position of distant viewing to one of empathic participation: "I learned to see Gaza through the eyes of its people," she writes, "not through the windshield of an army jeep" (Hass 1996, 5). But her real uniqueness lies in her ability to witness and thus have insight into both sides of the conflict. In a pivotal scene in Kedar's documentary we are presented with a first-hand account of Hass' agility to move across the conflict – both literally and psychologically – as she crosses sides during a clash in Ramallah in the spring of 2000, one that foreshadows the second intifada that will erupt a few months later. She is so close to the fighting on the Palestinian side that she is able to identify various National Front and Fatah factions. Rather than take cover, however, she walks across what appears to be a battle line, switching from the Palestinian side to the one where the Israeli Army is positioned. With a reverse view of the situation she sees young and exhausted Israeli soldiers sagging against the wall of a building and she observes:

> Now that I'm here with them, they don't seem bloodthirsty like it seems on the Palestinian side....You don't see them as being scary, they just want it to be over...They don't want to be here (Kedar 2001).

The effects of trauma

Hass' ability to move between entrenched sides is undoubtedly a testament to the potent influence of own familial history. Hass says early in Kedar's 2001 documentary:

I also feel like a refugee to some extent. I found that in Gaza, I identify
with what I call "permanent temporariness." As the daughter of refugees
from Eastern Europe, I can identify with that permanent temporariness
(Kedar 2001).

Hass' understanding of the refugees' sense of dispossession and
displacement comes directly to her through her parents' Holocaust past:
"...in my memory there will always be my parent's backward glance, their
last look at the beloved homes from which they were banished" (Hass
1996, 8). Indeed, it is not only her parents' past experience that has shaped
her, it is also the Holocaust itself that has imprinted upon Hass' psyche in
profound and immutable ways. "There is not a day in my life" Hass
confides in Kedar's 2001 documentary, "that I don't think about the
Holocaust."

Though predating her birth, it is the Holocaust and her parents'
particular experience of the Holocaust, that define much of Hass' life and
work. It is a past that she has absorbed rather than experienced: "my
parents' memories," she writes, were " told to me since my childhood until
they became my own" (Hass 1996, 5). The experience of the Holocaust
along with "a history of resisting injustice, speaking out, and fighting
back" were the sources of her parents' influential memories that imprinted
themselves upon her own psyche (Hass 1996, 6) The "scenes engraved on
their memories " she writes, "were stored in mine" (Hass 1996, 6).

One event in her mother's Holocaust past, in particular, Hass claims,
made a profound impact on her own psyche. She writes:

But of all their memories that had become my own, one stood out beyond
the others. One summer day in 1944, my mother was herded from a cattle
car along with the rest of its human cargo, which had been transported
from Belgrade to the concentration camp at Bergen-Belsen. She saw a
group of German women, some on foot, some on bicycles, slow down as
the strange procession went by and watch with indifferent curiosity on
their faces. For me, these women became a loathsome symbol of watching
from the sidelines, and at an early age I decided that my place was not
with the bystanders (Hass 1996, 11).

Hass' lasting reaction to her parents' memory is what Marianne Hirsch
defines as "postmemory," a phenomenon designated as the effect of
trauma transmitted across generations. Hirsch describes it as:

The experience of those who grow up dominated by narratives that
preceded their births, whose own belated stories are evacuated by the

stories of the previous generation shaped by traumatic experiences that can
be neither understood nor recreated (Hirsch 1997, 22).

Traumatic memory seems to imprint upon following generations as
postmemory because of its lasting and ongoing effects. While Hirsh's
concept of "postmemory" is encompassed by "both a specifically inter-
and transgenerational act of transfer, and the resonant aftereffects of
trauma," it appears most strongly articulated within the context of a
"particular relation to a parental past" (Hirsch 2012, 3-4). Thus although
her work revolves around a contemporary struggle, Hass' own parents'
history suggests the co-existence of two time-frames within the context of
Hass' life and work: her parents' Holocaust past is seemingly pressed
inside her work of witnessing and reporting the reality of the current
Palestinian occupation.

In the time-line of human history, the Holocaust stands alone – it is a
catastrophe unlike any other. Nevertheless, there are countless acts of
injustice, brutality and cruelty that reside within human history. For Hass,
the trauma of the Holocaust is therefore not the only past that haunts her
work. There are other fields of wounded memory that inhabit her writing,
and these, of course, revolve around Palestinian history. For Palestinians,
the event that begins their struggle is the "Nakba" ("catastrophe" in
Arabic) of 1948: "the collective Palestinian tragedy of uprooting,
dispossession, and deterritoralization with the establishment of the state of
Israel" (Bardenstein 1999, 153). Indeed both historic events – the
Holocaust and the Nakba – remain tragically connected in the chronology
of human history. Edward Said argues that both are catastrophes, he also
admonishes that while each must be acknowledged for the specificity of
their destruction, neither event is the same with the other. He writes:

> For there is a link to be made between what happened to the Jews in
> World War II and the catastrophe of the Palestinian people, but it cannot
> be made only rhetorically, or as an argument to demolish or diminish the
> true content both of the Holocaust and of 1948. Neither is equal to the
> other; similarly, neither one nor the other must be minimized. There is
> suffering and injustice enough for everyone. But unless the connection is
> made by which the Jewish tragedy is seen to have led directly to the
> Palestinian catastrophe by, let us call it "necessity" (rather than pure will),
> we cannot coexist as two communities of detached and uncommunicatingly
> separate suffering (Said 2001, 207-208).

In her effort to reveal the lethal consequences of the occupation, Hass
recognizes the legitimacy of both Jewish *and* Palestinian suffering and

258   Intersecting Traumas

memory when she makes the connection between her parents' Holocaust
losses and Palestinian losses:

> My parent's sense of longing and loss was passed on to me early in my
> childhood, and in Gaza their stories seemed echoed in the pain of the
> Palestinians – the stubborn way refugees clung to their lost villages, in the
> whiff of rusticity that hung even over people born long after the expulsion
> and flight (Hass 1996, 154).

Palestinian memory of loss, as in most other collectively experienced
tragedies, is invariably passed along in families, demonstrating the
ongoing nature of trauma, as it carries across generations. Although much
of Palestinian memory of the past is associated with dispossession and
exile, the past also signifies a time before the Nakba, a time remembered
with longing and signified by unbroken families, homes and villages. It is
this past that appears, ironically, more promising than the future and the
projected future Palestinians pass on to the next generation has become, in
a sense, the time of their past. The strength of such intergenerational
memories and projections are evident when Hass writes of a Palestinian
friend who still identifies with his family's village of origin long after it
was lost:

> I knew Abu Ali was from a village called Burayr, where Kibbutz Bror
> Hayil is today, that is, his family was from Burayr, he himself was born in
> the Jabalia refugee camp but had assimilated all his parents' memories,
> down to the colors of the wheat and corn, the sight of the plums and
> oranges and grapes, the smell of the fertile earth (Hass 1996, 150).

Carol B. Bardenstein, confirms this intergenerational connection to
loss in the Palestinian community in her examination of their symbolic use
of trees in poetry and art. She writes:

> At times, trees are fixated upon as isolated fragments of a remembered
> whole or intact Palestine, encapsulated, seemingly frozen memory-
> fragments of an idealized time before displacement into exile (Bardenstein
> 1999, 151).

Bardenstein also explains such a process when she highlights a passage
of verse by Palestinian-American poet Naomi Shihab Nye in which she
describes her Palestinian-born father's fixation with fig trees. "From his
point of dislocation and loss in the present," writes Bardenstein of Nye's
father:

He continually reactivated fig trees as sites of memory in a seemingly endless array of contexts, passing them on to his American-born daughter, who has never experienced the original or "primal" fig trees of Palestine, as she observes and absorbs her father's ongoing fixation in her own way (Bardenstein 1999, 151).

Although Hirsch's conceptual framework of postmemory was originally developed in relation to the children of Holocaust survivors, she contends that postmemory "may usefully describe other second-generation memories of cultural or collective traumatic events and experiences" (Hirsch 1997, 22). The transmission of one generation's memory to another is a powerful phenomenon, and Palestinian postmemory serves to keep the trauma of dislocation and loss continually present and profoundly felt. "I felt as if I belonged there," a Gazan man confesses to Hass about his family's lost Palestinian home "in a place where I had never lived" (Hass 1996, 160).

It is not just the role of memory in the Palestinian community that informs Hass' work, but also the precise role that memory plays in the ongoing occupation. Indeed the ongoing reality of the occupation creates new levels of trauma layered over an original one, thus the older event of dispossession and exile is held in relief against an ongoing crisis. The time of the present is therefore punctured with the time of the past: one is shaped in reality as it is lived through the events of the occupation; the other is shaped through remembrance of a more distant past.

Time, identity, trauma

Why do traumatic memories linger in this way? Hayden White's theory of the "modernist event" provides a possible answer when he suggests that the overwhelming scale of contemporary traumatic events – of which he considers the Holocaust to be "paradigmatic in Western European History" – are so inadequately understood and remain so severely unresolved that they continue to haunt the present (White 1996, 30). He writes that these events

cannot be simply forgotten and put out of mind, but neither can they be adequately remembered, which is to say, clearly and unambiguously identified as to their meaning and contextualized in the group memory in such a way as to reduce the shadow they cast over the groups capacity to go into the present and envision a future free of their debilitating effects (White 1996, 29).

An essential feature of traumatic events then, is that they often create ongoing and long-term effects that continue beyond their original historical occurrence. But traumatic events may linger and push their way back into the present, in part, because trauma is also itself oblivious to chronology. Maurice Blanchot points to these unique temporal markings of trauma when he writes that "...the experience of the disaster...obliges us to disengage ourselves from time as irreversible" (Blanchot 1986, 78). Lawrence Langer confirms this in his study of Holocaust testimonials when he demonstrates the ways memory of such a past signal a kind of disruption; one in which any sense of chronology "faces temporal dissolution" (Langer 1991, 3). This is what he defines as "wounded time," writing that if we are to understand this dimension of Holocaust testimonials:

> We forfeit the immunity from unnatural time that coherence and chronology afford us...if we are to master the meaning of wounded time, as it afflicts the voices in these testimonies, there appears to be no alternative to immersing ourselves in the shifting currents of its discontinuous flow (Langer 1991, 75).

But traumatic experiences can also appear to halt time and make the past seem more real, or desirable, than the present. As Hass points out many Palestinian refugees in the Gaza Strip, have committed their lost homes and villages to memory and transmitted that memory to the next generation. Growing up in Gaza, refugees know "of the villages only from parents and grandparents." But that transmitted knowledge, she writes. "challenges history and defies the passage of time with an individual and collective inner truth that refuses to die" (Hass 1996, 161). Such memories of the past also provide reprieve from desperate conditions. "Where space is scarce," Hass writes:

> There is at least room for memory and there are no limits to the dimension of time; the past might be real or beautified, the future more illusory than realistic, but both have the power to transport the refugee out of the present" (Hass 1996, 163).

Geoffrey Hartman reminds us of "the power of a traumatic episode to define an epoch" (Hartman 2003, 6). If trauma can define epochs, could it not also define a collective identity? Certainly many ethnic groups base their communal identity around their sense of shared history and tragedy. This appears true of both Jewish and Palestinian collective identities. Said confirms this when he writes: "the reality of a collective national trauma

contained for every Palestinian" resides within "the question of Palestine"
(Said [1979] 1992, xxxviii). Similarly, James E. Young notes that the role
"of historical trauma, in particular, has played a pivotal role in Jewish
national consciousness" (Young 1993, 210). The memory of the Holocaust
is, therefore, logically evident throughout Israel – a country constructed
specifically upon Jewish identity. "In every community," Young writes,
"in every corner of Israel's landscape, one is reminded of the Shoah by a
plaque, a building, dedication, an inscribed tablet" (Young 1993, 216).
Indeed, it seems rather obvious that the trauma of the Holocaust would
define a large part of post-World War Two Jewish identity, or that,
moreover, the Holocaust can be linked the formation of the state of Israel
in 1948 – a state created precisely around Jewish identity. But if White is
correct in saying that an event like the Holocaust disables it victims "to go
into the present" without feeling burdened by the "debilitating effects" of
such a past, what can be said of such a trauma in relation to the formation
of the state of Israel?

In an essay on Holocaust memorial culture in Israel, Young maps out
the very complicated manner with which Israeli national identity has
reckoned with the Holocaust. Young charts the complex process by which
Israel's early founders at first rejected making a connection between the
Holocaust and a national identity because they wanted to create a nation
that would counter "the Jew's traditional self-image as victim" with "new
Zionist ideals of strength and self-determination" (Young 1993, 213).
However, Young notes, the founders eventually did link "the state's raison
d'être to the Holocaust" when they realized

> its perverse debt to the Holocaust: it had, after all, seemed to prove the
> Zionist dictum that without a state and power to defend themselves, Jews
> in exile would always be vulnerable to just this kind of destruction (Young
> 1993, 211).

However, in a remarkable twist of history, Young continues, the early
founders reframed the Holocaust as the first battleground in a fight toward
Jewish self-determination and statehood: in this new narrative, the six
million Jews that were exterminated by the Nazis become "martyrs" and
"are recollected heroically as the first to fall in defense of the state"
(Young 1993, 214). The subsequent ideology created around Israel's
Holocaust memorial culture places the Holocaust in a sequence of events
that makes the eventual formation of the state of Israel the only possible
outcome for Jewish survival. The trauma of the Holocaust past is thus
redeemed through the fight for statehood: "the victims are memorable
primarily for the ways they demonstrate the need for fighters, who, in turn,

are remembered for their part in the state's founding" (Young 1993, 212). The Holocaust was thus evoked in the formation of a national mythology to construct a specific kind of Israeli identity; indeed, a post-Holocaust identity that was not based on irretrievable loss and mourning, but rather one constructed on the valorization and *necessity* of "fighting and self-preservation" (Young 1993, 212).

As early as 1977, Said understood the connection between the Holocaust and an Israeli national identity constructed around strength and self-protection. He writes:

> Two generations of men and women have been reared only on ideas like security, protection against extermination, minority sovereignty, an unappeasable need for weapons and their symbolism. Yet unless the pitiless logic of these concerns yields to some understanding of their human origins, the future will be still murderous (Said 1994, 32).

Indeed, the creation of the state of Israel can be evaluated within the context of a collective and national trauma. For if we acknowledge, as Said has, the "burden of fear" the Holocaust "places on all Jews" (Said 2001, 206), we understand the ever-ready Israeli response to any kind of perceived threat (whether real or imagined), the hyper-vigilant survival mechanisms set in place, the national identity based on "fighting and self-preservation" *as symptoms of a trauma*. Said himself recognizes the complexity of Israeli culpability in relation to the Palestinian Nakba and current occupation when he writes that Israeli Jews "are not white settlers of the stripe that colonized Algeria" (Said 2001, 271). But he also warns that: "the distortions of the Holocaust created distortions in its victims, which are replicated today in the victims of Zionism itself, that is, the Palestinians" (Said 2001, 209).

Regardless of whether the Holocaust has been used to construct Israeli national identity, or that the memory of the Holocaust returns across generations in disruptive and unresolved ways, or whether Palestinian memory of before the Nakba "defies the passage of time," it is clear that Jewish and Palestinian pasts converge onto the present landscapes inhabited by both peoples. In both Israeli and Palestinian identities then, it appears that past events continue to reassert themselves and push their ways back upon the present as the collective imagination of both groups circulate around historical traumas: one of extermination and another of displacement, exile and an ongoing occupation.

Post traumatic state disorder

The clinical terminology for the mental disorder of an individual whose traumatic past continues to pierce and disrupt their current experience of reality is Post Traumatic Stress Disorder (PTSD). The American Psychiatric Association only acknowledged this disorder in 1980, sometime after the Vietnam War had ended, after noting the large number of veterans who were involuntarily re-experiencing events associated with the war, even though the war had been over for some time. The unique element of this mental disorder is that its symptoms are not produced through any kind of illness, but rather specifically in relation to events themselves. Clinical psychologist Babette Rothschild notes:

> Most categories of diagnosis in the DSM are symptom-dependent...PTSD, on the other hand, is situation-dependent. That is, there must be an identifiable event that qualifies as "traumatic" for the diagnosis of PTSD to apply...in addition to experiencing a precipitating event, an individual...must have a symptom profile that includes a reexperiencing of the causal event (Rothschild 2003, 4).

In the pathology of Post Traumatic Stress Disorder, the sensation of re-experiencing the original trauma as if it was happening in the present creates a state of "hyperarousal", a symptom that causes the body's nervous system to literally "fight, flee or freeze;" in effect, to physically react to a threat that is no longer present (Rothschild 2003, 5). Thus traumatic experiences not only appear to contradict narrative and temporal coherence in the memory of individuals, but also, in fact, often produce temporal glitches within their lived experience by making the past appear more real than the present. Resisting against the naturally forward-moving chronologies of time, such a phenomenon impinges upon the experiential present when involuntary sensations and memories from the past surge forward in the form of "flashbacks." These sense-memories temporarily remove the subject from the conditions of the present and pull them to another time-frame that is, nevertheless, already past. Rothschild writes:

> Images, sensations and emotions can all be provoked...but they cannot be narrated (cohesively recounted) or understood. It is this mechanism that is behind the PTSD symptom of flashback – episodes of reliving the trauma as if it is happening now (Rothschild 2003, 11).

The power of post-traumatic symptoms is the force by which they reassert themselves back on to the present, even after the initial trauma is over. This occurs, in part, because traumatic events are themselves so overwhelming that, as Cathy Caruth has pointed out, they are often "partially unassimilated or "missed" experiences" (Caruth 1996, 124). Misapprehended during the time of their occurrence, memories of traumatic events often emerge later, after a period of postponement, through the symptoms of post-trauma. The strength of post-traumatic recollections occurs, moreover, "precisely in their temporal delay" (Caruth 1995, 9). Post-traumatic memories also achieve their strength in the way the past has been unconsciously engraved and preserved like a stencil: "traumatic recall remains insistent and unchanged to the precise extent that is has never, from the beginning, been fully integrated into understanding" (Caruth 1995, 153).

The fact that original traumas are often "missed" while they occur, that they are, moreover, unconsciously preserved in memory and then powerfully transmitted after a time of delay might explain why past tragedies are so powerfully transferred across generations and why they remain defining features within a groups' collective identity over time. Caruth writes: "since the traumatic event is not experienced as it occurs, it is fully evident only in connection with another place, and in another time" (Caruth 1995, 7). Moreover, if post-traumatic memory emerges later and if it is indeed a kind of etching of the past, it appears that it is history itself that is finally delivered through this temporal delay. Caruth writes:

> If PTSD must be understood as a pathological system, then it is not so much a symptom of the unconscious, as it is a symptom of history. The traumatized, we might say, carry an impossible history within them, or they become themselves the symptom of a history that they cannot entirely possess (Caruth 1995, 5).

If trauma can define an epoch, as Hartman (2003) notes, or the identity of a people or a nation, as Said (1995) and Young (1993) detail, could not post-trauma then also define epochs, nations and collective identities? And if the symptoms of post-trauma are evident in both the Israeli and Palestinian collective identities, what kind of contemporary reality does this create for both groups?

Indeed, while the post-trauma of a collective group would not produce the exact pathology of individuated sensations of the past appearing to be more real than the present, one could argue that both the Israeli and Palestinian identities are so encumbered by each group's unresolved histories, that the pasts of each side threaten to destabilize the realities of the present, just as involuntary flashbacks would work to destabilize a traumatized individual. In the Israeli and Palestinian collective identities, the past appears to be so active within contemporary reality that neither group can see the present without framing it through the phantasmagoric past. Beneath the surface of events and places, lie memories of other events and places. Fields of memory of pasts that are irretrievably over continue to reassert themselves back on to the present. The past returns in such a way that the forward flow of normal experiential time cannot be unhooked from history. The normal sense of chronological time becomes damaged. In both groups, spectral, memory-laden realities produce a temporality that cannot unravel toward a future that is free, as White reminds us, of the "debilitating effects" of the original traumas. Rather than unfolding and progressing into the future, the present is saturated with the past: *it is ruined with it.*

The Politics of Return

In many ways the continued return to the past, the spectral and phantasmagoric relationship to the past contained within each group's identity, accounts for some aspects of the seemingly irresolvable nature to this conflict. Indeed, both Israelis and Palestinians have, in large measure, constituted their identity through the politics of "returning," a multifaceted phenomenon that is structured, for each group, not just in temporal relations but also, significantly, in spatial dimensions. Temporal "returning", on the one hand, occurs as narratives and histories of rupture and displacement are actuated by individual and collective memories that reach back in time and across generations. This is true not just for traumatic memories but also of the more treasured memories of the pre-traumatic past (European lives before the Holocaust, and Palestinian lives before the Nakba). On the other hand, spatial "returning" is concretized as both groups lay claim to ownership of the same land – for Israelis, the rhetoric of "return" signifies going back to what had been an originary Biblical homeland; for Palestinians, returning means going back to their pre-1948 villages and homes. These separate visions of "returning" to one's "roots" are two visions of belonging that seemingly mutually exclude the other because they each vie for the same place as the site of their group's rightful homeland.

The complex rhetoric of "returning" for Hass is, moreover, filled with bitter irony. After surviving the Holocaust, her mother did "return" to her European home – then Yugoslavia, now Sarajevo – but "fled from the terrible void she had found in her real homeland" (Hass, 2011, 179). Because of Hass' European roots (yet in spite of her parent's tragic history there), she is often asked if she has ever thought of "returning" to Sarajevo. She writes:

Twice I have been asked whether I have ever thought of "returning" to Sarajevo, meaning returning to live there. I instantly saw beyond the words, and the shock at being asked such a question prevented me from commenting on its absurd terminology. How could I return to a place where I had never lived and only visited twice as a tourist? (Hass 2011, 179)

When well-meaning Palestinians ask her where she is from, she replies "I am from Jerusalem, I was born there." But to that they often retort: "But no, no, where did you really come from?" Of this attitude she writes: "They insist on giving me imagined roots in places, languages, and landscapes that are totally strange to me" (Hass, 2011, 179). When a French woman asked her why she did not think of returning, Hass had much harsher words about her: "Return to a continent that threw us out of the globe, out of the world of the living?...She was a European, a Christian, ignoring the perfectly familiar history that placed me exactly where I am, her history" (Hass 2011, 179).

These responses affirm Hass' stance toward history as a profound realist: the Holocaust was an historical event and the state of Israel was, in large measure, a response to that historical catastrophe. Hass was born in Israel, because of the Holocaust; for better or worse, it is her home, although, she admits she wishes her "parents had emigrated elsewhere" (Hass 2011, 179). History, as such, is simply a fact. "For many years, many Palestinians believed it was possible to undo history," she writes (Hass 2011, 179). But as a realist Hass also understands the problem is not just history: it is also ideology. Indeed the very rhetoric circulating around Israel's "Law of Return" – which mandates any person of Jewish heritage legal citizenship in the state of Israel – supersedes the reality of materialist history. This law, Hass writes, affirms "the alleged blood links supposedly shared by Jews all over the world and [ties] them all to the soil of the Holy Land" (Hass 2011, 176). She continues,

Much state violence has been exercised to make those acts of dispossession last, persist, and expand. The Law of Return is part and parcel of this violence, as it entitles every Jew on earth to more rights in this country than any Palestinian born in it possesses. The mythological return of the Jews has successfully made the literal return of Palestinians impossible (Hass 2011, 183).

Conclusion

Hass continues to be critical of both sides of the conflict – with Israel, as it imposes closures, blockades, fences, and checkpoints, encircling the

Palestinians and enforcing a deeper demographic separation; with the Palestinians, as the struggle with the occupation has moved from the secular Fatah and nationalist movements to Islamic groups like Hamas and Islamic Jihad. "The Palestinians", she wrote during the second intifada:

> are driven by the same misguided notion...more force and more killing...will teach the other side a lesson and foul their plans. The suicide bombs in Israel indicate impaired analytic ability on the part of most Palestinians (Hass 2003, 175).

Of the continued violence she warned: "Both sides are convinced that only more deadly and devastating force will restrain the opposing side. Both sides are dead wrong" (Hass 2003, 175). Though increasingly gloomy, Hass continues to anchor her writing in history, rather than conjecture or fear. When writing about the escalation of violent acts committed against Israeli civilians during the second intifada she has observed: "Israelis conclude that suicide bombings are the result of murderous tendencies in Palestinians.... they look to bio-religious explanations, not socio-historical ones" (Hass 2003, 174).

In the end, Hass' allegiance is not to a particular group, place or time but to reality. Hass has taken an inventory of reality and she has reckoned with it based on facts, not phantoms. What makes Hass' work truly forward thinking in relation to history is her ability to connect two traumas *but then to disconnect them*. Rather than dwelling on the Holocaust as a politicized site that justifies the occupation, she makes a profound leap forward. Like her parents, who as war refugees refused to take over the home of a Palestinian family in Jerusalem in 1949 because they recognized the family's plight as refugees just like their own, Hass recognizes the existence of two histories but then disconnects any justifiable causality between them. "So many people use the past to justify the present..." she says in Kedar's 2001 documentary,

> the Holocaust is exploited so much to justify things, or to connect unrelated things...For many Israelis, the Holocaust is a way or an excuse that justifies everything that was done or is being done. It justifies the entire cycle of the viction of the Palestinians. And for many Palestinians, being evicted by the Israelis justifies Holocaust denial or saying it didn't happen, that the Jews are lying.

By acknowledging both Jewish and Palestinian suffering, Hass underscores Said's call for "mutuality and coexistence" between both people (Said 2001, 231). A mutual regard of the suffering endured by both groups, would enable each, Said writes, "to admit the universality and integrity of the other's experience." Such an acknowledgement would allow both groups to move beyond the ongoing conflict, away from the "endless back-and-forth violence and dehumanization" thus helping them "begin to plan a common life together" (Said 2001, 208). Said's call for both groups to plan a peaceful co-existence together adds a temporal dimension to the conflict that is all too often suppressed by each group's allegiance to their separate pasts: it is a call to the future.

While defining each group's identity through their separate traumatic pasts is an important acknowledgment of history, cultural critic Gabriele Schwab warns in her writing on traumatic legacies, it can also be debilitating. She writes:

> The danger of emphasizing memory and mourning lies in using trauma as the foundation of identity. Such attachment to injury is problematic, especially in a "wound culture" oversaturated with stories and studies of trauma. An excessive emphasis on mourning may indeed contribute to an identitarian definition of cultural belonging by tying identity to victimization (Schwab 2010, 19).

Following Said, Schwab therefore argues that freedom from the grips of a traumatic past enables movement forward toward future resolution. She notes:

> It is one of the characteristics of trauma that makes the victim a prisoner of the past. This is why healing trauma also means a release from the past and an opening toward the future....A politics of redress therefore needs to be future-oriented and grounded in alliances across historical divides (Schwab 2010, 105).

The idea of travelling between such political and conflictual divides that would move beyond the corrosive effects of "competitive memory," "comparative victimization" and "identitarian competition" toward a more productive, shared and fair vision of the future resonates in the recent work of Michael Rothberg (2009, 4-5, 21). Through his investigation of the relationship "between the Holocaust and colonialism" as a strategy "for the rethinking of justice," Rothberg has harnessed the figuration of "multidirectional memory" to locate individual and collective memories that are "partially disengaged from exclusive versions of cultural identity" (Rothberg 2009, 21, 11). In doing so they become "ethical version[s]" of the past that are:

based on commitment to uncovering historical relatedness and working through the partial overlaps and conflicting claims that constitute the archives of memory and the terrain of politics (Rothberg 2009, 29).

For Rothberg the idea of "shared" or "related" memories and histories "of racism, spatial segregation, genocide, diasporic displacement, cultural destruction…" would not disregard the specificity of "powerful histories of division and difference" but rather create "complex acts of solidarity in which historical memory serves as a medium for the creation of new communal and political identities" (Rothberg 2009, 23, 11).

Indeed one could argue that Hass has always engaged in such "complex acts of solidarity" and across decades she has conjured ethical and communal bridges across the divide of differing histories. Indeed, she uses memories of the past, not to divide groups and histories, but to connect them. It is her parents' Holocaust past that allows her to see the tragedy of the Palestinian occupation. In doing so, Hass provides us with a third way through the conflict, neither Israeli nor Palestinian, but rather both; one that is intersubjective, where, as the philosopher Emmanuel Levinas writes, "the subject is *for the other*.." (Levinas 2003, 64). She describes a view of cypress, eucalyptus and mulberry trees that embodies this ethic: "to me so Israeli, to my friends so Palestinian…From the top of the hill, spread before us, was one country" (Hass 1996, 9).

Works Cited

Bardenstein, Carol B. 1999. Trees, Forest, and the Shaping of Palestinian and Israeli Collective Memory. In Acts of Memory. Cultural Recall in the Present. Edited by Mieke Bal, Jonathan Crewe, and Leo Spitzer. Hanover and London: University Press of New England.

Blanchot, Maurice. 1986. The Writing of the Disaster. Translated by Ann Smock. Lincoln: University of Nebraska Press.

Caruth, Cathy. 1995. Introduction. In Trauma. Explorations in Memory. Edited by Cathy Caruth. Baltimore and London: The Johns Hopkins University Press.

—. 1996. Unclaimed Experience. Trauma, Narrative, and History. Baltimore and London: The Johns Hopkins University Press.

Hartman, Geoffrey. 2003. On that Day. In Trauma at Home. Edited by Judith Greenberg. Lincoln and London: University of Nebraska Press.

Hass, Amira. 1996. Drinking the Sea at Gaza. Days and Nights in a Land Under Siege. Translated by Elana Wesley and Maxine Kaufman-Lacusta. New York: Henry Holt and Company.

—. 2003. Reporting from Ramallah. An Israeli Journalist in an Occupied Land. Translated by Rachel Leah Jones. Los Angeles and New York: Semiotext(e) Active Agents Series.

—. 2011. Between Two Returns. Rites of Return. Diaspora Poetics and the Politics of Memory. Edited by Marianne Hirsch and Nancy K. Miller. New York: Columbia University Press.

Hirsch, Marianne. 1997. Family Frames. Photography, Narrative and Postmemory. Cambridge, Massachusetts and London, England: Harvard University Press.

—. 2012. The Generation of Postmemory. Writing and Visual Culture After the Holocaust. New York: Columbia University Press.

Kedar, Yifat. 2001. Between the Lines. Video, 58 minutes. Israel. In Arabic and Hebrew.

Langer, Lawrence. 1991. Holocaust Testimonies. the Ruins of Memory. New Haven and London: Yale University Press.

Levinas, Emmanuel. 2003. Humanism of the Other. Translated by Nidra Poller. Urbana and Chicago: University of Illinois Press.

Rothberg, Michael. 2009. Multidirectional Memory. Remembering the Holocaust in the Age of Decolonization. Stanford, California: Stanford University Press.

Rothschild, Babette. 2003. The Body Remembers Casebook. Unifying Methods and Models in the Treatment of Trauma and PTSD. New York: W.W. Norton & Company, Inc.

Said, Edward. [1979] 1992. The Question of Palestine. New York: Vintage Books.

—. 1995. The Politics of Dispossession. The Struggle for Palestinian Self-Determination 1969-1994. New York: Vintage Books.

—. 2001. The End of the Peace Process. Oslo and After. New York: Vintage Books.

Schwab, Gabriele. 2010. Haunting Legacies. Violent Histories and Transgenerational Trauma. New York: Columbia University Press.

Wasserman, Tina. 2004. Between the Lines. Afterimage. The Journal of Media Arts and Cultural Criticism vol. 32(1)(July/August): 14.

White, Hayden. 1996. The Modernist Event. In The Persistence of History. Cinema, Television and the Modern Event. Edited by Vivian Sobchack. New York and London: Routledge.

Young, James E. 1993. The Texture of Memory. Holocaust Memorials and Meaning. New Haven and London: Yale University Press.

FROM INDIVIDUAL TRAGEDY TO SOCIETAL DISLOCATION: THE FILMIC REPRESENTATION OF TRAGEDY, DISLOCATION, AND CULTURAL TRAUMA IN THE DREYFUS AFFAIR[1]

NICO CARPENTIER

Introduction: the Dreyfus Affair

On December 22, 1894 Alfred Dreyfus was convicted by the Court-Martial of the Paris Military Government for high treason and deported to Devil's Island in French Guiana, which at the time belonged to the French colonial penal system. Although he received a pardon on September 19, 1899 (after a retrial in Rennes where his sentence was reduced to ten years imprisonment), it was not until July 12, 1906 that the French *Cour de Cassation* declared him innocent and ended Dreyfus's tragic Calvary.

His original conviction for espionage was based on extremely weak evidence (mainly a handwritten note, the *Bordereau* which was obtained from the German embassy), fed by feelings of antisemitism within the French army. Moreover, being convinced of his guilt and coming under pressure from the right-wing press (Bredin 1986, 80ff; Cahm 1994, 19)[2], the French Minister of War, General Auguste Mercier, unbeknown to Dreyfus's defense team, provided the judges with a secret dossier (containing more circumstantial evidence) to ensure that he would be convicted.

Although initially the majority of French society was convinced that the army staff captain was indeed a spy working for the German embassy, Dreyfus's family (and especially his brother Mathieu and wife Lucie) succeeded in mobilizing a small but influential group of supporters,[3] who became known as the Dreyfusards. At almost the same time, the new head of the French Intelligence Office, Major Georges Piquart, discovered new evidence (the so-called *Petit Bleu*), which pointed him to the real spy, Major Ferdinand Walsin-Esterhazy. The French general staff decided to protect Esterhazy and had Piquart removed from his position. A new forged piece of evidence (the *faux Henry*) was produced, and Esterhazy's name was removed from the *Petit Bleu* by Piquart's successor, Major Hubert-JosephHenry. A new inquiry was opened and as a result of the trial that followed, Esterhazy was proclaimed innocent.

J'accuse, Emile Zola's famous letter to the French president, Félix Faure, published on 13 January 1898, was the direct result of Esterhazy's acquittal and was aimed at provoking a new trial, this time against Zola (and unavoidably also against Alexandre Perrenx, manager of *L'Aurore*, in which *J'accuse* was published). During this new trial, which eventually led to their conviction and to Zola's flight to the UK, the French chief of staff, General Raoul de Boisdeffre, addressed the jury in the following threatening but illustrative way: "you are the nation. If the nation does not have confidence in the leaders of its army, in those who are responsible for the national defense, they are ready to leave to others that heavy task. You only have to say the word." (quoted in Johnson 1999, 97)

After the fall of the French Méline government on June 15, 1898 the new Minister of War, Jacques Cavaignac, re-opened the case, which uncovered the forged *faux Henry*, and led to Colonel Henry's suicide. The *Cour de Cassation,* on June 3, 1899 – following another long legal battle – annulled the verdict of the 1894 Court-Martial. At a new Court-Martial on September 9, 1899 in Rennes, Dreyfus's sentence was reduced to ten years imprisonment. On September 19, 1899 he pleaded for clemency and was pardoned. It took another seven years (till July 12, 1906) and another inquiry for the *Cour de Cassation* to annul this sentence, this time without re-referring Dreyfus to the Court-Martial. This (illegal) decision ended the long legal procedure and rehabilitated Dreyfus.

Outside the courtroom, the Dreyfus Affair had had a major destabilizing impact on French political and cultural life, but this was not the only disruptive event that occurred in France at that time. The Third Republic (1870-1940), which came into being after the defeat of Napoleon III in the Franco-Prussian war and the bloodily suppressed Paris Commune, was characterized by political instability, witness the 60 governments in France between 1870 and 1914 (Anderson 1977, 5). These events created the conditions of possibility for the rise of the strong nationalist and *revanchist* tendencies that characterized 19th century France.

France also had defined internal enemies, as antisemitism was increasing. Edouard Drumont's 1886 key work, *La France Juive*, applying a traditional scapegoat strategy to the French Jews. Drumont's newspaper *La Libre Parole* continued to rail against the French Jews until he lost control of it in 1910. It was his newspaper that published in cynical serial the list of "remittance men" involved in the Panama scandal,[4] transforming *La Libre Parole* from an insignificant sheet into a newspaper with a circulation of 100.000 (Bredin 1986, 518). The "Jewish threat" became intertwined with the "German threat"; before Russian and Polish immigrants began making their way to France, a large segment of the Jews in France had originated in Alsace (Johnson 1999, 6), which was considered being in alliance with Germany. Such outpourings of antisemitism marked an important shift in the articulation of antisemitism; it was no longer embedded only in a religious discourse, it was now also fed by radical nationalism and biological determinism.

It thus came as no real surprise that when colonel Jean-Conrad Sandherr and his Intelligence Office began to look for yet another spy, they rapidly decided that the "evidence" pointed to the Alsatian Jewish officer, Alfred Dreyfus, he was "their" traitor. Finding convincing evidence became of secondary importance. As Johnson (1999, 17) put it: "it was apparently assumed that every Jew was a potential traitor".

At its height in 1898-1899, the Affair polarized French society and its elites.[5] Arendt's (1985, 115) comment that "the disunity of the French people was apparent in each family" is illustrated by the famous cartoon of the anti-Dreyfusard Caran d'Ache,[6] which showed how a quiet family dinner could be reduced to a broil by raising the Dreyfus Affair. The embryonic group of Dreyfusards managed to spread its discourse through all layers of French society, while resistance to a retrial (or even the liberation of Dreyfus) led to the establishment of anti-Dreyfusard groups.

The Dreyfus Affair transcended the tragic faith of the individual person, Alfred Dreyfus, in being translated at the ideological level into a confrontation between two discursive orders. The nodal points[7] in the Dreyfusards' ideology were truth and justice, which made the socialist ideologist Jules Guesde refer to them as "les véritards-justiciards." The anti-Dreyfusards built their discursive order on the nodal points of "patriotism, the defense of the army; respect for legal positions and the maintenance of the principle of authority" (Anderson 1977, 21).

The intensity of the conflict turned these concepts into what Žižek (1989) called empty signifiers, pure signifiers without any signifieds. A series of conspiracy theories fed into the Affair on both sides. The Dreyfusards referred to the "Jesuit plot" and the "military plot", while the anti-Dreyfusards built their case on the "Jewish plot" and the "syndicate of treason". Both sets of conspiracy theories aspired to give meaning to an incomprehensible set of events, documents, strategies and interpretations, but at the same time provided the rhetorical armory for fighting the enemy (Griffiths 1991).

Fig. 12-1: Caran D'Ache in Boussel, 1960: 173

More fundamentally, the Affair was interlaced with a wide variety of ideological positions and contradictions, which simultaneously superseded the Affair in the strictest sense, and marked the entry of French society into the 20th century. Nationalism and antisemitism, but also (anti-) clericalism, (anti-) capitalism, (anti-) republicanism and (anti-) militarism played crucial roles in the Affair. Although some of these positions can be attributed to the Dreyfusard / anti-Dreyfusard dichotomy and were articulated in chains of equivalence with their nodal points (justice / truth versus patriotism / army / law and order), individual identifications often transcended or rearticulated these binary oppositions. For instance, not all anti-Dreyfusards were antisemites. These positions also turned out to be unstable and fluid over time, as illustrated by the discursive u-turn made by the socialist faction in the French parliament. It was Jean Jaurès who took the Dreyfusard cause to heart (Eley 2002, 87), bringing with him a large majority of the French socialists and thus "undermining left-wing antisemitism in France" (Johnson 1999, 104).

Dislocations, moral panics and cultural traumas

The complexity of these discursive structures and orders, and the multiplicity of events and strategies warrant the use of different perspectives to theorize the Affair. The intensity of the Affair and its impact on French politics and culture legitimize its articulation in Gramscian terms as an organic crisis, a concept defined by Smith (1999, 164) as: "dramatic collapse in popular identifications with institutionalized subject positions and political imaginaries." Within a related discourse-theoretical framework the term dislocation is used to indicate the moment of social crisis, which cannot be located within the discursive structure and severely disturbs the discursive structure. Dislocations destabilize hegemonic discourses and identities, and at the same time constitute a breeding ground for new discourses and identities (Laclau 1990, 39).

The Affair polarized French society as a result of the antagonism between Dreyfusards and anti-Dreyfusards and through the "clash of progressive individualism and organic solidarities" (Johnson 1999, 158) that lay behind it. In their emphasis on truth and justice the Dreyfusards privileged personal individual rights over the prerogatives of the state. In this sense the tragic faith of captain Dreyfus, which made him a victim of national (military) interest, acted as an almost perfect metaphor for the importance of human rights. The discursive order of the anti-Dreyfusards, in contrast, was built on preventing the army, which was France's safeguard against foreign invasions and "the necessary instrument of revenge needed to restore to France her integrity" (Bredin 1986, 534), from being weakened. It was also built on a belief in the impartiality of the law, so cherished as one of the great innovations of that century (Arendt 1985, 91).

The dislocation caused by the triumph of the Dreyfusards, opened up vital spaces to rearticulate the individual–state relationship. Human rights commanded a central position in political discourse, as illustrated by the establishment (on June 3, 1898) of the *Ligue des Droits de L'Homme.*[8] In addition, antisemitism was discredited in left-wing organizations. Bredin (1986, 530) describes how antisemitism was disarticulated from the socialist chain of equivalences, and firmly embedded in right-wing discourses: "left-wing parties and workers' unions would never again invoke the 'wisdom' of an antisemitic stance, for the Affair had definitely linked antisemitism with reactionary ideology." Thirdly, Theodor Herzl, the main proponent of political Zionism, was deeply influenced by the Affair and in February 1896 concluded in *The Jewish State* that the Jewish state was a necessity. Arendt (1985, 120) attributes major importance to this rearticulation of Jewish identity and to the role of the Affair in it: "The only visible result was that it [the Affair] gave birth to the Zionist movement – the only political answer Jews have ever found to antisemitism and the only ideology in which they have ever taken seriously a hostility that would place them in the center of world events."

Arendt's statement also allows the discursive opportunities opened up by the dislocation foreclosed in the course of time to be emphasized. Not all identities and discourses were rearticulated and the new discursive balances solidified again. Nationalism and militarism would rapidly regain their place in the French political landscape in the build-up to the First World War. Antisemitism would not disappear in France. Charles Maurras, an anti-Dreyfusard, became the leading ideologist of the monarchist, antisemitic and proto-fascist *Action Française*. And later, the anti-Jewish policies of the Vichy regime of Philippe Pétain, supporting the Hitlerian genocide, tragically confirmed the strength of French antisemitism.

The seriousness and intensity of the Affair seems to exclude the use of the concept of moral panic. Cohen's (1973, 9) reference to the necessary disappearance and/or submerging of a moral panic hardly matches the intensity of the Affair; Goode and Yehuda's (1994, 38) emphasis on the volatility and disproportionality of a moral crisis as defining characteristics seem to do less than justice to the Affair. Nevertheless, it is contended here that the concept of moral panic can be used to shed light on the first phase of the Dreyfus Affair and, more specifically, on the events that created the conditions of possibility for the arrest and conviction of Dreyfus. In analyzing the Affair, it should be kept in mind that what Bredin (1986, 516) calls the "political Affair", and Johnson (1999, 87ff) describes as the "grand Affaire" was concentrated on 1898 and 1899. The first trial, which took place in 1894, is an event – in terms of political significance and time – that must be isolated from the "grand Affaire".

The (first) trial against Dreyfus was preceded by a series of events and scandals that influenced its outcome, such as the Union Générale and Panama scandals, the assassination of the French president Marie-François Sadi Carnot on June 25, 1894 and a series of espionage scandals. Bredin

(1986, 47-48) mentions at least six persons who admitted to having spied and who were convicted of espionage. Within the context of the humiliating 1870/71-defeat, where the "general opinion was that France had lost the war not because it was victim of the balance of forces, but because it had been betrayed …, treason was the ultimate crime, which nothing could excuse or expiate" (Bredin 1986, 532). This "pathological obsession with spies" (Bredin 1986, 532), in 1892 became intertwined with antisemitism when the French newspaper *La Libre Parole* turned its attention to Jewish officers in the French army, denouncing them as potential spies. The hostility and accusations directed towards Jewish officers led to a series of duels and eventually to the death of the Jewish captain Armand Mayer. This provoked broad societal protest, which caused *La Libre Parole* to halt its campaign.

This fear of espionage, which became focused on the Jewish officers in the army, fits well with Goode and Yehuda's (1994) attributional[9] moral panic model. Their five indicators – concern, hostility, consensus, disproportionality and volatility (Goode and Yehuda 1994, 33-41) – can be identified. There was a "heightened level of concern on the behavior of a certain group or category and the consequences that the behavior [might] presumably cause for the rest of society" (Goode and Yehuda 1994, 33), and this led to hostility against Jewish officers in the French army. There was an important segment[10] of French society (and of the French army, see Bredin (1986, 533)) that accepted the problem as "real, serious and caused by the wrongdoing group members" (Goode and Yehuda 1994, 34). Echoing Hall et al.'s (1978, 52) argument, the political and military elites formed an integral part of "the circle out of which 'moral panics' develop". As the presumed threat was based on an antisemitic ideology, its disproportionality hardly needs to be argued. Finally, its abrupt cessation after the protests provoked by the death of captain Armand Mayer illustrates the volatility of the espionage panic.

Given the luxury of hindsight, it can be seen, of course, that this last point was rather more complex, as the espionage panic became one of the conditions of possibility of the dislocatory event of the Affair. In his approach to moral panic, Cohen (1973, 9) foresees the continuation and aggravation of moral panic: "[Sometimes] it has more serious and long-lasting repercussions and might produce such changes as those in legal and social policy or even in the way that society conceives itself." The Affair shows that moral panic does not have to last in order to have a lasting societal effect, but can contribute to and become incorporated into an organic crisis, that builds on a wider set of discourses.

The third theoretical notion that can be used to analyze the Affair, is the concept of cultural trauma. In contrast to the concept of moral panic, which provides us with a better understanding of the events that led to the Affair, the use of the cultural trauma concept is focused on the aftermath of the Affair. Here it is argued that the dislocation caused by the Affair produced a cultural trauma, which is explicitly not defined as an aggregate of individual traumata (see Kansteiner 2004, 209), but as a cultural phenomenon that "appears in the aftermath of a particular type of social change" (Sztompka 2000, 452). It builds on the assumption that "certain events are inherently traumatic for large collectives, such as nations or specific ethic groups" (Meek 2010, 1), although we might be careful with defining nations (and groups) as subjects, even if Butler (2004, 92) writes: "nations are not the same as individual psyches but both can be described as subjects, albeit of different orders." Sztompka lists four characteristics of cultural trauma, which all need to be present in conjunction: time (a sudden event), substance and scope (a radical and deep-cutting event), origins (an event that is inflicted upon us) and mental frame (an unexpected and shocking event). Again, the Affair seems to fit this theoretical model quite nicely, although its exogenous origins are debatable.[11] It should nevertheless be kept in mind that other dislocations and traumata – such as the 1870-71 war – preceded the trauma that occurred at the end of the 19th century.

Crucial to the process of cultural trauma are the dialectics of remembering and forgetting. Similar to the chosen approach towards cultural trauma, collective memory is not individualized but seen as a phenomenon that is situated "within discourses of people talking together about the past" (Radley 1990, 46, see also Singh et al. 1994). Collective memory thus becomes *How Societies Remember* – to quote Connerton's (1989) book title – and brings a temporal component into identity theory. The past becomes a collectively shaped temporal reference point (Eyerman 2001, 7), which provides societies and cultures with the building blocks for present-day identity constructions. Kaplan's (1999, 515) analysis of the Affair shows how crucial the memory of both the individual tragedy and the ideological struggle has remained for contemporary France:

> It belongs to the standard narrative which is a part of every educated Frenchmen's understanding of his country's past. To have been a Dreyfusard or anti-Dreyfusard was, for many years, a key point of an individual's self-identity. In its ultimate outcome the Dreyfus Affair is a subject of pride for the French: justice triumphed, an innocent man was vindicated and the Republic was saved.

Collective memory is not only fed through the discursive productions of different societal subsystems, such as academia, the art and media worlds (including of course film), and politics, but also through rituals and practices such as public commemorations, and through material objects, such as memorials, statutes and plaques.

Following De Certeau's argument in the *Writing of History* (1992), the unavoidable particularity[12] of discursive translations needs to be emphasized. Historical knowledge creates a narrative of a series of events and attempts to mould the infinite details of people's lives into a systematic discourse; often reducing those lives to "causes, politics, leaders and results" (Lewis 2002, 270). Apart from allowing me to acknowledge these constraints on the historical narrative expressed in this article, De Certeau's argument also highlights that the representation of events plays a crucial role in cultural remembering. To use Eyerman's (2001, 12) words: "how an event is remembered is intimately entwined with how it is represented." As direct access to (past or present) events is a realist illusion, the discursive mediation of those events becomes a condition of possibility for their continued existence within a society or culture. It is precisely through the process of representation that the individual tragedy of Dreyfus was transformed into the Affair that mobilized the entire French society, and provides us even today with identity markers and subject positions. Secondly, De Certeau's argument also highlights the discursive struggle (or, to use Hall's phrase: "the struggle to signify") that lies behind these representational processes. The meaning attributed to events is not stable, but the result of a process of cultural negotiation. Although its hegemonic truths are protected, contestation and attempted renegotiations always remain possible. For instance, the Dreyfus memorial in Paris has been an object of such struggle. Originally intended to be erected in the courtyard of the military school, it was almost three years before a final location was found for it after the army refused to house it. More dramatic, the statue was vandalized at the beginning of 2002. A yellow Star of David was painted on its plaque, accompanied by the words "Dirty Jew".

Dislocations and cultural traumas relating to the Affair cannot be seen in isolation from other historical events, tragedies, traumas and discourses. In the case of the Affair, the Shoah played a crucial role in how the Affair was remembered. In her book *The Origins of Totalitarianism*, Arendt (1985, 92) connects both histories and stresses the symbolic value of the Affair as heralding what was to come. But she also emphasizes that the Affair is remembered because of its prophetic strength: "The Dreyfus Affair in its political implications could survive because two of its elements grew in importance during the twentieth century. The first is the hatred of the Jews; the second, suspicion of the republic itself, of Parliament, and the state machine."

Films about the Affair

The French media, and especially the French press, played an important role in the Affair from the beginning. The press played out its relatively new role[13] to the maximum, as Miquel (1973, 16-17 – translated by Bredin 1986, 517) describes: "it was the press which made the Dreyfus case into the Dreyfus Affair and then the Dreyfus myth." Boussel (1960, 7-8) goes a step further, writing that "France had changed after the Affair. Protagonists and walk-ons benefited or suffered from that evolution of which the press was the first and almost only responsible instance" (my translation). The strength of the press should of course not be overestimated and certainly should not be fetishized. Bredin (1986, 518) remarks that "the press, despite its influence on public opinion, could not fully control that opinion. It amplified its movements; it could not create them." The press did play an important role both in providing its readership with information about the Affair, and even more so in stimulating the public debates, waged by journalists-writers-politicians as exemplified by the journalist-writer Zola and the journalist-politician Jaurès. As Whitney (1999) argues, during the Affair the press' opinionating role often dominated over its informational role: "The press played an integral role during the chaotic times of the Affair. Almost the entire press participated on one side or the other. The role of the press was no longer to inform, but to transmit opinions" (Whitney 1999 – my translation).

Whilst the polemics in the French (and international) press raged, film was making its first hesitant steps as a new medium. Through the Affair the medium of film – already from its conception – was confronted by concerns about authenticity and censorship. The first film made about the Affair was produced by one of Lumières' cameramen, Francis Doublier, while traveling in Russia. When asked for footage on the Affair he decided to fabricate a film, and in contrast to his later documentary-style films, he made explicit claims as to its authenticity (Bottomore 1984, 290). Unfortunately for him, the forgery was discovered soon afterwards.

A few years later, in August 1899 George Méliès, himself a Dreyfusard, reconstructed and dramatized the Dreyfus Affair in an 11-part, 15-minute long film. L'affaire Dreyfus focuses very much on the individual tragedy and covers the events from Dreyfus's arrest and degradation in 1894 up to the Rennes trial (Malthête-Méliès 1982;

Malthète 1992). Apart from being an "anomaly in [Méliès'] early filmmaking career" (Abel 1994, 92), *L'affaire Dreyfus* was also – according to Sadoul (1970, 28) – the first politically engaged film in motion picture history. At the same time,[14] Pathé issued its six-scène version of *L'affaire Dreyfus*. Both films were on the French market in the autumn of 1899. When the Méliès film was first shown, it provoked violent reactions among the spectators: "the police had to be called in to separate Dreyfusards and anti-Dreyfusards who were throwing things at each other and where about the smash the seats" (Bottomore 1984, 292-293) and was banned. The French government decided to ban the making or screening of any films on this subject[15]. The screening ban was lifted in 1950 (Ezra 2000, 69), but it was not until the 1970s that French film producers were allowed to make films on the Affair (Bottomore 1984, 293). In 1908, Pathé did decide to produce a new version of its *L'affaire Dreyfus* (by Ferdinand Zecca and Lucien Nonguet), but the film was distributed outside France (mainly in the U.S.A.).

A second wave of fictional films based on the Dreyfus Affair surfaced – not surprisingly – in the thirties. In Germany, Richard Oswald produced *Dreyfus* in 1930, with Fritz Kortner as Alfred Dreyfus. Milton Rosmer and F.W. Kraemer directed the British film *Dreyfus*, featuring Cedric Hardwicke as Alfred Dreyfus, which was released in 1931. The 1937 Hollywood version, entitled *The life of Emile Zola*, directed by William Dieterle, with Joseph Schildkraut as Dreyfus and Paul Muni as Zola, was the most successful of the Dreyfus films. As Singer (1988, 136) puts it: "Three Oscars […] is proof of the enthusiasm of the American public for miscarriages of justices to be repaired" (my translation).

Dreyfus's Jewish origins were barely mentioned in this second wave of films (Singer 1988, 136). However, this (important) element received more attention in the 1958 British film *I accuse!*, which was directed by José Ferrer, who also played Dreyfus in the film. This was followed by two German films made for television, the 1959 NWDR film *Affäre Dreyfus*, directed by Hanns Farenburg, and the 1968 ZDF film *Affäre Dreyfuss*, directed by Franz Josef Wild.

It took much longer for a film on the Affair to be produced in France: it was not until 1979 that Antenne2's eight-hour long film *Emile Zola ou la conscience humaine* by Stellio Lorenzi and Armand Lanoux was released, followed one year later by *La faute de monsieur Bertillon* by Alain Dhenaut (1980), which focused on the role of one of the graphologists. The German *Trotzdem!*, directed by Karl Fruchtmann for Radio Bremen in 1989, again focused more on Emile Zola. The 1990s saw three more films on the Affair: the 1991 television drama *Can a Jew be innocent?* directed by Jack Emery, the 1992 *Prisoner of honour* directed by Ken Russell, starring Richard Dreyfuss as Picquart and Kenneth Colley as Dreyfus (see Baron 2011); and in 1995 Arte's *L'affaire Dreyfus* directed by Yves Boisset, with Thierry Frémont as Dreyfus. After this series of films, the production of Dreyfus films ended, although the director Roman Polanski has, for several years, been announcing plans to produce a film on the Affair.[16]

Other formats than fictional films were used to narrate the Dreyfus Affair on screen. There was a series of documentaries, including Jean Vidal's 1954 *Zola*, Jean Vigne's 1965 12-minute *L'affaire Dreyfus*, Jean Chérasse's 1973 *Dreyfus ou l'intolérable vérité* and Peter Coltman's 1983 *The Dreyfus affair*. Documentary film production boomed in the 1990s and 2000s, with, for instance, Pierre Sorlin's *La raison d'état: Chronique de l'affaire Dreyfus* (1994), Paule Zajdermann's *Le sabre brisé* (1995) and Yves Jeuland's *Comme un Juif en France* (2007). Also interpretations of the Affair emanating from the art world found their way to the screen. For instance, the first part of *The accused – The Dreyfus trilogy* by George R. Whyte, the musical satire *Rage and outrage*, was televised in 1994. An earlier example is *Dreyfus*, a play directed by Hans Schweikart and recorded at the *Kammerspiele München* in 1975, which later (May 2003) was broadcast by the German *Theaterkanal*.

Representing past and present in Dieterle's
The Life of Zola

These films offer a remarkable collection of representations of the Affair and its protagonists. While one group of films offers a narrative on the Affair, others focus on some of the key players in the Affair. The film *Prisoner Of Honour* tells the story from Colonel Picquart's perspective, and *Emile Zola ou la conscience humaine, Trotzdem!*, and *The life of Emile Zola* all highlight the role of the French writer in the Affair.

In this chapter we focus on one of the Zola films, namely the 1937 U.S. film *The Life of Emile Zola* (LoEZ) and its historical reception (see Staiger 1992) in the U.S. LoEZ was produced by Warner First National, directed by William Dieterle, and featured Paul Muni and Joseph Schildkraut. It was based on the book *Zola and His Time* by Matthew Josephson[17]. This 116-minute movie is arguably the most successful of the films on the Affair (at least, as measured in terms of Oscars). It is especially relevant because of its temporal closeness to the Second World War; it was being produced at the time the German National-Socialist regime was already firmly in power.

Despite its success, it was a strictly biographical film, whose story was especially difficult to narrate because of the complexity of the Affair, the immobility and remoteness of Alfred Dreyfus (being locked away in a small cell on a remote island), and the discursive clashes that fed the Affair. For these reasons, the film was seen at the time as a film for "better-class audiences" (Film report and the Cinematograph Times 1937[18]), evidenced in the following comment:

> The producers have made no concession to the masses by inserting romance: they stuck to the lofty ideal of presenting a drama in the interest of truth and justice. Although its strongest appeal should be to class audiences, it should be played by every exhibitor, because of the prestige it will bring to his theatre. (Harrison's reports 1937)

In a 1983 interview, Warren Low, who edited LoEZ, talks about the enthusiastic reception of the film at its "big opening":

> At the big opening of the picture, the audience applauded this sequence [Muni/Zola's speech at the trial], and other scenes in the picture. It was the first time that I have ever witnessed a preview or an opening when the audience would applaud at different places throughout the picture. At the end, they went wild … "Bravo, bravo!" (Low interviewed by Nielson 1983, 19-21).

The need to reduce the complexity of the story was one reason for its zooming in on one protagonist (Zola). At the same time, this film was building on the biograph film tradition, which was flourishing at that time. However, the focus on Zola was only one of the many choices, and factual changes were made to the story and implemented in LoEZ.

This analysis does not pretend to investigate the film's historical accuracy. Following Rosenstone's (1995) and Toplin's (1996) approaches towards historical film, the analysis focuses on the representations of past and present that are offered in LoEZ and, specifically, the representations of individual tragedy in relation to the moral espionage panic and the dislocation of the Affair. In addition, it aims to deal with some of the questions relating to how these traumatic historical events are remembered and rearticulated as a history of the (American) present.

As LoEZ portrays Zola's entire life, it includes a much earlier and vital dislocation. The 1870-71 war is explicitly mentioned, and we are shown French troops triumphantly going to war, followed by shots of newspaper headlines announcing the defeat at Sedan and the capture of the Emperor (the ending of the Second Empire, and the beginning of the Third Republic). There is a scene in which Muni/Zola is shown expressing his dissatisfaction with the "unprepared" generals that led the war. However, the Parisian Commune, its defeat, and the resulting death and destruction in Paris, is not mentioned.

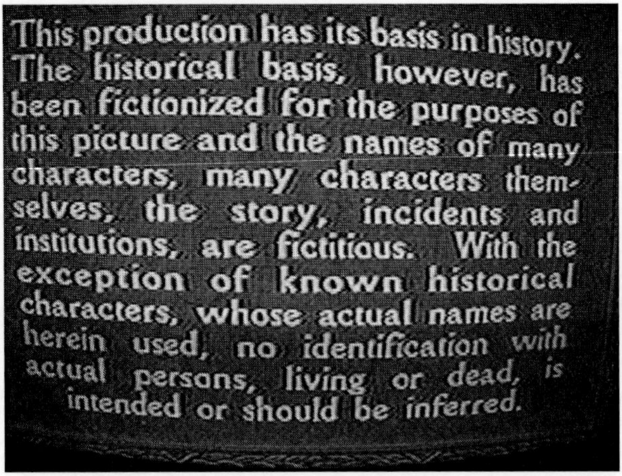

Fig. 12-2: The LoEZ screenshot 1: the disclaimer

The earlier scandals and the moral espionage panic are also almost entirely ignored,[19] but their mention is unavoidable in the depiction of the first investigation which led to the arrest of Alfred Dreyfus. When the *Bordereau* is brought to the French Intelligence Office, it is seen moving up the hierarchical ladder to the head of the office, Kingsford/Colonel Sandherr, and beyond. All the officers who read it, declaim it as "Outrageous" and "Inconceivable". Then the *Bordereau* is read out loud, almost in its entirety. Finally, the list of members of the General Staff is discussed. Esterhazy's name is mentioned, but he is considered trustworthy and the name of Dreyfus is finally settled on. The following description of this part of the scene can be found in *Magill's Survey of Cinema*: "As members of the staff look at the list of officers, seeking the possible traitor, the camera closes in on the name 'Captain Alfred Dreyfus' with the word Jew below it. A finger comes into the frame and a voice says, 'That's our man.' The word 'Jew' is never spoken during the entire film." (Magill's Survey of Cinema 1995)

LoEZ indeed contains no other reference to Dreyfus's Jewish origins or to antisemitism (see also Shindler 2014, 5). Some film reviews applauded this choice, as illustrated by the following evaluation: "In presenting the case of Capt. Dreyfus, the producer wisely avoided stressing the racial question" (Harrison's reports 1937). Archer Winsten in the *New York Post* (n.d.) expresses his surprise at its being "skimmed over" without it creating "an impression of unfortunate distortion." In *The Morning Telegraph*, Leo Mishkin writes:

> The fact that Dreyfus was a Jew and that his religion begot the inexplicable hatred against him, is mentioned, but played down in the film, but this is readily understandable and easily forgotten in the light of the greater theme to which the picture adheres (n.d.).

Fig. 12-3: The LoEZ screenshot 2: pointing to the (word) "Jew"

Other reviewers, however, deplore this omission. Kate Cameron of the *Daily News* calls it "a serious flaw" and in her article stresses the importance of antisemitism as an explanation for his arrest: "In 1894, an unreasoning wave of antisemitism swept through France. It was particularly virulent among army officers and was directly responsible for Dreyfus, a Jew, being falsely accused." The absence of more clear references to the moral espionage panic or the antisemitism that fed it, risks decontextualizing it. The lack of context leads some commentators to conclude: "Suddenly, Captain Alfred Dreyfus is found guilty" (Muni's greatest triumph yet 1937).

The circulating secondary texts do refer to Dreyfus's origins and to antisemitism, they do provide a context within which the entire film could be read in relationship to past (and present) antisemitism and intolerance. Warner itself (at least partially) supported this articulation in its press book, which contained a reprint of a letter from Louis Rittenberg (the editor of *American Hebrew*) written to "21 leaders of Jewry in New York" and dated August 3, 1937. The letter included the following paragraph:

Today, when prejudices are more rampant than ever, I feel grateful to those who have had the idealism and vision to produce a picture of such tremendous force on behalf of that greater understanding which humanity must have before people of different faith and opinion can live together in peace.

The actual dislocation caused by the Affair is narrated through an antagonistic structure, building on a traditional enemy-hero dichotomy, supported by the presence of a victim. Denby (1990, 34) summarized this as follows: "When he [Zola] publishes the Truth, he threatens the vested interests of people in power, who become his Enemies [...]." The main enemy in LoEZ is of course the army and its generals, partially in combination with the police, the judicial system and the political system, which are seen as accessories of the army.

The army is defined as a class in itself (witness the sentence spoken by Sondergaard/Lucie Dreyfus that they are about to "sacrifice one of their own class" when announcing O'Neill/Picquart's arrest), that is only interested in cting its honor and self-interest. Moreover, its representatives frequently proclaim that it "does not make mistakes", it colludes in protecting Esterhazy, and it treats Dreyfus and his family inhumanely. This inhumane treatment is represented by Schildkraut/Dreyfus being denied any physical contact with his wife when she visits him in his Paris cell, by his being shackled to his bed in his cell on Devil's Island, by the island having so many guards it becomes almost comical (see screenshot 3). The army's majors, colonels and generals become interchangeable; they flood the screen, creating a vague and non-individuated enemy identity (which discourages audience identification).

In the film, books fulfill a highly symbolic role in constructing the antagonism between hero and army. Zola's books are on display throughout the film, symbolizing his wisdom and intellectual capacity, which contrasts with the ignorance of the army generals, illustrated in the response of one of them to an enquiry about whether he has read Zola's "scandalous" The Downfall. He says that he: "doesn't read books, and certainly doesn't buy them." Finally, the army finds itself in a complex relationship with the French people, as "the people" (or "the mob", as Arendt calls them) are shown as supporting the army (in depictions of protest marches and mobs shouting abuse). At the same time, all authenticity of this support (and of the anti-Dreyfusard discourse) is demolished, in scenes showing provocateurs dressed in black (clearly linked to the army and its secret service) stirring up the masses. These filmic representations of the French people articulate them as a passive and manipulated mass, and create a structural opening for the rearticulation at the end of the film of the people's identity.

Fig. 12-4: The LoEZ screenshot 3: the guards on Devils' Island

The articulation of the enemy is juxtaposed with the individuated hero, who is "a great man [that] stand[s] alone – or rather, a great man is one who stands alone" (Denby 1990, 34). He is portrayed as self-assured, rational, eloquent, a man of letters, an intellectual. In one scene, Muni/Zola is even compared to Jesus, when, after sentence is pronounced, his lawyer points to a painting of Jesus' crucifixion and says "that too was a closed case." A critic writes the following about Zola, attributing him with super-individual powers: "Zola, when he thundered the 'I accuse' message that eventually exposed the army conspiracy against Dreyfus, was no longer an individual, he truly had become, as Anatole France later said of him, 'a monument of the conscience of Man'" (New York Times 1937).

In one of the film's key scenes, Muni/Zola receives a letter, informing him that his membership of the prestigious *Académie Française* is being considered. After a visit from Sondergaard/Lucie Dreyfus, who in the filmic narration successfully convinces him to write *J'accuse* and to become involved in the Affair, he is seen tearing up the letter, under the approving gaze of his old friend Sokoloff/Paul Cézanne (in a painting on the wall), symbolizing the avant-garde and anti-bourgeois. His resistance to *la pensée unique* in French society complicates his relationship with the French people, who are frequently interpellated by Muni/Zola('s ideology), but at first refuse to give in. This tension is only solved in the cathartic final scene of the film, when "the people" surround his coffin, and slowly and solemnly march past it to pay their last respects.

In LoEZ, the army (and the legal system) act as a constitutive outside, to emphasize Muni/Zola's heroism and self-sacrifice. A 1937 review of Zola's role in the Affair summarized it as follows: "The measure of his heroism is as great as the scope of the controversy" (Perjury, forgery, murder 1937). The most important threat to this heroic identity construction is the moment when he is seen fleeing the country to avoid imprisonment. Initially Muni/Zola refuses to flee in contrast to Barrat/Esterhazy's cowardice and treacherous behavior, but then reluctantly gives in to his friends who convince him to escape to the UK. They persuade him that it is "more courageous to be cowardly". However, Muni/Zola is shown to still be a presence in France through a poster displayed on the front door of the newspaper offices of *L'Aurore*, which headlines: "Truth is still on the march, read Zola's articles".

The evilness of the army and the heroism of the individuated Muni/Zola are further strengthened by the presence (or absence – as he is imprisoned) of the victim, Schildkraut/Alfred Dreyfus and his tragic faith. His identity construction is problematic: too strong a presence might pose a threat to Muni/Zola's individuated heroism; too strong an absence might render Muni/Zola's heroism unnecessary and incomprehensible. By including scenes showing Schildkraut/Dreyfus in captivity, his presence is activated, but often his character is invoked through his being talked about. The link with Zola is again symbolized by books, as we see Dreyfus receiving a copy of Zola's *(The belly of) Paris*. His suffering is also encapsulated by this book, when in a later scene the book is shown partially eaten by ants. His suffering is even more present when he is seen in his cell receiving a letter informing him that his sentence has been annulled and that he has been ordered back to France for the retrial in Rennes. His hair has turned almost completely white. Schildkraut/Dreyfus's devotion to the army (for instance, he says: "I've devoted my entire life to the army") creates a problematic relationship with the enemy-army, resolved by a disregard in the film of his being part of the military class.

Apart from the lawyer Crisp/Labori, the only other individuated quasi-hero is O'Neill/Picquart. Rather surprisingly, he is introduced early in the film's narration, critiquing the army's attitudes. Wearing an impeccable and light uniform (contrasting with most other uniforms which are dark), he is the only military witness to speak out on Muni/Zola's behalf during the trial. He too becomes a victim of the Affair, adding to the demonization of the army.

Fig. 12-5: The LoEZ screenshot 4: Schildkraut/Dreyfus set free

In contrast to these individuated heroes/victims, the Dreyfusard leadership (as a group) barely figures in this film, adding to the individuation of heroism and the disarticulation from organized activism. Apart from in the courtroom, in only one other scene is the group show sitting together in the offices of *L'Aurore*, contemplating what Muni/Zola will bring to them. This, of course, turns out to be *J'accuse*, which Muni/Zola then reads to the group. One other societal actor shares in the processes of heroization. The press is seen as a crucial (and impartial) informational source, not only in France during the Affair, but also in the filmic narration itself, providing the spectators with all the information necessary to understand the story line. This led one reviewer to remark: "Please note that even in that corrupt regime, there was still a free Press" (Opinion. The life of Emile Zola 1937). The opinionating and sometimes agitating role of the French press thus becomes disarticulated from the film's narration.

This film provides its audience with a set of specific articulations of the traumatic Dreyfus Affair. Its representations are unavoidably intertwined with the (1937) present. Despite the absence of explicit references to antisemitism, it contains a strong plea against "fanatical intolerance" (referred to in Muni/Zola's funeral oration), and against the vicissitudes, passivity and *manipulatedness* of the masses. In contrast, it emphasizes the importance of democracy and tolerance, referred to in the following review: "He [Zola] championed democracy, freedom of speech, and tolerance, which stand today more in need of support" (Zola. Man of Courage 1937).

Fig. 12-6: The LoEZ screenshot 5: O'Neill/Picquart at the witness stand

The LoEZ has thus become, as Denby (1990, 35) puts it, "an early example of Warner's anti-fascist drama." This is exemplified by the book burnings, a clear reference to the German National-Socialist regime, as Singer (2003, 17) remarks: "For instance, the Dieterle's film, we see a stake aimed at burning Zola's books, during the Dreyfus Affair in France. This is a purely fictitious event, but makes a clear reference to Nazi-Germany …." Although Germany's role in the Affair is not emphasized (presumably not to further complicate the narration), Nazi-Germany's presence is remarkably strong.

The pacifist theme also emerges at the end of the film, when on the evening of Muni/Zola's death, he is seen working on his new book *Justice*. Schildkraut/Dreyfus' reinstatement ceremony is to be on the next day,[20] but he cannot desist from working on "JUSTICE ('What matters the individual if the idea survives'), which he hopes will help prevent a world war." (Magill's Survey of Cinema 1995) Whether the film refers to the First or Second World War is left open. In conclusion, as Denby (1990, 35) puts it:

> The film offers many warnings of war and some discrete leftist popular-front rhetoric about the cure for injustice (i.e., socialism). Zola is portrayed as a writer with an instinctive sympathy for the down trodden. By degrees, this becomes the definition of what a writer is: he liberates the oppressed and shames the powerful.

Fig. 12-7: The LoEZ screenshot 6: the mob at work

Fig. 12-8: The LoEZ screenshot 7: books burning

Conclusion

In the history of the dislocatory Dreyfus Affair, there is a complex mixture of societal evolutions and structures, organizational characteristics and strategies, discourses on the Other and the Self, and diverging identities and subject positions, which superimpose and disconnect the Affair from the individual tragedy of Captain Dreyfus. During the Affair itself, Alfred Dreyfus is physically absent (being imprisoned), but at the same time is discursively extremely present, symbolizing the miscarriages of justice, the cruelty of the army and state, and the struggle for (individual) human rights. He in fact came close to becoming mere representation, unwillingly transformed into the object that divided France.

The Dreyfus films contain these contradictions, and have to reconcile the paradox of Dreyfus's present absence, especially when the focus is on some of the other protagonists in the Affair. These films need to narrate the story of Dreyfus's personal tragedy – in order to create a sense of historical factuality – but at the same time they locate the importance of these events outside the realm of his suffering. Strengthened by Hollywood's narrative tradition, in which the presence of the victim mainly supports the hero-enemy antagonism, this leads to the discursive erasure of the subject Dreyfus, in combination with a discursive focus on his tragedy as a point of access to the cultural trauma.

Although these Dreyfus films have become one of the many ways to commemorate the Affair, the specific spatial and temporal contexts in which they are produced alter its traumatic nature. The context allows for the rearticulation of historical narratives and the resymbolization of the tragedy according to its spatially and temporally delineated cultural needs. In this sense the Dreyfus films are not mere representations of an individual tragedy or a cultural trauma from the past. These representations "speak" to the (1937) present; they are not mere representations of French political and cultural history, but contain representations of "local" histories and futures. Among many other things, they carry warnings of a grim future and are celebrations of the then current culture sphere and ways of life.

In LoEZ, the moral espionage panic, and the two key forces in the Affair, antisemitism and nationalism, receive only limited attention. The lack of prominence given to antisemitism is indeed problematic, although the secondary texts repeatedly thematize this lack, providing their audiences with broadened interpretative frameworks. Moreover, the film's narration explicitly refers to and condemns intolerance and abuse of power. The army – a system of blind obedience – is articulated as the main societal enemy, threatening human rights and other democratic values. Its evilness and Muni/Zola's heroism are emphasized through the victimization of Schildkraut/Dreyfus and the representation of his suffering. Its representation of the masses as passive and manipulated by state agents, mindlessly accepting of state propaganda, also allows the film text to be read as an anti-totalitarian, anti-militarist, and anti-fascist critique.

Simultaneously, key signifiers such as individualism, liberty and freedom of speech, human rights, democracy, tolerance, "true" patriotism and heroism are strengthened, transposing the Affair into a U.S. context. On the one hand the anti-Dreyfusard camp is decontextualized and depoliticized, rendering its political motives incomprehensible by reducing these motives to self-interest (the army) or irrational behavior (the mob). This depoliticization contributes to the political nature of the anti-Dreyfusards being forgotten, disarticulating their practices and identities from the key signifier of patriotism. On the other hand we see one heroic individual reuniting the French nation, generating closure after the violent times of the Affair. Because of its focus on the hero, the organized and activist nature of the Dreyfusards is ignored, and the film shows how Muni/Zola leads France back to truth and justice (and liberty, as one American reviewer – Kate Cameron of the *Daily News* (n.d.) – adds). Through these mechanisms, the film optimistically signifies how rationalist and enlightened ideologies can overcome militarism, propaganda and mob passions. By showing how a nation comes to its senses after a dislocation, LoEZ projects the deep-rooted but illusionary hope that totalitarian regimes will eventually vanish and world conflict will be avoided.

Notes

[1] Special thanks to Sofie Van Bauwel, Roel Vande Winkel and Steven Vanden Broecke for their valuable help and comments, and to Katrina Stokes and Vicky Hedley of the British Film Institute, and Stephanie Boris of the Pacific Film Archive in assisting in my search for filmic and textual material.
[2] Other authors, for instance Kaplan (1999), have suggested that Mercier and the Intelligence Office consciously sacrificed Dreyfus to protect a disinformation campaign in relation to the new French 75mm rapid-fire field gun.
[3] Key Dreyfusards in this first phase were the writer-journalist Bernard Lazarre, the lawyers Louis Leblois and Edgar Demange, the vice-president of the senate Auguste Scheurer-Kestner and the deputy for Corsica and editor of Le Figaro, Emmanuel Aréne. Others were the philosophy professor Lucien Lévy-Brühl, the future Prime Minister Léon Blum, the librarian Lucien Herr, the protestant historian Gabriel Monod, the Radical senator Arthus Ranc, the more conservative

Jewish deputy Joseph Reinach and the former Minister of Justice Ludovic Trarieux, soon to be followed by Emile Zola and Georges Clemenceau (Johnson 1999, 62-65).
[4] The Panama Company went bankrupt in 1888, bringing ruin to some half a million middle-class Frenchmen. As the company had already been bankrupt for several years, "the press, half of Parliament, and all the higher officials" (Arendt 1985, 95) were bribed. According to Arendt, there were no Jews among the bribed members of parliament or on the company's board, but some of the middlemen (such as Jacques Reinach and Cornélius Herz) were Jewish. Another scandal that fed French antisemitism was the 1885 failure of the Union Générale, a Catholic banking establishment that tried to compete with Jewish capital.
[5] Duroselle (1964, 284-292) called the Affair a "pseudo-revolution of the elite."
[6] "A family dinner. Scene 1: Let's not discuss the Dreyfus Affair. Scene 2: They did."
[7] See Laclau and Mouffe's (1985) discourse theory.
[8] Johnson (1999, 99) calls the Ligue "the most enduring concrete legacy of the Affair" and describes how within the year it attracted 22,000 members. The rivalling Ligue de la Patrie Française counted more than 100,000 members.
[9] Critcher's (2003) refers to this model as attributional in contrast to processual models.
[10] The lack of a total consensus in France does not nullify the applicability of the moral panic model (Goode & Yehuda 1994, 34).
[11] The line of argument followed here is that the Dreyfus case and its injustices and collusions, were well embedded within the military and judicial system and then thrust upon French society as a whole.
[12] See also Laclau (1996) for a discussion on the relationship between the universal and the particular.
[13] The (potential) role of the French press had drastically changed following the liberal press law of July 29, 1881.
[14] The Pathé film is reported as lost (Abel 1994, 491). Its production year differs according to different sources. Singer (1988, 136) for instance dates it in 1902. In this text I follow Bottomore's (1984, 292) dating, supported by his reference to a description of the Pathé film in the British Journal of Photography of September 29, 1899.
[15] There is debate about the exact start of the ban (Datta 2013, 52).
[16] See, for instance, the June 26, 2014 Reuters report: http://www.reuters.com/article/2014/06/26/us-people-romanpolanski-idUSKBN0F12EM20140626.
[17] Screenwriters were Heinz Herald and Geza Herczeg, who – together with Norman Reilly Raine – also wrote the script.
[18] The reviews that were analysed are press cuttings that were archived by the BFI. All traceable bibliographical information is included in the reference list.
[19] One of the rare exceptions in the film's reviews is the following reference to another spy, who was mistakenly thought to be Dreyfus. "The officer D was a draughtsman, Dubois, who had been supplying the Germans with French gun designs" (Perjury, forgery, murder, September 18, 1937).

[20] Dreyfus was reinstated on July 12, 1906, Zola died on September 29, 1902. As is often the case in the films on the Affair, the last years are compressed.

Works Cited

Abel, Richard. 1994. The Ciné Goes to Town. French Cinema 1896-1914. Berkeley: University of California Press.

Anderson, Robert D. 1977. France 1870-1914. Politics and Society. London: Routledge and Kegan Paul.

Arendt, Hannah. 1985. The Origins of Totalitarism. San Diego: Harvest Books.

Baron, Lawrence (2011) The Dreyfus Affair According to HBO, in The Modern Jewish Experience in World Cinema. Edited by Lawrence Baron. Waltham: Brandeis University Press, 35-40.

Bottomore, Stephen. 1984. Dreyfus and Documentary. Sight and Sound, Autumn: 290-293.

Boussel, Patrice. 1960. L'Affaire Dreyfus et la Presse. Paris: Armand Colin.

Bredin, Jean-Denis. 1986. The Affair. The Case of Alfred Dreyfus. New York: George Braziller.

Butler, Judith. 2004. Precarious Life. The Powers of Mourning and Violence. London: Verso.

Cahm, Eric. 1996. The Dreyfus Affair in French Society and Politics. London/New York: Longman.

Cameron, Kate. N.d. Muni is Brilliant as the Immortal Zola. Daily News.

Cohen, Stanley. 1972. Folk Devils and Moral Panics. London: MacGibbon and Kee.

Connerton, Paul. 1989. How Societies Remember. Cambridge: Cambridge University Press.

Datta, Venita. 2013. The Dreyfus Affair as National Theatre. In Revising Dreyfus. Edited by Maya Balakirsky Katz. Leiden: Brill, 25-60.

de Certeau, Michel. 1992. The Writing of History. New York: Columbia University Press.

Denby, David. 1990. Emile and Louis and Mikhail and Václav. Première 3(13), August: 34-35.

Eyerman, Ron. 2001. Cultural Trauma: Slavery and the Formation of African American Identity. Cambridge: Cambridge University Press.

Ezra, Elizabeth. 2000. George Méliès. Manchester: Manchester University Press.

Film report and the Cinematograph Times. 1937. 967, September 25: 1.

Goode, Erich, and Nachman, Ben-Yehuda. 1994. Moral Panics. The Social Construction of Deviance. Oxford: Blackwell.

Griffiths, Richard. 1991. The Use of Abuse. The Polemics of the Dreyfus Affair and Its Aftermath. New York / Oxford: Berg.

Hall, Stuart, Critcher, Chas, Jefferson, Tony, Clarke, John, and Roberts, Brian. 1978. Policing the Crisis. Mugging, the State and Law and Order. London: Macmillan.

Harrison's reports. 1937. August 28: 139.

Johnson, Martin P. 1999. The Dreyfus Affair. London, Macmillan.

Kansteiner, Wulf. 2004. Genealogy of a Category Mistake. A Critical Intellectual History of the Cultural Trauma Metaphor. Rethinking History 8(2): 193-221.

Kaplan, Robert E. 1999. Making Sense of the Rennes Verdict: The Military Dimension of the Dreyfus Affair. Journal of Contemporary History 34: 499-515.

Laclau, Ernesto, and Mouffe, Chantal. 1985. Hegemony and Socialist Strategy. Towards a Radical Democratic Politics. London: Verso.

Laclau, Ernesto. 1990. New Reflections on the Revolution of our Time. London: Verso.

—. 1996. Emancipations. London, Verso.

Lewis, Jeff. 2002. Cultural Studies. The Basics. London: Routledge.

Magill, Frank N. (ed.) 1997. Magill's Survey of Cinema. http://library.dialog.com/bluesheets/html/bl0299.html

Malthète, Jacques. 1992. "L'Affaire Dreyfus" de Georges Méliès. Les Cahiers Naturalistes 66: 317-322.

Malthète-Méliès, Madeleine. 1982. L'Affaire Dreyfus de Georges Méliès. Cahiers de la Cinémathèque 35-36: 166-167.

Meek, Allen. 2010. Trauma and Media. Theories, Histories and Images. New York: Routledge.

Miquel, Pierre. 1973. L'Affaire Dreyfus. Paris: PUF.

Mishkin, Leo. N.d. "Life of Zola" an Inspired, Profound and Effective Screen Biography, The Morning Telegraph.

Muni's Greatest Triumph Yet. Epic "Zola" Film that Holds and Thrills. 1937. The Daily Film Renter, March 21.

Nielson, Ray. 1983. Reviewing the Classics. Things to Come (1936) & The Life of Emile Zola (1937). American Cinemeditor 33(2/3), summer/ autumn: 17-21.

Opinion. The life of Emile Zola. 1937. Daily Express, September 21.

Perjury, Forgery, Murder. 1937. Scholastic, September 18.

Radley, Alan. 1990. Artefacts, Memory and a Sense of the Past. In Collective Remembering. Edited by D. Middleton and D. Edwards. London, Sage: 46-59.

Rosenstone, Robert A. 1995. Visions of the Past. The Challenge of Film to our Idea of History. Cambridge and London: Harvard University Press.

Sadoul, Georges. 1970. George Méliès. Paris: Seghers.

Shindler, Colin. 2014. Hollywood Goes to War. Films and American Society, 1939-1952. New York: Routledge.

Singer, Claude. 1988. Dreyfus. In Dictionnaire des Personnages du Cinema. Edited by Gilles Horvilleur. Paris: Bordas: 136.

—. 2003. Le Juif Süss et la Propagande Nazi. L'Histoire Confisquée. Paris: Les belles lettres.

Singh, Amritjit, Skerrett, Joseph, and Hogan, Robert E. (eds.). 1994. Memory, Narrative, and Identity. New Essays in Ethnic American Literatures. Boston: Northeastern University Press.

Smith, Anna Marie. 1999. Laclau and Mouffe. The Radical Democratic Imaginary. London and New York: Routledge.

Staiger, Janet. 1992. Interpreting films. Studies in the Historical Reception of American Cinema. Princeton: Princeton University Press.

Sztompka, Piotr. 2000. Cultural Trauma. The Other Face of Social Change. European Journal of Social Theory 3: 449-466.

Toplin, Robert Brent. 1996. History by Hollywood. The Use and Abuse of the American Past. Urbana: University of Illinois Press.

Warner. 1937. Press Book. New York, Warner.

Whitney, Virginia. 1999. L'Affaire Dreyfus et La Presse. Downloaded on 15 September 2004 from: http://home.wlu.edu/~lambethj/Dreyfus/whitney/indexdreyfus.html.

Winsten, Archer. N.d. "Life of Emile Zola" at Hollywood Theatre. New York Post.

Žižek, Slavoj. 1989. The Sublime Object of Ideology. London, New York: Verso.

Zola. Man of Courage. 1937. Scholastic, September 18.

ABOUT THE AUTHORS

Rebecca A. Adelman
After earning her Ph.D. in Comparative Studies from The Ohio State University in 2009, Rebecca A. Adelman joined the Department of Media & Communication Studies at the University of Maryland, Baltimore County (UMBC) as an Assistant Professor, where her research and teaching interests include visual culture, citizenship, and cultural studies of terrorism and war. She has published on spectatorship, transparency, and visual ethics, methodologies, and pedagogies as they intersect with militarized violence. Her first book, *Beyond the Checkpoint: Visual Practices in America's Global War on Terror* (University of Massachusetts Press, 2014), maps the visual circuits linking the terrorized American nation-state, its citizens, and its enemies by exploring the practices of image creation, circulation, and consumption that animate these relationships. Contact: adelman.27@osu.edu

Stephanie Athey
Stephanie Athey is Associate Professor in the Department of Humanities at Lasell College and Director of the Honors Program. She was a 2006 Visiting Scholar at Columbia University's Center for the Study of Human Rights and is working on a book titled, *Torture's Echo: Sponsoring Violence through Rituals of Debate*. Editor of *Sharpened Edge: Women of Color, Resistance and Writing* and author of several essays on torture, eugenic feminisms, race and reproductive health, and colonial discourse in the Americas. Contact: SAthey@Lasell.edu

Nico Carpentier
Nico Carpentier is Associate Professor at the Communication Studies Department of the Vrije Universiteit Brussel (VUB - Free University of Brussels) and Lecturer at Charles University in Prague. He is a research fellow at Loughborough University and the Cyprus University of Technology. He is also an executive board member of the International Association for Media and Communication Research (IAMCR) and he was vice-president of the European Communication Research and Education Association (ECREA) from 2008 to 2012. His theoretical focus is on discourse theory, his research interests are situated in the relationship between media, journalism, politics and culture, especially towards social

domains such as war & conflict, ideology, participation and democracy. More information about him can be found at: http://homepages.vub.ac.be/ ~ncarpent/ Contact: nico.carpentier@vub.ac.be

Gordon Coonfield
Gordon Coonfield is Associate Professor of Communication and Director of Graduate Studies in Communication at Villanova University. He teaches courses in cultural studies, gender, visual communication and media studies. His research approaches the study of media and visual culture, and the modes of subjectivation that emerge at their confluence through the philosophy of Gilles Deleuze and Félix Guattari. Correspondence to: Department of Communication, Villanova University, 800 Lancaster Ave., Villanova, PA (USA), 19085; 610-519-7754 (voice). Contact: gordon.coonfield@villanova.edu

Karen J. Hall
Karen J. Hall works on militarist material culture. She is currently an academic advisor at the College of Arts and Sciences of Syracuse University. A longtime activist in Syracuse's peace and social justice community, she dedicates her research and teaching to raising awareness in the U.S. of the multitude of costs and effects of militarism. She has published articles on war toys and first person shooter video games. Contact: kjhall@syr.edu

Kylo-Patrick Hart
Kylo-Patrick R. Hart (Ph.D., University of Michigan) is professor and chair of the Department of Film, Television, and Digital Media at Texas Christian University, where he teaches courses in film and television history, theory, and criticism and queer media studies. He is the author or editor of several books about media, including *The AIDS Movie: Representing a Pandemic in Film and Television*, *Film and Sexual Politics*, *Film and Television Stardom*, *Mediated Deviance and Social Otherness: Interrogating Influential Representations*, and *Queer Males in Contemporary Cinema: Becoming Visible*. Contact: k.hart@tcu.edu.

Marc Lafleur
Marc Lafleur is a Contract Faculty member at the Department of Anthropology of York University in Toronto, Canada, and Head of Medical Anthropology at Idea Couture, a global strategic innovation and experience design firm. His Ph.D. addressed post-Cold War nuclear weapons politics and culture, specifically nuclear weapons memorializations,

nuclear museums and nuclear tourism, and the different ways in which these challenge traditional forms of anti-nuclear activism. Contact: mlafleur@yorku.ca

Christina Lane
Christina Lane is Associate Professor in the Department of Cinema and Interactive Media and Director of the Norton Herrick Center for Motion Picture Studies at The University of Miami in Coral Gables, FL. She is the author of Feminist Hollywood: From Born in Flames to Point Break (Wayne State UP), Magnolia (Wiley-Blackwell) and a number of journal and anthology articles. Contact: Contact: clane@miami.edu

Vincent Stephens
Vincent Stephens specializes in depictions of social pluralism in post-WWII popular culture. Since August 2011 he has been the Director of Multicultural Student Services at Bucknell University. Previously he was a Postdoctoral Faculty Fellow in the Humanities at Syracuse University. Vincent completed his Ph.D. in American Studies at the University of Maryland College Park in May 2005, and earned a B. S. in Mass Communication from Emerson College and an M.A. in Popular Culture Studies from Bowling Green State University. He has published articles for *All About Jazz Online,* essays in the academic journals African-American Review, American Music, The Journal of Popular Culture, *Popular Music,* and *Popular Music & Society,* and chapters in *Common Culture: Reading and Writing About American Popular Culture* (5th edition), *The Continuum Encyclopedia of Popular Music of the World, Volume VIII,* and *Masquerade: A Panorama.* Stephens is also co-editor, with Anthony Stewart, of *Post Racial America? An Interdisciplinary Study* (forthcoming Rowman & Littlfield). Contact: vls008@bucknell.edu

Tina Wasserman
Tina Wasserman is a faculty member in the Visual and Critical Studies Department at The School of the Museum of Fine Arts, Boston. She has published essays and chapters on film and visual culture with Intellect and Wallflower Press and in Quarterly Review of Film and Video, *Afterimage: The Journal of Media Arts and Cultural Criticism, C Magazine, New Art Examiner, Dialogue* and others. She has a Ph.D. in Cinema Studies from New York University. Contact: tina.wasserman@smfa.edu

Metasebia Woldemariam
Metasebia Woldemariam is an associate professor of communication and media studies at Plymouth State University in New Hampshire. She received her Ph.D. from the Joint Program in Communication offered by the Université du Québec à Montréal, Concordia University and the Université de Montréal. Her research interests include African media and cultural studies, feminist media scholarship, and international/developmental communication. Prior to joining the faculty at Plymouth State University, she worked as a research associate for the ORBICOM Network for UNESCO Chairs in Communications in Montreal, Quebec. In Canada, she taught courses at Concordia University and McGill University. Contact: mwoldemariam@plymouth.edu

Usha Zacharias
Usha Zacharias worked on the cultural politics of gender, media and citizenship in the context of globalization and the rise of fundamentalisms. She was currently Associate Professor at the Department of Communication, Westfield State College, where she thought International Communication, Film and Gender, Intercultural Communication and Media Criticism. She died on 30 September 2013. Her brother, Ajit Zacharias, kindly agreed to act as a contact person for those interested in her work. Also, a website (at www.ushazacharias.com) is being constructed to archive her work. Contact: zacharia@levy.org

AUTHOR INDEX

SUBJECT INDEX

monogamy, 211
MOO, 193
moral panic, 275, 276, 277, 278, 294
morality, 73, 107, 161, 166, 171, 183, 202, 203, 212, 213, 225, 226, 231
mother, 27, 30, 31, 32, 33, 34, 35, 38, 40, 41, 44, 54, 55, 56, 58, 59, 60, 63, 65, 67, 68, 70, 71, 72, 73, 140, 141, 209, 210, 216, 218, 222, 247, 251, 256, 265
mourning, 13, 23, 25, 28, 31, 34, 37, 38, 112, 225, 235, 262, 268
multiplicity, 52, 195, 222, 246, 275
Muni, Paul, 281, 282, 283, 285, 287, 288, 289, 290, 293, 295, 296
Munich, 52
museum, 10, 79, 229, 230, 232, 233, 234, 237, 238, 239, 245, 247
mutilation, 9, 110, 140
myopic, 184
myth, 8, 39, 52, 98, 124, 211, 220, 221, 227, 262, 280
Nagasaki, 230, 231, 234, 237, 238, 242
Nakba, 257, 258, 262, 265
Napoleon, Bonaparte, 272
narration, 3, 10, 11, 15, 18, 23, 24, 25, 26, 28, 30, 31, 32, 33, 34, 35, 36, 37, 38, 40, 41, 44, 54, 55, 56, 58, 67, 68, 69, 70, 71, 72, 73, 77, 79, 81, 82, 83, 84, 86, 91, 92, 93, 95, 99, 100, 109, 111, 114, 115, 117, 126, 128, 129, 130, 133, 134, 135, 137, 138, 141, 142, 143, 144, 149, 151, 152, 153, 154, 155, 156, 162, 168, 171, 172, 174, 175, 179, 181, 182, 185, 187, 204, 207, 208, 215, 216, 226, 239, 246, 247, 248, 256, 257, 258, 261, 263, 268, 278, 279, 282, 283, 286, 287, 288, 289, 290, 292
nation, 1, 2, 4, 7, 11, 15, 18, 24, 25, 28, 29, 34, 36, 42, 43, 52, 53, 54, 56, 64, 68, 69, 70, 89, 98, 112, 113, 115, 117, 124, 126, 127, 128, 130, 131, 132, 133, 135, 137, 139, 140, 144, 161, 162, 164, 165, 166, 168, 191, 201, 202, 203, 204, 205, 206, 207, 208, 209, 210, 212, 214, 215, 217, 220, 221, 222, 224, 225, 229, 230, 231, 237, 239, 242, 260, 261, 262, 264, 272, 275, 278, 293
National Atomic Museum, 238, 239
nationalism, 108, 111, 122, 124, 129, 130, 134, 139, 140, 141, 202, 203, 206, 214, 221, 224, 229, 267, 272, 273, 292
NATO, 98, 99, 121, 144
Navy, 100, 160, 170
Nazism, 11, 17, 53, 63, 64, 78, 93, 128, 184, 186, 203, 261, 282, 290, 297
NBC, 99, 111, 115, 137, 141
negotiation, 7, 10, 41, 53, 56, 57, 64, 108, 125, 161, 188, 201, 202, 205, 207, 208, 217, 223, 252, 279
neighbor, 32, 85, 86, 208
Nell, 68
Netherlands, 197
network, 51, 111, 129, 132, 138, 141, 153, 157, 162
neutrality, 7, 16, 41, 190, 203, 213, 217
New Mexico, 229, 230, 232, 238, 249
New York Post, 285
New York Times, 80, 81, 117, 137, 138, 142, 144, 145, 147, 151, 166, 172, 173, 174, 175, 176, 197, 287
New Yorker, 129, 130, 174
news, 7, 8, 19, 20, 33, 36, 44, 50, 81, 93, 99, 100, 111, 113, 114, 115, 116, 117, 118, 125, 126, 129, 132, 134, 137, 139, 141, 144, 148, 151, 152, 153, 154, 155, 156, 159, 160, 161, 164,

psychiatry, 4, 9, 53, 54, 55, 56, 58,
61, 65, 67, 71, 73, 114, 135, 159,
162, 164, 171, 202, 207, 216, 263
public, 2, 8, 25, 26, 28, 32, 37, 38,
43, 48, 63, 67, 77, 81, 82, 91, 92,
93, 97, 98, 109, 113, 122, 125,
126, 127, 129, 131, 139, 140,
141, 142, 148, 149, 153, 156,
159, 163, 166, 175, 179, 182,
183, 187, 188, 195, 199, 201,
203, 206, 210, 211, 213, 216,
222, 226, 227, 229, 230, 234,
235, 242, 245, 246, 279, 280, 281
public sphere, 126, 142, 213, 222,
229, 230, 234, 235, 242, 245, 246
punishment, 9, 18, 134, 151, 168,
172, 203
race, 24, 25, 28, 31, 39, 42, 86, 88,
122, 123, 129, 130, 139, 144,
148, 161, 163, 165, 167, 204,
205, 206, 207, 214, 221, 222,
224, 284
racism, 39, 89, 163, 206, 269
radicalism, 4, 19, 24, 32, 38, 88,
135, 136, 168, 197, 207, 214,
215, 244, 273, 278
radio, 77, 84, 85, 86, 89, 91, 93, 99,
132, 134, 142
Radio Bremen, 281
Radio-Télévision Libre des Mille
Collines, 86
Ramallah, 251, 255, 270
rape, 57, 86, 147, 149, 150, 158,
159, 167, 193
rationality, 3, 57, 69, 134, 149, 155,
205, 213, 237, 241, 245, 287, 293
reader, 7, 11, 93, 94, 154, 181, 182,
186, 187, 198, 224, 280
Reagan, Ronald, 214
realism, 10, 51, 56, 70, 82, 83, 84,
222, 260, 266, 279
reality, 19, 26, 30, 39, 41, 42, 51,
59, 60, 64, 69, 77, 79, 80, 84, 97,
101, 108, 109, 110, 111, 150,
185, 208, 244, 257, 259, 260,
263, 264, 266, 267

refugee, 77, 83, 88, 93, 251, 254,
255, 256, 258, 260, 267
regime, 4, 37, 83, 89, 157, 234, 276,
282, 289, 290, 293
religion, 27, 43, 124, 139, 141, 161,
163, 188, 201, 202, 205, 206,
207, 209, 212, 213, 216, 217,
219, 221, 267, 273, 285
representation, 3, 6, 7, 8, 9, 10, 11,
12, 13, 14, 15, 16, 17, 18, 28, 29,
32, 33, 34, 35, 37, 38, 39, 40, 42,
43, 51, 56, 58, 60, 70, 77, 78, 79,
80, 81, 82, 83, 84, 86, 87, 91, 92,
93, 94, 105, 106, 110, 112, 131,
148, 149, 150, 153, 154, 155,
156, 157, 165, 166, 167, 169,
173, 182, 184, 185, 201, 210,
211, 220, 222, 245, 279, 282,
283, 286, 289, 292, 293
republicanism, 274, 280
resistance, 6, 13, 14, 25, 97, 100,
125, 131, 138, 154, 169, 188,
206, 214, 222, 246, 256, 273, 287
Reuters, 114, 144, 294
Rice, Condoleeza, 131, 132
righteousness, 97, 203, 218, 230,
236, 239
rights, 2, 15, 31, 36, 54, 67, 97, 113,
115, 126, 130, 132, 133, 135,
137, 139, 154, 167, 169, 172,
181, 191, 204, 207, 213, 223,
224, 226, 234, 244, 253, 254,
266, 271, 275, 276, 292, 293
ritual, 9, 15, 20, 30, 31, 59, 149,
150, 157, 161, 163, 164, 165,
167, 169, 172, 181, 185, 188,
195, 197, 199, 279
Roosevelt, Theodor, 203, 237
Rosmer, Milton, 281
Roth, Philip, 81, 92, 93, 201, 208,
210, 214, 215, 216, 217, 218,
221, 222, 223, 224, 227
Rumsfeld, Donald, 121, 122, 123,
129, 130, 131, 132, 133, 137,
143, 144